THE LETTERS OF MARY PENRY

PIETIST, MORAVIAN, AND ANABAPTIST STUDIES

EDITED BY SCOTT PAUL GORDON

THE LETTERS OF MARY PENRY

A Single Moravian Woman in Early America

The Pennsylvania State University Press
University Park, Pennsylvania

Letters held in the Penralley Collection used by permission of Llyfrgell
Genedlaethol Cymru / The National Library of Wales and the Rhayader
Museum and Gallery (CARAD). Letters held at the Historical Society
of Pennsylvania; Jacobsburg Historical Society; Library Company of
Philadelphia; Linden Hall Archives; Moravian Archives, Bethlehem,
Pennsylvania; Moravian Archives, Winston-Salem, North Carolina;
and Rubenstein Rare Book and Manuscript Library, Duke University,
used by permission.

Library of Congress Cataloging-in-Publication Data

Names: Penry, Mary, 1735–1804, author. | Gordon, Scott Paul, 1965– editor.
Title: The letters of Mary Penry : a single Moravian woman in early America
    / edited by Scott Paul Gordon.
Other titles: Pietist, Moravian, and Anabaptist studies.
Description: University Park, Pennsylvania : The Pennsylvania State
    University Press, [2018] | Series: Pietist, Moravian, and Anabaptist
    studies | Includes bibliographical references and index.
Summary: "A collection of letters by Mary Penry (1735–1804), who
    immigrated to America from Wales and lived in Moravian communities
    for more than forty years. Offers a sustained view of the spiritual and
    social life of a single woman in early America"—Provided by publisher.
Identifiers: LCCN 2018007931 | ISBN 9780271081083 (cloth : alk. paper)
Subjects: LCSH: Penry, Mary, 1735–1804—Correspondence. |
    Moravian women—Pennsylvania—Correspondence. | Single women—
    Pennsylvania—Correspondence. | Moravians—Pennsylvania—Social life
    and customs—18th century. | Moravians—Pennsylvania—Social life
    and customs—19th century. | Single women—Pennsylvania—Social life
    and customs—18th century. | Single women—Pennsylvania—Social life
    and customs—19th century.
Classification: LCC BX8593.P46 A4 2018 | DDC 284/.6092 [B]—dc23
LC record available at https://lccn.loc.gov/2018007931

The Pennsylvania State University Press is a member of the Association
of University Presses.

It is the policy of The Pennsylvania State University Press to use acid-free
paper. Publications on uncoated stock satisfy the minimum requirements of
American National Standard for Information Sciences—Permanence of
Paper for Printed Library Material, ANSI Z39.48–1992.

CONTENTS

ILLUSTRATIONS

ACKNOWLEDGMENTS

This volume would be impossible without the generosity of the institutions that possess Penry's letters: the Rhayader Museum and the National Library of Wales, the Moravian Archives in Bethlehem and in Winston-Salem, the Historical Society of Pennsylvania, the Library Company of Philadelphia, the Jacobsburg Historical Society, the David M. Rubenstein Rare Book and Manuscript Library at Duke University, the Joseph Downs Collection of Manuscripts and Printed Ephemera at Winterthur, and Linden Hall in Lititz. At Linden Hall, archivist Joey Yocum and assistant archivist Kate Yeager were especially generous with their time, as were four volunteers at the Lititz Moravian Church Archives: Marian Shatto, Tom Wentzel, Nancy Sandercox, and Bob Sandercox. I wish Bob could see this volume.

Invitations to present the Moravian Historical Society's Annual Meeting Lecture in 2012 and the Jeanette Barres Zug Lecture in 2014 provided opportunities to talk about Mary Penry to engaged audiences who asked superb questions. Those lectures appeared in the *Journal of Moravian History* and in *The Hinge*, and I thank the editors of both publications for letting me use previously published material in the introduction to this volume.

I am grateful to Edward Quinter for translating material for this volume; to Monica Najar, Linda Yankaskas, and Jeremy Zallen for critiquing a draft of the introduction; to Jennifer Lewis for digging in Welsh records for information about Penry's genealogy; to Louise Benson James for touring me around Wales on a beautiful spring Friday; to Lehigh University's Lawrence Henry Gipson Institute for Eighteenth-Century Studies for financial support; to the readers for Pennsylvania State University Press, whose suggestions have improved this volume substantially; and to Kathryn Yahner of Pennsylvania State University Press, with whom it has been a true pleasure to work.

I thank Katie Faull, Dashielle Horn, Dawn Keetley, Jeffrey Long, Seth Moglen, Monica Najar, Christina Petterson, Heather Reinert, Megan van Ravenswaay, and Lanie Yaswinksi for conversations over many years that helped shape this volume. I owe profound debts to Craig Atwood, who urged me to submit this manuscript to the series he edits; to Tom McCullough, assistant archivist at the Moravian Archives in Bethlehem, who helped me in more ways and more often than I can recall; and especially to Paul Peucker, the archivist in Bethlehem, who supported this project at every stage of its life, when it was new and when (I imagine) it began to seem old. Nobody endured more conversations about this project than did James Dinh. For his encouragement—in all things—I am very lucky.

My parents, Lois Gordon (1927–2016) and Melvin Gordon (1925–2014), did not live to see this volume in print. Both offered, for fifty years, unqualified support and encouragement in whatever I chose to do. I dedicate this volume, with love and gratitude, to them.

GENEALOGICAL CHARTS

PENRY GENEALOGY

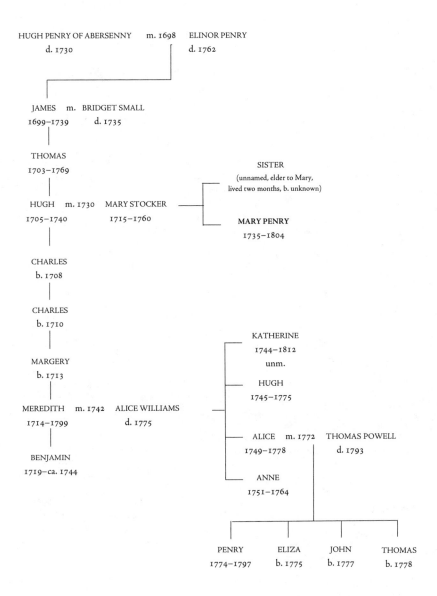

HUGH PENRY OF ABERSENNY   m. 1698   ELINOR PENRY
d. 1730   d. 1762

JAMES   m.   BRIDGET SMALL
1699–1739   d. 1735

THOMAS
1703–1769

HUGH   m. 1730   MARY STOCKER
1705–1740   1715–1760

SISTER
(unnamed, elder to Mary,
lived two months, b. unknown)

MARY PENRY
1735–1804

CHARLES
b. 1708

CHARLES
b. 1710

MARGERY
b. 1713

KATHERINE
1744–1812
unm.

HUGH
1745–1775

MEREDITH   m. 1742   ALICE WILLIAMS
1714–1799   d. 1775

ALICE   m. 1772   THOMAS POWELL
1749–1778   d. 1793

BENJAMIN
1719–ca. 1744

ANNE
1751–1764

PENRY   ELIZA   JOHN   THOMAS
1774–1797   b. 1775   b. 1777   b. 1778

STOCKER GENEALOGY

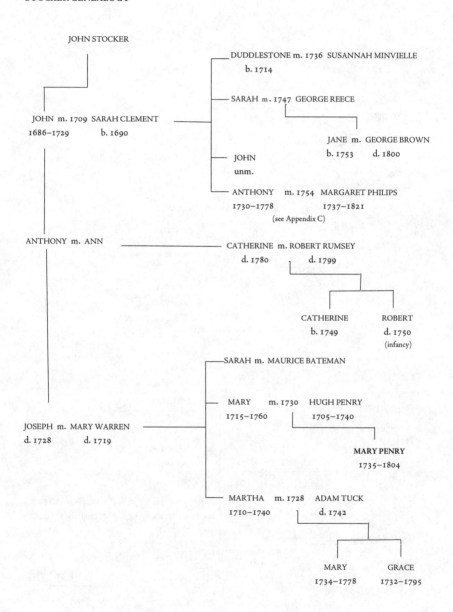

JOHN STOCKER

DUDDLESTONE m. 1736 SUSANNAH MINVIELLE
b. 1714

SARAH m. 1747 GEORGE REECE

JOHN m. 1709 SARAH CLEMENT
1686–1729   b. 1690

JANE m. GEORGE BROWN
b. 1753   d. 1800

JOHN
unm.

ANTHONY   m. 1754 MARGARET PHILIPS
1730–1778   1737–1821
(see Appendix C)

ANTHONY m. ANN

CATHERINE m. ROBERT RUMSEY
d. 1780   d. 1799

CATHERINE   ROBERT
b. 1749   d. 1750
(infancy)

SARAH m. MAURICE BATEMAN

MARY   m. 1730 HUGH PENRY
1715–1760   1705–1740

MARY PENRY
1735–1804

JOSEPH m. MARY WARREN
d. 1728   d. 1719

MARTHA   m. 1728 ADAM TUCK
1710–1740   d. 1742

MARY   GRACE
1734–1778   1732–1795

This volume includes all the surviving letters by Mary Penry that are known to me, except eight business letters related to the single sisters' textile industry. Appendix D prints one of these letters and identifies the others' locations. This volume does not print letters (in Penry's hand) that she wrote for others; it does not print the diary of the Lititz single sisters' choir that Penry kept from 1762 to 1804; and it does not print the financial accounts she produced each year.

All the texts printed in this volume, except Letters 9 and 10 and Penry's memoir (*lebenslauf*; see Appendix A), were written in English. These three exceptions were written in German. Unlike most eighteenth-century Moravians, however, Penry did not use German script (*Kurrentschrift*); she used Latin script, as she did when she wrote in English. For these three German-language texts, I have provided English translations and, immediately following, transcriptions of the originals.

At the top of each letter, I identify the addressee, the letter's date, and the place it was written. Penry's date and location, which she sometimes placed at the letter's top and sometimes at its bottom, I have placed at the top of the letter flush with the right margin. I have placed Penry's salutation flush with the left margin and her signature flush with the right margin. I have placed elements of her farewell flush with the right margin only when she has clearly separated that element from the sentence of which it is part. An unnumbered note at the bottom of each letter identifies the collection that contains the letter and the form of the source text: ALS (autograph letter signed by Penry), Copy (contemporary manuscript copy, with the copyist identified when possible), Printed Copy (document transcribed from a printed source), or Typed Copy (document transcribed from a typescript when the original manuscript no longer exists). This note also reports on other marks on the letter (e.g., the address, the endorsement) and any information about its delivery.

Even the most conservative transcription, determined to be faithful to the original manuscript, changes that manuscript by rendering it in print. I have not reproduced Penry's line breaks, and I have regularized the indentation of her paragraphs. Penry often did not use a period to end a sentence if that sentence concluded at the end of a line; she often used an uppercase letter at the start of a line even when a new sentence had not begun; and she often omitted a period in the middle of a line, leaving variable-sized spaces where one sentence ended and another began. It would be impossible to reproduce such features without reproducing Penry's line breaks, and there is no good reason to attempt to do so. Therefore, I have added punctuation at the end of sentences and removed the uppercase letters that appear at the start of a new line. I have added such end punctuation sparingly to preserve Penry's tendency to string related sentences and phrases together with commas and her fondness for punctuating with dashes (though I have regularized these as em dashes).

Penry's handwriting was clear throughout her life. Her words are rarely difficult to decipher, except when the manuscript itself is damaged. There are remarkably few cancelled words or interlinear insertions. I have preserved Penry's spelling except on very rare occasions, and in such cases I have placed my emendations in brackets. I have marked the places where damage to the text has left words impossible to recover with "[*missing*]" and, for those spots where I could not make out a word, "[*illegible*]." When missing words, however, could be easily reconstructed, I have placed my reconstruction within brackets. Where Penry underlined a word, I have substituted italics. I have also expanded abbreviations and superscripts (e.g., "B^r" becomes "Brother," "Philad^a" becomes "Philadelphia").

Heavily edited excerpts of sixteen letters were published in the following issues of *The Moravian*:

Volume 58: no. 43 (October 22, 1913): 687–88; no. 47 (November 19, 1913): 751; no. 49 (December 3, 1913): 773; no. 51 (December 17, 1913): 805.

Volume 59: no. 1 (January 7, 1914): 11; no. 3 (January 21, 1914): 43–45; no. 5 (February 4, 1914): 75; no. 7 (February 18, 1914): 107; no. 9 (March 4, 1914): 139; no. 11 (March 18, 1914): 171–72; no. 13 (April 1, 1914): 203–4; no. 15 (April 15, 1914): 235–36; no. 17 (April 29, 1914): 267; no. 19 (May 13, 1914): 299; no. 23 (June 10, 1914): 363; no. 27 (July 8, 1914): 427–28; no. 31 (August 5, 1914): 491; no. 33 (August 19, 1914): 523; no. 37 (September 16, 1914): 587–88; no. 39 (September 30, 1914): 619–20; no. 41 (October 14, 1914): 651; no. 43 (October 28, 1914): 683.

Volume 60: no. 9 (March 3, 1915): 139–40; no. 13 (March 31, 1915): 203–4; no. 15 (April 14, 1915): 235; no. 17 (April 28, 1915): 267.

Information in notes about individuals' births, deaths, and marriages, and about their movements within Moravian communities (or their departure from Moravian communities altogether), derives from congregational diaries, membership catalogs, and church registers, which are identified in the bibliography.

ABBREVIATIONS

ALS   Autograph letter signed by Mary Penry
HSP   Historical Society of Pennsylvania
LCHS   Lancaster County Historical Society
LOC   Library of Congress
MAB   Moravian Archives
MASP   Moravian Archives, Southern Province
MP   Mary Penry
NAK   National Archives, Kew
NLW   National Library of Wales
PCA   Powys County Archives

INTRODUCTION

The letters of Mary Penry (1735–1804) offer a sustained glimpse into the spiritual and social life of an ordinary eighteenth-century American woman over a period of forty-five years. Mary Penry emigrated from Wales with her widowed mother in 1744 and lived for a decade in cosmopolitan Philadelphia. For the rest of her life, nearly fifty years, she lived in Bethlehem and Lititz, small Moravian communities in Pennsylvania, as a single woman or, in Moravian terminology, a "single sister." Few eighteenth-century American women produced such a prodigious amount of first-person writing as did Penry, and little survives of what they produced.[1] Penry appears as a minor character in two famous diaries: both Elizabeth Drinker, whose diary of staccato entries extends from 1758 to 1807, and Hannah Callender Sansom, whose diary records a trip to Bethlehem in 1761, were Penry's schoolmates, and both describe their visits with her. In her own letters, of course, Penry speaks in her own voice. Hers is a not an early American voice we have heard before: deeply devout and garrulous, always, but also witty, plaintive, worldly-wise, curious, heartbroken, joyous, prophetic, bold, irreverent.

Penry may have been an "ordinary" woman, but she is unusual in an important way for historians of early America: she writes, self-consciously, as a single woman at a time when singleness was rare. A recent study of revolutionary

---

1. Fewer than two dozen book-length volumes of first-person writing—letters, diaries, or journals—by eighteenth-century American women have appeared in print in the last century. In addition to collections that excerpt women's writing—such as Evans, *Weathering the Storm*; and Skidmore, *Strength in Weakness*—see Greene, *Journal* (1923); Hulton, *Letters of a Loyalist Lady* (1927); Cowles, *Diaries* (1931); Shippen, *Journal Book* (1935); Knight, *Journal of Madam Knight* (1938); Morris, *Her Journal* (1949); Pinckney, *Letterbook* (1972); Cooper, *Diary* (1981); Burr, *Journal* (1984); Wister, *Journal and Occasional Writings* (1987); Drinker, *Diary* (1991); Murray, *From Gloucester to Philadelphia in 1790* (1998), *Letters I Left Behind* (2005), and *Letters of Loss and Love* (2009); Sansom, *Diary* (2010); Heaton, *World of Hannah Heaton* (2003); Franks, *Letters* (2004); Clark, *Voices from an Early American Convent* (2009); Warren, *Selected Letters* (2009); Adams, *Letters* (2016); and Osborne, *Collected Writings* (2017).

America tells the story of four women—the Philadelphian Deborah Reed Franklin, the Mohawk Margaret Brant, the Virginian Elizabeth Dutoy Porter, and her enslaved African Peg—to "represent the major varieties of women's experience" in eighteenth-century America.[2] Rural, urban, white, black, native, wealthy, impoverished: these women are various indeed. But all were married. Penry's letters, by contrast, offer the perspective of a woman who chose to remain single. "I desire to spend and be spent," she wrote, "in the Service of the *Virgin Choir*" (Letter 64). This choice to remain single was made possible by the Moravian communities in which Penry lived. In both Bethlehem and Lititz, single women lived together in great stone buildings, which Moravians called "choir" houses. In these choir houses, which still stand, Moravian single sisters lived, worked, and worshipped alongside one another. They also laughed, played music, gossiped, and mourned their dead. These Moravian communities offered Penry not only the rare opportunity to remain single but also to have a career that fulfilled her, as she worked at varied occupations, including bookkeeper and translator, that supported her and her community.

The early American culture that surrounded these Moravian communities pressured young women to marry to survive. This pressure was not equally intense everywhere in early America. Unmarried women, as Karin Wulf has shown, could find economic opportunities in urban environments. Some religious groups that emphasized the spiritual equality of men and women, including Pennsylvania's Quakers, encouraged women of means to imagine fulfilling lives independent of marriage. In general, however, early Americans tended to conflate "woman" with "wife," which ensured women's subordination and dependence. Unmarried women, as Wulf summarizes, "defied the presumption of masculine authority over women" on which Anglo-American society was organized.[3] They remain invisible, too, in most recent scholarship: "virtually every woman in 17th and 18th century America," one recent textbook asserts, "eventually married."[4] Few systematic studies reveal what percentage of women in early America actually remained single. In New England, where "religious and behavioral norms were supposed to be inculcated voluntarily within the family," singleness was very rare. A study of late seventeenth-century Hingham, Massachusetts, found that only 3.4 percent of women did not marry.[5] One study of Quakers near Philadelphia between 1681 and 1735 found that 14 percent of women never married; another

---

2. Gundersen, *To Be Useful*, 15.
3. Wulf, *Not All Wives*, 1–6. See also Chambers-Schiller, *Liberty*.
4. Kamensky, *Colonial Mosaic*, 58.
5. Seeman, "Better to Marry Than to Burn," 398, 403.

study of two New Jersey Quaker meetings before 1786 found that about 10 percent of women had not married by the age of fifty. The rate of Quaker women who had not married by age fifty rose later in the eighteenth century to 23.5 percent, which roughly matches the rate of women among the Philadelphia gentry who had not married by fifty (17.6 percent before 1775, 23.2 percent from 1775 to 1800). But historians emphasize that these rates of singleness are unusually high, enabled by extraordinary economic circumstances or religious beliefs. Among the general population, the rate of singleness was much lower.[6]

Cohorts of Moravian women tell a very different story and reveal the rare opportunity that these settlements offered to single women. Visitors to Bethlehem between 1754 and 1773, for instance, would have found that about 54 percent of the community's women were single, having never married (an additional 6 to 9 percent were widows).[7] Some of these women, of course, would marry. But the number of those who, like Penry, chose to *remain* single throughout their life was high. In 1758, for instance, Penry lived with ninety-three others in Bethlehem's single sisters' house. Over half of these women (60 percent) were born in America. Most of the rest had emigrated from Germany, but some women had been born in Norway, France, England, and Wales. Among the group were three Native Americans (a Wampanoag, a Delaware, and a Mohican), an African American (born in Trenton), and an African (born in Guinea). It was a remarkably diverse group of women. An astonishing 42 percent of these women remained single sisters for their entire life. Half of these women lived into their sixties and many into their seventies and eighties, and so most spent more than four decades as single sisters in a Moravian choir house.[8]

Anna Nitschmann (1715–1760) established the first house for single women in 1730 at Herrnhut, a small village on the estate of Count Nicholas Ludwig von Zinzendorf (1700–1760), about sixty miles from today's Dresden. In 1727 Zinzendorf collaborated with a group of religious refugees, to whom he had given sanctuary, to renew or reinvent a pre-Lutheran Protestant church called the Ancient Brethren. For more than thirty years Zinzendorf led an evangelical movement that spread Moravian piety throughout the Atlantic.

---

6. Klepp, "Fragmented Knowledge," 231–33; Wells, "Quaker Marriage Patterns," 426–28. See also Wulf, *Not All Wives*, 13.

7. Smaby, *Transformation*, 54–56; Wulf, *Not All Wives*, 76. Gundersen conflates women who were unmarried at a given time with those who remained single throughout their life. See *To Be Useful*, 54.

8. Four left the Moravian church entirely, while the rest married within the church. The statistics in this paragraph analyze a November 1758 single sisters' membership catalog. See Catalogs of the Single Sisters and Girls in Bethlehem, 1754–60, BethSS 26, MAB.

Moravians assured listeners that anybody would find salvation who accepted the simple truth that only Christ's sacrifice enabled unworthy human beings to find the grace to do good, and Moravian hymns and sermons centered devotion on Christ's bloody wounds as the source of such grace. Individuals were encouraged to cultivate a personal relationship with their Savior. Their piety and simplicity, approximating the practice of the early apostles, attracted followers from every rank of society, including the evangelists George Whitefield and Charles and John Wesley.[9] Zinzendorf expanded the Pietist tendency to encourage worship in small bands by organizing his movement into "choirs," which were groups of people of the same gender at a similar stage of life: single men worshiped with other single men, single women with single women, married couples with married couples, widows with widows. This arrangement offered an extraordinary amount of authority to women, who, as a group of single sisters remarked, were "led and guided by people like themselves, which . . . elsewhere in the whole world is not usual."[10] Herrnhut's single men and single women began to live together in separate residences. This model was reproduced in Moravian settlements around the globe in which the church owned all property, permitted only Moravians to establish residences, and closely controlled the economic and social activities of these residents.

Most recent scholarship on eighteenth-century Moravians in America has focused on these settlement communities, Bethlehem in Pennsylvania and Salem (later Winston-Salem) in North Carolina. But such places were rare in the Moravian Atlantic in the decades after the church's renewal. More common were the mission stations that Moravians established in the Caribbean islands, Africa, Greenland, and throughout colonial America from Georgia to New York. In missions, a Moravian couple (or two) would minister to a congregation of enslaved men and women in the West Indies or to a community of Native Americans who had converted to Christianity. In addition to numerous missions, Moravians also established churches in urban centers, including New York City, Philadelphia, Lancaster, and York.[11] In these urban areas, a pastor held services, sometimes in German and in English, and often supervised a school for boys and girls. Church members lived dispersed in family homes, and church authorities did not monitor or control their economic lives. Many non-Moravians attended services, even though they had

---

9. For the early Moravian church and its evangelical efforts, see Atwood, *Community of the Cross*, 21–40; Engel, *Religion and Profit*, 13–38; and Sensbach, *Rebecca's Revival*.

10. Smaby, "Only Brothers," 158, and "Gender Prescriptions."

11. See Ritter, *Moravian Church in Philadelphia*; Stocker, *History of the Moravian Church*; Albright, *Moravian Congregation at York*; and Gordon, "Entangled by the World."

not been admitted either as provisional members or as full members who participated in Holy Communion.

None of these Moravian communities relegated single women to the "usual despised State of Old Maids" (Letter 52). Only "in the world outside" of Moravian communities, Zinzendorf affirmed, was "an old maid . . . mocked and scorned." Zinzendorf did not, however, always speak of the single life and married life equally. He often depicted marriage as the proper trajectory for all single women: "The actual profession of a Single Sister when she is in the Congregation," he stated in an address to the single sisters in 1747, "is to enter into marriage." When Jean-François Reynier joined the Moravians at Marienborn in late 1739, he was told that single people were only "half people."[12] The choir system established in Moravian communities in the 1730s and the practices and piety in those houses, however, provided a powerful counterweight to such statements. The choir system was, as Craig Atwood writes, a "practical expression of Zinzendorf's theory that the earthly existence of the Son of God has sanctified *all* aspects of human life"[13]—including singleness. A "Choir-Ode" for the single sisters in the 1759 *Litany-Book*, for instance, reminded single sisters that:

> In old Times was Virginity
> Preserved but indiff'rently;
> For one did scarce a Virgin see,
> But she was a Bride immediately.
>
> The first Change happen'd in this Plan,
> When the Creator was made Man;
> And from that awful Hour we date
> The Honour of the Virgin-State.[14]

Regular ceremonies and festivals (e.g., May 4 was the single sisters' festival), hymns, and litanies particular to these choir houses valorized the state of singleness. These daily routines and this organized piety sustained Penry's faith.

The popularity of the single sisters' choir took Bethlehem's founders by surprise. Initially there were few single sisters in Bethlehem, and church authorities did not expect the number to grow: most single sisters, they thought, would quickly marry. But by 1746 the numbers of single women

---

12. Zinzendorf sermon in Smaby, "Gender Prescriptions," 86; Zinzendorf address to the single sisters in Faull, *Moravian Women's Memoirs*, 139n2. See also Fogleman, *Two Troubled Souls*, 81.

13. Atwood, *Community of the Cross*, 176.

14. *Litany-Book*, 280.

outgrew the space allotted to them. Authorities moved them to Nazareth, a Moravian community a few miles north, but the choir's continued growth convinced authorities to find a place for it back in Bethlehem. The community built a new house for its single brothers and, when the brothers vacated their building, twenty-one single sisters (and twenty-eight older girls) returned to Bethlehem in November 1748 to occupy it.[15] When Mary Penry arrived in Bethlehem in 1756, about seventy-five single sisters lived in the house, which had been enlarged by an extension to the north in 1752 and would be further enlarged in 1773 by an extension to the east. By 1760, over one hundred single sisters (and many older girls) lived in the house, a number that would remain stable for the next forty years.[16]

Penry's early experience did not promise a life in a Moravian choir house. Born in 1735 in Abergavenny, Wales, Penry moved after the death of her father, Hugh Penry (1705–1740), to Bristol with her mother, Mary Stocker Penry (1715–1760). Moravian evangelists had worked in Bristol and in Wales in the late 1730s and early 1740s. Their message of simple piety, based in the celebration of Christ's sacrifice, together with universal access to salvation found a receptive audience.[17] But Penry's family, attached to the Anglican church, had no contact with this movement. In 1744 mother and daughter immigrated to America, invited to Philadelphia by a cousin who was married to a rich Quaker merchant, William Attwood. The Penrys arrived on September 16 and moved into the Attwoods' home. A powerful man, Attwood served on Philadelphia's city council and was elected mayor during these years (1747–1748). He was involved in the transatlantic trade and had a diverse set of financial interests. In the 1720s he was vending "Sundrey Sorts of European Goods," including raisins, garlic, hats, and nails; he invested in the Colebrookdale Iron Furnace in the 1730s; and in the 1740s he had his own ship and wharf, where in 1748 the volunteer militia, formed to defend Philadelphia and the Delaware River during King George's War, erected a ten-foot-thick breastwork and a battery of thirteen guns. Attwood also sold slaves. Only a few men—among them William Allen, Israel Pemberton, Isaac Norris, and Anthony Morris—contributed more than the fifty pounds

---

15. Smaby, "Forming the Single Sisters' Choir." Moravian children were raised in a community nursery, after which boys and girls were separated. Girls entered the little girls' choir at the age of four and the older (or great) girls' choir at twelve or so. In their late teens, girls were eligible to join the single sisters' choir. See Smaby, *Transformation*, 10.

16. Catalogs of the Single Sisters and Girls in Bethlehem, MAB.

17. Jenkins, *Moravian Brethren in North Wales*; Dresser, "Moravians in Bristol"; Podmore, *Moravian Church in England*, 88–96.

that Attwood gave to the Philadelphia Hospital for the Relief of the Poor.[18] The Penrys' relative, Ann Attwood, died in 1747 of yellow fever, and subsequent events, as Penry tells them, resemble an eighteenth-century novel.[19]

This wealthy Quaker seems to have forced Penry's mother, who was living in (and perhaps confined to) his home, to marry him. "Attwood was a terrible person . . . who had little concern for either God or his fellow man," Penry wrote. But he "cajoled my mother so much, she did in fact marry him, albeit of necessity" (Appendix A). What she meant by "of necessity" is unclear— perhaps financial exigency, perhaps something darker. Mary Stocker Penry gave birth to Attwood's child, a daughter Elisabeth, on January 20, 1751; two months later she married him. The Philadelphia Quaker Monthly Meeting immediately began a process to disown Attwood, citing his "irregular & Scandalous conduct in diverse respects."[20] Penry called her time in this household an "Egyptian Bondage" (Letter 30). Attwood died on June 25, 1754. His will left £1,000 to his male cousins but only twenty shillings to Mary Stocker Penry (later Attwood) and the same amount to "Mary Penry junior."[21] The widow probably claimed her dower right, which in Pennsylvania entitled her to a third of Attwood's real property (his home, with rights to use the yard for any chickens she had) but no part of his personal property. "The law's emphasis on real property, appropriate for an agricultural community," Lisa Wilson notes, "failed to take into account the increasing importance of personal wealth." Mary Attwood, however, seems to have lived comfortably after her second husband's death.[22]

Penry's life in Philadelphia in her stepfather's house mixed suffering with opportunity. Penry learned to keep accounts, since the merchant Attwood required her to write "day and Night when ever Bus'ness required" (Letter 30). She would use these skills for the rest of her life. She gained a very different sort of education from the Quaker Anthony Benezet. The great abolitionist began teaching at the Friends School in 1743 and began a girls' school

---

18. *American Weekly Mercury*, October 10, 1723; *Pennsylvania Gazette*, July 19, 1744, April 28, 1748, May 29, 1755; Withington, "Pennsylvania Gleanings," 469; Roth, *Mayors of Philadelphia*, 1:44–51. Only eight of 360 men contributed more than Attwood did.

19. Ann Attwood died on August 26, 1747. See Births and Burials, 1686–1807, Philadelphia Monthly Meeting, Quaker Meeting Records; and Balch, *Letters and Papers*, 9–10.

20. Attwood married the widowed Mary Penry on March 16, 1751 (Jordan, "Pennsylvania Marriage Licenses," 72), not 1747 as MP states (Appendix A); for Attwood's disownment, see March 29, April 26, May 31, 1751, Minutes, 1740–55, Philadelphia Monthly Meeting, Quaker Meeting Records.

21. William Attwood, Last Will and Testament, February 5, 1750, Will Book K-185, Register of Wills Office. William Attwood composed this will as a widower.

22. Wilson, *Life After Death*, 30 (see also Salmon, *Women and the Law of Property in Early America*, 141–84). See below for Mary Attwood's financial circumstances upon her death.

there in summer 1754.[23] In the mid-1740s, however, he taught Penry alongside Elizabeth Sandwith (later Drinker), Hannah Callender (later Sansom), and Timothy Matlack (later a leading Pennsylvania revolutionary)—all of whom Penry referred to as school chums at "good Master Benezets school" (Letter 60). Benezet likely taught these children in a private setting, perhaps in the home of one of the girls. Penry learned French, maybe from Maria Jeanne Reynier, a friend of Benezet who taught the young Callender; Rebecca Birchall, who taught Drinker, may have taught Penry as well.[24] The most important development in these years, however, was that Penry and her mother began to frequent the Moravian church in Philadelphia after her stepfather died.

In June 1755 Thomas Yarrell, the Moravian pastor in Philadelphia, described some new attendees. Mary Attwood is "much Affected with our preaching and loves us much," he remarked, adding that although "in past times [she] was not used to go out of her house any where"—William Attwood seems to have confined his wife to their home—she "now comes constantly to church." Of Mary Penry, Yarrell noted simply, "Our saviour works in her heart."[25] Penry visited the settlement town of Bethlehem, some sixty miles north of Philadelphia, in early December 1755 and asked permission to remain. "Mary Penry, a Single woman from Philadelphia, was spoke with," authorities recorded. "The usual Questions being put to her, & the dangerous Situation of the Times with Regard to the Indians being laid before her, she declared that if she might be permitted to stay, she had much rather undergo any Hardships with the Sisters than go to Philadelphia again."[26] Some of the twenty-four "usual Questions" inquired into Penry's ties to the world ("Have you promised your self in Marriage to any Person?" "Are you embroiled in Suits of Law with any one by Means whereof you may be hereafter molested?") and probed her spiritual circumstances ("Is the Salvation of your Soul your Chief Concern?").[27] For reasons left unrecorded, Penry's request to move to Bethlehem was rejected.

---

23. Before 1754, girls appear in Friends School records only as sisters of male students. See Anthony Benezet Papers, Box 14, and Teachers' Accounts, Box 7, both in MC 1115, William Penn Charter School Archives. For Benezet, see Jackson, *Let This Voice Be Heard*, 20–24. For Quaker education, see Rosenberg, "World Within"; and Fatherly, *Gentlewomen and Learned Ladies*, 69.

24. Sansom, *Diary*, 12, 330; Drinker, *Diary*, 1:99.

25. Thomas Yarrell to Augustus Gottlieb Spangenberg, June 18, 1755, PhB II (Letters from Philadelphia up to 1760), MAB.

26. December 5, 1755, Journal of the Commission of the Brethren, 1752–60, BethCong 239, MAB. For Bethlehem during the French and Indian War, see Levering, *History*, 297–343.

27. Questions to Be Asked Discretionally by the Committee for the Regulation of Temporal Affairs in the Church or Congregation of the United Brethren at Bethlehem Previous to the Admission of Persons Permitted to Reside Amongst Them, Box: Economy Papers, 1742–61, MAB.

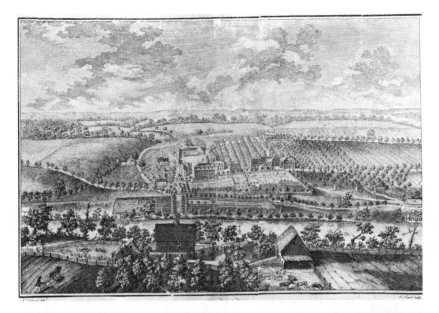

Figure 1 Nicholas Garrison, "A View of Bethlehem, one of the Brethren's Principal Settlements, in Pennsylvania," 1757. Mary Penry lived from 1756 to 1762 in the single sister's house, the last building (*on the right*) in the line of structures that face the Lehigh River. Reproduced by permission of the Moravian Archives, Bethlehem, Pennsylvania.

Penry returned to Philadelphia. Mary Attwood, who did not want to separate from her daughter, thought about moving with both daughters to Bethlehem or to Lancaster or York. Yarrell thought that "Philadelphia for the present is the best place for both Mother and Daughter." In January 1756, both mother and daughter were formally admitted to Philadelphia's Moravian congregation: Christian Seidel, present at the service, noted the "tears of love and joy" that they shed. Elisabeth Attwood, the young daughter of Mary and William Attwood, participated in the life of the congregation and pleased everybody in March by singing a Moravian hymn in German. (The girl died on September 26, 1758, and was buried in the Moravian graveyard in Philadelphia.) Penry, however, continued to beg for permission to move to Bethlehem. In May 1756, Mary Attwood asked Yarrell "how it will be determined about her daughter Molly if she comes to Bethlehem or not."[28]

28. Thomas Yarrell to Augustus Gottlieb Spangenberg, December 16, 1755, PhB II (Letters from Philadelphia up to 1760); January 25, 1756, [Christian Seidel], Journal from His Visit to Philadelphia and Jersey, TravJournals 146; Catalog of Moravians, Friends, and Children Deceased in Philadelphia, 1744–68, MC Phila I.514; May 5, 1756, Diary of the Philadelphia Congregation, MC Phila I.7–8, 192, all in MAB.

Permission soon came. On June 16, 1756, Mary Penry left Philadelphia to join the Moravian settlement at Bethlehem.

The Philadelphia she left had about seventeen thousand inhabitants. It had recently become the largest city in colonial America, surging ahead of Boston but not yet overtaken by New York. Bethlehem in 1756 comprised about eight hundred men, women, and children.[29] The frontier town had recently fortified itself in anticipation of an Indian attack. Religious, social, and economic life was organized by choirs; the community raised small children in a nursery, a practice that freed adults to undertake the missionary work that was the settlement's primary goal. In these years (1741–62), Bethlehem featured an extraordinary social arrangement usually referred to as the General Economy or "communal housekeeping." One of the questions asked of those who wished to move to Bethlehem described this Economy: "Do you know that we here live together in Common, and that no One receives any Wages for his Work, but are like Children in one House, contented with necessary Food and Rayment?"[30] Everyone in Bethlehem contributed his or her labor and, in exchange, received housing, food, clothing, medical care, and educational opportunities. A 1752 list identifies thirty-six different trades in which Bethlehem's men and women worked. Whites, blacks, and Native Americans lived together, worked together, worshiped together, and were buried together in what was perhaps the most egalitarian community of its time.[31]

Penry felt that by moving to a Moravian settlement community she had left "the World." "It pleased our dear Saviour in my 19th year," she wrote to her Welsh relatives, "to give me a gracious call in my heart to bring me off from the World and the things of it, to fix me on him" (Letter 3). The sense of detaching oneself from the world was central to the experience of joining a settlement community, and memoirs often depict family and friends as impediments to one's effort to orient oneself away from the "world."[32] Indeed, writers frequently mistook Moravian single sisters for nuns, confined to massive stone houses and isolated from the world. A 1773 visitor to Bethlehem, who thought Moravians "resembl[ed] the Roman Catholicks," regretted that single women were "Cloistered up." In 1784 Ezra Stiles called the single sisters'

29. Smith, "Death and Life," 865; Memorabilia, 1756, Diary of the Congregation at Bethlehem, BethCong 15, MAB.

30. Questions to Be Asked Discretionally, MAB. On January 25, 1757, Penry promised to abide by the congregation's rules and regulations. See Declarations at the Reception, 1757, Box: Economy Papers, MAB.

31. For early Bethlehem, see Levering, *History*; Gollin, *Moravians in Two Worlds*; Smaby, *Transformation*; Moglen, "Excess and Utopia."

32. Faull, *Moravian Women's Memoirs*, 42, 88.

house a "Nunnery," and Henry Wadsworth Longfellow's "Hymn of the Moravian Nuns of Bethlehem" (1825) drew on this impression. Some scholars, surprisingly, continue to describe single sisters as "cloister[ed]" or as "sequestered under the strictest rule from the world . . . like novices, protected behind the garden walls of a village monastery."[33]

The lines that separated Moravian communities from the communities around them were not walls: they were boundaries, clearly drawn but capable of being crossed, even by single women. We learn from Penry's letters that the worldview of a Pietist woman was not as limited or as insular as we may expect. Katherine Carté Engel has documented the extensive *commercial* activities that connected Bethlehem's choir houses to the surrounding communities.[34] Many Moravians, including single sisters such as Penry, also preserved persistent and deeply felt *social* ties with the world beyond Moravian settlements. Penry's experience reveals the many and varied affiliations that tethered her to the world. Every week Penry wrote to her mother, who covered her daughter's purchases from the community store. Indeed, Mary Attwood visited Bethlehem each year until her death in May 1760.[35] Penry traveled frequently to visit friends in Lancaster, Philadelphia, Harrisburg, and Baltimore. She kept informed about politics from newspapers and from her correspondents, and she sent information to her friends, hoping that they would respond in kind. "I am a great Politician," she confided to a friend, "but am very careful of speaking my Sentiments" (Letter 37). Penry's letters were both how she kept connected to the world and the surviving traces of these many affiliations. These social ties, which Penry's letters document extensively, supplemented the relationships that became central for individuals who joined a settlement community: the individuals' relationship with their Savior and with the new family of choir members with whom they lived and worked.

The Moravian single sisters became Penry's family, but Penry never shed her pre-Moravian identity or ties. Indeed, she struggled to reconnect where

---

33. Hills, "Summer Jaunt," 209; Ezra Stiles, "Itineraries," 3:659, Ezra Stiles Papers, 1727–95, Beinecke Rare Book and Manuscript Library, Yale University; Ferguson, *God's Fields*, 273; Southern, "Strangers Below," 87. For efforts to distinguish single sisters' houses from convents, see the *London Chronicle*, June 29, 1780, 1; Judith Sargent Murray to Dorcas Babson Sargent, June 22, 1790, in *From Gloucester to Philadelphia*, 139.

34. Engel, *Religion and Profit*.

35. The three pounds that MP spent in 1759 was "paid by her Mother." See Ledger of the Store at Bethlehem, 1768–75 (Ledger C), BethStore 102, MAB. Mary Attwood left her estate to her daughter. In May 1763, after sending MP £147 of "Goods & Effects" and clearing substantial debts, the executor still had £308.6.1 in hand. These funds may have been transferred to MP in Lititz. See Mary Attwood, Last Will and Testament, November 12, 1758, Will Book L-538, Estate Inventory, October 20, 1760, Administrative Account, May 25, 1763, Register of Wills Office.

Figure 2   Abersenny, in Defynnog, Wales, where Mary Penry's grandfather lived. Author's photo.

connections had been severed. She tried to contact her Welsh relatives when she was in her twenties but did not hear back from them for over thirty years; as a result, she felt abandoned for most of her life. Her longing for this connection solidified a Welsh identity that otherwise might have never taken hold in this woman who barely remembered a Wales she left as a young child. Family always reminded Penry of what she had lost—not just lost fellowship but also a loss of status and wealth, which her parents' families had possessed generations earlier. She heard from her mother of the great Welsh estates that the Penry family built: Hugh Penry, vicar of Llywel and Devynock, erected the mansion Llwyncyntefin in 1634; his grandson built Penpont; and Mary Penry's grandfather had lived in a house called Abersenny (Letter 47). But times had changed. "It has pleased the Lord to humble our Family," Penry admitted. Theophilus Jones's 1809 *History of the County of Brecknock* referred to the few living Penrys as "very poor," and Penry herself joked that if one were to "place an u between the n and r" in her name, it is "what we are brought to" (Letters 36 and 37).[36] When Mary Stocker (Penry's mother) married the impoverished Hugh Penry, her family, which slave labor on Barbados

---

36. Jones, *History of the County of Brecknock*, 2:678.

sugar plantations had made wealthy, disinherited her.[37] In the 1760s Mary Penry would reconcile with her mother's family. Her cousin, Anthony Stocker, had immigrated to Philadelphia and prospered as a merchant, and during the 1790s whenever she traveled to Philadelphia she lodged with his widow. Indeed, Margaret Phillips Stocker became her closest friend. But this intimate contact with the Stockers, living "in the greatest affluence," only emphasized her own "Constrained Circumstances" (Letter 31) and reminded her of what she and her mother had been denied.

During the 1760s Penry even tried to recover a substantial inheritance out of which, she believed, her mother had been cheated. Mary Stocker's marriage to Hugh Penry led her father's family—the Stockers—to disinherit her. A larger inheritance was due from her maternal grandfather, Commodore Thomas Warren. Warren's two daughters each had a daughter: when one granddaughter ("Miss Day") died unmarried and without children, an estate of £300 a year should have passed to the other, Mary Penry's mother (Letter 9). Penry recruited the help of Moravian authorities to recover these funds. She found that, without skill at negotiating the British legal system and funds to enable a lawsuit, a right was difficult to assert. Her efforts were unsuccessful. She indulged a tendency, which she understood was a "weakness," to "lament at the loss of Fortune" throughout her life (Letter 54). At other times, however, she considered these deprivations as blessings: "it matters little wether we have earthly treasure or not," she wrote. "I believe most certainly that it was good for me that I have been afflicted—It has weand my heart from this world and its vanities" (Letter 31). Penry's sense of having been deprived of things rightfully hers—family as well as fortune—never left her.

One of Penry's first challenges when she moved to Bethlehem was to learn German, the primary language of most residents and the language in which religious services were held and records were kept. Penry was a quick study. When in 1762 she moved to Lititz, a small community about eight miles north of Lancaster, authorities assigned her responsibility for the daily diary of the single sisters' choir. She wrote this diary for more than forty years, in German, and regularly produced membership catalogs and financial records for the single sisters' choir, also in German. Penry thought that "the Constant use of the German Tongue, all our Meetings being in that Language and near 40 Years constant dwelling with Germans," caused "a Material Injury" to her "English tongue." She asked her cousins to pardon her "Germanisms. . . . The

---

37. See Appendix B. A legacy due to MP's mother from her stepmother was also denied (Letter 6).

Figure 3   Detail of Samuel Reincke, "View of Lititz," 1809. The parsonage and church stand between the single sisters' house in which Mary Penry lived from 1762 to 1804 (*on the left*) and the single brothers' house (*on the right*). Reproduced by permission of the Moravian Church Museum and Archives, Lititz, Pennsylvania.

Monosyllables in particular . . . are either too frequent, or wrong placed" (Letters 37 and 48). But her letters, most of which were written in English, indicate that Penry moved easily between English and German.[38]

The Moravian community at Lititz, to which Penry moved in 1762, was even smaller than was Bethlehem. The settlement at Lititz had been established only in 1756, developing from the nearby town and country congregation of Warwick, where church members lived on scattered family farms. In 1761, only 257 individuals (ninety-seven of whom were children) lived at Lititz and Warwick. Lititz consisted of a school, a large mill, a church and parsonage, several private dwellings, a store, and a brothers' house and sisters' house. (Philadelphia's Moravian congregation had raised more than fifty pounds, including ten shillings from Mary Attwood, toward the construction of this

---

38. For work on translation and bilingualism in the eighteenth century, see Erben, *Harmony of the Spirits*; Weber, "Translation as a Prism"; McMurran, *Spread of Novels*, 1–26, and "Crèvecoeur's Transatlantic Bilingualism"; and von Morzé, "Cultural Transfer in the German Atlantic."

sisters' house in Lititz.) The single brothers had occupied their house in October 1758, but no women yet resided in the single sisters' house. The bishop Matthias Hehl (1705–1787) and his wife lived there, and the congregation met for services in its first-floor meeting hall (*saal*)—that is, until the first group of single women, including Penry, arrived in May and June 1762.[39] By the end of 1764, thirty-one women lived in this single sisters' house. Thirty years later, Penry reported that "we are 56 in Number of different ages, from 15 to Sixty" (Letter 41). At sixty, Penry was the oldest woman in the house.

Moravian authorities wished that their settlement places were insulated from the storms of local and national politics, but political strife often visited Lititz. In December 1763 several Paxton Boys, fresh from slaughtering fourteen Conestoga Indians at the Lancaster workhouse, threatened Lititz, shooting off their guns and shouting "God damn you, Moravians." During the Revolutionary War, the Continental Army established a hospital in the Lititz brothers' house. At one point, six armed soldiers entered Penry's sisters' house, apparently in search of blankets.[40] The Revolution also interrupted transatlantic communication, severing permanently Penry's ties to several friends in Great Britain. (Few letters from this period survive.) The early republic's partisan strife also reached small villages such as Lititz. Penry's letters trace her responses to the major political events of late eighteenth-century America—the Jay Treaty, the XYZ Affair, French attacks on American shipping, the end of Washington's presidency, the beginning of Adams's, the rise of Jefferson—that intensified the partisan divisions between the emergent Republican Party, aligned with revolutionary France, and the Federalist Party of Washington and Adams. Penry's friends knew her political preferences: "I read no *Demo's* paper," she reminded her friend Elizabeth Drinker (Letter 63), and her disgust for figures such as Thomas Paine and for the "Pernicious Doctrine" advanced by the French Revolution once got her in trouble with the Speaker of Pennsylvania's Assembly.

Penry described the single sisters' house in which she lived as an "Azylum." She meant primarily that the choir house was a *religious* refuge that protected her from the spiritual dangers of the wider world. But Moravian choir houses also served Penry and others as an *economic* refuge. They offered a place of security from an early American social and economic world that posed particular dangers to single women for whom the promise of America had turned out to be an illusion. Many single women and their families were

---

39. For early Lititz, see Brickenstein, "Sketch of the Early History of Lititz."
40. Gordon, "Paxton Boys and the Moravians"; Jordan, "Military Hospitals"; Beck, "Military Hospital."

casualties of the Atlantic system, swept to America by the promise of a better life and better opportunities only to discover, once here, that their hard work guaranteed them nothing. Following our urge to tell stories of immigrant success, we often overlook these people. Moravian single sisters' houses embraced women whose circumstances had left them little hope. "These Houses," Penry boasted, "have prov'd an Azylum for Numbers, who had they been left to seek their Bread in the midst of a deluding World, might have been led astray into the Paths of Vice, which has been the Misfortune of but too many Young Persons of our Sex" (Letter 18). Young women were not invited to join Moravian communities to save them from economic peril: one's worldly circumstances, unfortunate or privileged, did not earn one admission to a choir house. No woman entered a Moravian community unless church authorities trusted that she was awakened spiritually, and authorities rejected many requests to join the community. But if women such as Penry were not welcomed *because* they were in precarious domestic or economic situations, they were welcomed *from* such circumstances. The strict spiritual standard for admission to Moravian communities was not used to exclude the most vulnerable individuals in early American society.[41]

Penry's experience enabled her to see the hard truths about immigrants' lives, and she warned her Welsh cousins about stories of a better life in America. The "first outbreak of America fever" in Wales began in 1791, with Welsh immigration reaching its peak in 1794–97. This Welsh immigration was part of a large wave of immigration from Great Britain in the 1790s. In the summer of 1791 alone, between three and four thousand Irish arrived in Philadelphia. Penry believed that most immigrants "with tears lament they ever left their Country" and are "half distracted, at finding things so vastly different from the discription given them" (Letter 42). Many immigrants "expected riches and liberty," a Scotsman in Baltimore wrote in 1803, "but found nothing but a struggle to keep themselves alive."[42] The Moravian sisters' houses made room for poor immigrant women, giving some a chance at a fulfilling life. Worried about her young Welsh cousin, Penry opined that "a Single woman of her age seems somehow so unprotected in the midst of the World! I never experienced *this* because in my twentieth year I came to live among a House, full of Maidens, and have continued among them ever since" (Letter 71). Penry thought about returning to Wales after her mother died. But she would have returned penniless, and in such circumstances, she asked,

41. See Gordon, "Asylum."

42. Williams, *Search for Beulah Land*, 30, 130; Durey, *Transatlantic Radicals*, 1–2, quotation at 178; Davies, "Very Different Springs," 376.

"to whom should the helpless *Maiden* go?" (Letter 37). Penry's life in America constitutes an answer to that question. If she were lucky, the "helpless *Maiden*" could "go" to a Moravian single sisters' house, which offered economic and social, as well as spiritual, asylum.

Penry's letters reveal how the different spaces in the sisters' house shaped this diverse community that lived together within it. All the single sisters gathered for worship services, for some meals, and to sleep; but for much of the day they met in smaller groups of six to eight, organized according to the forms of labor in which they were engaged. "Every appartment in which we Sisters live together," Penry wrote, "may be calld a little Family" (Letter 41). Penry's eight "Room Companions" spun cotton for their livelihood, but Penry spent her days differently: she sat at "a Window·fronting the Street" in a "large Room," "a round Table before me, behind me my Bureau with a Closet on the Top, sometimes, indeed most frequent writing at my Desk" (Letter 37). Late in life, Penry "removed into a little Room to myself" in the sisters' house. This room, "exactly 10 Feet Square," was a private *workspace*. Penry continued to sleep "in the large Hall with the rest of the Family" and spent evenings "sometimes in one room sometimes in another but never in my Room unless I have something particular to do" (Letter 66). Penry was given privacy only to do her work: she was not provided private space for personal reasons, nor did she desire it.

Penry served as "Clerk" for the single sisters' house in Lititz. "I keep the Accounts of our House," she wrote, "and write letters of Busness" (Letter 29). She was responsible for recording and reporting to church authorities the business activities of the single sisters' choir, including their spinning industries and their girls' school, and for corresponding with those outside Lititz about these activities. Contacts from her years in Philadelphia, the Shippens and the Franklins, purchased spun cotton from the single sisters in Lititz during the 1770s.[43] Penry also kept, as we have seen, the daily diary of her choir, in which she described the comings and goings of the single sisters, reported the arrival and departure of visitors, noted the choir's religious services and the spiritual milestones of its members, and remarked on events in the larger world that affected the choir. Penry was also responsible for guiding visitors around the community, and she was paid to translate documents. She earned income, too, by embroidery and tambour (embroidery on a frame), traveling to Lancaster to diversify her skills in April 1774.[44] Other

---

43. See Appendix D. For MP's invoices to the family of Elizabeth Henry, a student at the girls' school, see Elizabeth Henry, Accounts, 1779–81, Box 10:14, Henry Family Papers, 1759–1909, Accession Number 1209, Hagley Museum and Library.

44. Brickenstein, "Sketch of the Early History of Lititz," 371.

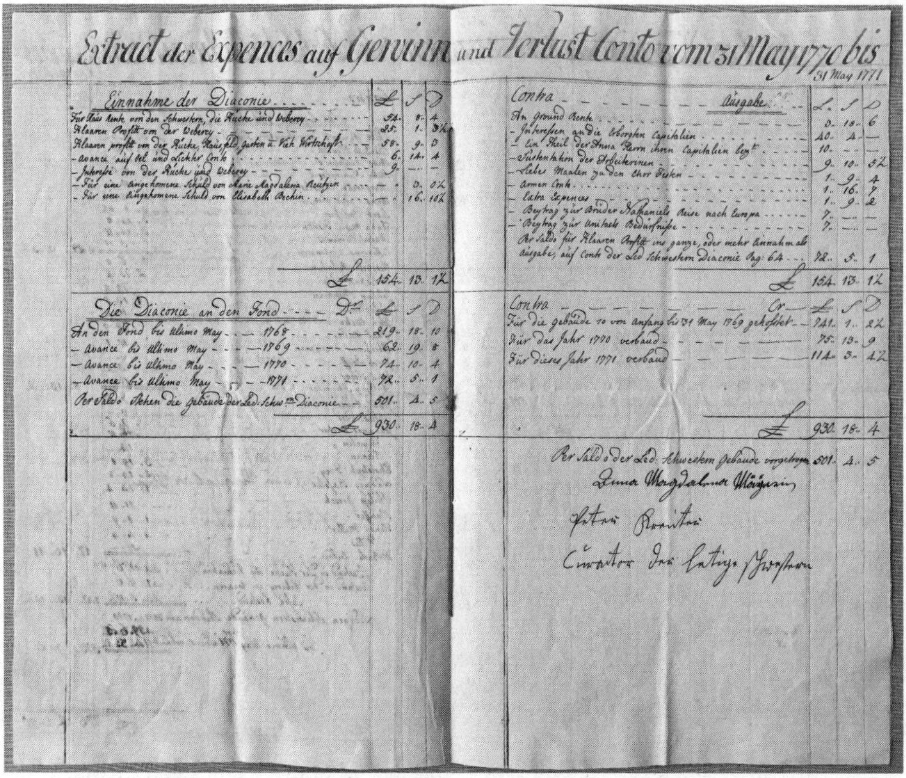

Extract der Expences auf Gewinn und Verlust Conto vom 31 May 1770 bis 31 May 1771

Einnahme der Diaconie	£	s	d
Für Haus Rente von den Schwestern, die Küche und Weberey	54	8	4
Klaaren Profit von der Weberey	25	1	3½
Klaaren profit von der Küche, Haus, feld, garten u. Vieh Wirtschaft	58	9	3
avance auf Oel und Lichter Conto	6	14	4
Interesse von der Küche und Weberey	9	—	—
Für eine eingekomene Schuld von Marie Magdalena Reutzin	—	3	0½
Für eine eingekomene Schuld von Elisabeth Beckin	—	16	10½
£	154	13	1½

Contra — Ausgabe	£	s	d
An ground Rent	3	18	6
Interessen an die erborgten Capitalien	40	4	—
ein Theil der Anna Herrn ihren Capitalien bezt.	10	—	—
Sustentation der Arbeiterinen	9	10	5½
Liebes Maalen zu den Chor Festen	1	9	4
armen Conto	1	16	7
extra Expences	1	9	2
Beytrag zur Bruder Nathaniels Reise nach Europa	7	—	—
Beytrag zur Unitaets Bedürfnisse	7	—	—
Per Saldo für Klaaren Profit ins ganze, oder mehr Einnahm als ausgabe, auf Conto der Led. Schwestern Diaconie Pag. 64	72	5	1
£	154	13	1½

Die Diaconie an den Fond — Dr.	£	s	d
An den Fond bis ultimo May 1768	219	18	10
avance bis ultimo May 1769	62	19	8
avance bis ultimo May 1770	74	10	4
avance bis ultimo May 1771	72	5	1
Per Saldo stehen die Gebäude der Led. Schwn. Diaconie	501	4	5
£	930	18	4

Contra — Cr.	£	s	d
Für die Gebäude so von anfang bis 31 May 1769 gekostet	741	1	2½
Für das Jahr 1770 verbaut	75	13	9
Für dieses Jahr 1771 verbaut	114	3	4½
£	930	18	4

Per Saldo der Led. Schwestern Gebäude vorgetragen 501. 4. 5

Anna Magdalena Wägerin

Figure 4 A page from the Lititz single sisters' financial accounts from 1771. Mary Penry produced such accounts each May. Reproduced by permission of the Moravian Archives, Bethlehem, Pennsylvania.

single sisters in Lititz performed different tasks: they wove muslin, flax, and wool; spun cotton; worked as mantua makers and seamstresses; labored outdoors at gardening, hay making, and reaping; baked bread; and washed and mended for the single men (Letter 41). In Bethlehem, single sisters tended livestock, as Hannah Callender found when during her visit she was awakened by "one Hundred Cows, a number of them with Bells, a venerable goat and two she goats" driven into "town by two Sisters."[45] Other women in Lititz's single sisters' house served as spiritual leaders and helped in other ways to administer the large community of women.

45. Sansom, *Diary*, 154.

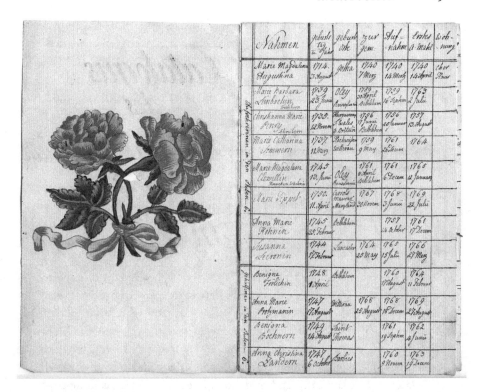

Figure 5   From the Lititz single sisters' membership catalog, 1780. Mary Penry produced these catalogs regularly. She probably drew the decorative rose on the left-hand page. Reproduced by permission of the Moravian Archives, Bethlehem, Pennsylvania.

The single sisters at Lititz were paid for their labor (as they were at Bethlehem after 1762, when its General Economy ended). The single sisters still ate, worked, and slept alongside one another. But each woman paid for items or services that under the General Economy she would have received in exchange for her labor. Penry paid £0.2.6 each week for room and board, which guaranteed her a "good plain Dinner, of Meat Broth," seasonal vegetables, and tea for breakfast and in the afternoon. She contributed a bit more for materials for a fire and for candles and to have her clothes washed (Letter 41). The transition from communal housekeeping to wage labor may have made some single sisters anxious about how they could earn money to support these expenses. Bethlehem's authorities orchestrated the transition from the General Economy to ensure that each single sister would be able to earn a living. A planning document reveals that authorities expected several single sisters to become seamstresses, while others would make linens, wash and mend clothes, work in the garden and kitchen, make and bleach twine, and help with the harvest and with the animals. They proposed that, if a resident of the single sisters' house familiar with linen weaving would start a weaving shop, the single sisters would be given part of a field to sow flax or hemp, which later they could prepare and spin.[46] Even with a wage economy, these choir houses insulated single sisters from the precariousness of the early American economy. Penry never worried that she would become destitute. Her community would care for her even if she could no longer contribute economically, as she wrote of a single sister too sick to labor: "She will want for Nothing as long as she lives, and will be attended with the very same care and tenderness as one in affluent Circumstances" (Letter 27). Penry prayed that she would never become a burden to her community.

Penry spent her life writing. Some of this labor involved business correspondence, as we have seen, and she wrote letters for those who did not speak English well. In the 1760s and 1770s, Penry was paid to translate for the church (Letter 70). To knit together the far-flung communities of the Moravian diaspora, authorities established an ambitious system by which reports from mission stations, settlement places, and urban churches were copied, circulated transatlantically, and read aloud in each Moravian community.[47] Scribes in Bethlehem and at Nazareth Hall (an educational institution north of Bethlehem), for instance, produced seven copies of the Bethlehem and Nazareth diaries for Philadelphia, New York, Newport, Europe, the West Indies, and varied mission stations; they copied other materials for the town and country congregations; and for Jamaica and Bethabara, North Carolina, they copied the vast and varied "congregation accounts" (Gemeinnachrichten), which were letters and reports collected from around the Moravian diaspora.[48] Copyists were not enough: German-language texts had to be translated for English-speaking Moravian churches. In the 1760s, Penry herself was responsible for translating the Gemeinnachrichten. She translated discourses on watchwords, pastoral conferences, sermons by bishop August Gottlieb Spangenberg, travel journals to Surinam, dozens of letters from Jamaica and Barbados and from missionaries in Greenland, diaries from Russia and Ire-

---

46. Projects for the Intended Change of the Bethlehem Economy, re: Single Sisters, 1761, Box: Transition Period 1761–72, MAB.

47. See Wessel, "Connecting Congregations"; Beachy, "Manuscript Missions"; Schutt, "Complex Connections."

48. A Description of Duties Assigned to Copyists in Bethlehem and Nazareth in the 1760s, PHC 262, MAB.

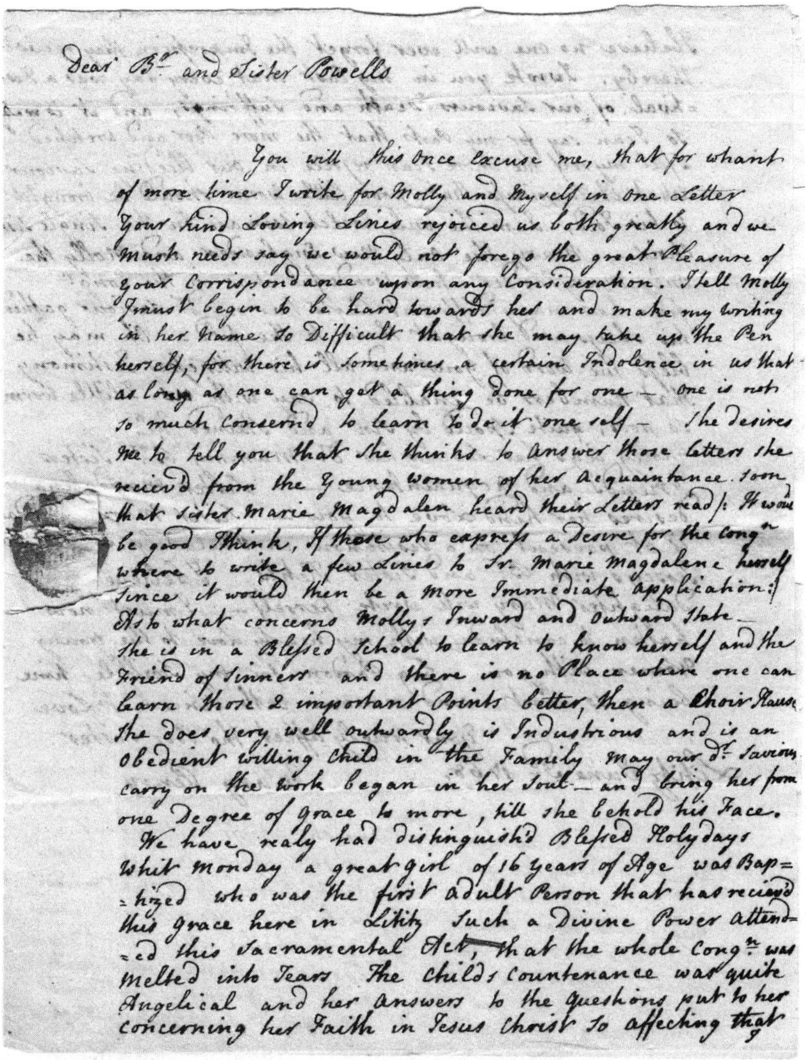

Figure 6   The first page of a 1768 letter from Mary Penry to Joseph and Martha Powell (Letter 14 in this volume). Reproduced by permission of the Moravian Archives, Bethlehem, Pennsylvania.

land, reports from Lusatia and Copenhagen, memoirs of deceased members from around the world, congregational diaries from a half dozen mission stations in the West Indies, results of synods in America and in Europe, and comprehensive histories of the annual work of the entire Moravian church that were composed at Zeist, the Moravian center in the Netherlands. Her work on these congregation accounts continued at least until 1774, when she worked on extracts from congregational diaries from Russia and Labrador.[49]

In addition to these duties, Penry spent substantial amounts of time writing to her friends and relatives. Penry's letters (and correspondents) reveal the complex sources of her sense of self: a Welsh nation she barely remembered, a cosmopolitan Philadelphia in which she briefly lived in affluence, an egalitarian Moravian spiritual community in which she spent her adult life. These letters reveal the strands out of which Penry wove her identity.[50] Even more, they functioned to "maintain and extend . . . social networks" that could be mobilized to her own or her friends' social, spiritual, or economic benefit.[51] Penry used her letters to spark relationships between her varied correspondents. She urged her unmarried Welsh cousin to write to the Moravian single sisters at Haverfordwest, and she tried to connect her Lititz friends to Elizabeth Drinker by asking the former to deliver letters to the latter. Relying on friends to carry correspondence could serve this social purpose: it also avoided the costs of using the postal system. The post imposed a financial burden, usually on the friends who received her letters (since recipients typically paid the cost of postage of letters circulated within the United States) and sometimes on Penry herself (since by the 1790s she could send letters "post paid" at offices in Lancaster or Philadelphia, and she paid the cost of letters sent transatlantically) (Letters 33 and 66). Most of Penry's letters describe how they have been transmitted, express frustration at letters that lay for long periods at merchants' shops (Letters 49 and 52), or ask about letters that may have been lost. The letters collected here hint at a much larger body of work. While some letters miscarried, many others, successfully delivered, no longer survive. Extant letters mention regular correspondence with Nancy Vaughn at Haverfordwest, with Molly Gwillim of Abergavenny, with her cousin Jenny Brown in New Haven, and with the minister Christoph Gottfried Peter in New York. Nearly a dozen letters to Elizabeth Drinker are lost.[52] Penry's weekly correspondence with her mother

---

49. Congregation Accounts, Box: Old English Translations II (Gemein Nachrichten); Congregation Accounts 1774, Items 39–40, Box: G.N. / Engl. 1750–89, New York Ser. I; February 1–May 31, 1768, Diary of the Friedenshütten Congregation, MissInd 131.5, all in MAB.

50. Gerber, *Authors of Their Lives*. For founding texts on epistolary writing and an overview of the field, see Stanton, *Female Autograph*; Altman, *Epistolarity*; and Gaul and Harris, *Letters and Cultural Transformation*, 1–12.

51. See O'Neill, *Opened Letter*, 1–46, quotation at 1. See also Dierks, *In My Power*.

52. For letters, now lost, that Drinker received, see August 16, December 28, 1797, January 18, March 16, December 31, 1799, May 26, 1800, July 22, 1802, March 24, May 18, and November 16, 1803, in Drinker, *Diary*, 2:953, 990, 1131, 1146, 1251, 1303, 1536, 1367, 3:1651, 1704.

between 1756 and 1760 is lost. The greatest loss in volume is likely Penry's correspondence with her cousin, Margaret Stocker, in Philadelphia.

Most of the vast materials that survive in Moravian archives were produced by the men who led the church, although writings by Moravian women (e.g., spiritual memoirs, diaries of single sisters' choirs, reports from mission stations) survive as well. Much of this material, since it was read aloud in congregation or choir meetings, constituted the daily diet of ordinary Moravians. But little evidence survives to indicate how Moravians assimilated these lessons that were addressed to them. Some such evidence is available through congregational records, especially the minutes of overseers' committees, which capture much about ordinary Moravians' daily lives. But these sources dwell disproportionately on the tensions that such committees were established to manage. Even the memoirs (*Lebensläufe*) in which Moravian men and women described their spiritual journey were composed to be read in public, with an awareness of generic expectations, and so tend to offer an idealized version of Moravian life.[53] An extensive personal correspondence such as Penry's is extremely rare and offers an unusual opportunity to examine how an ordinary church member received, understood, and disseminated the ideas and lessons she heard over the course of fifty years.[54]

Moravians documented more of their lives than did most early Americans, but even they, as Leland Ferguson has written, "did not write down most of what they thought or did."[55] Penry recorded more than did most Moravians. Most of her correspondents were not Moravians, and some were not Americans, so she felt obliged to explain the young American republic and the principles and practices of her church to those who knew nothing of them. She composed a thousand-word history of the Moravian church, describing the martyrdom of John Hus in 1415, the church's efforts to preserve unbroken apostolic succession, and its revival in the 1720s (Letter 41). In describing and explaining daily life in a Moravian community to outsiders, Penry's letters contain information not typically found in Moravian records because these take the everyday and the normal for granted. Her sharp eye and skillful pen also recorded life beyond Moravian settlements: an ox roasted on the frozen Delaware, air balloons that some had proposed for transatlantic travel, a visit to Philadelphia's "African church," and the suppression of the Whiskey Rebellion. She reports on economic matters from food prices to politicians' salaries to the fluctuating rent prices in Philadelphia and land prices in Pennsylvania's

---

53. See Faull, *Moravian Women's Memoirs*; Smaby, *Transformation*, 125–44.
54. See Peucker, "In the Blue Cabinet," 7–8; Petterson and Faull, "Speaking About Marriage."
55. Ferguson, *God's Fields*, 34.

backcountry. International and national politics absorbed her. Church leaders forbade members from taking sides in partisan disputes ("It is a Stated Rule in our Congregations that none of their Members engage in Politics or Parties" [Letter 37]), but Penry expressed her allegiances openly in her letters. She mourned when her hero Washington "surrenderd" his office after two terms, had hopes for John Adams, and despised Jefferson.

Penry's Federalist, Anglophile political identity, which emerged from her life in a conservative religious community (and as a British immigrant who never fully embraced America), was fostered by the newspapers she read. Jeffrey Pasley has shown that, in the absence of a consistent party system in the early republic, newspapers were the "fabric that held the parties together between elections and conventions, connected voters and activists to the larger party, and linked the different political levels and geographic regions of the country." Partisan newspapers not only helped create the parties themselves but also created "a sense of membership, identity, and common cause among political activists and voters." Mary Penry's eager consumption and dissemination of political news makes it clear that even readers who were neither activists nor voters—women, for instance—were similarly energized by a newspaper's "common rhetoric and common ideas" into committed partisans.[56] It is not surprising that Penry mentions William Cobbett so often: his *Porcupine's Gazette* taught her how to understand global events. Penry, in turn, attempted to recruit her correspondents into seeing things similarly.

Penry's enjoyment of politics was part of the culture of elite women in eighteenth-century Philadelphia in which Penry grew to adulthood. Deborah Norris assured her friend Sarah Wistar that, while she would express her "sentiments freely" in letters, "Politicks . . . are not our province."[57] Many disagreed. Wealthy Philadelphia women, tied by marriage or friendship to political leaders, were expected to be "knowledgeable about current political developments," to form "their own opinions about issues," and to discuss these opinions with others.[58] In different circumstances, Penry may well have been an exemplary republican mother or wife, who, as Linda Kerber and Jan Lewis have argued, influenced public affairs by fostering her husband's virtue, by educating her children to become virtuous citizens, or even at times by "direct participation" in "public affairs" or "political ritual[s]."[59] Penry's church discouraged this ambition—by men or by women—to engage in

---

56. Pasley, "*Tyranny of Printers*," 11–12.
57. Norris, "A dear dear friend," 502.
58. Fatherly, *Gentlewomen and Learned Ladies*, 133–34.
59. Kerber, *Women of the Republic*, 159, 277; Lewis, "Republican Wife."

public affairs, a prohibition that Penry embraced. But her many years in Moravian communities did not lead Penry to cease forming or expressing her own opinions or to lose interest in local or global politics. When she traded political information with Elizabeth Drinker in the 1790s, Penry reaffirmed the elite class status she and Drinker had shared decades earlier.

Penry's relentless curiosity, her diligent efforts to describe and interpret what she saw for others, makes these letters indispensable to historians of early America. But to treat these letters merely as records of early American political culture is to miss Penry's deep piety. John Woolf Jordan, the librarian at the Historical Society of Pennsylvania, used his editorial scalpel to excise most of Penry's enthusiastic devotion when he reprinted sixteen of her letters in *The Moravian* from 1913 to 1915. He transformed Penry into a historian much like himself, curious about the political, cultural, and economic life of the early republic. But Penry's letters burst with personal testimonies of her devotion to her Savior and record her lifelong efforts to eliminate self so that she could receive grace. They reveal what it feels like to believe that, when individuals become "gladly passive to let good be done to us" (as Zinzendorf promised in a 1746 lecture preached in London), the grace to do good works will follow.[60]

Penry credited her Savior for all her accomplishments, convinced, as Moravian piety taught, that she could not have achieved them on her own. Penry told her Welsh relatives that it was impossible "to think even a good thought—without his Assistance." "There is no *Merit* in *the Creature*," she added. "Everything which renders *us lovely*, is his pure free gift alone" (Letters 42 and 43).[61] This deep belief both in natural depravity ("there is no *Merit* in *the Creature*") and in the necessity and availability of grace (which "renders *us lovely*") fills Penry's letters. Natural depravity held that, due to the fall, human beings—unaided, independent, alone—were unable to perform worthy actions. "The most perfect thing which proceeds from man," John Calvin's 1536 *Institutes of the Christian Religion* had insisted, "is always polluted by some stain." Zinzendorf's lectures on the 1530 Augsburg Confession distilled its second article—since "the fall of Adam, all men begotten in the natural way are born with sin" and no "man can be justified before God by his own strength"—into a memorable hymn that began, "I do believe, since Adam's Fall, / That Mankind are by Nature all / Nothing but Sin."[62] The workings of grace, however, enable sinful human beings to think good thoughts, to

---

60. Zinzendorf, *Nine Public Lectures*, 70.

61. See Zinzendorf, "Third Sermon," in Atwood, *Collection of Sermons*, 45.

62. Calvin, *Institutes*, 2:92; Zinzendorf, *Twenty-One Discourses*, 36.

perform good deeds, to live worthwhile lives. Such deeds, then, derive not from "self" but from the presence of another, of Christ, in one's thoughts and actions. This paradox meant that the only way to lay claim to thoughts or actions that were "pleasing in his Sight" (Letter 69) was to disown agency for them. The notion that only by eliminating self can one find the strength to act worthily is not unique to Moravian piety; elsewhere I have analyzed its pervasive presence in seventeenth- and eighteenth-century British thought.[63] But not every Protestant group lived these paradoxes to the same degree: Moravians in settlement communities such as Bethlehem or Lititz, as Atwood has shown in *Community of the Cross*, lived them intensely.

In Moravian communities, the rhythm of daily life (e.g., services, hymns, litanies, festival days) reminded individuals that they *were* special recipients of their Savior's grace. Penry told friends in Bethlehem in 1768 that "every day thro out the Year we have and injoy his near Presence in his Suffering Form" (Letter 13). Penry's spiritual memoir offers the individual version of this communal assurance. In Lititz, she wrote:

> the dear Savior taught me the hard way for the well-being of my poor heart. This allowed me to see my inherent depravity even more. But I still was not cured. Because I rejected admitting to my true nature, and tried to help myself by my own means, I only slipped deeper into despair. I continued on in this sad state until the Savior granted me the grace to reveal my entire former journey of faith to our then Choir Helper, Sister Maria Magdalena, in an open and truthful manner. Even so it was difficult to recognize myself as such a totally lacking sinner. (Appendix A)

Penry insists that self-reliance ("tried to help myself by my own means") only impeded her ability to receive grace. Even the decision to consult her choir helper is not really hers: her Savior prompts it ("the Savior granted me the grace to reveal my . . . journey of faith").[64] The hymns, litanies, and prayers that structured daily life in Moravian communities aimed to ensure that this grace remained unforgettable. The adjustments after Zinzendorf's death did not eliminate these communal and individual structures that reinforced this conviction.[65] The intense focus on the crucified Christ's wounds, the practice that reminded Moravians of the grace they had received and thus of the

---

63. Gordon, *Power of the Passive Self* and "Glad Passivity."
64. For conversations with choir helpers, see Faull, *Speaking to Body and Soul.*
65. Peucker, *Time of Sifting;* Atwood, "Deep in the Side of Jesus."

source of the good works they performed, persisted throughout the eighteenth century in communities such as Lititz and Bethlehem.

Penry's piety shaped the way she understood the global events she described with such curiosity and in such detail. Her religious millenarianism fit all the happenings in early America and across the globe within a narrative of the end of times. Like so many of her contemporaries, Penry was obsessed with the fever of prophecy that the French Revolution and European war revived as the year 1800 approached. "That we are in the *last* Days, I think beyond a doubt," Penry wrote in 1794, "but how Many Years before the end of those days—God only knows." Penry's confidence that "we live in the last days" did not disappear once the year 1800 had passed (Letters 34 and 71). She watched events in America and in Europe to trace the approach of these end times. Organizing all her observations is her conviction that nothing happened without divine approval: "I am Confident God—and not Chance—is the director of our Affairs" (Letter 57). Penry believed that "history was in the throes of great providential events," and these contemporary events found "their ultimate eschatological meaning" within a divine narrative that Penry did not question.[66] It was her responsibility to interpret what she observed so that it conformed to the divine order she knew existed. This story, of the preparation by the Savior for the final gathering, was the only one worth following and telling.

On May 4, 1804, Penry wrote one last time in the diary of the single sisters' choir. Another hand completed the entry for that date. Penry had been sick off and on for six months, as her cousin Margaret Stocker in Philadelphia knew. Although she "had been in bad health from the first of november," Penry had written Stocker encouraging letters in November, at Christmas, and after New Year's. On March 31, 1804, Penry told Stocker that "she had been ill with a cramp in her breast an Inflamatory fever but the worst was over." She was absorbed in routine business, "settling her Books and drawing out accounts belonging to the Society as she always did Every year" in May. Penry's last letter, describing severe health problems (Letter 74), did not reach Stocker until after Penry's death on May 17, 1804. Mary Penry had lived sixty-eight busy years. Stocker heard the news the next day and wrote a long letter to Penry's surviving Welsh relatives: "it was a great Shock," Stocker assured Katherine Penry and Eliza Powell. Elizabeth Drinker heard on May 20 that Penry had died. A lengthy death notice appeared on May 23 in *Poulson's American Daily Advertiser*, placed there, Drinker believed, by the Stockers, and was picked up by several newspapers on America's East Coast.

---

66. Bloch, *Visionary Republic*, 150–51. See also Juster, *Doomsayers*.

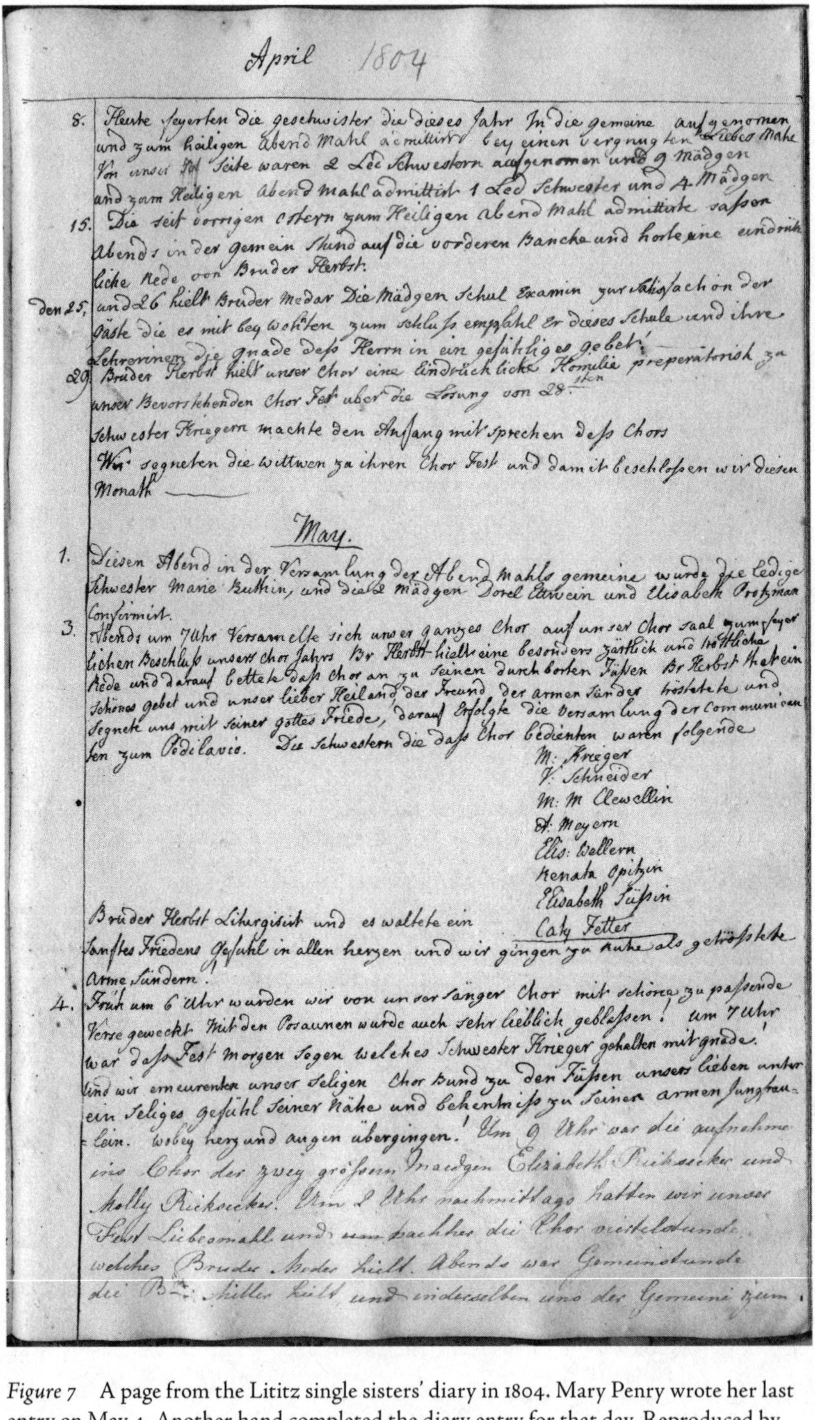

April 1804

8. Heute feyerten die geschwister die dieses Jahr In die gemeine aufgenomen und zum heiligen Abend Mahl admittirt bey einen vergnugten Liebes Mahl Von unser Seite waren 2 Led Schwestern aufgenomen und 9 Mädgen und zum Heiligen Abend Mahl admittirt 1 Led Schwester und 4 Mädgen

15. Die seit vorrigen Ostern zum Heiligen Abend Mahl admittirte sassen Abends in der gemein Stund auf die vorderen Banche und horte eine eindrückliche Rede von Bruder Herbst.

den 25, und 26 hielt Bruder Medar die Mädgen schul Examin zur satisfaction der Gäste die es mit beg wohnten zum schluss empfahl Er dieses schule und ihre Lehrerinen die gnade dess Herrn in ein gefühliges gebet.

29. Bruder Herbst hielt unser Chor eine eindrückliche Homilie preperatorish zu unser Bevorstehenden Chor Fest uber die Losung von 28sten

Schwester Kriegern machte den Anfang mit sprechen dess Chors

Wir segneten die wittwen zu ihren Chor Fest und damit beschlossen wir diesen Monath

May.

1. Diesen Abend in der Versamlung der Abend Mahls gemeine wurde die ledige Schwester Marie Buthin, und diese Mädgen Dorel Elwein und Elisabeth Protzman Confirmirt.

3. Abends um 7 Uhr Versamelte sich unser ganzes Chor auf unser Chor saal zum feyerlichen Beschluss unsers Chor Jahrs Br Herbst hielt eine besonders zärtlich und kräftliche Rede und darauf bettete dass Chor an zu seinen durchborten Füssen Br Herbst that ein schönes gebet und unser lieber Heiland der Freund der armen Sünder tröstete und segnete uns mit seiner gottes Friede, darauf Erfolgte die Versamlung der Communicanten zum Pedilavio. Die Schwestern die dass Chor bedienten waren folgende

M. Krieger
V. Schneider
M. M Clewellin
A. Meyern
Elis: Wellern
Renata Opitzin
Elisabeth Füssin
Caty Fetter

Bruder Herbst Liturgisirt und es waltete ein sanftes Friedens Gefühl in allen herzen und wir gingen zu Ruhe als getröstete Arme Sündern.

4. Früh um 6 Uhr wurden wir von unser sänger Chor mit schöne zu passende Verse geweckt Mit den Posaunen wurde auch sehr lieblich geblassen! um 7 Uhr war dass Fest morgen Segen welches Schwester Krieger gehalten mit gnade! und wir erneurenten unser seligen Chor Bund zu den Füssen unsers lieben unter ein seliges gefühl seiner Nähe und bekentniss zu seinen armen Jungfraulein. wobey herz und augen übergingen! Um 9 Uhr war die aufnahme ins Chor der zwey grössern Maedgen Elizabeth Ricksecker und Molly Ricksecker. Um 2 Uhr nachmittags hatten wir unser Fest Liebesmahl und nachher die Chor viertelstunde welches Bruder Meder hielt. Abends war Gemeinstunde die Br. Miller hielt, und in derselben uns der Gemeine zum

Figure 7 A page from the Lititz single sisters' diary in 1804. Mary Penry wrote her last entry on May 4. Another hand completed the diary entry for that day. Reproduced by permission of the Moravian Archives, Bethlehem, Pennsylvania.

Penry's friend Anna Rosina Kliest, a single sister in Bethlehem, quoted the published death notice in full in a letter to the Moravian missionary John Heckewelder in Ohio.[67]

Penry's will disposed of the few personal effects she had possessed. Most of this consisted of clothing and furniture (two chairs, two tables, and a desk), but Penry also had books and pictures. The bulk of this small estate, including the silver that she had used to host vespers (tea cups and saucers, tongs, a strainer, a sugar dish), went to Anna Margareta Krieger, the steward (*Vorsteherin*) of the single sisters' house, for the choir's use.[68] Four teaspoons were dispersed to friends. The Stockers arranged to have Penry's silver watch, promised to her niece in Wales, sent across the Atlantic to a merchant in Bristol, who received it safely in February 1806 and transferred it to Eliza Powell.[69]

Penry's most valuable legacy had already been distributed: her letters. After Penry's death many correspondents preserved the letters they had received over the decades. John Woolf Jordan first rediscovered these letters in the 1880s. He received the letters that Penry wrote to Elizabeth Drinker from her great-grandson, Henry Drinker Biddle, and presented them to the headmaster of Linden Hall, the girls' school that was founded during Penry's time in Lititz.[70] In 1911, visiting Britain, Jordan learned of Penry's letters to her Welsh cousins. He published bowdlerized versions of sixteen letters in *The Moravian*. Readers enjoyed them and Jordan announced that he was

---

67. Mary Stocker to Katherine Penry, May 30, 1804, Penralley Collection 1399, NLW; May 20, 1804, Drinker, *Diary*, 3:1744 (Drinker heard both that gout and asthma caused MP's death: May 23–24, 1804, *Diary*, 3:1745); Anna Rosina Kliest to John Heckewelder, June 2, 1804, GriderColl.f.19, MAB; Poulson's *American Daily Advertiser*, May 23, 1804, 3. See also Philadelphia's *Evening Post*, May 23, 1804, 3; Harrisburg's *Oracle of Dauphin*, June 2, 1804, 3; and Portland, Maine's *Eastern Argus*, September 27, 1804, 4. The notice read, "DIED, on the 16th inst. at Leditz, in Lancaster county, in the 69th year of her age, Miss Mary Penry. This Lady was born in Wales, and came young into this county. Being early impressed with a sense of Religion, she retired to Bethlehem in the year 1757, and afterwards removed to Leditz, where she spent the last thirty years of her life, in the peaceful enjoyment of all the happiness, which arises from the cultivating and directing a vigorous understanding, and the most benevolent affections to the noblest objects. In her occasional excursions from her beloved retirement, she diffused cheerfulness and knowledge by her conversation among a numerous circle of acquaintances. She lived likewise by her letters in a state of friendship with many learned and pious persons of different denominations in Europe, and different parts of America." The notice concluded with an "extract from one of her last letters," which appears as Letter 73 in this volume.

68. Mary Penry, Last Will and Testament, August 1, 1803, Will Book H-504, Microfilm 299F; Estate Inventory, July 23, 1804, Inv 1804 F001 P; Administrative Account, December 13, 1804, AdAcct 1804 F001 P, all in LCHS. Margaret Stocker wrote that MP's "cloaths [went] to Some of the Singel Sister in the house with her and a small book of Sermonds & a gold ring to me, Her Bed chairs bookcase &c to be Sold and the money to be for the benefit of their Sick poor." Margaret Stocker to Katherine Penry, April 15, 1805, Penralley Collection 1400, NLW.

69. Thomas Daniel to Katherine Penry, February 6, 1806, Penralley Collection 1403, NLW.

70. John Woolf Jordan to C. D. Kreider, September 17, 1903, Linden Hall Archives.

"preparing to publish" the letters "in book form."[71] In this effort Jordan may have collaborated with Elizabeth Lehman Myers, who was gathering materials for *A Century of Moravian Sisters*, published in 1918. Myers transcribed fifteen of the letters that Jordan had printed, added short excerpts from four letters to Drinker, and retyped some biographical paragraphs that Jordan had published in *The Moravian* in 1913.[72] Neither Jordan nor Myers, however, published Penry's letters.

The 1804 death notice in the *Daily Advertiser* is the only trace in the public papers of Mary Penry's life or death. The notice got many details incorrect, including the year Penry moved to Bethlehem and the date of her death. But it captured the central activity of her life: "She lived . . . by her letters in a state of friendship with many learned and pious persons of different denominations in Europe, and different parts of America." Penry did indeed live "by her letters." These letters connected her to the Europe she had left and to the cities of early America, especially Philadelphia, in which she had lived or that she had visited. This volume gathers together that writing that survives, scattered still, as her correspondents were, around the globe.

---

71. *The Moravian* 60, no. 21 (May 26, 1915): 331.
72. PP MEL 19, MAB.

LETTERS

❧ I. TO THE CONGREGATION[1]

1755

Philadelphia, Pennsylvania

Dear Brethren & Sisters

I am a Poor Creature deeply Wo[u]nded by Satan & the World and now desiring to bid an Eternal Adieu to What to my Sorrow has proved so hurtful to me. This therefore is the Reason that I Apply myself to our Saviours Congregation begging that they will have Compasion Upon me for his Sake who has Shed his blood for me a poor Creature Utterly Unworthy of the least of his Mercies.[2] Oh I beg you will not Cast me Out for by Experience I know that if I return back I can not think Otherwise but I Shall be cast away. Dear Saviour to thee I must Apply myself have Mercy Upon me And give me the Priveledge to live Wholly for thee. Thou knowest the Weakness of My heart thou knowst the World was a bitter Enemy to me in bringing me Astray from the[e] then hear my Prayers and lead me not into Temptation but deliver me from Evil give me leave to be thine to live under the Care of thy Congregation for thee. Now I humbly beg the Brethren & Sisters to take my case into Consideration have Compasion on my Youth the time of life when the World has most power over one. And as most of them knows the Danger of it let me pray them to give me Shellter amongst them from it. May my dear Saviour hear and Answer this Request is the Earnest Prayer of

Mary Penry

ALS: BethCong 525, MAB.

1. This letter is MP's request to join the Moravian congregation at Bethlehem. Such letters were required. In June 1755, Thomas Yarrell (1721–1795) included "Mary Penry, Mrs. Attwood's Daughter" among "those who have wrote to be rec'd" into the Philadelphia congregation, describing MP as "a Young Woman our saviour works on her heart She loves the brethren and our Saviour in her degree." See Thomas Yarrell to Augustus Gottlieb Spangenberg, June 18, 1755, PhB II (Letters from Philadelphia up to 1760), MAB.

2. "poor Creature Utterly Unworthy": MP employs mainstream Moravian rhetoric, in which individuals identified themselves as depraved sinners, often likening themselves to lowly creatures such as worms (Letters 4 and 14), entirely dependent on Christ's grace.

2. TO POLLY GORDON[1]

May 5, 1759

Bethlehem, Pennsylvania

May the 5th 1759

Dear Miss Gorden,

I had the Pleasure of Yours of the 26th of April which I had long expected as my mamma gave me hopes of a letter Soon and as it allways does it rejoiced me to hear you had Not forgot your Unworthy friend who is Scarce worth thinking off. I thank you Kindly for your wishes for my happiness, But my dear Friend I am far from desiring that exalted frame or dispos[it]ion of mind. All I wish is Continually to feel my self a poor but Redeem'd Sinner who Cannot Subsist one Minute without the Preventing grace of my Crucified Saviour who has Revealed himself to me as Suffering for my Sins and dying for my Iniquities,[2] For Me, who So long have rejected the kind offers of his grace to Contemplate his Stupendius love, that forc'd him down from his throne to take our Nature upon him that he might die to redeem us. This is the only Object, I think deserves any Attention, Thro' him I have access to his Heavenly Father being assured Whosoever hath the Son hath the Father allso, For in him dwelleth all the fullness of the Godhead Bodily,[3] Not that it is in my Power to bring any thing of my own to render me acceptable in the Sight of God, Nothing but the blood of the Imaculate Lamb will have any Plea before the Throne.[4] You Say my dear you desire and are Pleased to hear of the Welfare of your Friends and the Publick, I think it is laudible in you, far be it from me to think to bind any one to Certain rules as if they Could Not be happy in Whatever State of life the Lord has Placed them in, for my part I Sincerely wish happiness to all my fellow Creatures and am bound in duty to pray for the Goverment Under which we Injoy Liberty of Conscience and Freedom, But as for Concerning my Self any further with the Affairs of the World I think my self a poor Insignificant thing that Im Sure never Shall be of any Service in it and when I go hence Shall not be miss'd by any one Except my Mamma,[5] being in Possession of the heaven I desire (as much as I can enjoy this Side Eternity), In knowing my Self to be a Poor but Redeemed Sinner for the Sake of the Atoneing blood of Christ Injoying the Antipast of a blest hereaffter, In his love which when faith shall be turn'd into Sight will be Perfect, When I shall see him Face to Face on whom I Now believe and I have Indeed found Something so engaging in my dear Saviours love to me a Poor Creature that it has Indeed took Up all my Attention, and I look upon that time lost when my mind is taken up with any thing else. Not that I Pretend to be Perfect. No I find Occasion enough to humble my Self in the dust before his Footstool,[6] Confessing my Self a Poor Sinful Mortal that Stands in Continual Need of his grace from Day to Day, But I find him a gracious and Merciful Saviour that is Readyer to forgive than I to ask. Who would not Serve so good a Master? My Reason for Saying I did not Want to make a Moravian of you proceeded from this, as I writ so free to you you might perhaps have Thought, as many does, that we want to bring ever[y] one over to our way if we Speak or Write a little Serius to them which is not my desire.[7] I like to leave every one to the guidance of the holy Spirit which will lead Us into all truth. It is true in one Scence we must and I hope are of one faith for Christ is the General Saviour of us all and the[re] is no Salvation in any other but in him. Neither is he Confined to this or that Perswasion But as many as receive him to them give he power to become the Children of God even to them that believe on his Name. And I heartily Wish my dear Miss Gorden may (if She has not) Experience that true Happiness which every one may attain to that will accept of It, which is no Enthusiastick Rapture,[8] but a Solid Foundation in his death and Suff'rings a Childlike Reliance on him from day to day to give us his grace to keep Close to him and to follow the directions of his holy Spirit which will be a Lanthorn to our feet and guide our Steps in his Paths.[9] This is the Foundation of which my house is built which Cannot fall Since it is Grounded on the Rock of Ages.

My Whole Wish is to Continue humble and Low, att his feet I desire to keep my Seat and listen to that Small Still Voice which only wispers Love, which teaches me What is his will, which tells me what to do and Covers me with Shame when I, Do Not his will Persue.[10]

Now my dear Friend I belive by this time I have tired you, so will Hasten to a Conclusion, and may our dear Saviour Watch over you and keep you (In a World full of Temptations) from every Danger and give you temporal and eternal Happiness in him the Fountain from whence all true happiness flows. Could [I] but have hopes of Seeing you here, an hours Conversation would be a greater Satisfaction then 20 letters. Please to give my kind Love to your Mamma Grandmama and your Sister Dolly[11] which concludes me your Affectionate but Unworthy Friend

Mary Penry

ALS: Saltar Family Correspondence, David M. Rubenstein Rare Book and Manuscript Library, Duke University. Addressed "To Miss Gordon, | In Philadelphia." Endorsed "1759 M. Penry."

1. Mary (Polly) Gordon (b. 1733). Her stepbrother, the painter Henry Benbridge (1743–1812)—whose widowed mother, Mary Clark Benbridge (d. 1778), married the widower Thomas Gordon (ca. 1712–1772) in 1751—worried in the 1760s that none of his sisters would marry. But Polly's sister Dorothy (1738–1781) married Lawrence Saltar (1737–1783) in 1769, and her sister Elizabeth (1752–1818) married John Saltar (1733–1802) in 1774. See Saltar, "Fanny Saltar's Reminiscences"; and Henry Benbridge to Elizabeth Gordon, December 9, 1769, Collection 777, Ph-32, Joseph Downs Collection of Manuscripts and Printed Ephemera, Winterthur Library.

2. "Preventing grace": divine grace that precedes and enables the action of the human will.

3. 1 John 2:23; Colossians 2:9.

4. "Not . . . in my Power": one is incapable by means of one's own will to act worthily without grace.

5. "Affairs of the World": Moravians avoided engaging in public life, as MP explained in Letter 46. Zinzendorf urged Moravians to "[escape] out of the World's Way" (Twenty-One Discourses, 275) and to not swear public oaths, serve on juries, or use civil courts. Moravians deferred to established governments, except when they demanded military service (from which a 1749 Act of Parliament released Moravians). This principle of nonengagement was difficult to maintain during civil conflicts.

6. "dust before his Footstool": MP may refer here to Isaiah 49:23. This exact phrase is used satirically in Jonathan Swift's 1726 Gulliver's Travels, 204.

7. "did not Want to make a Moravian of you": Zinzendorf resisted the formation of a separate "Moravian church," encouraging believers to remain in their confessional denominations. See Letter 41, note 16.

8. "Enthusiastick Rapture": MP shares the eighteenth-century suspicion of enthusiasm, portraying it as a momentary effusion and contrasting it with "Solid Foundation." See Letter 49, note 9.

9. Psalm 119:105.

10. "listen . . . . his will Persue": Gambold, Collection of Hymns, 2:47.

11. "your Mamma . . . Sister Dolly": see above, note 1.

₰ 3. TO RELATIVES IN WALES

July 13, 1760
Bethlehem, Pennsylvania

Bethlehem in Pennsylvania
July the 13th 1760

Honoured Unkle

It is now full 16 years since I have heard from any off my dear Papas Family which allmost makes me Question if ever I shall. But if these lines has the good Fortune to reach my dear Unkle Billy or any of my Fathers Brothers Hands let it serve to Inform you that your Brother Hugh Penrys Daughter is living and earnestly longs to hear from you.[1] Tho so far Distant and Perhaps forgotten by her Friends I have no other motive to write you but filial affection, I ask no other Favour but a few lines in answer to this, as our dear Lord has been graciously Pleased to give my Mamma a competency tho' we live not in affluence yet we need not be a Burthen to any one.[2] I have these many years had a great desire to write but where to direct to I knew not, this kept me back till in October 1759 I writ to my aunt Sally Bateman in Narboth and entreated her to Inquire if any of my dear Relations was alive.[3] In April 1760 I receivd an answer dated the 25 of January wherin she told me she could give me no Information as she liv'd 3 score miles distant. This determin'd me to write my Self and beg my aunt to forward it as I hope she will. It is some Incouragement to me that the way is open within Sixty miles and that I hope a Post can take it, what a joy it will be to me if I am Successful in this, the Pleasing hopes of Seeing a few lines from you draws tears from my eyes. Indeed my dear Unkle tho' I was so young when I came to america yet I cannot forgett that I was born in Brechnockshire and that I have so many near and dear Friends there. Indeed I only know it from my dear Mamma for I have never had the Scrape of a pen from any one in Wales. When I think on this and that I am so far removed from them that I have not one Relation but my Mother in this Country and have not so much as the Pleasure of hearing from them, this often makes me Melancholy. Now I have made a trial. If this fails (hard as it is to me) I must give up all hopes in this life, But hope in the life to come to See you all (thro the Merits of our dear Redeemer) assembled among those who have washd their Robes and made them White in the Blood of the Lamb.[4] If it is Possible for the Departed Spirits in heaven to know one another I am Sure my joy will be inexpressible to meet you there[5]— Oh my dear Unkle could you but be Sencible of the tenderness which overwhelms my heart att the Writing of this you'd see a Proof of the force of Blood. I should be very glad to hear Perticulars of my Family and If my Grandmama is yet living which [I] doubt of as She was in years when I left England.[6] If she is, pray present my most Respectful Love and Duty to her as allso to my Unkles and aunts dear to me, but allmost unknown, to Miss Sally Penry my dear godmother and Miss Molly Guillim.[7] My Unkle Benjamin died I think in the year 45. My Unkle Charles I think I remember as he often visited Mama in Bristol and once I Remember Seeing my Unkle Thomas. You my dear Unkle Billy I do not Remember I have seen att least I was very Young if I did tho my Mama has often talk'd of you and my Unkle the dockter.[8] (To give you an account of my Self) It pleased our dear Saviour in my 19th year to give me a gracious call in my heart to bring me off from the World and the things of it, to fix me on him in obedience to this call I left Philadelphia In the [year] 1756 and came with the full Consent of my Mama to live att Bethlehem which is 60 miles distant from Philadelphia in a congregation of the United Brethren where I live in the Single Sisters house.[9] I have these 4 years enjoyed an uninterupted Tranquility and happiness, I live for and to him who died for me and know of no happiness to Compare to this, To Jesus all [our soul] directed is, and I have bound my Self for ever his. Oh he has drawn me with the Cords of Love, His Satisfying Sweetness now I prove, He [hath deserved] me, free my Self I give, He has redeem'd me, To him will I live[10]—I have the Pleasure to See my dear Mamma once a year and [hear from] her by letter every week. In April She was here and made a stay of 3 weeks.[11] Now my dear Unkle I know not what to Say further but that [I remain] with the greatest Respect and Love, your ever dutiful Neice.

Mary Penry

P.S. This comes by a Vessel belonging to the Brethren called the Co[ncord. The] Captains name is Jacobson, and Sails out of New York.[12] [Please write and] send your letter to my aunt Bateman who will forward it.[13]

ALS: Penralley Collection 1353, NLW.

1. Hugh Penry of Abersenny (d. 1730) married in 1698. See Brecon St. Mary Church Register, PCA. He and his wife, Elinor (d. 1762), had several children, including James (1699–1739), a cleric; Thomas (1703–1769), a doctor; Hugh (1705–1740), MP's father; Charles (b. 1710); Meredith (1714–1799); and Benjamin (b. 1719), who died before MP left for America in 1744 (Letter 36). See Defynnog Church Register, PCA. In this letter MP addresses "Unkle Billy," so she also recalled a brother William. It was Meredith Penry who replied over thirty years later (Letter 29).

2. MP moved into Bethlehem's single sisters' house in June 1756. Her widowed mother, Mary Attwood, lived in Philadelphia.

3. "Narboth": Narberth, about ten miles northeast of Milford Haven in Wales. "Sally Bateman": MP's mother's sister, Sarah Stocker, had married Maurice Bateman, a surgeon. See Letter 6. MP often asks after from this aunt in later years.

4. Revelation 7:14.

5. "If it is Possible for the Departed Spirits in heaven to know one another": a popular topic among eighteenth-century novelists and divines. Richard Polwhele wrote that "when on the last day our souls shall be re-united to our glorified bodies, we shall be enabled to recognize those with whose persons we are here familiarly acquainted" (*Discourses*, 1:188). See also Radcliffe, *Romance of the Forest*, 274. MP ponders this question often; see Letters 5, 37, 43, 44, 48, 69, and 73.

6. Elinor Penry, who married Hugh Penry of Abergavenny (MP's grandfather) in 1698, was still living: she died in 1762. See Brecon St. John Evangelist Church Register, PCA.

7. "Sally Penry": likely Sarah Penry (b. 1700), daughter of Thomas and Margaret Penry of Llwyncyntefin. Thomas Penry of Llwyncyntefin may have been the brother of Hugh Penry of Abergavenny. "Miss Molly Guillim": a Mary Gwillim, probably unmarried, died in Abergavenny in January 1794. See Abergavenny St. Mary's Church Register, PCA. MP often asks in later letters after Gwillim, with whom she corresponded before the American Revolution.

8. For Hugh Penry's brothers, see above, note 1.

9. See Appendix A (and this volume's introduction) for an account of MP's early years.

10. "To Jesus . . . will I live": Gambold, *Collection of Hymns*, 2:162–63.

11. Mary Attwood visited Bethlehem and Nazareth in late April and early May 1760.

12. The *Concord*, captained by Christian Jacobsen (d. 1782), arrived in New York from London on June 14, 1760. Jacobsen had captained the *Irene* on several transatlantic voyages, including its last (1757–58). By the end of 1760 he had a new vessel, the *Hope*. Jacobsen retired to Staten Island and married Ann Van Deventer.

13. "aunt Bateman": see above, note 3.

❧ 4. TO UNKNOWN[1]

[1760]

Bethlehem, Pennsylvania

My dearest mother frequently told me when in health, that if she should be called home to our dear Saviour without seeing & taking leave of me she would beg for permission to visit me after her decease. I entreated her not to come, alledging my weakness, & that I could not support it. Well my dear, said she, see you I must, & if I have leave, I will visit you in your sleep & converse with you without putting you in fear. This she told me very positive the last time I saw her, which was in May 1760. She departed this life the 21st of September the same year.[2] As I did not hear one word of her illness & received the account of her decease eight days after, I found it very hard to reconcile myself, & grieved & lamented more than I ought to have done. I was as much desireous of her appearing to me as I had been against it, & frequently walked out of evening's alone in hope of seeing her. About ten days after her death I went to bed very much depressed indeed & lamented my loss of so tender a mother (as she had been to me) with many tears. In this situation of mind I fell asleep & had the following dream or more properly *Vision*, for such it really was!

Methought I was in a place in the open air, & looking upwards, I saw my dear Mama descend & come gently towards me, in a robe of such a dazzling brightness that it exceeded every thing I ever saw in my life. She seated herself by me, & thus she spoke to me. My dear child! I have asked & obtained leave of our dear Saviour to come to you, as I have observed the concern you are under & am now ready to answer any questions which you have to ask. Upon this I looked steadfastly at her, but was quickly obliged to cast down my eyes, for although I knew every feature in her face, yet her countenance shone with such a brightness that I could no more bear to look at her, than at the sun at Noon-day. Yet I was not sensible of the least fear or terror. As she had frequently expressed a great fear of death, the first thing which I asked was, wether she had an easy departure? To which she replied, My dear I was not sensible of the pains of death, my dear Saviour had taken away the sting. As soon as I departed I approached our Saviour's feet as a poor worm, & met with a most gracious reception.[3] He then took a book in his hand & held it open, in which my name was wrote in such large characters that all the saints & Angels could read it—& then our Saviour pronounced these words: Mary Attwood! because thou hast kept the word of my patience, so have I kept thee from the hour of temptation! She then paused, as if to give me time for recollection—And indeed my thoughts were manyfold. I felt such a secret curiosity to know what *manner* she was happy & had not courage to speak my thoughts, which she seemed to perceive. However with a faultering voice I said: And are you indeed happy! Here she assumed a serious countenance, & in a very ernest tone of voice spoke as follows. It is not permitted me to tell you what my degree of happiness is! Enough that I am happy. As happy as is consistant for me to be—more happiness would do me no good & with less I should not be contented. She then took occasion from my asking her this question to rebuke my curiosity. You know my dear child said she, that our favorite theme was usually the life to come, but I charge you, not to pry too deep into those mysteries—poor mortals pretend to describe what they can scarce form an idea of, for the tongues of Men & of Angels cannot describe the unutterable happiness of the blessed spirits with our Saviour! After pausing a little, she asked wether the stroke (meaning her death) was not much lighter than what I had expected? I said yes—Upon which she replied, I beged our Saviour to make it easy to you—Your Sister Anna Rosel behaved very kind to you—I stood by when she told you of my decease.[4] She then as near as I recollect spoke as follows: Our Saviour together with his perfect Congregation, often visits sometimes one, sometimes the other Congregation, & there we pitch our Tents, were your eyes opened to see the numbers which surround you, you would then have reason to say your meeting hall is too small. When our Saviour observes among the members of the Congregation an indifference toward him, he says, Arise, let us go hence, but he never goes away without leaving a fire of love in those hearts who become sensible of their errors, that they burn with desire after his appearing.—And you, my dear child, do you not depend upon this & comfort yourself with saying Our Savour is gracious, merciful & long suffering. It is most certainly true that he is so, but do you not try his patience too much, for he will not bear so much from his selected children, as from worldlings. You have now lost your Mother, and are an Orphan, do not put your trust in any one, but in our Saviour, take him for your Father, your friend, & your all. He has promised to supply my place toward you, & that he will do an hundred fold! Make him your only object & have no other, above all let his suffrings be weighty to your heart. Jesus martyr! Jesus martyr! She repeated (holding up her hands to heaven) Jesus' death! Jesus' sufferings! O what powerful words! For this we continually fall at his feet & adore him. Do not be impatient my child, to come to our Saviour, in two or three hours, after my reckoning, you will be with me. She then seemed to be going, I beg[g]ed her to stay a little longer. No, was the answer, No my child, I cannot leave heaven for you. I then asked her to come again to which she said No, this time, but no more—I am called and must go to my Order—& then she ascended in a tract of light—I looked after her till she disappeared, & then awoke in a peculiar situation of heart & mind which it is not in my power to describe.

Mary Penry

Copy (unknown hand): Henry Family Papers, 1740–1989, Series 6, Box 1:20, Jacobsburg Historical Society.

1. A second copy of this account, which omits the first three hundred words and features more standard spelling, survives. See Commonplace Book, Box: Lancaster Misc. I, MAB. Other copies circulated as well; Esther Duché Hill (1760–1835) recalled that when she was in England (1777–92) her grandmother sent her MP's "remarkable Dream of her Mother." See Esther Duché Hill to Mary Hopkinson, August 17, 1800, Redwood Collection, Am. 12905, HSP. An English Moravian commonplace book from Bristol or Bath, now lost, contained "a dream sent from Philadelphia in 1787," surely MP's.

2. Mary Attwood died on September 21, 1760.

3. "poor worm": see Letter 2, note 4.

4. Anna Rosina Anders (1727–1803), known as Anna Rosel, served as the single sisters' spiritual adviser in Bethlehem from 1748 to 1764. Her memoir appears in Faull, *Moravian Women's Memoirs*, 5–9.

❧ 5. TO POLLY GORDON[1]

March 1, 1762
Bethlehem, Pennsylvania

Bethlehem March the 1st 1762

My dear Miss Gorden

It is so long since I have heard from you that I believe this, must ask if you are yet in the land of the Living; Mrs Stocker is indeed so kind as to let me know now and then how my Miss Gorden does, but as she has been ill, it was some weeks before I rec'd a Letter from her and that very short as she was yet but weak.[2] Some time ago she inform'd me, you had been dangerously Ill but was on the Recovery at the time she wrote. Now dear Miss Polly I beg if you are able, you would let me hear of your Welfare by a few lines as I can assure you this little Billet comes fraught with Love and a tender Sollicitude to know how you do, for my dear Friend tho' our Accquaintance is not so many Years Standing, yet when I examine my Heart, there is none of my old Friends that is so dear to me as your Self. To you, I can write free, without fearing to be ridiculed as unfashionable, To you I can write That I enjoy so much Happiness in living for and to my Lord, and you can understand me as you experience that Happiness your self. I often think, if it is Possible after this Life to know Those in heaven who was dear to one on Earth That the Sight of my dear Friend would be an addition to my Felicity.[3] May we both, is my humble petition answer the Charactor which Mary had, having Chose the Better part which it is our own fault if we lose

> We know the Weakness of our Souls
> But Jesus is our Stay
> Our kind Redeemer has engag'd
> To lead us on our Way
> And He'l forever prove the same
> Tho' we to change are prone
> Our welfare He will ere promote
> Who chose us for his Own.[4]

This is my Comfort that He is my Shepherd who will with his Power and grace defend me (while I put my Trust in him) from all assaults of the Evil One. Now my much lov'd Friend I must conclude being in great haste to Send this away as the oppertunity goes soon and Remain your truly Affectionate Friend

M: Penry

ALS: Saltar Family Correspondence, David M. Rubenstein Rare Book and Manuscript Library, Duke University. Addressed "For | Miss Gordon | In Philadelphia | Per favour | Mrs Stocker." Endorsed "No 8 | 1762."

1. See Letter 2.
2. "Mrs Stocker": Margaret Stocker. See Appendix C.
3. "if it is Possible . . . who was dear to one": see Letter 3, note 5.
4. "We know . . . for his Own": Gambold, *Collection of Hymns*, 1:338.

🕮 6. TO FRIEDRICH VON MARSCHALL[1]

July 19, 1763

Lititz, Pennsylvania

Lititz July the 19th 1763

Dear Brother Marschall

Shall I take the Liberty to make a Request to you and Trouble you with my affairs, indeed I can hardly perswade myself to incommode you with it, Yet knowing your Readyness to assist the poorest Child that stands in need, I am embolden'd to address my self to you and beg your kind assistance.

In a Letter which I lately receiv'd from a Friend in Wales, I am Inform'd of a Legacy supposed to be left my Mamma at the Decease of her step Mother; the Legacy is in it self very triffling being but 10 pounds per Annum yet as it is 17 Years Since it is fallen to us it amounts to a pretty sum. I have writ, to Brother Okely for his advice what to do in the Affair, and I have receiv'd his answer.[2] I must own I am very Indifferent about [it my]self. Yet as I have not sought for it, but hear of it by Chance, I will not lay it quite aside but endeavor by gentle means to obtain it.

I cannot bear the thoughts of a Law Suit besides the grounds are to[o] Insignificant to build on as I have nothing to show, nothing to plead but hearsay.[3]

I have thought wether it would not be better to write a Letter to my Aunt (who is the Person from whom the money must come) and ask herself for Information. I am the Readyer to do this as she is in Some Measure under the Care of the Brethren in Hertford West.[4] Would therefore ask Brother Marschall, if you will be so kind as to convey a Letter for me to my Aunt, under cover to some Brother there, who would be kind enough to see a little into the Affair, and should she not write a Satisfactory answer that I might from him Obtain some further Light.[5]

It is above 3 Years since I heard a Word from my aunt tho' I have writ her 4 or 5 letters. In her last she tells me she lives at a Place call'd Narboth, near Milford Haven, that she first heard the Gosple from Brother Gussenbaur, and Miss Patty Vaughan, that she has visited the Congregation at Hertford to her great Blessing.[6] But her husband was an Enemy to the Brethren.

I should be much concern'd to draw my Aunts displeasure on me by any Violent proceedings as it may in the end be for Nothing, especially as I know not what her Circumstances are, her husband is a Docter and in good Bussiness. Yet she is a Mother of Children and such a sum of money as it amounts to, might Ruin her. Therefore am very desireous to know a little how she is Situated before I proceed further.

It is true my circumstances are not extraordinary and if our Saviour says it proper that I should have an addition I should be thankful. If not, I am quite contented. I want for Nothing. Neither do I believe I ever shall as long as I continue faithful to our Saviour and his Congregation.

Will you be so kind Dear Brother and let me know If I may Write, and trouble you with the letter, as I am desireous to do it as soon as may be, and should I obtain [no o]ther Satisfaction than hearing from my Aunt, that would be a very great pleasure to me.

Please to give my Respectful Love to dear Sister Marschall and a kiss to your dear little Baby.[7]

Sisters Mag. and Annal desire the same,[8] which Concludes me with much Respect dear Brother Your Most

Affectionate Sister &
Humble Servant
Mary Penry

P.S. My Aunts Name is Sarah Bateman. Her Husband, Maurice Bateman, Surgeon at Narboth. She is my Mammas Sister by the Fathers Side. Her Maiden Name was Stocker.[9]

ALS: PP MFr 2, MAB.

1. Friedrich von Marschall (1721–1802) joined the Moravian church in 1739 and married Hedwig Elizabeth von Schweinitz (1724–1795) in 1750. He arrived in America in 1761 to oversee all Moravian congregations in Pennsylvania and adjoining areas. He held this position until 1764, when he left to assume the same role in Wachovia, the Moravians' hundred-thousand-acre tract in North Carolina.

2. John Okely (1721–1792) emigrated from Bedford, England, in 1742. He served as scrivener and conveyancer at Bethlehem until he dissociated from the Moravians because of conflicts over the land between Bethlehem and Nazareth. See Jordan, "John Okely." MP spent several years without success trying to obtain this legacy. See Letters 7, 9, and 10.

3. "Law Suit": Moravians preferred "the rapid disposition of internal disputes without resort to worldly legal means." Engel, *Religion and Profit*, 34.

4. "Hertford West": Haverfordwest, a Moravian community in Wales, officially settled in 1763, although itinerant Moravian preachers had worked there for over a decade by that time.

5. "some Brother there": Marschall suggested Thomas Sims, whom MP contacted. He did not reply (Letter 9).

6. Haverfordwest lies midway between Narberth (ten miles west) and Milford Haven (ten miles south). John Balthasar Gussenbauer (1711–1789), involved with early Moravian activities in England at Fetter Lane, was in Bristol during the late 1740s and labored at Haverfordwest from 1756 to 1763. "Miss Patty Vaughan": Margaret (Patty) Vaughn (1726–1803), one of four Vaughn sisters attached to the Moravian church. She lived near Haverfordwest at Trecwn, an estate owned by her brother, admiral John Vaughn (ca. 1713–1789). Patty and two of her sisters remained single: Joanna Vaughn (1723–1799) and Anne (Nancy) Vaughn (1717–1798), who in 1764 moved from Bedford to the Haverfordwest's sisters' house. See Catalog of the Congregation at Haverfordwest, 1763–1849; Diary of the Haverfordwest Congregation, 1763–1805; and Register of Burials, Haverfordwest, Archive Book 125–26, all in Moravian Church Archives. MP often asked her Welsh relatives about Nancy Vaughn, with whom she had corresponded before the American Revolution. A third sister, Dorothy Vaughn (1721–1781), drew her husband, Joseph Foster-Barnham (1729–1789), to the Moravian church, after which he invited Moravian missionaries to his Jamaican plantation Mesopotamia. See Dunn, *Tale of Two Plantations*, 31, 228.

7. "dear little Baby": Christian Friedrich von Marschall (1762–1764), the von Marschalls' first American-born child.

8. "Sisters Mag. and Annal": Anna Magdalena Meyer (1710–1780), the first spiritual overseer (*Pflegerin*) of the Lititz single sisters' house, and Anna Schäffer (1730–1797), the *Pflegerin's* helper. On April 30, 1764, Schäffer married Samuel Herr (1716–1773), who became the pastor in York; in December 1774, the widowed Anna Herr married Ewald Gustav Shewkirk (1725–1805), who soon after became the pastor in New York.

9. "Sarah Bateman": See Letter 3, note 3.

ఇ 7. TO FRIEDRICH VON MARSCHALL[1]

August 9, 1765

Lititz, Pennsylvania

Lititz August the 9th 1765

Dear Brother Marschall,

Mr Weiss has now [been] here, and I am as Wise as ever I was for there has not been any [thing] done since I left Philadelphia.[2] I know not wether I writ you dear [Brother] that Mr William Logan had promis'd me to, state such question[s] as He thought necessary in the affair, and send two copies over to Bristol to two of his Corrispondants there, Gentlemen capable of answering, or procuring answers, to these questions;[3] as he look'd upon it a highly necessary step; that we might know what Measures to take, this I took to be doing Sufficient as I have heard certain that Miss Day and her Father are both living, and in very good circumstances.[4] But Neither has this been done, undoubtedly my Cousins Delitariness is in a great Measure the Reason of it, for He and Weiss both Promised to call on Mr Logan and give him the questions they desired to have resolved—Weiss says he is quite tired of waiting so often on Mr Stocker for no purpose as he never can meet with Him at home, or att liesure to receive his Visits[5]—As to Mr Humphreys, the Person whom my Cousin pitch'd upon to draw up the Paper with Captain Wall &c. Deposition[6]—Mr Weiss says by Several Expressions he has dropt, He seems to know more of the affair than anyone. But it is likewise to be observ'd He seems more inclin'd to serve my Friends in England against me, than to act as my Friend.

I heard something of it before I left town—told my Cousin of it and He promised to go to him, and as he is very intimate with him endeavour to Sift him and try to get out of him what he knows but this is not done—Weiss says Mr Humphreys told him—if any Monies was to fall to me, he was sure they would send it me, But if I made any demand against a Landed Estate I should never get it—When I first talk'd with Weiss, I beg'd him not to envolve me in great Affairs at this Juncture. Then, He was for driving it to the uttermost. Now he repeats my own Words, says, let us wait till We have better and Surer ground to build on—very true, but let me get those grounds, thats all [missing] at Present. Why yes he says, quite right, but tis not my Fault [missing] you don't, you draw back—(O these laywers)

I have writ to my [Cous]in and press'd him to conclude this one part—it may be [long] before I undertake another—

Upon shewing Weiss The State of the Case, relating to my Mammas Mothers Fortune—He told me, he did not give that up as lost, but that if I had 100 Sterling to spare He really beliv'd I might recover it, but as that is not so, I am deaf to such Proposals. I writ my Cousin he should try to recover his Legacy which his Uncle left each of his Brothers Children, and then I could get Mine, and by that means be enabled to fee my Lawyer. This is all that I have ask'd both Weiss and Stocker, for it is hitherto been only asking questions receiving fair Promises and nothing brought to a Conclusion.

I can assure you dear Brother I am heartily tired of this Much Ado About Nothing, as I believe you are with hearing of it—Mr Stocker is I believe offended at me for not accepting a genourous offer (in his Opinion) which he made me[7]—but that gives me no Manner of uneasiness—

I have now related to you Dear Brother what I know my self and can only wait with Patience the Result—

This I can assure you it is the least of my Concerns—whatever you (as my dear Brother in our Dearest Saviour, and much nearer Related to me thro his Precious Blood than any of my Natural Relations—) think proper to Advise me, I shall follow and will not do any thing contrary to it—I submit my self as a Child to your Dirrections—and conclude with tenderest love to dear Sister Marschall. Your ever affectionate Sister

and truly obliged Servant
Mary Penry

Dear Sister Magdalena begs a hearty Salutation to your Self & Spouse, in which all our Sisters Join.[8]

ALS: PP MFr 2, MAB. Addressed "To | Dear Brother | Marshall | In | Bethlehem."

1. See Letter 6.
2. Lewis Weiss (1717–1796), lawyer and judge in Philadelphia. See Jordan, "Lewis Weiss." MP left for Philadelphia on June 30, 1765, and returned to Lititz on July 13.
3. William Logan (1717–1776), attorney for the Penn family. His father, James Logan (1674–1751), was William Penn's personal secretary, a member of Pennsylvania's Provincial Council for over forty years, Pennsylvania's chief justice (1731–39), and its governor (1736–38). His son was George Logan (Letter 53, note 4).
4. "Miss Day": see this volume's introduction.
5. "my Cousins Delitariness": Anthony Stocker, a Philadelphia merchant. See Appendix C.
6. "My Humphreys . . . Captain Wall": unidentified.
7. "genourous offer": Anthony Stocker invited MP to live with his family, but "happily settled in the Congregation" she refused, which "produced a Coolness of some years" (Letter 41).
8. Anna Magdalena Meyer. See Letter 6, note 8.

🐚 8. TO POLLY GORDON[1]
August 25, 1765
Lititz, Pennsylvania

Lititz August the 25 1765

Dear Miss Gordon
My ever Beloved Friend

Having fully recover'd all the Fatigues of Body and Mind, Which the Journey and Noisy City Occassion'd, I think it is high time to make my Acknowledgements to my dear Friend for the Tenderness with which you treated me on my late Visit.[2] It is true I cannot express the deep Sence I have of your Kindnesses, tho' my Heart is truely Sencible of them and never shall forgett it, and knowing how undeserving I am in myself the greater is my Obligations—What a Pleasure would it be to me, could I hope one day to have the favour of your Company in my Peaceful Dwelling a few Hours, I flatter my self to one of your Taste I could render your Visit agreeable, as your Inclinations (if I Judge right) is more for quietness and calm Repose than the so call'd Pleasures of the World—

Yet my dear Miss Gordon I can Scarce hope for this Satisfaction and must content my Self with Conversing with you thro' the Pen. But altho' we are Separated, our Souls *can* have an Intercourse If we Unite in one Object and both make that equally our Concern (as I hope we do) if our Dear Redeemer be our Only Happiness if we know of none out of Him if the Meditation on his Death & Suffring is what Alone takes up our thoughts—then we may call our selves *Kindred Souls*—Relations by the Blood of Jesus—O there is Nothing else can make Life Supportable, for When we behold ourselves in the true Light—as poor Fallen creatures who are utterly Lost had not our dear Reedeemer had Compassion on us, and given his Life to redeem us. The greatness of our Ransom Price, Convinces us of the greatness of our Offences, so that [it is] no Wonder when a Poor Pardon'd Sinner is taken up Continually in Contemplation on their Suff'ring Lord

"Thro all Lifes Hours and Stations, I'm under Obligations, The highest to thee Lamb"
"Thy Death and Passion ever, Till Soul and Body Sever, Shall in my hearts recess prevail"[3]

Time will not Permit me to enlarge can only add my Service to your dear Mamma & Sisters, and beg you to excuse this Incoherent Stile as the

Opper[tu]nity just now presents and I'm in such haste, can scarce read what I write. Adieu my dear Miss Gordon! Believe me to be unchangeably your

ever Faithful & Affectionate Friend

M. Penry

ALS: Saltar Family Correspondence, David M. Rubenstein Rare Book and Manuscript Library, Duke University. Addressed "To | Miss Gorden | In | Philadelphia." Endorsed "No 11 | P Penry."

1. See Letter 2.
2. MP left for Philadelphia on June 30 and returned to Lititz on July 13, 1765.
3. "Thro all . . . hearts recess prevail": MP links two separated verses in Gambold, *Collection of Hymns*, 1:256.

৯৶ 9. TO NATHANAEL SEIDEL[1]
October 13, 1766
Lititz, Pennsylvania

Lititz October 13th 1766

Valued and dear Brother

I come to you now like a child approaching her beloved father, asking advice for my affairs. Dear Sister Marie Magdalen suggested I do so. Yesterday evening I received a letter from Wales, stating a female relative of mine passed on 9 months ago. I am a rightful heir and find it's high time I get in touch with the proper persons. But I'm unfamiliar with the correct procedure in such matters. I also have no one here in Lititz to advise me. Therefore dear Brother I request you most kindly to ask Brothers Okely, Ettwein and Dettmers (or someone he finds suitable) what to do in this matter.[2] Commodore Thomas Warren left his estate to two daughters as co-heirs with the stipulation that one sister with her heirs should bequeath the other, should she die without heirs.[3] One sister was my mother's mother. The other is Miss Day's mother who recently died unmarried and without children. My own blessed mother recommended the urgency herein and said my claim is indisputable. Two years ago I wrote to a Brother Thomas Syms in Bristol.[4] I was advised to do this by our dear Brother Marschall. But I didn't receive any reply. I just recently received my baptismal certificate along with a letter from my godparent, which I want to send along, in order to see if it is valid. Apparently the amount will be £300 per year, but I can't say with certainty how much it might be. According to what my late mother told me, my relative's father wants to persuade her to cut off the entail. She doesn't want it to appear that she had it in her power to do so. If that's true, I have little hope, for she wasn't my friend. My mother thought however she isn't able to surrender it to anyone else during her lifetime. My present circumstances don't permit me to move forward without resolving this. For this reason I'm anxious to hear where I stand before I presume anything. Nonetheless I should take appropriate measures and do something to resolve it before it is too late. I look forward to your advice. And should the precious Savior see to it that I receive some financial gain, I will view it as nothing less than as His matter that He entrusted to me to act according to His will. And should He grant me through grace the proper disposition of my heart, I could then joyfully proceed. But should our dear Saviour determine that my heart is changing due to these circumstances, may He then protect me through grace. Mr William Logan in Philadelphia is acquainted with me since I arrived here in this country. He promised to provide a letter of attestation if I ask him.[5] The Captain of the ship on which I came will do the same. Mr. Edward Shippen in Lancaster promised he would also do this, as well as others.[6] Dear Brother Nathaniel please let me know very soon what I should do. Of course, it lies solely in the hands of our dear Saviour, to whose will I completely surrender. I have no doubt He will guide me.

Please give my warmest greetings to Sister Anna Johanna. Sisters Marie Magdalena and Magdalena wish to send the same.[7] I remain your poor child.

Mary Penry

P.S. Warren's last will and testament is registered in London.[8] I also request you return what I included in this post.

[German original]
Theuerer und lieber Bruder,

Ich komme nun zu euch, wie ein Kind zu ihren lieben Vater um Rath zu fragen wegen meine Sachen, so wie mir die liebe Schwester Marie Magdlen gerathen hat. Gestern abend kriegte ich einen Brief von Wales, mit der Nachricht dass meine Verwandtin in England, dessen Erbin ich bin, nun schon vor 9 Monathe aus der Zeit gegangen, also es ist jetzo hohe Zeit dass ich mich melde. Wie aber, dass weiss ich nicht, den ich bin solche Sachen ganz [fremd], habe auch niemand hier in Lititz, der mir rathen kann. Darum bitte ich, lieber Bruder, sey so gut und redte mit Br. Okely, Etwein, Dettmers (wem Er vor Gut befind) und frage was darein zu thun ist.

Die Sache ist so: Commodore Thomas Warren hinterliess 2 Töchter Mitterben seine Estate mit dem Beding, dass die eine Schwester und ihre Erbe der andere ererben solte, wo sie keine hinterliess. Der eine Schwester war meine Mamma ihr Mutter, der ander eben die Miss Day ihrer, welches nun als ledig gestorben ist. Meine seelige Mutter hat mir die Sache gar angelegentlich recomandirt und gesagt, meine Recht sey indisputable. Vor etwa 2 Jahren schrieb ich auf Anrathen unser lieben Br. Marschalls einen Bruder in Bristol nahmens Thomas Syms, habe aber kein Antwort bekommen. Ich habe letztens mein Taufschein nebst ein Brief von mein Bathen bekommen, welches ich hiermit schicken will, um zu sehen, ob es gültig ist. Es heist, dass es wird 300 Pfund des Jahrs seyn. Ich kan aber nicht sagen gewiss, wie viel es ist. Meine seelige Mamma hat mir gesagt, dass meine Verwandtin ihr Vater wolte sie perswadiren, den Intail abzuschneiden. Sie aber wolte nicht, dass es also scheint, sie hat es doch in ihrer Macht gehabt. Wenn dass wahr ist, so habe ich wenig Hoffnung, den sie ist nicht mein Freund gewesen, doch meynte meine Mutter, sie könt nicht mehr als auf ihr Leben die Sache jemand anders übergeben. Meine Umstände erlauben mir nicht weit zu gehen, ohne dass die Sach gewiss ist. Desswegen möchte gerne höhre, wie es aussieht, ehe ich viel wage. Indessen aber solte ich doch etwas drinne thun, ehe es zu spät ist, und bitte um gerathen zu werde. Solte Es der liebe Heiland so machen, dass ich was gewinne, so sehe ich es nicht anders an als seine Sache, dass Er mir anvertrauet, um vor Ihm zu handeln, und wenn Er mir aus Gnad die Herzens Stellung verleiht, die ich jetzo habe, so kan ich mich mit Freudigkeit drin mühen. Wo aber der liebe Heiland vorsehen solte, dass mein Herz sich ändern soll mit meine Umstände, den soll Er mich in Genaden davor bewahren. Mr William Logan in Philadelphia kennt mich [s]eit ich im Land bin und hat mir versprochen ein Attestat zu geben, wenn ich es fordern wird, desgleichen der Capitain, der mich ins Land gebracht hat; Mr. Edward Shippen in Lancaster hat eines gleiches versprochen, und so sind ihrer mehrer. Der lieber Bruder Nathaniel werd so gut seyn und mir bald zu wissen thun, was ich machen soll. Es kömmt gewiss lediglich auf dem lieben Heiland an, zu dessen Wille ich es gänzlich überlasse und zweifle nicht daran, Er wird dass beste rathen. Ich bitte meinen herzlichsten Gruss an die liebe Schw. Anna Johanna, unser lieben Schw. Marie Magdlen und Magdalena thun eines gleiches. Ich verbleibe Euer armes kind.

Mary Penry

P.S. Mr. Warrens Testament ist in London regestrird. Ich wolte auch bitten dass inliegende wieder zu bekommen.

ALS: PHC 261.7, MAB. Addressed "An | Den l. Brüder | Nathaniel | In | Bethlehem." This letter, written in German, has been translated and transcribed by Edward Quinter.

1. Nathanael Seidel (1718–1782) traveled back and forth between America and Europe from 1742 and 1761, after which he oversaw all Moravian congregations in Pennsylvania and adjoining areas until his death.

2. John Okely (1721–1792), Johannes Ettwein (1721–1802), and Ferdinand Philipp Jacob Detmers (1718–1801) were Moravian authorities in Bethlehem. Ettwein, who led Bethlehem during the American Revolution, married Johanette Maria Kimbel (1725–1773) in 1746. They arrived in Pennsylvania in 1754 and served in Wachovia, North Carolina, until returning to Bethlehem to help Nathanael Seidel (see above, note 1) reorganize Bethlehem's economy after 1762.

3. In the 1690s, commodore Thomas Warren, captain of the HMS *Windsor*, commanded a squadron that captured Captain Kidd—but then let him escape. Warren seems to have died in 1699 at Madagascar. See Charnock, *Biographia Navalis*, 2:290; and Zacks, *Pirate Hunter*, 32–39. Warren's will divided his estate equally among his wife and children and stipulated that, if any child died, his or her portion "be equally divided between my said loveing Wife and the survivors or survivor of my said Children." MP contends that this "entail" prevented the surviving children from disposing of their inheritance as they wished. See Thomas Warren, Last Will and Testament, 1694, and A Codicil, 1695, PROB 11/456/196, NAK.

4. Thomas Sims (1709–1795) and his wife, Elizabeth (1721–1781), arrived in Bristol from Bedford in September 1761 and opened a school there. He was introduced as the congregation secretary in December. See September 9, 1761, Diary of the Bristol Congregation, 1756–63, DM451/1; and December 27, 1761, Bristol Congregation Committee Book, 1755–67, DM451/7, both in Special Collections, Arts and Social Sciences Library, University of Bristol.

5. William Logan (1717–1776), an attorney for the Penn family. See Letter 7, note 3.

6. Edward Shippen (1703–1781), Lancaster's leading citizen. Shippen and his wife, Mary Shippen (1706–1778), moved to Lancaster in 1753 when the governor appointed him to lucrative offices. They lived on the corner of Duke and Orange Streets. Shippen had flourished as a fur trader and been Philadelphia's mayor in 1744. The Shippens purchased spun cotton from the single sisters. See Appendix D.

7. "Anna Johanna": Nathanael Seidel's wife, Anna Johanna Piesch Seidel (1726–1788). "Marie Magdalena": Maria Magdalena Augustine (1714–1784), the spiritual overseer (*Pflegerin*) of Lititz's single sisters' choir. "Magdalena": Anna Magdalena Meyer, the first *Pflegerin* of the Lititz single sisters' house (see Letter 6, note 8), whose duties Augustine assumed on December 10, 1763, when she arrived in Lititz from Bethlehem.

8. Thomas Warren, Last Will and Testament, NAK.

❧ 10. TO NATHANAEL SEIDEL[1]

October 30, 1766

Philadelphia, Pennsylvania

Philadelphia October 30th 1766

Dear Brother Nathaniel

I can't neglect to write a few lines to Br. Okely, to inform that everything that can be done for now is completed. The dear Savior has allowed me to find grace among people, so that they gladly gave of their own what was asked of them.[2] I appeared everywhere with my Moravian bonnet. They showed their approval of this. I am very appreciative of how dear Brother Nathaniel supported me so faithfully in this matter. I must also mention my thanks to Br. Okely, who worked so tirelessly to settle everything. The expenses come to £2.13.0. But now I long for my dear choir house. There's nothing attractive here for me, only commotion and vanity. Please relay a tender greeting to Sister Anna Johanna. I remain your poor child,

Mary Penry

[German original]
Lieber Bruder Nathaniel,

Ich kan es doch nicht unterlassen, mit Br. Okely ein par Zeilen zu schreiben und ihm zu sagen, dass nun alles vollendet ist, was vor die Zeit zu thun. Der liebe Heiland hat mich lassen Gnade vor den Menschen finden, so dass sie gerne das ihrige in der Sache, was mann ihnen gebeten, gethan haben. Ich erschiene überall in der Gemeinhaube, worüber sie ihren *Wohlgefallen* bezeugten. Ich bin den lieben Br. Nathaniel viel Dank schuldig, dass er meiner in diese Sache so treulich angenomen. Muss auch sagen, das Br. Okely unermüdet ist gewesen, alles zur Stande zu bringen. Die Umkosten machten £2.13.0. Nun sehne mich nach mein liebes Chor-Haus, finde hier keinen Charm—nichts als Unruhe und Eitelkeit. Ich bitte ein zärtliche Gruss an die liebe Schw. Anna Johanna und verbleibe euer armes Kind,

Mary Penry

ALS: PhB VI, MAB. Addressed "An | Der liebe Bruder | Nathaniel | In | Bethlehem." This letter, written in German, has been translated and transcribed by Edward Quinter.

1. See Letter 9.
2. The Philadelphia community may have taken up a collection for MP to defray the costs of her communications regarding the lawsuit.

🐦 11. TO NATHANAEL SEIDEL[1]
December 1, 1767
Lititz, Pennsylvania

Lititz the 1st of December 1767

Dear Brother Nathaniel,

Our dear Friend Sally Toon has desired me to write a few lines to you in her Name as follows:[2] That she has brought her Daughter Molly here According to her Promise, and given her up to our dear Saviour and the Congregation. She says she was a little too hasty in telling her upon the Road she would bring her to Bethlehem and was a little uneasy fearing Molly might more incline to go to Bethlehem, than too Stay here, But she being ask'd in her Mothers Presence if it was all one to her, she declared herself intirely given up to our dear Saviours Will and Provided she had but leave to Stay in the Congregation it was the same to her, here or Bethlehem—which has made her Mother easy again.[3] She desires her kind Love to your Self and Spouse—Likewise Brother Sydrik[4]—all Friends in general and Commends herself to your Faithful Remembrance—

Your Poor Polly—and her daughter Molly begs leave to Salute yourself and dear Sister Anna Johana. Molly likewise begs a Salutation to Sister Krogstrups Sisters and to the 2 Sisters Ashley[5]—I remain with respect and Love

Your Poor Child
Mary Penry

ALS: Letters from Lititz, 1765–69, LE: VI, MAB. Addressed "To | Dear Brother | Nathaniel | at | Bethlehem."

1. See Letter 9.

2. "Sally Toon": born Sarah Palmer. She married Benjamin Chitty, her children with whom included Benjamin Chitty (1743–1822), who lived in Carroll's Manor, Salem, and Lititz. After Chitty's death, Sarah married Henry Tippet. Their son became a leather-dresser, while their daughter, Mary (Molly) Tippet (1750–1829), figures frequently in MP's letters (see below, note 3). After Tippet's death, Sarah married Robert Toon. Their two children followed Mary Tippet to Lititz. Samuel Toon/Tune (1763–1821) arrived in December 1774, living with Samuel Fockel (1719–1799) before entering the single brothers' house; he left Lititz in 1783 for Bethlehem and later Emmaus, where he was involved in the Fries Rebellion of 1799. Catherine Toon (1761–1780) arrived in 1779, sick with consumption, and lived only six more months. Sally Toon died in early 1770 (Letter 15).

3. Mary Tippet (1750–1829) was born in Carroll's Manor, Maryland. During Nathanael Seidel's visit in October 1767, she was given permission to move to Bethlehem, "agreeable to the inward impulse of her Heart." See Joseph Powell to Nathanael Seidel, November 21, 1767. Box: MyA: Maryland, MAB. She and her mother stopped in Lititz on November 29, where Tippet remained rather than continuing to Bethlehem. Tippet entered the Lititz single sisters' house in 1768 (Letter 12, note 2) and became spiritual leader of the choir in 1784. Tippet served the same role in Bethlehem from 1798 to 1809, after which she returned to Lititz and resumed leadership of the single sisters' choir. She retired from her duties in 1817.

4. Daniel Sydrich (1727–1790) emigrated from Herrnhut to Bethlehem in 1750, served at the boys' schools in Emmaus and Christiansbrunn, and pastored in Philadelphia, Hope (New Jersey), and Graceham (Maryland), where he met Sarah Toon and Mary Tippet. Sydrich died in Lititz, where his wife continued to live. See Letter 37, note 38.

5. In 1757 Otto Christian Krogstrup (1714–1785) married Anna Burnet (1724–1784), eldest daughter of George Burnet and Ismaiah Thomas Burnet (b. 1696) of New York. Ismaiah Burnet was an early member of New York's Moravian congregation. Anna Burnet's two younger sisters—Elizabeth (1730–1790), who had taught in the girls' school since 1757, and Jane (1735–1776)—were at this time single sisters in Bethlehem. Molly Tippet knew the Krogstrups from Carroll's Manor, where Krogstrup ministered from 1764 to 1767. Patience Ashley (1735–1820) and Anna Rosina Ashley (1739–1819) were both in Bethlehem's single sister's house at this time, though Patience married Adam Von Erd (1722–1789) on December 18.

ᴥ 12. TO JOSEPH POWELL AND MARTHA POWELL[1]
March 20, 1768
Lititz, Pennsylvania

Sunday March the 20th 1768

Dear Brother and Sister

I am desired to write you a few lines from our dear Molly, to inform you that at length the long wish'd for Hour has Struck and that she has now our dear Lords Approbation to dwell in our House.[2] She will therefore move hither tomorrow. She is full of thanks to Sister Fenstermakern who has thus long been a kind Mother to her and Still more so towards our dear Saviour for the favour she has so long wish'd to have that is for leave to dwell in the choir House—We dont question but that it will be a very Particular Joy and Satisfaction to you both as likewise to her dear Mother whom you will be so kind as to inform of this Event—and beg of her to send Mollys things as soon as she can, Particularly her Bed.[3] And if it were Possible for her Mother to send her a Chest to put her Cloaths in, that is a necessary thing that she cannot well do without and do dear Brother beg her to send a Bundle of Quils allong for me, I will Pay Molly the cost.

Molly begs her kind Love to you both and to her dear Mammy Brothers Sisters Friends and acquaintance. She is in a pretty Frame and we hope she will become a Joy to our Saviour and his People—Sister Mary Magdalen desires her Love to you and Congratulates you to this your Daughters Election of Grace Sister Magdalena does the Same[4]—Your daughter Mary and your little Country woman take no small share in this our Sisters Happiness and if it lies in our Power to be any ways Conducieve to the same you may depend on our not neglecting it. Please to give our kind Loves to Mollys Mammy.—

I remain dear Brother and Sister—Sincerely your

Affectionate Sister
Mary Penry

ALS: PP PJos 1, MAB. Addressed "To | Dear | Brother | Joseph Powell | at | Carrols Manor."

1. Joseph Powell (1711–1774), born on the border of England with Wales, married Martha Prichett (1704–1774) in 1742. The couple came to America that year, serving at Shamokin, Jamaica, Staten Island, and Carroll's Manor, where they arrived in 1766. They returned to Bethlehem in 1772.

2. "Molly": Mary Tippet. See Letter 11, note 3. When she arrived in Lititz, Tippet lived with Anna Barbara (1709–1790) and John Christian Fenstermacher (1697–1767), who died a week after Tippet arrived. See Maria Magdalena Augustine to Joseph Powell and Martha Powell, December 1, 1767, PP PJos 1, MAB. For Barbara Fenstermacher's memoir, see Faull, *Moravian Women's Memoirs*, 87–89.

3. "dear Mother": Sally Toon. See Letter 11, note 2.

4. "Mary Magdalen . . . Magdalena": Maria Magdalena Augustine and Anna Magdalena Mayer. See Letter 9, note 7.

🐦 13. TO JOSEPH POWELL AND MARTHA POWELL[1]
April 25, 1768
Lititz, Pennsylvania

Lititz April the 25th 1768

Dear Mammy and Daddy Powell

Tho I am obliged to make use of a Borrow'd Pen to write you Yet I know you will accept of my poor Salutations in this Manner untill I am able to write with my own Hand which I hope I shall be one day able to do.[2] It is not in my Power to express the filial Love and Gratitude which My Heart feels toward you in Words, but you will believe the truth of what I say tho' express'd in so Short a Manner. I am quite happily Situated in my dear Choir House and hope and pray that our dear Saviour may form me according to his Heart[3]—I have writ a letter to Mammy that you will be so kind as to give to her. I wish very much to see you once here, then I will tell you more than I can write—but wherever I am, no Place nor Absence can ever alter the tender Love I bear you. But I am and remain your ever loving Daughter

Mary Tippet

Accept of the tenderest Love and Salutations from your little Worthless Polly—It is really a great Pleasure to me to have it in my Power to Oblige you by loving your dear Daughter Molly—I hope she will grow up as a tender Plant of Grace in our Virgin Garden water'd with his Precious Blood untill being fully blown she be transplanted to his Arms and Bosom—

We have had exceeding blessed Holydays: God's dear Lamb in Purple dy'd in his Figure bloody, Midst us walk'd & shewd his Side to the Church his Body[4]—Indeed every day thro out the Year we have and injoy his near Presence in his Suffering Form, and what will it be for unspeakable Joy when we shall close embrace upon our knees those Seals of our Election—

I remain your ever loving

Polly

ALS: PP PJos 1, MAB. Addressed "To | Mr | Joseph Powell | att | Carrols Mannor."

1. See Letter 12.
2. This first paragraph, from Mary Tippet, is in MP's hand.
3. See Letter 12.
4. "God's dear Lamb . . . the Church his Body": Gambold, *Collection of Hymns*, 2:224.

ᘓ 14. TO JOSEPH POWELL AND MARTHA POWELL[1]
June 3, 1768
Lititz, Pennsylvania

Lititz June 3rd 1768

Dear Brother and Sister Powells

You will this once Excuse me, that for whant of more time I write for Molly and Myself in one Letter.[2] Your kind Loving Lines rejoiced us both greatly and we must needs say we would not forego the great Pleasure of your Corrispondance upon any Consideration. I tell Molly I must begin to be hard towards her and make my writing in her Name so Difficult that she may take up the Pen herself, for there is sometimes a certain Indolence in us that as long as one can get a thing done for one—one is not so much concernd to learn to do it one self—She desires me to tell you that she thinks to answer those letters she receiv'd from the Young Women of her acquaintance soon, that Sister Marie Magdalen heard their Letters read (It would be good I think if those who express a Desire for the Congregation [were] to write a few Lines to Sister Marie Magdalene herself since it would then be a more Immediate application).[3] As to what concerns Mollys Inward and Outward State—She is in a Blessed School to learn to know herself and the Friend of Sinners and there is no Place where one can learn those 2 important Points better, then a Choir House. She does very well outwardly is Industrious and is an Obedient willing Child in the Family. May our dear Saviour carry on the Work began in her Soul—and bring her from one Degree of Grace to more, till she behold his Face.

We have really had distinguish'd Blessed Holydays. Whit Monday a great girl of 16 years of Age was Baptized who was the first Adult Person that had receiv'd this grace here in Lititz.[4] Such a Divine Power attended this Sacramental Act, that the whole Congregation was Melted into Tears. The Childs Countenance was quite Angelical and her answers to the Questions put to her concerning her Faith in Jesus Christ so affecting that I believe no one will ever forget the Impression they receiv'd thereby. I wrote you in my last that every day was a Festival of our Saviours Death and Suff'rings, and it is really so. I can say for my Part that the more Poor and wretched I feel my self the more I can rejoice in our bleeding Saviour. What A Happiness that I poor little Worm should be brought to his Fold. I am the only Welch woman in the Single Sisters Choir—Mary the only New Englander and Molly the only Marylander.[5] How wonderful it is in the Congregation from how many different Parts has our dear Saviour gather'd his sheep and brought them to the fold—Oh may he bless the Word of your and all his wittnesses Testimony that Numbers be enabled to say with us: I little Worm so poor, quite spoil'd by Sin and Stained &c.[6]

Molly begs her Love to her dear Mammy Brothers Sisters Friends and Acquaintance—Sister Magdalena desires her kind Love to you—Sister Marie Magdalen is at present on a Visitation in Philadelphia and the Jerseys with Brother and Sister Hehls.[7] I believe your daughter Mary will write herself—I must now hasten to conclude with my hearty Love to the young Women with you, beg Pardon for my Scribble time being so short and remain with sincerest Love

Your truely Affectionate tho Poor Sister

Mary Penry

ALS: PP PJos 1, MAB. Addressed "To | Mr | Joseph Powell | att | Carrolls Mannour | Maryland."

1. See Letter 12.

2. "Molly": Mary Tippet. See Letter 11, note 3.

3. "Marie Magdalen": Maria Magdalena Augustine. See Letter 9, note 7.

4. "great girl of 16 years of Age": Anna Christina Kreiter (1752–1838) was baptized on May 23, 1768, and remained a single sister in Lititz until her death.

5. Mary Ashley (1734–1791), from New England, had arrived in Lititz from Bethlehem in May 1764 to work as a linen weaver in the single sisters' house. Her sisters, Patience and Anna Rosina, were in Bethlehem. See Letter 11, note 5. She left Lititz for Bethlehem on October 1, 1771, on her way to Jamaica. Her husband, John Miller, died in Jamaica in 1781, and the widow returned to Bethlehem in 1785. "Molly": Mary Tippet was from Maryland.

6. "I little Worm . . . Sin and Stained": Gambold, *Collection of Hymns*, 2:372. See Letter 1, note 2.

7. Matthias Hehl (1705–1787), married in 1737 to Anna Maria Jaehne (1716–1777), immigrated to Pennsylvania in 1751 and moved to Lititz in 1756. For thirty years he was principal pastor in Lititz and as bishop responsible for many congregations. Maria Magdalena Augustine (see Letter 9, note 7) and the Hehls left Lititz on May 26 and returned on June 10, 1768.

15. TO JOSEPH POWELL AND MARTHA POWELL[1]

March 5, 1770

Lititz, Pennsylvania

Lititz March the 5th 1770

Dear Brother and Sister Powells

Your kind Letter of the 23rd of February we receiv'd last Evening. The Letter was deliverd to Sister Mary Magdalen to whom I read the Contents.[2] She then sent for Molly and broke the News to her, with her usual Tenderness and Maternal Affection. Molly is much affected, yet resignd to our Saviours Will and in the midst of those Tears which she cannot avoid shedding for the loss of a Mother, she yet rejoices that she hast passd the Turbulent waves of this Life (to which *she* has been more Particular[l]y exposed) and is arrived at the Haven of Rest.[3]

Molly['s] chief Concern now is about the children, whom she fears will be scattered about in the World, she trusts her good Daddy and Mamme Powell will do what they can to see them settled and begs to be inform'd how they are disposed off. She observes no mention has been made of her Brother Benjamin and wonders at it saying both he and his wife has had the small Pox—she hopes they did not forsake mammy in her Distress.[4] Likewise she takes Notice that Daddy and Mammy Powell was only once to see her Mammy and reckons that it was allmost 3 weeks before her End.—These Scruples she has intreated me to inform you off—A few lines from you will remove them. Another thing: when her Mammy was here, some Sisters bespoke Feathers of her—and she gave Molly the Money they was to cost— These feathers are in Friedricks town—(according to the last Letter she receiv'd). We hope they will come safe, and that the Payment will not be demanded of poor Molly, who has bought a Bed ticken for the same, since it would fall heavy on her to raise it and is doubtless the whole of her Fortune.[5] It is something remarkable that last Thursday the Room Door where Molly lives softly opend (as tho' some one look'd in) of its own accord and Molly directly said she was the Person meant by that Sign. She has nothing against it if should please our Saviour to take one or more of her 3 Brothers to himself. She desires her kind Love to both of you and to her Brothers and Sisters longs much to hear further &c. Sister Marie Magdlen salutes you tenderly, and bids me tell you she is much rejoiced, that our savior has brought diese Schaafgen aufs Trokkene—er wird wissen was sie meynt.[6] Marie Ashley desires her kind love to you,[7] and now be pleas'd to accept of the same in the tenderest Manner from your

Truely affectionate Sister
Mary Penry

P.S. Sister Mary Magdalen desires her kind Love to the Single women— Please to salute them from us likewise.

ALS: PP PJos 1, MAB. Addressed "To | Mr | Joseph Powell | at | Carrols Manour." Endorsed "Pennry."

1. See Letter 12.

2. One of the few native English speakers in Lititz, MP translated correspondence in English and wrote letters in English for German speakers. See also Letter 70, note 3.

3. Daniel Sydrich heard via the same communication that "Sally Toon departed this life." See Daniel Sydrich to Joseph Powell, March 5, 1770, PP PJos 1, MAB.

4. "Brother Benjamin": Benjamin Chitty (see Letter 11, note 2), who married Mary Padget (1746–1788) in 1765. Both moved to Hope, North Carolina, around 1780. Widowed, Chitty moved to Lititz in 1792.

5. "ticken": cover.

6. "Marie Magdlen": Letter 9, note 7. "diese Schaafgen aufs Trokkene—er wird wissen was sie meynt": this sheep on to dry land—he will know what she means (German).

7. Mary Ashley: see Letter 14, note 5.

৵ 16. TO MARY SHIPPEN[1]

October 17, 1774

Lititz, Pennsylvania

Lititz October 17th 1774

Dear Maddam!

I hope your Goodness will excuse this address, dictated by sincere Love and accompanied with a *Drop of Honey from the Rock Christ* which will undoubtedly meet with a good Reception at your Hands.[2] This little Treatise is so much in Esteem with us, that there is scarce one among us, children and grown Persons who have not one, and the most have it in both Languages, English and German. This little Treatise is a Consice discription of our Doctrine—we subscribe to it one and all with our whole heart, and I must Confess it is a peculiar Pleasure to me That an English Christian of Former times has left us so fine a Testimony of that Truth which in these days alas is much rejected! I should have sent this some time agon, but I must own I sufferd myself to be deterrd by the Fear of being Troublesome with the Scribble—But having wrote Mr Shippen and sent his Stockings,[3] I could no longer refrain addressing you, and assuring you that I frequently reflect with Pleasure on the last conversation we had together, which has indeared you to me greatly. An affection between Christians (according to the true Sense of the Word) is lasting—begining here in Time and Continuing in Eternity. As my whole desire is to be found in Him my dearest Lord & Saviour—the next wish is to be in Unity of Spirit with his *Children*. This my sole motive for Writing and I assure you dear Maddam that I am in Sincerity your affectionate Friend

and humble Servant

Mary Penry

ALS: Dreer Collection, Box 21:46, HSP. Addressed "To | Mrs | Shippen | In | Lancaster | With a small | Pamphlet."

1. See Letter 9, note 6.

2. Thomas Wilcox's *A Choice Drop of Honey from the Rock Christ* (London, 1690) was reprinted frequently in colonial America. In 1774 Henry Miller printed a German version in Philadelphia.

3. For this letter and for the single sisters' textile industry, see Appendix D.

17. TO POLLY ROBERTS[1]
September 23, 1780
Lititz, Pennsylvania

Lititz September 23rd 1780

Dear Mrs Roberts,

I cannot refrain taking the first oppertunity which came to my Knowledge since my Return Home[2]—To salute and thank you for your Kindness to me—a grateful Sense of your Favours I shall ever Retain tho it has not pleased the Lord to put it in my Power to express my acknowledgements any otherwise than the above—However a generous Mind takes the greatest Pleasure in confering obligations on those from whom they can expect no Return—which is exactly *Your Case*, and *Mine*—

The young woman that I found so ill at my Return, continues so. Tomorrow is the 9th day Since she was taken, so that its possible her illness will take a Turn one way or the other. Her earnest desire is, to depart and be with Christ, and her Friends would fain have her a little longer with them—which Side will prevail is allso uncertain.[3]

Please to give my Respects to your good Husband, and to Mrs Becom when you see her.[4] I should be very glad to hear that your Aunt Webb had been to see you, and behaved to you with all the Kindness of so near a Relation. I think you are both call'd to love each other, not only by Relationship, but the still closer Band of Unity in our Common Lord and Heavenly Father whose children you desire to be. I have only to add that I shall ever Remain My dear Mrs Roberts Obliged Friend & servant

Mary Penry

Pray Excuse my Scrible being in Haste

ALS: Wetherill, Jones, and Roberts Families Papers, 1683–1904, Box 1:15, 94x122.209, Winterthur Library. Addressed "To | Mrs Roberts | In | Lancaster."

1. Mary (Polly) Roberts was married to the Lancaster hatter John Roberts, whose shop in these years was near the Court House. In 1791 Roberts moved his hat shop to East Orange Street, next to the Presbyterian meeting house, where he sold beaver and raccoon hats. See Hostetter, "News-

papers," 158. From 1801 to 1806, John Roberts represented Lancaster in the Pennsylvania Assembly, and he died on May 3, 1809. See *Wahre Amerikaner*, May 6, 1809, 3.

2. Two single sisters—Marie Catherine Koch (1745–1802) and Elizabeth Hopson (1756–1808)—traveled with MP to Lancaster on September 18 and returned on September 21, 1780.

3. "young woman": this sister must have recovered. Maria Dorothea Glotz (1754–1780) died of consumption on September 19, 1780, before MP returned to Lititz.

4. "Mrs Becom": Mary Henry Bickham (1735–1806), who had married one of Lancaster's leading citizens, James Bickham (1730–1789), in 1776.

&♥ 18. TO ELIZABETH DRINKER[1]
October 23, 1783
Lititz, Pennsylvania

Lititz October 23rd 1783

My dear Friend Betsy Drinker!

Eighteen or 19 Years are past since we last saw each other in your House in Philadelphia.[2] I had some thoughts of coming to town this Summer but Sickness in our Family, and one thing or other has put it off untill the Season was too far advanced to admit of travelling. Wether the coming year (if I live to see it) will admit of my leaving home is uncertain, especially as we have a great undertaking before us which is the Building of an Addition to our dwelling House.[3] Tho indeed my Presence is no other way Necessary, than as I keep the Accounts it were Possible my Service would be wanted—It is this Circumstance my dear Betsy which Occasions my troubling you with a Letter—

In our Youth a Strickt intimacy and Friendship Subsisted between us—wether on your Side every Spirit is extinguish'd or not, is to me uncertain.[4] Thus much I can say of my self and that with truth, that the Name of Besty Sandwith is still dear to me. As your name Drinker is not so fluent with me you will Pardon my making use of your Maiden Name to Express my Regard. The sence I have of Love & Tenderness towards you has emboldend me to send you the inclosed, in hopes your wonted Goodness and those Generous Sentiments you possessd in Youth have increased with your Years—you may depend on the thankful Prayers and Acknowledgments of our whole Family and we Confidently hope yea firmly believe that what you bestow on us will be abundantly made up to you and yours—The enclosed writing will explain at large what I have here intimated—I shall hope for a few lines from you in answer to this which if sent to the Brethren's School House or Church in Philadelphia will safely come to my Hands—

Although I have frequently wrote you without being favoured with an answer—I beseech you do not this time put me to shame but let me have a few lines from you—which will be an Encouragement to me to Corrispond with my Worthey Friend I trust to our Mutual Satisfaction—I have only to add my most hearty Love to your self, Spouse and Children. [I pray] you will be so kind as to send the enclosed to my Friend Hannah Sansom (formerly Callendar) if Living—if not, Commit it to the Flames.[5]

I remain with the greatest Esteem your Sincerely Affectionate Friend

Mary Penry

P.S. As soon as the inclosd paper has deliverd its Message—I beseech you to burn it—that it may fall into no other hands but yours—

[Enclosure] The Single Sisters at Lititz, being very much Straightened for Room, and in want of many Conveniences absolutely Necessary for so large a Family, are under the Necessity of building an addition to their dwelling House.[6]

Many of our Friends and well wishers having expressd their Satisfaction in observing the good Order and Industry here maintaind, which has, and we hope will further prove serviceable to the *State*—Have encouraged us to request such of our kind Friends whose easy Circumstances admit, and their Generosity incline them, to assist an undertaking which we trust is allow'd to be laudible. The Intent of This, as well as all our Choir Houses is no other, than to a School for Piety, Virtue and Industry.—Certain it is! These Houses have prov'd an Azylum for Numbers, who had they been left to seek their Bread in the midst of a deluding World, might have been led astray into the Paths of Vice, which has been the Misfortune of but too many Young Persons of our Sex, whose Case we commiserate.—We have no Fund to this undertaking. We depend solely on the Blessing of our Heavenly Father (who has promised to take care of the Orphan and the helpless) and the kind assistance of our Friends and well wishers. All those who are disposed to a generous *Donation*, may be assured of our warmest thanks, and Prayers for their Spiritual and Temporal Wellfare, the only way in our power to shew our gratitude.

Our gracious Redeemer, has promised that even a draught of Water bestow'd on his Children shall not be unrewarded,[7] and will certainly never suffer our kind Benefactors to want themselves what they so generously bestow on us.

ALS: Linden Hall Archives. Addressed "To | Mrs | Elizabeth Drinker | @ Philadelphia | To the care of Miss Widdyfeld." Endorsed "Lititz October 23 | Mary Penry."

1. Elizabeth Sandwith Drinker (1735–1807), MP's childhood friend and long-time correspondent. See Appendix C.

2. Although MP was in Philadelphia in summer 1765 and in October 1766, Drinker's diary mentions no meeting at these times. MP may not have seen Drinker in Philadelphia in "Eighteen or 19 Years," but on a 1771 visit to Lititz Drinker "mett with Molly Penry." See August 26, 1771, Drinker, *Diary*, 1:167.

3. The cornerstone of an addition to the single sisters' house was laid on May 25, 1784, and the building was completed in summer 1785.

4. MP and Drinker (then Sandwith) were both taught by Anthony Benezet. See Letter 52, note 5, and the introduction to this volume.

5. Hannah Callender (1737–1801), a schoolmate of MP and Elizabeth Drinker, had married Samuel Sansom (1739–1824) in 1762. See Sansom, *Diary*, for her trip to Bethlehem and visit with MP in 1761.

6. "so large a Family": at the end of 1784, fifty-five women lived in the Lititz single sisters' house.

7. Matthew 10:42.

❧ 19. TO JOHANN ANDREAS HUEBNER[1]
April 16, 1784
Lititz, Pennsylvania

Lititz 16 April 1784

Dear Brother Hübner,

It is with no small Pleasure that I undertake the Commission Brother *Dans* has given me, to answer your Letter. He would fain have done it himself, but is really incapable as he has such a Violent Cough that it is scarce Possible for him to write a Line—and I must say that it seems highly Probable that it is a Consumptive Cough, as he has a slow Hectic Fever and most of those Signs which Indicate that Disorder. They both took it extreemly kind that you wrote them concerning their little Darling and return you their most hearty thanks. They are greatly Rejoiced that the same Letter which brought them the first News of their Daughters illness inform'd them of her recovery.[2] They desire their kind Salutations to Brother Hübner, His Spouse and Sister Anna Johanna.—Thus far my Commission.

Now my good Brother Hübner I am desired to salute you both tenderly from my dear Sister Marie Magdlen, Marie Tippet, and M. B. Leinbachin and to inquire after your Health as likewise to tell you that we have had blessed Holydays[3]—and that our 2 Dear Visitants have keept several anointed Meetings[4]—which we hope will not be fruitless—

The Cellar to our New Building is almost finish'd and it begins to have the Prospect that our Prayers will be answer'd and we shall in time have more Room, which we greatly Want.[5] Our Heavenly Father himself must provide for his poor Maidens and we believe and trust he will do it. It is he who has the hearts in his Disposition and can incline them to help his poor Children in their Necessity.

Our good Brother and Sister Hübners we know take a large Share in our Wellfare and will give their Blessing to our undertakings, and when our House is finish'd, you will rejoice us with a Visit. But we hope to see you *this* Sommer in our present Dwelling as well as next year in our New One— Please to give kind Love to Sister Anna Johanna and I remain Dear Brother your Affectionate—tho poor unworthy

M: Penry

ALS: Letters from Lititz, 1770–89, LF: V, MAB. Addressed "To | the Reverend Brother | Hübner | @ | Bethlehem." Endorsed "received April 20th by Brother Ettwein | answered May 29th 1784."

1. Johann Andreas Huebner (1737–1809), born in Berthelsdorf, served as pastor in Bethlehem from 1780 to 1790 and was the first principal of the boarding school for girls. Huebner was conse-crated bishop in 1790 and moved to Lititz, where he replaced Matthias Hehl as superintendent of Moravian congregations in southern Pennsylvania and Maryland. He returned to Europe to attend the General Synod of 1801.

2. Simon Danz (1744–1789), landlord of Lititz's Zum Acker inn. He sent his eldest daughter, Maria Barbara Danz (1780–1797), to Bethlehem for schooling.

3. Maria Barbara Leinbach, the steward (*Vorsteherin*) of the single sisters' house in Lititz. See Letter 24, note 4.

4. Johannes Ettwein (see Letter 9, note 2) and John Augustus Klingsohr (1746–1798) visited Lititz from April 3 to April 20, 1784.

5. See Letter 18, note 3 and enclosure.

᠈᠊᠍᠍ 20. TO CATHERINE WISTAR[1]
   August 12, 1786
   Lititz, Pennsylvania

Lititz August 12th 1786

My dear Friend

I was in hopes ere this of seeing you here, or at least of hearing from you. My last informd you that I was just going to sett off to Lancaster, w[h]ere I had Bus'ness which detain'd me 2 Days[2]—Since then I heard by a Friend from Philadelphia that our good Friend Morton was so low that they were obliged to hasten to town and it is most Likely that he has bid adieu to Pain and Sickness and is safely arrived in the Kingdom of Heaven—I must own I feel deeply Affected for his dear Friends, who will doubtless be allmost inconsoleable for their Loss—for we are so selfish we cannot but with the uttmost Reluctance part with such dear Friends, notwithstanding we are Convinced our Loss is their great gain—[3]

The sweet Composure which appeard in the Countenance of that Young Gentleman seem'd to me to evince his aproaching Exit from a World of Vanity to enter The true Haven of Bliss—but the more this was Visible and the sweeter his Behaviour the More his Friends will suffer at their Loss. Our Lord himself be their Comforter. He gave, and he has taken back to himself that Soul which was his by Creation and Redemption to which he has a double right—I shall not venture to write Mrs Pemberton till some time is pass'd and her Grief is somewhat subsided[4]—That Family is a Strong proof, that neither Riches nor Honour can purchase Happiness—Or *theirs* would have been uninterrupted. Nothing but the Love of Jesus Christ, shed abroad in our Hearts by the Holy Spirit is productive of Substantial good[5]—and this cannot be destroyd by death, Nay then it attains to everlasting duration.

My dear Friend I could wish to see you here before you leave these Parts[6]—and should that not be Possible do let me have a line where and how I am to direct to you and be pleas'd to send that Book with care back, it is not Mine, and as Soon as you have perused it, should be glad to have it in my Power to return it—

I have not forgot the Promise I made you to send you Some of my Drawings but must beg you to have a little Patience till the Flies give me some Respite, as they are really so troublesome I can scarce write, much less draw in Peace—Please to make my love Acceptable to your Brother and Sister—I have that Piece finish'd for your Cousin Caty Hains, but shall keep it untill a safe Conveyance offers of Sending[7]—I have only to add that I remain my dear Friend your Sincerely Affectionate

Mary Penry

ALS: Catharine Franklin Sharples (1768–1824) Family Papers, Collection 3062, Series Three, Box 1:24, HSP. Addressed "To | Miss Caty: Wistar | @ Ephrata." Endorsed "No 2 | Maria Penry one of the | Sisters at Letitz | August 12—1780 | answered."

1. Catherine Franklin Wistar (1768–1824), the granddaughter of the famous immigrant Caspar Wistar (1696–1752; regarding whom see Beiler, *Immigrant Entrepreneur*). In 1802 she married the widower Abraham Sharples (1748–1835), a successful miller in Chester County. Both served on the committee for the Quaker Westtown School (see Letter 66, note 19).

2. "My last": this letter is lost.

3. Robert Morton (1760–1786) would die on August 18, 1786. In 1784 he married his stepsister, Hannah Pemberton (1755–1788), the daughter of the Quaker leader James Pemberton (1723–1809). For Morton's revolutionary experience, see Morton, "Diary."

4. "Mrs Pemberton": James Pemberton's third wife, Phebe Lewis Morton (1738–1812), was the widow of Samuel Morton (1730–1773)—so Robert Morton's mother.

5. Romans 5:5.

6. Catherine Wistar, along with her family, lived at Ephrata in the summer of 1786 while two of her siblings were undergoing medical treatment. See Letter 22, note 4. Eight miles northeast of Lititz, Ephrata was founded in 1732 as a monastic religious community by Conrad Beissel (1691–1768). See Reichmann and Doll, eds., *Ephrata as Seen by Contemporaries*; Alderfer, *Ephrata Commune*; and Bach, *Voices of the Turtledoves*.

7. Catherine Haines (1761–1809) and Catherine Wistar were first cousins: Haines's mother, Margaret Wistar Haines (1729–1793), was the sister of Caspar Wistar (1740–1811) and thus Catherine Wistar's aunt.

ॐ 21. TO CATHERINE WISTAR[1]
September 18, 1786
Lititz, Pennsylvania

Lititz September 18th 1786
Monday Night

Respected Friend Caty Wistar!

The hopes of seeing you at Ephrata shortly, has hitherto made me delay writing, as I expected to have the Pleasure of a Verbal Intercourse; but being to day half way on the Road, and obliged to turn back on Account of the Hammer Creek being unpassable, I set down to inform you of the Grief my disapointment has given me—[2]

You may be assured that the Inhabitants of Ephrata are no Impediment to my coming to see you! I have nothing to Object to *them*, as I do not Mind a little Tittle tattle which if *true* is no hurt to me nor my People—And, if I come there it is *you* that I visit and not them—and can keep from those to whom I am not Wellcome—Altho I belive Petronella has some Regard for me att least she seems glad to see me[3]—The real cause of my not coming is the want of a Conveyance—it has been such a Busy time that neither waggon nor horse was to be hired, and on foot its too much for me to come and go in one day—The Stage waggon from Bethlehem being here, I embraced the oppertunity, after Dinner a Company of us sat out to Docter Fahnstocks—Myself and one more intending to stay there over Night[4]—to visit you tomorrow and then walk home—but was forc'd to turn back at the Hammer Creek—It will be now at least 14 days before I can get a Horse—and if you should leave Ephrata before that then I have no call thither at present—We have a pretty dark Strip'd Cotton in the Loom if you could but come and look at it, I wish you would try[5]—I write this with the Bethlehem Stage which returns to Beth'lem on Wednessday or Thursday.

I have not heard from Caty Hains since she left you tho I have wrote her a long Letter 2 weeks ago—Isaac Kaggy was here last week and told me our Friend Morton was gone to Rest[6]—I shall write by a Neighbour who is going Next Week to town to Katy and to Mrs Pemberton—My dear Friend do let me hear from you if you send any Letter by Fahnstocks Children who go to School in Ephrata I shall receive it safe.

I thought a quarter Sheet of Paper would be more than I should use but I am afraid I shall tire you with my Scribble which being wrote by Candle Light is really scarce Legible—You will find me a very plain writer. I cannot bear any formalities which has occasion'd me to Contract my Corrispondancy to a small Number of Friends, who do not Expect anything of the kind from me. My dear Miss Caty, if I know myself I am really no Hypocrite, and I esteem my Friends and Respect them Notwithstanding I use no Compliments—I am also quite certain at the very *first sight* wether I can call the Person my Friend! You my dear made a very tender Impression on my Mind, and you may be where you will—as little as my Regard may be worth your Acceptance—I shall allways Rejoice to hear of your Wellfare (give me leave to add) both Spiritual and Temporal—I have no news to relate, except what is within my Circle, our Church roof is raisd and God be thank'd no one hurt, but one Man who bruis'd his Finger[7]—We are all well in Health, and Happy in our sweet Azylum of Peace. Now and then, we have a Sight of *Vanity Fair* when the Beax and Belles from Lancaster call upon us, and take a View of our House, sometimes I suppose full of Pity at our Confinement *as they think*—but I never can observe that any of our Girls would wish to change Stations with them. As for myself I'm out of the Question, my time is over—having been 30 Years a Recluse, I have only to think on my approaching Change, My Years reminding me that it cannot be far off— Well you will wish I would come to the close of this Epistle. My Paper is full and your Patience Exhausted, farewell my dear Miss Caty I remain yours Sincerely

Mary Penry

ALS: Catharine Franklin Sharples (1768–1824) Family Papers, Collection 3062, Series Three, Box 1:24, HSP.

1. See Letter 20.

2. "Ephrata": see Letter 20, note 6. Hammer Creek is a tributary of Cocalico Creek in Lancaster County.

3. Maria Höcker (d. 1791), known as Petronella at Ephrata. She helped teach in the Sunday school run by her father, Ludwig Höcker (d. 1792; known at Ephrata as Brother Obed).

4. In 1786 Casper Fahnstock (1722–1808), a Sabbatarian from Ephrata, purchased an inn on the road from Philadelphia to Lancaster. In 1794 he built a larger inn. See Sachse, *Wayside Inns*, 21.

5. For the single sisters' textile industry, see Appendix D.

6. Isaac Kaegy (ca. 1763–1789), who ran for sheriff of Lancaster County in 1787, died on July 29, 1789. See Lerbscher and Calvin, "Items of Interest," 107; *Neue Unpartheyische Lancaster Zeitung, und Anzeigs-Nachrichten*, October 17, 1787. Regarding "Friend Morton," see Letter 20, note 3.

7. "our Church roof": the Lancaster Moravian William Henry (1729–1786) submitted a design for the new church in November 1785. Its cornerstone was laid on June 7, 1786, and the church was consecrated on August 13, 1787.

22. TO CATHERINE WISTAR[1]

November 3, 1786

Lititz, Pennsylvania

Lititz November 3rd 1786

Much esteemed Friend!

Your kind Favour I duely receivd, and to my great Satisfaction, to hear of your safe Arival to the Arms of your Friends, whom Absence has more endear'd to you—I can easily immagine what a Person of your Sensibility must feel at rejoining those dear Connexions, and Sincerely Congratulate you on the Occassion. I am perhaps more Particularly Affected with *your* Joy on Returning home, as *myself* so lately as the last Saturday had the great Pleasure to see two of my Relations, one I had not seen near 3 Years, and the other not in 20.[2]

At such times, and on such Occassions, I am at a loss wether to call that tender Sensibility a Happiness or a Misfortune[3]—For altho when my heart expands to receive my Friends, and the feelings of Consanguinity and Friendship are inexpressibly sweet—yet Seperation is so Distressful, that I sometimes think those are more happy who have a cooler Temper. I believe few Persons have sufferd more than I have—when I conceive an Esteem for a Friend I could wish to enjoy their Company & Conversation, and when that is not Attainable it gives me Pain, which would not be the case if I had more Indifference. However upon the whole I will not give up those pleasing Sensations for fear of the painful ones since I can hope from time [to] time to have them renew'd and indeed here—I live as [it] were at the Fountain Head where Friendships Cultivated in Religion are as lasting as our Being.

I have frequently recolected the Solitary Mead at Ephrata, and the leave I took of my Friend—I feel no Inclination now, to Revisit those Scenes which that Pretty Company of you and your Friends, renderd so agreeable. It seems Docter Gideon is in great Credit with the Philadelphians, My Cousin came to Consult him and Perhaps may next Summer become one of his Patients;[4] should that be the case—She intends to reside at Lititz rather than at Ephrata, which to be sure is quite Natural as she has her Relation here.

I had the Pleasure of a Letter from your Valueable Cousin Kitty Haines[5]—To whom I have been a very Troublesome Corrispondant. She has been so kind as to procure me some Shades of Embroidering Silk—If wishes could restore her to Health—mine would certainly procure her that Blessing. But if our great Physcician Heal the Maladies of our Sin Sick Soul—we will not repine at the weakness of our Mortal Tent—knowing that sooner or later—it must be broken down and Oh what a blessed Change will that be when this Corruptable shall put on incorruption and this Mortal Immortality!

I am at [a] Loss what to entertain you with that will be agreeable. My Life goes on here in one regular Course. Seldom any thing new happens. Among the Many Visitants which Curiosity brings hither I seldom find any thing suiting my taste and an Insiped Formality is all I have to observe—

The Building of our Church goes on pretty brisk, so that we have somes hopes it will be finish'd early in the Spring.[6] We have thro Mercy had a Healthy fall. We have none Sick in our Village—We have not much to Spin for Strangers but having purchased a Bag of Cotton we are not without work—which is likewise a great Blessing—we have a large Quantity of Spun Cotton on hand and twisted 3 thread at 2/ the Skain from 12 Skains to the Pound to 30, so that if you or any of your Friends have any occassion for Stockings or to be wove—we can supply you—18 Skains to the Pound which the general sort for Stockings is 12/ ready for knitting—and so on in Proportion to the fineness—[7]

And now my dear Friend I will hasten to conclude my tiresome Epistle which is so Dry and wholly destitute of any thing agreeable that I am quite asshamed to send it you—You see what you are to expect in Such an Old Fashiond Corrispondant, and will repent the encouragement you have given me to adress you. All the Sisters in my Apartment Salute you—Those 2 in Particular who bore me Company in my last Visit to you—Inclosed I send you the Coppy of the Conversion of a poor Simple Man—it is Short & Sweet. If this be agreeable shall in my Next send you another Piece—For your Valueable Manuscripts[8]—I have only to add Sister Mollys Tippets kind Love, be pleased to make mine Acceptable to good Good Father & Mother—Your Brother & Sister Molly and believe me to be and remain your Sincerely affectionate

Friend and Obliged humble Servant
Mary Penry

ALS: Catharine Franklin Sharples (1768–1824) Family Papers, Collection 3062, Series Three, Box 1:24, HSP. Endorsed "No 4 | Maria Penry | a Sister at Letitz."

1. See Letter 20.
2. "two of my Relations": Margaret Stocker and her son, John Clement Stocker, who had been in Britain for many years. See Appendix C.
3. "tender Sensibility": fine feeling, considered in the eighteenth century both a blessing and a curse. See Mullan, *Sentiment and Sociability*. Throughout her letters, MP strives to display this elite quality of sensibility and praises others for possessing this same quality.
4. Christian Eckstein (1717–1787), known as Doctor Gideon, arrived at Ephrata in 1743 and was a physician of some repute. The Wistars spent June to September 1786 at Ephrata, while two of their children, Thomas (1767–1814) and Mary (1772–1810)—the "Brother & Sister Molly" mentioned below—were under Gideon's care.
5. Haines and Wistar were first cousins. See Letter 20, note 7.
6. "The Building of our Church": see Letter 21, note 7.
7. For the single sisters' textile industry, see Appendix D.
8. "your Valueable Manuscripts": Catherine Wistar kept a commonplace book (a collection of extracts from others' writings), the second volume of which survives. See Commonplace Book, vol. 2, Catherine Franklin Sharples Family Papers, Collection 3062, HSP. It does not contain the "Conversion of a poor Simple Man," which may have been a Moravian memoir (*lebenslauf*).

➋ 23. TO CATHERINE HAINES[1]
November 3, 1786
Lititz, Pennsylvania

November 3rd 1786

Kitty Haines,

—Your sensations at meeting your Friends, answer so much to my own feelings, that I believe I can form a just idea of them. I had the trial last saturday on seeing two, tho second Cousins, yet such dear Relations that I cannot look on them but as my own Brother & Sister[2]—the reason is obvious my poverty is so great I have neither Father, Mother, Brother or Sister—which causes me to transfer all the affection due to those on these. The Family is remarkable for their tender regard for each other. Our Grand Fathers were Brothers and their Affection for each other was so great that the one surviv'd his Brother but 6 months—these my Relations are so kind as to impart to me my share in the Family attachments and I believe they are as sensible of my affection—I am glad you give me some hopes of seeing you here again. We shall then not meet strangers, but Friends and Acquaintance—in the Interim shou'd one or both of us (as may be the case) be called to our eternal Home and we depart in Peace, we shall then meet in the Realms of Bliss! where all sorrow and tears shall be done away. Your ill state of Health, and my Age and the infirmities attendant on it, must certainly bring the thoughts of a perhaps, short stay here very close—for myself my desire is to be found in Jesus, my Saviour and my God! who call'd me at a very early time of life, from the sinful Vanities of this world, to an Azylum of Peace—I have experienced the life of Riches and Honour, I have had my share in all the so call'd Pleasures which Youth and Affluence render still more pleasing, in vain I sought for Happiness therein—it constantly evaded my search—till the Holy Spirit turn'd my eyes inward, and gave me sight as well of my own depravity, as of the means to be purified and made happy, and I must confess, that only in and through his mercy and grace, I enjoy *any* Happiness either Spiritual or Temporal; without the Sensations of my Saviour's love nothing is sweet, nothing is desirable—and his residence in my Heart illumines, what other wise would be dark & dreary and turns my Desart into Canaan.³—Tis' this gives me: an Orphan separate from all the Connexion of nature: to find Fathers, Mother Brethren, & Sisters, ever ready to assist me, allways patiently bearing with my weakness and infirmities, Rejoicing when they can contribute to any thing towards making my Journey through this Vale of Tears easy—and bearing a kind part in my Afflictions which is in a manner delivering me from them—after this faint description of my situation you will not be surprised at my choice—tho' Sensible that I am in myself a poor Creature undeserving the least regard. Yet in and thro the Meritorious sufferings and Death of Jesus, I rejoice in God my Saviour who has regarded the low state of his Handmaiden—Set me free from the Slavery of Sin & Satan—And I now live a monument of his Mercy display'd to the worst of Sinners—

Maria P—a Sister of the Convent [illegible]

Copy (by Catherine Wistar): Catharine Franklin Sharples (1768–1824) Family Papers, Collection 3062, Series Three, Box 1:24, HSP. Endorsed "Extracts of a letter from | Maria P to Kitty H | Letitz November 3rd 1786."

1. Haines and Wistar were first cousins. See Letter 20, note 7. This letter is in Wistar's hand; she copied this extract from a lost letter to Haines.
2. The Stockers. See Letter 22, note 2.
3. "my own depravity . . . Desart into Canaan": see Letter 1, note 2, and this volume's introduction.

🐦 24. TO ELIZABETH DRINKER[1]

March 29, 1788

Lititz, Pennsylvania

Lititz 29 March 1788

My dearest Friend

I should not wonder if you thought I was determined to be Silent—because you wish'd me to write—[were] all the Letters I have wrote in Imagination to be reallities I fear you'd wish me to dessist. Thou dear Companion of my Youthful Years—The Friend I ever lovd with heart Sincere—Nor time nor Absence can The Bond dissolve—Such are my Sentiments when I think on my beloved Betsy Sandwith. My Friend Drinker its very true I am not so *very* Intimate with—but If you will not forget that you once was a Sandwith—I will with Joy recognize *Betsy Drinker*. It is happy for you that I am at a distance. Since the renewal of our Friendship in that well known *Councill Chamber*[2]—the long Blank of 25 or 30 Years is overlook'd and seems to me as though no Impediment had been and I should wish to enjoy a great deal of your Company. What shall I write my Friend that will be agreeable. In my Situation I have very little that can afford much entertainment unless you like to be entertain'd with Serious Subjects. Of these, we had this winter enough to employ a descriptive Pen. I will venture to relate some of them. The 9th of december a Worthey Friend I may say Venerable Father, one of the first of our Elders *Matthew Hehl* departed to the Joy of our Lord.[3] I was Present at his death to my great Edification—the 18th of January we lost our good & Faithful Manager of our Temporal Affairs after a Painful Illness of 6 Weeks—her Place is Suply'd by one (we hope) Suitable Person.[4] This Circumstance gave me more than Usual Imployment in closing our Accounts at her Decease—And that is as no sooner Compleated than I was Confined to my Chamber near 4 Weeks under a Course of Medicines for a Stubborn Rash in my Face.[5] It is 8 or 10 days since my Quarantine (as I may call it) is over.

You my dear Hold not with the Celebration of *Festivals*,[6] yet bear with me if I attempt a small Discription of what we Stile the Passion Week; but I must first Premise—that the Doctrine of our blessed Saviours Meritorious Life especially his Death and Suffrings is Our Constant Theme from *One* Easter to the *other*. Nevertheless That Season which the Church has apointed and set apart for a Solemn Meditation on His Suffrings, Death Burial and Resurrection, is indeed a Season peculiarly Bless'd to my heart. And as the last week *was* that happy Season, I know you will excuse my entertaining you with an account of our Solemnities Since you will believe the Impression is Still fresh in my Mind. Every Evening of the Week a Portion of Scripture[7]—The Simple plain Account which the Evangelists have given, of what may [*missing*] to have happend on each day of the Week—Is read with a [*missing*] heart To an Attentive Auditory, and on Good Friday as [it is] call'd, In the different Meetings of the Whole day Nothing [*missing*] but the Continuation of the Evangelists Account of the different Scenes of our Lord Suffrings—On Saterday his Burial and on Sunday his Glorious Resurrection—We had this time a Funeral on Good Friday, a Single Sister dying on the Wednesday before.[8] One and thirty Years I have kept these in *Truth* Holy Days, here and in Bethlehem and I must say it is every Year New to me—My heart accompanies My Redeemer From the Mount of Olives and the Garden, there where He was in such an Agony that he Sweated Blood, to Mount Calvary &c. And this to Redeem *My Soul.* I could enlarge on this Subject—But Judging of your Sensations by my own, think I have said Enough on this Subject. For after all, the feelings of the heart cannot be express'd in Words!

I must now turn to another Subject—I cannot but think a Journey would be of great Service to you, and I please my Self with making out a very Agreeable One—You first go to Downing, that is but One days Journey.[9] There you will chuse to Spend some days. From thence you proceed to Lancaster—and then you will come to Lititz. What a pretty Tour, that will be—and how joyfully should I receive you! Think upon it and let me know your Thoughts—I cannot return your Book with this Opportunity. The Man is a Stranger to me and affraid to take any Small Parcell for fear it should be Stolen—It is a great Hardship to get any little thing to or from Philadelphia.

Now my dear I will only add: Je vous Aime de tout mon Coeur et je reste votre fidelle aimie Jusque la Mort[10]

Marie Penrie

Je vous prie Eccrive Moi—Je vous reponderoi.[11]
And do any thing to Oblige you—or Yours that is in my Power.
My Love to your Spouse, and worthy Friend Able James.[12]

ALS: Linden Hall Archives. Addressed "To | Mrs Elizabeth Drinker | @ Philadelphia | To the care of | Mr Bartow." Endorsed "Lititz March 29, 1788 | Mary Penry."

1. See Letter 18.

2. *"Councill Chamber"*: the governor's council chamber in what is now Independence Hall. In the 1780s, both this council chamber and the assembly room contained patriotic paintings that the public could view, as Hannah Sansom did. See October 24, 1785, Sansom, *Diary*, 307. They must have

"renew[ed]" their friendship in Philadelphia while MP visited from May 28 to June 18, 1787. Drinker's diary from 1787 does not survive.

3. *"Matthew Hehl"*: see Letter 14, note 7. Hehl had actually died on December 4, 1787.

4. Maria Barbara Leinbach (1739–1788), the steward (*Vorsteherin*) of the single sisters' choir, responsible for its financial activities, died on January 18. Mary Tippet, already the spiritual leader (*Pflegerin*) of the choir, temporarily assumed her duties, but Anna Margareta Krieger (1758–1842) took over by February. Krieger remained the *Vorsteherin* of the single sisters' choir until she left for Salem, North Carolina, where in November 1807 she became both *Pflegerin* and *Vorsteherin* of the single sisters' house there.

5. "Rash in my Face": see Letter 65 to Benjamin Rush.

6. MP assumes that Drinker, a Quaker, did not recognize holidays such as Christmas or Easter.

7. "Every Evening of the Week a Portion of Scripture": the Moravian's Holy Week manual, first composed in 1757. Samuel Lieberkuehn (1710–1777) produced a new version in 1768, translated into English as *The Harmony of the Four Gospels; or, The History of Our Lord and Saviour Jesus Christ* (London, 1771).

8. Anna Christina Zander (1747–1788) died on March 19.

9. Downings was the halfway station between Philadelphia and Lancaster, at the eastern end of the village of Downingtown and thirty-three miles from the Philadelphia courthouse. Sachse, *Wayside Inns*, 22.

10. "Je vous Aime . . . Jusque la Mort": I love you with all my heart and remain your faithful friend until death (French).

11. "Je vous . . . reponderoi": please write me and I will respond (French).

12. Abel James (d. 1790) was Henry Drinker's business partner.

❧ 25. TO ELIZABETH DRINKER[1]

August 9, 1788

Lititz, Pennsylvania

Lititz August the 9th 1788

My dearest Friend!

My last Letter to you Consisting in a Verbal Message from the Lips of your Beloved Son, was doubtless more Acceptable than 20 written Letters would have been;[2] however not being likely to receive an answer in the same Way I must again have recourse to the Pen, tho Age and Infirmities has pretty near blunted the Edge. You Reciev'd I hope the little Book, which was a pleasant Recreation for an Idle hour and a Renewal of my Request for the Magazines which your Son agreed to send to the Care of Ann Edge at Downings to be by them forwarded to Friend Cope at Lancaster and thus we settled that affair wether it will be productive of any thing time will shew[3]—I very much wish'd you had health and Spirits to take a Tour of the same kind with your Son—Tho', if Collecting in of Debts was some part of his Bus'ness I would recal my Wish since that is too Vexatious for a Person who would travel for their Health. If you are really better in your health as your Son Said you were (tho these Young Men are Strangers to the Complaints of Old Women and for that Reason their information not wholly to be depended on) I may put in a Plea for a Letter now and then—In order to give me a Subject which a Corrispondant on One Side only, as I may say, is Certainly very much at a loss for—The Paragraph at the beginning of Common Corrispondance I am in good Health hoping these lines will find you in the Same is become Obsol[e]te and must be exchangd for One of later date—and tis *you* that are as I observd above by writing me, to put me in a way to write without that hearty tho Old Fashiond Introduction—As for myself nothing *new* as I may say happens that is of Conscequence to any one beyond my Circle so that its not worth Communicating—Unless one was certain those Communications were agreeable to the Corrispondant. This you will say is very trifling Scrible—your Censure is just, I will tell you honestly that this time the Enquiry after your Health is certainly and sincerely my first Motive and the Second is to recomend the Packet directed to your Care—and to beg you to send it carefully to My Esteemed Friend Sally Graff.[4] It is a little Book which I send her, Neither a Novel or a Play, but purely texts of Scripture for every day of the Year[5]—You will judge of the extreem Haste I am in, both the Incoherence of the Stile and the wretched writing is a Sufficient Proof. Adieu Ma tres Chere Amie. J suis votree Fiddelle[6]

My kind Love to your Sister—to your good Spouse & Chilldren

M Penry

ALS: Linden Hall Archives. Addressed "Mrs | Elizabeth Drinker | In Front Street near Race Street | Philadelphia." Endorsed "Lititz August 9, 1788 | Mary Penry."

1. See Letter 18.

2. Elizabeth Drinker's eldest son, William, stopped in Lititz on a business "tour," as MP mentions later in this letter.

3. Caleb Cope (1736–1824), whose home stood at what is now 26 North Lime Street, housed Major John Andre when he was confined in Lancaster in 1776. Cope carried letters between MP and Drinker. See Drinker, *Diary*, 2:1487. He moved to Burlington, New Jersey, in 1813.

4. Sarah Nicholson married George Graff on December 28.

5. "texts of Scripture for every day of the Year": Zinzendorf began the tradition of "watchwords" (*Losungen*) on May 3, 1728, when he provided the Herrnhut congregation with a scriptural text to guide devotions each day. Beginning in 1731, small volumes were printed that contained two scriptural verses, one from the Old Testament and one from the New Testament, each followed by a hymn (or "antiphone"), so that Moravian communities around the globe would meditate on the same watchword each day. In subsequent letters, MP often copies entries from the annual *Daily Words and Doctrinal Texts of the Brethren's Congregation*.

6. "J suis votree Fiddelle": I am your faithful (French).

🐛 26. TO ELIZABETH DRINKER[1]

November 26, 1790

Lititz, Pennsylvania

Lititz 26 November 1790

Mon tres Chere Amie

I sitt down to *converse* with you in a total ignorance how or when it will come to your *Ears*. I will even write and should an Oppertunity serve it is ready. In the first place accept of my Sincere thanks for all your Kindness and in particular your last favour which I got out of Bed to receive.[2] I sat out on Friday at allmost 8 O Clock. My Companions [were] first Mr Tilt and his wife lately arrived from Halifax.[3] He is a Brittish Officer who during the War was a Prisoner at Lancaster, and there married and after his Release took his wife to Halifax and was going to Lancaster to see her Relations, with them was their 2 children—Twins of 7 Year old. In this Company I travelld till the first Stage, when we took in an Irish Gentlewoman who with her Husband arrived in the last ship from Ireland. These last came so far as Fahnstocks in a chair but could get no Carriage further, neither could the Man get a Horse to hire and was obliged to travel on Foot.[4] At Downings we spent an agreeable Evening and sat out early on Saterday in hopes of being at Lancaster by day light but herein we was greatly disapointed as you shall hear.[5] Fourteen Miles below Lancaster the axle tree of our hind Wheels broke, we had just time to unlight before the Wheel dropt off and also received no hurt.

We all footed it to the Sign of the Hat 2 Miles from the place where we left the Stage.[6] After an ordinary Dinner and a Melancholy Prospect of spending our Sunday perhaps here, it was a *favour* to obtain a Country Waggon without a cover—and no other Seats than Bundles of Straw. Into this Vehicle we went with all our Package and our Irish Gentleman who seem'd to think humble riding was better than Proud walking on Foot. We came safe to Lancaster after 8 OClock in the Evening. We unlighted from our Coach at the Entrance into town and walk'd Soberly to our respective Quarters after taking an affectionate leave of each other for we had been very good Company together, Politness and good Nature had lessen'd every difficulty.

Sunday Morning a Carriage from Lititz took me home to the mutual Joy of myself and my dear Companions. I have no Wish now that cannot be gratified, but the Sight and Converse of my dear Friends and the latter is in some Measure to be attaind with the Pen. I am extreemly desirous of an Intimate Corrispondance with my dear Betsy, but you must write me your self[7]—You have no manner of Reason to aprehend that *one* Person either hears or see's our Corrispondance—I write when and how, and to whom I please, in perfect Freedom, and it is at my own choice to comunicate my Corrispondance or not. Whatever Subject you think proper to start shall be answerd to the best of my Ability, and with the Privacy suiting Friends.[8]

Be pleased to give my kind love to your good Spouse and all your Children and kiss your little Eliza for me, my kind love to Sister Polly[9]—and embracing you tenderly I conclude your Sincerely affectionate Friend

Marie Penrie

ALS: Linden Hall Archives.

1. See Letter 18.

2. On September 16 MP left Lititz for Philadelphia. While there she visited with Drinker for tea and dinner, returning to Lititz on November 14, 1790. See September 24, October 23, 1790, Drinker, *Diary*, 1:452, 455.

3. Thomas Tilt served as quartermaster to the British light infantry of the 80th Regiment of foot, which served under Cornwallis at Yorktown. British prisoners, initially confined to Winchester, Virginia, were marched to York and Lancaster. When they arrived in May 1782, they found a large number of other British prisoners already there. See "List of British Prisoners of Warr Brought to Lancaster . . . April 1781," Peter Force Papers and Collection, Series 9, Microfilm Reel 106, Manuscript Division, LOC. A payment warrant suggests that Tilt was in Lancaster from October 20, 1781, to June 24, 1782.

4. "Fahnstocks": Letter 21, note 4.

5. That is, while it was still light out.

6. During the American Revolution, Samuel Smith was the proprietor of this inn.

7. "Intimate Corrispondence": in requesting this relationship, MP not only asks Drinker to share her private sentiments but also lays claim to the sensibility that embraces such exchanges. See Letter 22, note 3.

8. "Privacy suiting Friends": MP assures Drinker that church authorities do not read their correspondence. Earlier, under different circumstances, Zinzendorf advocated inspecting letters for inappropriate disclosures about the church. See Atwood, "Zinzendorf's 1749 Reprimand," 68.

9. Regarding "little Eliza" (Elizabeth Downing, Drinker's granddaughter) and "Sister Polly" (Drinker's sister, Mary Sandwith), see Appendix C.

？❦ 27. TO BENJAMIN RUSH[1]

April 21, 1791

Lititz, Pennsylvania

Lititz April 21st 1791

Dear Sir!

I cannot sufficiently express the scence I have of your kindness in that you condescended to write me yourself.

As I well knew how precious your time is, I had not the last Expectation of any other answer than thro the medium of Mrs Stockers letter—or I should have applied immediately to yourself.

The answer was detaind so long, that despairing of receiving any, we applied to a german Docter at Lancaster,[2] who I believe did all in his power to relieve our poor Patient,[3] but we cannot say that the chief complaints are removed; and indeed we have very little hopes they ever will. The german doctor advised frequent Emetic's and she was every Evening anointed with a certain oil which have had that Effect,[4] it has prevented the Convulsions from breaking out with the violence they had done for a Considerable time when I stated her Case to Mrs Stocker.[5] It is surprizing that she casts up such Quantities of Gall, which causes her to find great Relief from the frequent use of Emetics. Animal food does not agree with her as well as vegetables. She is frequently obliged to fast owing to her Jaw being so Stiff, that she cannot open her Mouth. At such times we contrive to feed her with a tea Spoon with good Soups &c.

Nothing relieves this Complaint but a gentle emetic, which forces open the Jaw—when this Cramp or Convulsion is in her Stomach & Bowels she has violent pains, and a Supression of Urine—This we can remove with a gentle Purge—but it only shifts its Station from one part to the other. She is now (taking all together) as well as usual since we have known her—but must Constantly be attended like a Sick Person, and we have great reason to fear was we to relax in the least with our attendance the Convulsions would return since they have never wholy left her. She has been constantly taking Medicines these 9 Months, yet have we hitherto not been able to have her so far restored as to contribute to her Mantainance by any kind of work, which notwithstanding she very well knows is neither desired nor expected, yet this makes her low spirited, as she is but young, she wishes she could just obtain such a degree of health, as might enable her to earn her livelihood, but if the Lord does not think fitting, she must be resignd and thankful that her lot is cast where it is, as she will want for Nothing as long as she lives, and will be attended with the very same care and tenderness as one in affluent Circumstances.

And now Sir having given you as circumstantial account of our poor patient as I am able, and letting you know the German *Doctor* is mov'd away from Lancaster—we shall follow your advice in every Particular only waiting for a line from Mrs Stocker (since I would not willingly put you to the trouble). I beg leave to ask wether it is *quick Lime* that you meant when you mentiond from 1 to 2 grains of the *Powder of Lime?* Secondly wether you find it Necessary to give any further Directions or wether we are Simply to follow your Prescription in the Letter you was so kind to Write? I beg pardon for intruding on your Patience with so much tautology and here will close this Subject.

But now Sir give me leave to tell you, by writing to me you have drawn yourself into a Scrape—you have exposed yourself to the tiresome redundances of my Pen, and tho' to console you in some Measure I promise I will be very careful not to trouble you again, unless urged by the greatest Necessity, or moved to write an *answer* (which out of pure Regard I desire you would not give me any cause of writing). Thus much premised I shall go on without fear and not concern myself about the length of my Letter—its being the first, and possibly the last—I shall have the Honour of writing *Doctor Rush*. My dear *Doctor* your *Merrits* as a *Physician* are beyond my Conception, and like all in my Class, I stand at an humble distance and admire the goodness of our god who has bestowd such inestimable gifts upon you for the benifit of such Numbers as have the happiness to be under your Care—Yet dear *Doctor* I confess all the shining qualities which adorn your Charactor in every stage and calling of your Life, would be an Indifferent matter to me, unless perhaps moved by a selfish principle when in distress (which indeed is something I cannot bear). O my dear Sir! It is the *Christian* I admire, my heart glows towards the Man who in this degenerate age, placed in so Conspicious a Station & surrounded by all the Tribe of fashionable Unbelievers—is not Ashamed of Christ—but is ever ready to confess his tender attachment to the loving and beloved Jesus! This gives you the finest oppertunity of attending your Patients in double capacity and adminestring to the Health of the Soul, as well as the Body. May your Labours in both respects be crownd with Success! and may the Lord continue to bless your Spiritual and Temporal Concerns is my Sincere Prayer! I beg you will be pleased to give my most Respectful love to your dear Spouse, and give me leave to subscribe myself your affectionate Friend, and obliged humble Servant

Mary Penry

ALS: Rush Family Papers, Correspondence, Box 13:48, Library Company of Philadelphia. Endorsed "Mary Penry | Recommended | Lime—Wine | cordial diet—frictions exercise | Bandages to her limbs | & body | May 7th 1791."

1. Benjamin Rush (1746–1813), the premier physician in early America.
2. "german Docter at Lancaster": perhaps Abraham Neff (1719–1793), who lived on Orange Street just above Lime, near MP's friends, the Robertses. Adam Simon Kuhn (1713–1780) had been the most prominent German physician in Lancaster; his son, Adam Kuhn (1741–1817), also a physician, had moved to Philadelphia by 1768.
3. "poor Patient": unidentified.
4. "Emetic's": substances that produce vomiting.
5. "Mrs Stocker": see Appendix C.

❧ 28. TO FRANCIS ALISON[1]

July 1, 1792
Lititz, Pennsylvania

Lititz July 1st 1792

Dear Sir!

The bearer of this Mr Matthew Eggert, the Steward of the Single Brethrens House in Lititz,[2] Waits upon you Sir to ask your advice, in Regard to the loan of their House for the Use of the Hospital as they, the Brethren have receiv'd no maner of Payment (which they was promised). Mr Eggert intends to apply—but being a Stranger to the terms under which the Brethren vacated their dwelling house for the use of the Hospital.[3] We think none can better advise him than you Sir who was the Senior Surgeon of that Hospital—and as you gave so many Proofs of your Friendship for the Congregation at Lititz during your Residence here we put so much Confidence in you Sir that you Will not Refuse Mr Eggert your Councill and Assistance in this affair.

Miss Tippet joins in this Request, being Convinced in our own Minds beforehand of your granting our Request[4]—Our joint Love to good Mrs Alison and your whole Family Concludes me—Sir your Sincere Friend and humble Servant

Mary Penry

ALS: Society Small Collection, 1681–1996, Collection 22B, Box 1, HSP. Addressed "Docter | Alison | Near Newport | Honnourd by | Mr Matthew Eggert | 2 D C." Endorsed "Miss Penry | July 1, 1792."

1. The son of the Presbyterian minister Francis Alison (1705–1779), Francis Alison, Jr. (1751–1813), supervised the Continental Army hospital in Lititz from December 1777 to August 1778. See Radbill, "Francis Alison," 248. In the Lititz single sisters' diary for August 29, 1778, MP wrote, "Dr. Allison maintained order and discipline to the best of his ability. The soldiers being quartered so near us, we were subjected to all manner of inconvenience and care, but the Lord commanded his dear angels to keep watch over us, so that we might not be harmed. In this, Dr. Allison—so influenced by the Lord—was of much assistance, for he acted toward us like a father, taking every precaution that we should not be incommoded in the slightest degree by the soldiers or their wives." See Beck, "Extracts," 701.

2. Matthew Eggert (1763–1831), who had taught at Nazareth Hall (1786–91), was warden of the Lititz single brothers' house (1792–1802) until he married Maria Ruppert (1777–1854). He later taught at the Bethlehem boys' school (1808–14). Eggert left Lititz for Philadelphia on July 2, 1792.

3. Bethlehem's single brothers' house had also served as a Continental Army hospital. In October 1779 Bethlehem's authorities submitted to Congress a bill for the expense of repairing the building. See Jordan, "Military Hospitals."

4. "Miss Tippet": see Letter 11, note 3.

☙ 29. TO MEREDITH PENRY AND KATHERINE PENRY[1]
May 2, 1793
Lititz, Pennsylvania

Lititz May the 2nd 1793

Honoured Uncle and dearest Cousin!

Its not in my power to express the heart felt Pleasure your dear letter gave me which I received the 25th of April.[2] Imagine to yourselves how great must be my Joy, after almost 49 years to receive the first line from my dear Fathers Family for whom, and for my Native Country I have ever had a strong Predilection. After living near Six years in the Single Sisters House at Bethlehem I removed to Lititz which is about 70 Miles from Bethlehem, and Sixty from Philadelphia.[3] Either at my first coming here in the year 1761 or shortly after my Mammas decease in the year 1760 I wrote to my dear Grandmamma and Uncle. Miss Gwillim of Abergavenny with whom I have Corrisponded untill of Late years informed me, that my Letters arrived safe and that my Grandma dyed shortly after—but from the family I did not receive a line and indeed Miss Gwillim wrote me they *would not* write and beg'd me to make no further attempts.[4] This has frequently occasiond me *sorrowful* hours. I look'd on my Situation—an *Orphan* in a *Strange Country* to be melancholy enough, without the aditional grief of being forsaken by my Relations to whom I had given no Offence, and from whom I ask'd no Favour but a Letter. Indeed my Mamma was not so attach'd to my Father's Family as I could have wish'd, because I felt more tenderness for them than for my Mammas Relations. She has frequently told me that my Grandmama Penry was very much displeased with her for taking me to America. My dear Mamma's sole aim was to procure an Independent Fortune for me, which she was intirely disapointed off, and I have my whole Life been *Dependant* on my own Industry and the Friendship of Strangers.[5] The Step my dear Mamma had taken occasioned I believe a Coolness and during her Lifetime I heard nothing from you. After her death I seemd to want the Consolation of my Relations, for blessed be the Lord I allways had good Friends—yet Nature drew me towards *you.* It was a tender Call but it was not heeded and I thought my Lot hard—Yet let me not Murmer. I have far far greater reason to adore and praise his Name! I never have wanted my needful food—or Raiment to put on.[6]

My Situation is precisely the same as described in my letter to my uncle.[7] I keep the Accounts of our House, and write letters of Busness. As the Lord as bless'd me with very good eyes—I embroider Satin for Pincushions and work Tambour, an easy pleasing employment, which provide for my Necessaries.

Fortune I have none, but am happy in the love and care of my Friends.[8] A Distant Relation of my Mamma's Second Cousins to me reside in Philadelphia whom I visit once in 2 or three years are very kind to me when I am with them and bear my Expenses when I go to the City. I have been some weeks with them on such a visit.[9] Anything further I never ask'd—nor was it offer'd—they see I am not in want and they make no Enquiries into my Circumstances. Was I to give you a detail of the Troubles and disapointments my dear Mamma and I have met with, since we left England it would take up Sheets of Paper, and in the end aford you little Satisfaction. Let me therefore dearest Uncle and Cousin endeavour to relate something more pleasing and forget what is past. Altho it has been my Lot to suffer many and Severe troubles, and my Constrain'd Circumstances prevent me from the Enjoyment of many Convieniences my Family and birth made me hope for—Yet to the praise and Glory of my Lord and Saviour I must say that ever Since I have join'd the Brethren's Congregation I have led a quiet and happy Life. Retired from the World and its Vanities, my whole Concern is to make my calling and Election sure—In looking unto Jesus, the Author and Finisher of our Faith I enjoy a Contentment & Peace of Mind which this World can neither give nor deprive me off.[10] My age is so far advanced as well as doubtless that of my honoured Uncle that I fear our Corrispondance will not be of long duration. Yet God only knows how long we may Continue in this Vale of Tears. Let us then make good use of our time while we can, and write frequently. I shall write twice more this Summer—If we continue our Neutrality our Corrispondance will not be interrupted by the war—American Vessels can pass at all times[11]—but none else—I beg you will favour me with an account of our dear Family, in which you cannot be too prolix—Adieu my most honoured Uncle and dearest Cousin receive my unfeigned thanks for your stepping forth to Enquire after your (as it were) forsaken Niece and Cousin—please to present my Duty and Love to all and every of the worthy Relatives. I am with true heart Affection—Your *Dutifull Niece* and Affectionate

Cousin

Mary Penry

Please to direct To Mary Penry at Lititz Lancaster County State of Pennsylvania

ALS: Penralley Collection 1359, NLW. Addressed "Mr Meredith Penry | Streut Brecon | Brecknockshire | South Wales." Endorsed "Brecon | This Letter came to hand | July 6th 1793 | Answered it July 13th 1793."

1. Meredith Penry (1714–1799) married Alice Williams (1717–1775) in 1742 and labored as a tanner. His unmarried daughter, Katherine Penry (1744–1812), lived with him. So did Eliza Powell (b. 1775), his granddaughter, whose parents—Alice (Penry) Powell (1749–1778) and Thomas Powell (d. 1793)— had both died. See Brecon St. Johns Church Register, Defynnog Church Register, PCA. Eliza's older brother, Penry Powell (1774–1797), is mentioned frequently in later letters.

2. This letter, sent from Wales on December 14, 1792, was the first that MP received from her relatives, to whom she had written in 1760 (Letter 3).

3. The Lititz single sisters' diary begins on March 25, 1762, in MP's handwriting, although MP arrived in Lititz on June 3, 1762 (not 1761, as she states here).

4. "Miss Gwillim": see Letter 3, note 7; "Grandma": Elinor Penry died in March 1762 (Letter 3, note 6).

5. For MP's inability to secure her inheritance, see this volume's introduction.

6. "needful food—or Raiment": *Collection of Hymns* (1743), 257. See also Matthew 6:25.

7. Presumably Letter 3, written over thirty years earlier.

8. "Tambour": embroidery on a frame.

9. "A Distant Relation": the Stockers. See Appendix C.

10. Hebrews 12:2.

11. "our Neutrality": after France declared war on Britain in February 1793, the United States adopted a policy of neutrality—officially proclaimed by George Washington in May. This policy led to Thomas Jefferson's resignation as secretary of state in December.

⁓ 30. TO MEREDITH PENRY AND KATHERINE PENRY[1]

May 20, 1793

Lititz, Pennsylvania

Lititz May 20th 1795

Honour'd Uncle and dearest Cousin

This is my second Letter since the receipt of your favour of December the 14th 1792.[2] In hopes *that* will reach your hands, I will not repeat, what that Letter contains. My life in America was during the first 10 years—one Scene of Affliction tho in outward prosperity! We came over in the year 1744 and 1746 my Mothers Relation dyed—upon which Mamma took our Passage to return to England but the Widdower made use of so many Intreaties to prevail on her to stay one year longer that she consented. And in the end he prevaild on her to accept his Hand.[3] With him she led a most unhappy Life, which was renderd more bitter, by reflections on her Happiness with my dear Papa. She has frequently given me the most pleasing relations, of my dearest Father and her Mutual regard, which often made me lament his loss anew. No one can conceive the Egyptian Bondage I was under with this Step Father!—But enough of that—My great Inheritance at his Death—was twenty Shillings—which I was too proud to accept of—So that I have nothing to thank him for unless for my Education[4]—and that I in a manner repaid by my Dilligence in his Counter, where I sometimes wrote day and Night when ever Bus'ness required. In the year 1760 I buried my dear Mother. Happy for me I had been 4 years before that settled at Bethlehem, or I believe it would have been still harder to me—An Orphan in a foreign Country—Yet God be thank'd not *friendless*. About 4 years ago I was acquainted with a Surgeon named Lewis, who told me he knew several of Our Family.[5] He was born in Brecknockshire (if I am not mistaken). He mention'd a Penry who was a Methodist minister, I suposed it must be a Brothers son of my Fathers[6]—He was in *our* congregation but a few weeks before his death tho he had lived in One of our Congregations at Carolina some years. During the Warr in America I waited upon Some Gentlemen who were Prisoners among the Americans, and came to see our Place, to shew them our House; being introduced to them as an English woman I was ask'd my Name and the place of my Birth, at the hearing of which One in Particular seemd greatly surprized, said he was well acquaintd with some of my Family—and press'd me to write home, he would take care of my Letter—but I declined, as I knew not who to adress my Letter to—neither did I think any one thought on me.[7]

Oh how much do I owe to my Great and Good Saviour, who has never left nor forsaken me, from my Youth up till now, neither will he leave me in Old Age—but Continue (I humbly trust) to supply all my wants thro the short time I may reasonably expect to stay in this Mortality.

Should I depart this Life before you receive this—you may depend on hearing from my Friends, the account of my Decease—

I indeed shall now be content to live a little longer, to enjoy the pleasure of interchanging a few letters with you. I could wish to hear how old my dear Uncle is—and dearest Cousin you forgot to Sign your Name—I want to know wether you are a Mary as well as myself. I am the only welch woman in our Congregations in America. The 2 Bretheren Gambold and Lewis lye burried side by side in Bethlehem—the *only* Welch Men among us.[8] I hope to receive a long letter from you with an accurate account of our Family—Miss Gwillim of Abergavenny invited me to her and promised to leave me what she had at her decease, I immagine she has been dead some years.[9] One of my Mamma's Relations (her first Cousin Kitty Stocker, now a Widdow of the name of Rumsey)[10] wrote me some years Since with Miss Gwillim, near whom she resides; I answered her Letter but never heard from her Since, if you can convey my Compliments to her—I shall take it kind—as likewise to Miss Gwillim, if living.

In Haverford West I have had Corrispondance with Miss Nancy Vaughan a Single Sister there—which has been dropt Since the troubles in America began.[11] We have thro Gods Mercy, the enjoyment of Peace and Quiet. May our good Lord bless you with Spiritual and Temporal Benefits. So prays— your dutiful Niece & affectionate Cousin.

In haste

Mary Penry

P.S. You can direct to Me—to the care of Mr John Clement Stocker Merchant in Philadelphia who is my Cousin[12]

ALS: Penralley Collection 1360, NLW. Addressed "Mr | Meredith Penry | Struet Brecon | Brecknockshire | South Wales." Endorsed "This Letter came to hand | from Talgarth July 30th | 1793 | Brought to Trevecka by a | Minister from America | Answered it August 24 | sent it to Bristol 30th Instant."[13]

1. See Letter 29.

2. Letter 29 was the first.

3. Anne (Stocker) Attwood actually died in 1747. The widower, William Attwood, married the widow Mary Penry in 1751. See Appendix B and this volume's introduction.

4. William Attwood's will provided only twenty shillings to MP and to her mother. See Last Will and Testament, Register of Wills Office. For MP's education at Anthony Benezet's school, see this volume's introduction.

5. John Lewis (1744–1788), born in South Wales, married Catherine Eliza Lembke (1750–1810) in 1783. The couple moved to Salem, North Carolina, where Lewis served as the community doctor. For complaints about his drinking and high fees, see Long, "Medical Care," 280–81. Lewis died soon after he returned to Pennsylvania.

6. "a Penry who was a Methodist minister": unidentified. See also Letter 37, note 7.

7. MP later identifies this officer as "Major Rice Price." See Letter 42, note 3. Several men by this name lived in Brecon at this time. Many British officers and soldiers were confined in Lancaster from 1775 to 1780. No officer by this name, however, appears in Ford, *British Officers Serving in the American Revolution*, nor in the many lists of prisoners that survive among the Peter Force Papers and Collection, Series 9, Microfilm Reels 103–4, Manuscript Division, LOC.

8. Hector Gambold (1719–1788), born in South Wales, joined the Moravians at Oxford and came to America in 1742. He married Helen Craig (1718–1792) and served in several Moravian congregations, including Staten Island (1763–84). Their son was John Gambold, one of MP's correspondents (see Letter 32). For John Lewis, see note 5 above.

9. "Miss Gwillim": see Letter 3, note 7.

10. Catherine Stocker married Robert Rumsey, a cleric at St. Michael's Church, Cwmdu, near Abergavenny. In 1749 they had a daughter, Catherine (see Letter 51), and in 1750 a son Robert, who lived only a month. Catherine Stocker Rumsey died in 1780. She was not a widow, however: her husband, the Reverend Robert Rusmey, lived until 1799. See *Rumsey v. Stocker*, 1743, C 11/339/32, NAK; Robert Rumsey, Last Will and Testament, 1799, BR/1799/20, NAK; and Llantilio Pertholey Church Register, PCA.

11. For Haverfordwest and for Anne (Nancy) Vaughn, see Letter 6, note 6.

12. Regarding John Clement Stocker, the son of Anthony Stocker and Margaret Stocker, see Appendix C.

13. "Trevecka": Trefeca, a Welsh town home to Methodist leader Howell Harris. It is about twelve miles from Brecon, where Meredith Penry lived.

డ్రి 31. TO MEREDITH PENRY AND KATHERINE PENRY[1]
June 4, 1793
Lititz, Pennsylvania

Lititz June the 4th 1793

Honourd Uncle and dearest Cousin!

This is my Third *Letter* since the receit of your kind *Letters*,[2] both of which came to my hands, the first in April, the other in May. It being possible that my *three* Letters may come safe I will vary my stile and avoid repetition—should on the contrary but one reach you, I trust that one will be sufficient to satisfy you concerning my Wellfare. I have wrote pretty quick in Succession, that I might lay hold of the Early Ships in the Spring[3]—and shall now wait till the fall of the year before I write again and in the mean while hope to hear from you a more circumstantial Account of our Family than were prudent in a *publick Letter*. Thus much I expect before hand, that Neither Wealth nor Grandeur is to be met with in the Penrys Family—The Wheel of fortune has turn'd us to the *Bottom*. If we can but Submit to set thus Low, we may perhaps be hapier than many who are now at the Top—My Grandfather Penry, had he been a better Oeconomist, might have left his Children and Grand Children in Affluence—but let us not reflect upon the dead! I am thankful that I have been bless'd with resignation to the Lords dispensations—he doubtless has his infinitely wise and good reasons in *all* his dispensations, and provided we have treasure in heaven, it matters little wether we have earthly treasure or not. I believe most certainly that it was good for me that I have been afflicted—It has weand my heart from this world and its vanities, and being now Aged, my time here below will not be many years more, and provided I can have the Necessaries of Life, to me it will be all one wether I die worth 50 Pounds or 50 pence. Undoubtedly many little Convieniences which render Life comfortable, are wanting—Yet since such things are not absolutely Necessaries—why should we sigh after them. Yet I confess my frailty that I sometimes have thought my Lot rather hard, being deprived of my Maternal fortune thro the baseness of those, who have enrich'd themselves, by spoiling the Widdow—and the Orphan[4]—When on the contrary I compare my Situation with that of my Relations in Philadelphia who live indeed in the greatest affluence I find they are not so happy as I am in my Constrained Circumstances.[5]—I have in my former Letter informd you that these relations are my second Cousins, my Grandfather Stocker, and their Grandfather, were *own Brothers*. Another of my Grandfather Stockers brothers Children was living some years agon at Abergavenny a Widdow of the name of Rumsey[6]—I believe—tho perhaps I may have mistook the name since its many years past, that I have not heard from her. Ever since it has pleased my Gracious Saviour to bring me to the Knowledge of my own Sinful State by Nature and the Riches of his redeeming Grace in (which Glory be to his Holy Name) I have an Interest—and that he has given me a place among his Children, I am realy in an Azylum of peace and Happiness. Days and Years pass on without an Material Change in my way of Life. His Mercies are so Many, and his Long suffring so great, that I am humbled in the dust at the recolection of my own unworthyness, and his unspeakable Love. May he continue (as I humbly trust he will) my kind and Compassionate Saviour—untill he takes me to the Arms of his Mercy—And may he bless *you* my dear Uncle and *Cousins*—with all my dear Relatives—by filling your hearts with *his* Peace which no vissisitudes of this Mortal Life can deprive us off—unless we willfully withdraw ourselves from his protection. Amen, Amen. I remain your Dutiful Niece and Affectionate Cousin

Mary Penry

P.S. Direct to Mary Penry at Lititz, Lancaster County—State of Pennsylvania North America
To the Care of Mr John Clements Stocker Merchant Philadelphia

ALS: Penralley Collection 1361, NLW. Addressed "Mr | Meredith Penry | Struet Brecon | Brecknockshire | South Wales." Endorsed "received this Letter by Post | September the 23rd 1793 | answered this July 20th | sent from Bristol in July or | August by one Capt Goodwrich | in the Ship Severn."

1. See Letter 29.
2. Letters 29 and 30 were the first two.
3. "Early Ships in the Spring": since shipping was seasonal, sending letters to Great Britain "required a complex understanding of the workings of Atlantic . . . shipping." O'Neill, *Opened Letter*, 34–36.
4. For MP's inheritance, see this volume's introduction.
5. "Relations in Philadelphia": the Stockers. See Appendix C.
6. "Widdow . . . Rumsey": see Letter 30, note 10.

❧ 32. TO JOHN GAMBOLD[1]

October 4, 1793

Lititz, Pennsylvania

Lititz 4th October 93

My dear Brother

The Salutation you sent me in the little note to your Step Mother, had a Surprizing Effect[2]—I was moved to answer with a Letter or a scrible for I expect every Minute the Man will set out. Your Step Mother desires her love and I am to tell you that Young Peter Rixegger went off from Bethlehem, where he had been placed, and Gredel Friedrick to York town under the Pretence to visit her Mother—there they *met*, and *married*.[3] I suppose you will immagine this has given much trouble and uneasiness. That Brother Muller is Married to Anna Johana Levering and Betsy Henry to Br Johan Molther you will doubtless hear[4]—That the poor Philadelphians are dead or dying by 50ties 100dreds and 3 [to] 400 in a day and the disorder not yet abated.[5] We can hear very little from thence. None are sufferd to come to Lancaster nor indeed any where without performing quarantine. Those who have forsaken the City and lockd up their Houses are likely to be great loosers in their Property by thieves and Robbers who plunder where they can— Billy Wistar who fled to Lancaster being desired to return to the City—his House was in Danger—answerd if I loose all I have in the World I cannot go I am not prepared for death.[6] This summer I was 5 Weeks in Bethlehem. Spent many agreeable Hours with your Sister Betsy and at Nazareth with Nancy—Nancy is in a poor State of health but Betsy is cheerful and hearty[7]—Müllers are calld to Emaus Molthers to Hebron Peters to New York[8]—We in Lititz have all had the Influenza—George Sturgeus made a happy Exit out of this world in a sore throat and John Müllers eldest Daughter[9]—Dishong and his Sister has left us,[10] poor Tschudy is alone in the Weavers Shop[11]—But surely you will be quite vex'd at my Incoherent Nonsense—you see I would fain have wrote you Something agreeable but time forbids. Farewell my good Brother. Our Saviour bless your Spiritual and temporal Concerns and may you have a more pleasing prospect in your Brethrens Choir in Salem than Bethlehem or Lititz have—Brother Strohle is Single Brethren Labourer here—and Frühauf at Bethlehem[12]—Sister M Krieger desires Love as does your Step Mother.[13] I remain your Sincerely Affectionate

M Penry

ALS: Correspondence of John Gambold, Drawer A-45, MASP. Addressed "Mr | John Gambold | Salem | North Carolina."

1. John Gambold (1760–1827) served briefly (1790–91) as helper of the single brothers' choir in Lititz, before assuming the same role in Salem in November 1791. In 1805 he returned to Lititz to marry Anna Rosina Kliest (see Letter 37, note 33); the couple ministered to Cherokees at Springplace from 1805 to 1812. See McClinton, *Moravian Springplace Mission*.

2. "your Step Mother": affectionate term for MP's friend Mary Tippet. See Letter 11, note 3.

3. Peter Rickseker (1770–1836) and Margaret (Gretel) Frederick (1769–1850) later returned to Lititz, where they lived out their lives.

4. In Bethlehem on September 18, 1793, Georg Gottfried Müller (1762–1821) married Anna Johanna Levering (1759–1822), and Johannes Molther (1759–1834) married Elizabeth Henry (1765–1798).

5. "poor Philadelphians": about 10 percent of Philadelphia's residents, five thousand individuals, died between August and November 1793 when yellow fever visited the city. Historians estimate that 1,100 people died when the disease returned in 1797 and 3,500 in 1798. The 1799 and 1802 epidemics caused fewer deaths, but panic drove larger numbers of people from Philadelphia, perhaps twenty thousand people in all between 1797 and 1802. See Letters 33, 51–52, 54, 57, 71, and 73.

6. "Billy Wistar": William Wistar (1746–1801), the nephew of Caspar Wistar (1696–1752) and a cousin of MP's friend Catherine Wistar, a prominent Philadelphia merchant. See Rubicam, "Wistar-Wister Family."

7. Elizabeth Gambold (1747–1811) and Anna (Nancy) Gambold (1756–1834), who had suffered a severe fall.

8. For the Müllers and Molthers, see above, note 4. For the Peters, see Letter 33, note 13. Emmaus (about fifteen miles southwest of Bethlehem) and Hebron (about twenty miles north of Lititz) were small Moravian communities.

9. George Sturgis (1775–1793), a weaver, died on September 15, 1793, and Elizabeth Müller (1788–1793) died on September 11.

10. David (b. 1774) Digeon (Dishong/Dijon) returned to his family at Hebron in September 1793, perhaps because of a weak mental state. See Andreas Albrecht, Jr., to John Gambold, October 4, 1793, Correspondence of John Gambold, Drawer A-45, MASP. His sister Maria (b. 1773) left as well. They were the eldest of many Digeon children: Catherina (b. 1775), Henrich (b. 1777), George (1779–1779), Susanna (b. 1780), Elisabeth (b. 1781), Christian (1783–1787), George (1786–1789), and Maria Barbara (b. 1787). Their father, Johann David Digeon (b. 1749), worked as a shoemaker in Lititz from 1762 to 1770 and, after marrying Catherine Schweitzer (b. 1746), at Hebron. Their grandfather, David Digeon (1722–1777), was "demented" during the last twenty years of his life in Bethlehem. See Engel, *Religion and Profit*, 209.

11. Matthias Gottfried Tshudy (1771–1852), a weaver. By June 1794, Jacob Chitty (1784–1850) had joined Tshudy. See Andreas Albrecht, Jr., to John Gambold, June 11, 1794, Correspondence of John Gambold, Drawer A-45, MASP.

12. "more pleasing prospect": due to marriages, deaths, and departures, the population of Lititz's single brothers' house had "declin[ed] rapidly." See Albrecht, Jr., to Gambold, October 4, 1793, MASP. Ludwig Strohle (1767–1827) remained the leader of Lititz's single brothers until 1799, when he married Catherina Roth (1774–1853). The couple moved to Schoeneck and, later, to North Carolina. Johann Friedrich Früauff (1762–1839) served Bethlehem's single brothers until he married Johanna Elisabeth von Schweinitz in 1798.

13. "M Krieger": see Letter 24, note 4.

33. TO MEREDITH PENRY, KATHERINE PENRY, AND ELIZA POWELL[1]

February 3, 1794
Lititz, Pennsylvania

Lititz February 3rd 1794

Honour'd Uncle and dearest Cousins

Your sweet Letter I received the 31 of January in the Evening. It was too dark for me to read it, I only turn'd to the Name, kiss'd it and bath'd it with my tears, and it was some time before I could recover my self so far as to be able to read it thro. The *war*, the danger of *Privateers* both *Algerine* and *Christian*, quite sunk my Spirits and I frequently lamented that a Corrispondance so much desired on both Sides should be liable to so many impediments and I allmost despaired of seeing a line from you.[2] A thousand times I wish'd that I had given you such directions that your letters to me might be given to the Minester of the Brethrens Church at Bristol who would then take proper care to inclose it in a Packett with those letters of our Congregation Members to America—because in these dangerous times a Single Letter, and that directed to a woman, is not much thought off—tho to *me* the loss of one line from *you* would be irreparable. Yours is dated the 13th of July—I wrote 3 Letters by 3 different Conveyances the first in May which a friend at Philadelphia put on board a Bristol Vessel. The 2nd and 3rd I gave to the care of our Minesters to be inclosed in their Packets to England[3]—true it is this method may be more Expensive but if you are satisfied I will rather forgo a *Necessary* piece of Cloathing than not receive letters from you. As it is, I am amazed at the triffling Postage your letters cost me. The 3 letters cost but 4/.[4] I feel your *Tenderness*, I acknowledge your *kindness*. Yet do not take it *amiss* if I observe, that you cannot be Compleat judges of my Sensations, because you were never so Circumstanced. You have had Relations around you—I have none, and 6000 miles seperate me from *you*. I only mention this to Paliate in some Measure the Warmth of my Expressions! I cannot remember the least Trace of my dear Father. Uncle Benjamin and Charles I remember but not Uncle Merideth.[5] Here let me beseech you to Humour me and when you mention Grandma Penry Uncles Aunts and Cousins—do not exclude poor *me* but write *our* Grandma *our* Uncle, and when you mention your dear Father—do write: *your* dear Uncle. When you only write in the first Person *my* it grieves me—dont you think I am very silly, perhaps I am. Forgive me. I cannot remember any thing of Mrs Parsons but Mamma used to speak a good deal of *our* Grandpa's Brothers Family—one of the daughter[s] I believe was my God Mother and I was to have been calld Sally after her, but my

Father would have me calld Mary.—*But* as I observed in my first Letter, my Mamma seem'd more attach'd to her own Family than to mine—and very seldom spoke of *you*. With Miss Gwillim of Abergavenny she corrisponded, and after her decease I continued the Correspondance, and it was she that inform'd me, *our* Grandma lived to receive my Letter, which tho never answerd, was yet a great Consolation to me. I have likewise Corrisponded with miss Nancy Vaughn at Haverford West and she acquainted me of my Aunt Batemans decease—to whom I always wrote under Cover to Miss Vaughn—but since my Cousin Bateman was not kind enough to write me one word—I declined asking her—a first Cousin of my Mamma's Cath: Rumsey at Abergavenny wrote me twice.[6] I duely acknowledged the favour— but since the warr between England and America broke out, all Corrispon-dance with my Native Country ceased till it became happily renew'd thro your kind cares. During the war numbers of the English Officers who were taken Prisoners by the Americans came to see our little village and it being my Office to attend Strangers and shew them the House[7]—I was introduced to one of them as his Country Woman—He very eagerly inquired my Name and told me he was perfectly acquainted with my Family, seem'd uncom-monly surprized to meet with one of the Family here and very Politely offer'd to take Letters home, which I declined, as he was a Stranger to me, and an officer, I could not bring my self to trust him with a letter. He promised to tell you that he had seen and conversed with me—I thank'd him—but had no notion he would keep his word—You best know if he has or not—His name I cannot call to mind. Gloomy indeed, is the account you have given me of *our* Family—it was partly what I expected having heard a good deal from my Mamma—and Miss Gwillim—place an u between the n and r in our Name—it allmost is what we are brought to. Well what ever *is* is best—as Pope says when we are laid in our graves it may be said How Loved how Honourd—*now* avails thee not, to whom related, or by whom begot. A heap of Dust alone remains of *thee*, Tis all *thou* art, and all the *Proud* shall be.[8] Pride of Family is one of my weaknesses—which all the Frowns of Fortune has never been capable of curing—Grace alone can and does convince me the Pride of Family is all a cheat—who's truely good alone is truely great.[9] In the Eye of the World, an unblemish'd Charactor is true greatness—*This* with all Humility be it acknowledged, I can claim, as for the goods off Fortune— thats out of the Question. I have all that is *Necessary*—and if ever I sigh for Affluence it is when I hear the distresses of others and *Particular* my Friends. Then indeed I wish it were in my power to display my regard in *deeds* as well as words. And one thing indeed I have the advantage of you—I neither see nor hear those Griefs and troubles which afflict you and which I cannot (any more than yourselves) mitigate. How kind how Consolatory are your Loving and pious Wishes. My Troubles have indeed been Sanctified to me! One of our Brethren kindly said to me: *you*, are one of the Tribe of Levy, who was to have no Inheritance among their Brethren because the Lord was to be their *Portion*. Be it so and I am happy.[10] I should be glad to hear wether you are in Communion with the Church of England or have joind another Community. My Aunt Bateman was some time before her decease a hearer of the Brethren. I suppose you have some of them in your Parts. At Haverford West there is a small congregation. Several of the Vaughns Family live there.[11] In the End there is but one *Saving* Faith (be the outward denominations ever so various) and all who live in *that* Faith will undoubtedly be saved. Thankful very thankful I am by the stile of your Letter to perceive Piety and Love to the beloved and loving Jesus is deeply grounded in your heart. Indeed the World seems at present to be worse than ever, and true Christianity at a very low Ebb. Philadelphia has been visited the latter part of the last Summer with a Malignant Fever which carried off more than 3000 persons but they seem to have forgot it allready.[12] With us it has been a healthy season—The disorder did not penetrate into the Country which caused numbers, *some* thousands to leave the City and move into the Country. We hear they are now they *think* out of danger. The Cold weather stop'd the Progress of the disease. *You* need be in no aprehension from this Letter. I shall send it off to New York via Bethlehem. It will not pass any Infected place. The Reverend Brother I send this letter to, lived some years at Fullneck in Yorkshire. He married an English Sister there. They are both my very intimate Friends.[13] I have requested him to write on the back of the Letter the Name of the Person to whose care he sends it, that you may send yours to the same Person. For altho' I desired you in a former Letter to direct to the care of my cousin Stocker at Philadelphia I would now rather wish you did not. Should the disorder break out again in the Summer as some people apprehend it will—He will leave the City—and if a Ship arives there they will hasten away as fast as possible. Give my tender love to my Cousin your dear Niece and thank her in my name for assisting her Aunt in writing to me. Tell her I wish to know her Name—I should be glad to know my dear Uncles age—I was born the 12th of November (according to the new Stile) 1735.[14] Tell my dear Uncle that I feel a tenderness for him truely filial. He is but *one Remove* from my dear dear ever lamented Father who I shall never never forget—Oh my honourd Uncle how eagerly did I look for some mention of you, and how my tears flowed when I read that you sent me your Blessing—precious Blessing how much do I prize it. Love me my dear Uncle your poor Orphan Niece—and console yourself that hitherto preventing grace has preserved [me] from behaving unworthy of the Name and Family of Penrys.[15] I am so attach'd to the name, that I am fond of being called *Penry*, instead of Polly. Are you not weary Cousin Kitty, of reading this long Epistle—For *yoursake* I will conclude. As for *me* I could go on and fill the Paper, but enough for this time as I shall write you more than once this year. I send my Uncle a Watch Paper as a small token of my love.[16]

Adieu Honour'd and tenderly beloved Uncle. Adieu, my dearest Cousin Kitty and your niece likewise my dear Cousin—Affectionate Love to those dear Relatives you communicate this to. Believe me to be and remain in our dearest Lord & Saviour your *Dutiful Niece* and *Affectionate Cousin*,

Mary Penry

I may say this is the first letter I have wrote these 3 Months, at least of any consequence having had the Rheumatism in my right arm which for the time it lasted, allmost made it useless—Otherwise I have a very steady hand and good eyes. I never use Spectacles and can embroider and do any kind of fine work—My Mamma said I resembled my Grandmamma Penry more than any one of my other Relations—She allways said I was a true *Penry*. My sisters desire a kind Salutation to you—we are just going to drink tea—O what would I give [if] you could sett and drink tea with us

ALS: Penralley Collection 1362, NLW. Addressed "Mr | Meredith Penry | Struet Brecon | Brecknockshire | South Wales." Endorsed "Received this Letter by post | June 20th 1794 | Answered this Letter July 20th 1794 | sent off from | Bristol in the | latter end of July | or the beginning of | August by Captain Goodwrich | Ship Severn."

1. See Letter 29.

2. "The *war*": after Portugal, which had protected American shipping, signed a treaty with Algiers in 1793, Algerine privateers seized eleven American merchant vessels. In early 1794 president George Washington asked Congress to fund a naval force to protect American shipping, and in March Congress authorized the creation of a fleet of six vessels. See Letter 46, note 5.

3. "I wrote 3 Letters": Letters 29–31.

4. "triffling Postage your letters cost me": MP paid to send these three letters across the Atlantic.

5. Regarding MP's father's brothers, see Letter 3.

6. "Miss Gwillim": see Letter 3, note 7; "Nancy Vaughn": see Letter 6, note 6; "Aunt Batemans": see Letter 3, note 3; "Cath: Rumsey": see Letter 30, note 10.

7. "my Office to attend Strangers": MP served as *fremdendeiner*, the individual responsible for supervising strangers visiting the community.

8. MP quotes from two poems by Alexander Pope, whose *Essay on Man* (1733–34) had stated that "Whatever IS, is RIGHT" (3:i:51), which others quickly paraphrased as "whatever is, is best." See Rusticus in the *Daily Gazetteer*, August 26, 1738. Pope's *Elegy to the Memory of an Unfortunate Lady* (1717) included the lines "How Loved how Honourd ... all the *Proud* shall be" (2:345).

9. Proverbial, popularized by Daniel Defoe's 1701 *True-Born Englishman*: "For fame of families is all a cheat, / 'Tis personal virtue only makes us great" (58). It appeared as an epigraph in the *North Briton* 55 (July 2, 1768) and was reprinted in an American newspaper later that year. A closer variation

appeared in Butler's 1795 *Arithmetical Questions*: "The pride of family is all a cheat, / The virtuous only are the truly great" (51).

10. See Joshua 13:14.

11. "a hearer": although not a member of the Moravian Haverfordwest congregation, Sarah Bateman (Letter 3, note 3) attended services. For Haverfordwest and the Vaughns, see Letter 6, note 6.

12. "Malignant Fever": yellow fever. See Letter 32, note 5.

13. Christoph Gottfried Peter (1760–1797), having served at Moravian schools at Niesky (1785–86) and Fulneck (1786–91), married Sarah Bailey (1756–1820) and immigrated to America. He stayed first in Lititz and then ministered in Hebron from 1791 to 1793 and in New York from 1793 until his death. MP stood as sponsor of their first child, Joseph Gottfried Peter, born on June 8, 1792. See Letter 41, note 37. After her husband's death, Sarah Bailey Peter married the Nazareth storekeeper John Ljungberg (1737–1808).

14. "new Stile": a New Style date follows the Gregorian calendar, which was adopted in Great Britain and its colonies in 1752. The Gregorian calendar was eleven days ahead of the Julian calendar (Old Style). MP's baptism was recorded on November 1, 1735 (Old Style). See Abergavenny St. Mary's Church Register, PCA.

15. "preventing grace": see Letter 2, note 2.

16. "Watch Paper": or watch piece, a small piece of fabric or paper designed to be put inside a watchcase, in part to protect the watch from dust. See O'Connell, *London 1753*, 138–40. A small watch piece, a floral decoration with verse, created by MP survives. See Penralley Collection 1367, NLW.

34. TO ELIZABETH DRINKER[1]

March 10, 1794
Lititz, Pennsylvania

Lititz March the 10th 1794

My dearest Friend!

But is it true, is my dearest Betsy still with us poor Mortals, or has she taken her flight to the realms of Light? who can resolve this question, and ease my Anxiety? I have examind Carys List of the dead,[2] but I did not find your Name. This has encouraged me to adress a Letter to you which I should have done many Weeks agon had I not been disabled from holding my pen by a Rheumatic pain in my arm—The first use I have made of my recovered strength is to enquire after my Friends. As Mr Reich and his Spouse—Betsy Bartow, as was—are going to your City—together with a dear Friend of Mine who has the Charge of the Single Women here, her name is Mary Tippet, she will be 8 or ten days in town and will lodge with Mrs Bartow.[3] I wish you would Step and see her—I must own I have a certain what shall I call it *Vanity*. I am *proud* of my *Friends*—I want her to see *my* Betsy of whom she has so frequently heard me Speak—like—a—loving—Faithful—Friend.[4]— What think you of the Prophecy? It might be dangerous to ask what think you of the *times*. Can it be proved, the Inscription was really found on that Stone which had lain near 600 years—then I should have Faith in the Prophecy![5] That we are in the *last* Days, I think beyond a doubt but how Many Years before the end of those days—God only knows. Was the Prophecy to be depended upon, I think I should not be unwilling to live the 6 coming Years—But Gods will be done—do give my love to your Sister—all your Children and Grand Children—to my Friend Hannah Sansom and her Children, and send me a few lines by the Bearer of this.[6] If your City should continue healthy, I think to come to town some time in June. God grant you may not have a second Visitation, I fear it would be Worse than the first.[7] Adieu Mon Amie—Ma Tres chere amie—votres Fidelle

M. Penrie

Respectful Love to your Spouse

ALS: Linden Hall Archives. Addressed "Mrs | Elizabeth Drinker | Philadelphia | Honourd by | Miss Tippet." Endorsed "Lititz March 10 1794 | Mary Penry."

1. See Letter 18.
2. Mathew Carey, *A Short Account of the Malignant Fever Lately Prevalent in Philadelphia* (Philadelphia, 1794).
3. Elizabeth Bartow (1769–1799) married Johann Christian Reich (1757–1811), a clerk in Bethlehem's store. The travelers stayed with Elizabeth Bartow Reich's parents, Sarah Benezet Bartow (1746–1818) and Thomas Bartow (1736–1793), who lived on Second Street between Arch and Race Streets (Drinker lived a block east on Front Street). For Mary Tippet, see Letter 11, note 3. Tippet and the Reichs stayed longer than expected, leaving for Philadelphia on March 12 and returning on April 1, 1794.
4. The women did meet, as Drinker recorded. See March 18, 1794, *Diary*, 1:548.
5. The *Pennsylvania Gazette*, February 19, 1794, 2, reported on this prophecy, "engraved on a flag stone, two yard square . . . supposed to have lain near 600 years under an old wall," which predicted that "the Millenium" would arrive in 1800. See also Bloch, *Visionary Republic*, 162–63.
6. For Hannah Callender Sansom, see Letter 18, note 5.
7. MP did not visit Philadelphia in summer 1794, but her relatives visited Lititz. See Letter 35, note 3.

ॐ **35. TO MEREDITH PENRY AND KATHERINE PENRY**[1]
September 21, 1794
Lititz, Pennsylvania

Lititz, September 21, 1794

Honoured Uncle and dear Cousin,

I wrote you in the spring shortly after the receipt of your affectionate lines but am afraid that letter miscarried, it looked rather gloomy, the sea was infested with so many ships of war, continually making depredations on each other's property—that I had no heart to send any letters after that wrote in the spring. Now things seem rather more promising for ships to England, and having seen in the newspaper that a vessel will sail for London the next week, I determined to sit down and converse with you at my leisure. I entertained some hopes of your writing once more this year, and perhaps you have, though I was not so happy to receive any more than one. I wrote you three letters last year, you mention the receipt of one only.[2]

You remember I lost my dear Father in the year '40. I was then too young to be sensible of my loss, but after I had been a few years in America, the thoughts that if my Father had lived I should never have left my native country, and then perhaps not have had so many troubles, these thoughts wounded me to the quick.

The 16th instant it was fifty years ago that I landed at Philadelphia, and yet my warmth of affection for my dear country is as great as though I had not left it above a twelve month. I feel much concerned when anything threatens the welfare of the kingdom, and I sincerely pray for it as well as for America, in which country I have it's true, had severe trials, yet I have enjoyed, and live in the enjoyment of, unspeakable blessings. As we are a people who wish to be at peace with all men, it does not become me to reflect on any one nation or people, but I pity and pray for all those who are afflicted, and Europe has at present numbers in that situation with whom I sympathize most heartily, and I cannot help fearing our time will come sooner or later.

This summer Mrs Stocker, the widow of my Cousin, Anthony Stocker, who lives at Philadelphia in great affluence, came with her youngest daughter to see me, and spent three weeks here to our mutual satisfaction.[3] She shows me a great deal of tenderness, but I always put the best side outwards, and give her no trouble on my account. She was extremely pleased that I had heard from you, and she and her daughter, my Cousin, Peggy Stocker, desired their love to Uncle and Cousin Kitty.

I sent you in my last letter a little love token which one of my sisters sent me to my birthday—in this I enclose the initials of your names, which one of my friends cut for me; accept them in love.

If I knew how to send you my picture you should have it. I was drawn about 38 years ago in the dress the sisters wear, and it is thought a very good likeness.[4] Stocker's family have it, but I believe they would give it up was you to desire it. You must know I am a *Penry*, very little of the Stocker's family. I was thought by my Mamma to resemble our Grandma Penry; if so, she was *not* handsome.[5]

You will think I shall never come to the close of this epistle. I cannot tell how to leave off yet I have nothing to entertain you with. I go on in my quiet way of life, happy and contented, my eyesight, through mercy, is so good that I write this by candle light without spectacles, for I never have used any. I can embroider silk and do any kind of needlework as well as I could thirty years ago. It is true, I have so much to write, and writing very quick, I have lost my once good hand, and am become a scribbler, however, I depend on your goodness to pardon that and whatsoever faults may be in this, as I am really too much in haste to take that care I ought to.

My birthday is the 12th of November, I was born in 1735.

I remain, dear Uncle and Cousins,

Your dutiful niece and affectionate cousin,

Mary Penry

P.S. I know not the name of my *Cousin*, your niece.[6]

Printed Copy: *The Moravian* 59, no. 5 (February 4, 1914): 75.

1. See Letter 29.

2. See Letters 29–31.

3. Margaret Stocker visited Lititz with her daughter Peggy on July 2, 1794. Her grandson, Andrew Potts, arrived a few days later. See Appendix C. MP accompanied them to Lancaster on July 27 and returned on August 6.

4. "my picture": probably painted by Johann Valentine Haidt (1700–1780). The portrait was "drawn 40 years ago—when she was 22 or 23 years old—in the Moravian dress." See July 15, 1798, Drinker, *Diary*, 2:1053–54. Hanging in the Stockers' Philadelphia home, the portrait was damaged during the Revolutionary War. MP never sent the portrait to her Welsh relatives. Instead, George Fetter (1768–1801), brother of Sally Fetter (see Letter 68, note 15), produced a miniature, which she did send. Fetter produced many watercolors, including views of Bethlehem in 1793 and 1797 (Schwarz, *Bethlehem on the Lehigh* and *Picturesque Sand Island*). See Letters 37, 42, 53, 55, 57, 64, and 71.

5. "she was *not* handsome": see Letter 37, note 3.

6. "my *Cousin*, your niece": Eliza Powell. See Letter 29.

ꙮ 36. TO MEREDITH PENRY AND KATHERINE PENRY[1]
March 5, 1795
Lititz, Pennsylvania

Lititz March the 5th 1795

Honourd Uncle and dear Cousin!

I again take my Pen in hand to converse with you, which is the fourth Letter I have wrote within these twelve months—wether any *one* have come to hand I know not, Corrispondance to Europe is very precarious at present, which I am very sorry for, as we cannot expect to hear from each other much longer, at our time of Life. I am in continual dread of hearing of my honourd

Uncles decease, and its a very short time that I have been favour'd with the *knowledge* of him. One way I have to reconcile myself to the loss of all, and every Friend, that is: the sweet hopes of meeting them in the Kingdom of Heaven, to which blessed Place we are hastning. I hope you will never experience the Sensations which I have felt, to look on myself as a poor Orphan, banish'd as I might say from my Native Country, and all my dear Relatives— but I will not grieve you with repetitions—You have sought after me, and given me the unspeakable Satisfaction of claiming a Connexion I thought intirely dissolved. My Cousins from Philadelphia, spent 3 weeks with me last Summer on a Visit, and behave with great tenderness and Respect, more so, than usual, so that it has pleased the Lord to give me many Comforts in my old age, which was denied my Youth. If health and Life be spared me, I shall this year, go to make a Stay of some weeks with them in Philadelphia.[2] I have not been there these 4 years. I long impatiently to hear from you—and I hope a Letter is on the way. The last I receiv'd from you came to hand the 2nd of February, also 13 long Months are past since the Receipt of those dear Letters! I know of nothing new to write you, I continue in my usual quiet happy way of Life. I have God be praised, my Eyesight and all my Faculties as good as I had 20 years ago. I feel the Infirmities of Age its true, but am thankful it is no worse. I wonder wether Miss Gwillim is living or dead?—but I think I ask'd this question in a former letter. I have not heard from Haverford West these many years, Nancy Vaughn used to write me once a year, but ever since the troubles broke out with us, we have both dropt our Corrispondance.[3] I frequently in Idea pay you a Visit and talk with you Hours together, and wish I could see my dearest Fathers Brother! Perhaps he resembles him—then I could form some Idea of a Father, whom I may say I never had the Happiness to know—yet how vain, how idle this wish, I ought to be ashamed to wish for impossibilities, it is time for me to think of meeting you in a better place, and I submit, thankful for the Blessings I have, and daily receive! May our dear Saviour give me Strength to overcome that Attachment to my Relations, which too frequently draws my heart from him. We are here in the Vale of Tears, and it is in vain to expect Perfect Happiness in anything out of Christ. To know, and be found in him, is the only lasting good, to believe in him, and live to him, will smooth the most rugged Path thro this Life—and yet a few years, or Perhaps Months, all Sorrow and sighing will be over, and we shall be at Peace. Let us often meet at the Throne of Grace in Supplication for each other—It has pleased the Lord to humble our Family, let us Submit to his dispensations without murmering, true Godliness is better than Riches. Our Forefathers were perhaps with all their wealth and Honours, not so happy as many of their poor descendants. Be pleased to give my kind love occasionly to our dear Relations and tell them: not to be ashamed of me, notwithstanding I am poor, for my Charactor is no disgrace to them. And now ever Honour'd Uncle, may our dear Redeemer be himself your Staff and Stay, in your Old Age, and whenever the Hour shall come that he calls you to himself, may he take you in the Arms of his Mercy and give you to behold his Face with Joy, in his Heavenly Kingdom. Amen Amen! My dear Cousin Kitty, you *weep* at these lines, I expect it—but part you must one day or other, and when the time comes, our Lord will give you strength to Support the separation. Your Letters are in a Stile that Convinces me *you know* in whom you believe, and to whom you are to aply in times of distress. You *may* be call'd first—but I think, was I to chuse, I would not wish the ancient Father the *pain* of surviving his faithful daughter. You my *young* Cousin, I beseech to be kind to your dear Aunt, and assist her in taking care of your Grand Papa—write me my love, write in your Grandpa and Aunts name, and write me in your *Own Name* that I may know *what* my young Cousins name is, of which I am ignorant. Adieu dearly beloved 3. I send each of you a Kiss just here—but my dear *uncle* you must give a threefold Kiss From his poor Niece.

Mary Penry

P.S. 6 Kisses are here inclosed to each of you and 4 for my uncle, my lips has been as it were glewd to the paper more than 20 times. When you write to Uncle Charle's daughter, please to give my very kind Love to her, and tell her I remember Uncle Charles perfectly well, as I can likewise remember Uncle Thomas, and Benjamin who dyed before we left England—4

ALS: Penralley Collection 1365, NLW. Addressed "Mr. Meredith Penry | Struet Brecon | Brecknockshire | South Wales | Per Diana | Captain Mason." Endorsed "Received this Letter per post | May 15th 1795 | Answered it June 2nd 1795."

1. See Letter 29.

2. See Letter 35, note 3.

3. "Miss Gwillim": see Letter 3, note 7. For Haverfordwest and Anne (Nancy) Vaughn, see Letter 6, note 6.

4. Regarding MP's father's brothers, see Letter 3, note 1.

2❦ 37. TO MEREDITH PENRY, KATHERINE PENRY, AND
ELIZA POWELL[1]

July 2, 1795
Lititz, Pennsylvania

Lititz July 2nd 179[5][2]

Dearly beloved and ever Honourd Uncle! And most beloved Cousins

After having long lamented and mournd after you and suposed the unpitying Enemies had Captur'd Vessels with Letters to the poor orphan, from her Friends on the 20th day of June I was most agreeable surprized by one of my Friends who full of Joy presented me your Letter! As my Cousin Betsy very justly observes the Pen is too feeble to express the Sensations of the heart—Each of us knows by Experience what those feelings are but it is not in the Power of Language to describe them. The Gloves were received as a Token of your love and as such lookd upon inestimable—yet I am sure that you will not take it amiss when I tell you the Initials of your Names workd with your Own Hair was a far greater Present. Will only observe my Hair is of the same Colour as yours. If I can get a good Conveyance I shall send you a piece of my own Work which I have now in Hand and shall work part of it with my own Hair. I am not very Grey for my Age, which I believe is in a great Measure owing to my having scarce any Complaint in my Head. Indeed I may say I hardly know what the Head Ach is: Dear Uncle and Cousins I beg pardon for insinuating that our Grandmama was not Handsome[3]—I had been frequently told that I resembled her—and my Looking Glass always telling me I had nothing to boast off—I may as you observe have done her a piece of injustice—but many plain people resemble Handsome Person[s] in some degree—When I was young I had a delicate Skin and very Fine Hair. This I can *now* say without Vanity, and even to this day my Relations in Philadelphia often wish they had *my* Hair. I am rather under the common size in Stature—and ever since I was forty years of age am grown fat and have lost my Gentility. I have most excellent Eyes for use—but not beauty—dark Grey—am near sighted, yet not so much so, as to hold my work close to my Nose. I never have used Spectacles and believe never shall. The small Pox which I had in England spoild the little Beauty which I ever had. Tho I was not *seamd* as they call it and have very little traces of it at present.[4] Will you forgive my descending to these Particulars of myself—I seem to wish that when you endeavour to form an Idea of *your American* you may not draw a frightful, altho no Handsome Picture. This much I must add: I am allways taken to be *younger* than I really am, as I am Plump the Wrinkles are not so visible as they would be, were I lean and haggard. As to my Picture I cannot but repeat my wishes that it was with you—but shall make no attempts to withdraw it from the Hands it is now in unless it should be offerd me—Could I get once more Possession of it I would destroy it—for its not worth sending over the Seas, and I am allways thinking after my decease it will one time or another be sold at Auction—well let it be so, it will be no Injury to me. How silly I am to waste a thought upon it.[5]

I have seen the Reverend Mr Cooke you mention some years agon when he first came to America. I had the Pleasure to show him our House and he expressed his Satisfaction at what He saw and heard.[6] I was very much taken with him. He seemd to be a most amiable sweet Man! had I then known what you have now inform'd me I should certainly have let him known who I was. I have never heard of him since. It is true I have some Friends among the Methodists which I *highly* esteem—but I never heard *one* of their teachers Preach. I have a very good Opinion of them in the whole, but I cannot say I aprove of their Manners in their Worship which I have been told is something terrifying. Pardon my freedom of Expression, perhaps they are dearer to you than I know—and I would on no Account grieve you! I remember Many years ago I was told one Mr Penry was a Methodist Minester—but wether He was of our Family or no I could not find out.[7] I must again repeat that altho I am in no Connection with the Methodists I have a great Respect for them and believe the far greater Part of their Preachers are faithful Labourers in the Lords Vineyard. The Church of England which I shall ever Esteem as my Mother Church, teaches us universal Charity—The Brethrens Church of which I am an humble Member believe that whosoever believeth in the Lord Jesus shall be saved. I don't aprehend that it wil after this Life be ask'd us to what Denomination of Christians we belong'd? Our dear Saviour ask'd 3 times: "Simon Son of Jona lovest thou me"? *This* is the grand Point—for our Lord says, *"If ye love me ye will keep my Commandments."*[8] I have the Satisfaction to hope my 3 dear Friends agree with me in this grand Matter—and its like the Balsam pourd on my heart—that in this degenerate age (*of Reason*) *you* are not ashamed to Confess *your Faith in, and Love to,* the Crucified *Redeemer of lost Man.*

My dear Uncle wishes to know the Particulars of the threatened Insurrection.[9] It was far back in the Western Counties and took its Rise from an Excise being laid on a liquor call'd *wisky* which is a Spirit distilld from Rye of which the Farmers in those parts made a very lucrative Trade. *Wisky* in America is as pernicious to the Commonallity as *Gin* in England. Those Persons who distilld this Liquor are settled so far back that they cannot sell their grain to the advantage they draw from *Wisky*. I believe the Real design of the Excise which was laid on the Stills in proportion to their size was to render the article more scarce because so many poor People ruin themselves and Families by too free Use of this Spirit. The Insurgents are call'd *Wisky Boys*. It is plain they did not expect such Resistance—for at first they was very bold bidding Defiance to the Laws, and Using the Officers who had to collect the Excise very ill both in their Persons and properties. But when the Militia from the different States Assembled and Marched against them some fled, others submitted and no blood was spill'd,[10] which is a great Happiness, and will be an instructive Lesson to others who we may say stood on tip toe to see how this would end—and had our Rulers submitted to Remove what the *Wisky Boys* called a Burthen—others might have pleaded their Grievance wether Real or imaginary, till in the End the whole Constitution would have been overturnd. We have great Reason to be thankful for the Man who is at the Helm of government in the United States of America—our Excellent *Washington*, a Descendant from *our* brave General *Monk*.[11] Will not this please you my dear Uncle! is he not a branch of *our* family. O my dear Niece methinks I hear you say: How vain you are. 60 Years of age and so full of Family Pride. Have you forgot the old adage—Gentility without ability[12]— you know what that is like—very true. Dear Uncle I stand Corrected—But I am your Brothers Daughter—and my dear Cousin Kitty says in her dear Letter she has been preserv'd from doing any thing unworthy the *name of Penry*! There my Uncle, your Daughter spoke, what your *Niece* has so often said, that I must own my Face glow'd on reading the sentence and my intimates to whom I communicated it said: *That is just like you.*

I must further say I am a great Politician but am very careful of speaking my Sentiments—and this has hitherto prevented me from introducing those Subjects in a Letter which must cross the Seas and by falling into wrong Hands involve my *Brethren* in trouble since *their* sentiments might be judged by *mine*, however different they might be in reality. It is a Stated Rule in our Congregations that none of their Members engage in Politics or Parties. We have Brethren Setled under so many different Rulers who are united together under One Head our Lord and Saviour Jesus Christ—that in *every* Place where we are, we are calld to pray for the safety and Wellfare of *that Place* and to be obedient to *those* that bear Rule over us, and to live at *Peace with all Men*![13] Our Lord will Ever live and ever Reign, all attempts to dethrone him will fail. Altho sometimes his Enemies enjoy a short lived Triumph it is quickly over, and those who will not kiss his Scepter, must bend under his Rod.[14] The Maker justly claims that world he made. In this the right of Providence is laid. Our Actions uses, nor Controuls our will, But bids the doubting sons of Men be still. What strange events can strike with more surprize Than those which frequent meet the wandering Eyes—Yet taught by these confess the Allmighty just, And where you cant unriddle—learn to *trust*.[15] Such reflections my Honourd Uncle calm my Spirits and enable me to look with coolness on all the Various Changes which have taken place within these 20 years! Not that my heart is insensible to the Distresses of Europe in General and England in Particular of which Melancholy tales are related from the Publick Prints. You are pleased to stile me your dear *American*, any tittle, provided that of *Niece* and Cousin be retaind, is agreeable—but *your Niece* and your *Cousin* glories in being an European—The Map of *Our* Country, under a glass hangs over My Chair and I look often over it with Peculiar Pleasure, you may depend I stay longest at Brecon and seem to penetrate even to your Presence—but no friendly Voice salutes my Ear, and as I *look* in Silence in like manner I withdraw Silently from it, and set down praying for Resignation to my Lot![16]

The 2 letters you tell me you put on board the Severn Captain Goodwrich are lost. I read the account of that Vessels being captured by the French and said Oh I certainly had Letters on Board.[17] I have only 4 Letters of yours in my Hands, and one of the 4 is a Copy of your first Letter. The Dates are as follows: 1st the 14 December 1792—2nd Coppy same Date—3rd July 13th 1793—4th 20 December 1974. To which I have wrote 8 or 10 in answer. I imagine if you could put your Letters on board an *American* ship they will stand a better chance of coming Safe. However God be thank'd there seems to be hopes of *Peace*. Should our Mercyful Lord grant us that Blessing we may then Expect better Fortune with our Letters. Our worthy Bishop is now writing to Europe—He forwarded my last wrote last April or May I forgot which. I trust you either have, or will soon receive it. If Nothing unforseen Prevents me I shall go to Philadelphia in the Month of September on a visit to my Cousin Stockers of a few weeks there.[18] I shall write by one of the Fall Vessels and perhaps have it in my Power to send you the promised *Piece* of my own work. My dear Uncle you could not have planted Peas here in December, tho we had what we call a very mild Winter frequent Snows by quickly succeeded by a thaw and frequent Rains the whole Spring with frosty Nights in May which has injured the Fruit so that the Apples and Peaches fall off the Trees. At this time we have the 3rd Rainy day. The Harvest being I might say before the Door makes it rather disagreeable to think of because the heavy Rains beats down the grain. Bread is very high with us at Present, owing to the sending so much Flour abroad, and this article has raised the Price of all kinds of Provisions, even in this Land of Plenty. And altho we have a pleasing Prospect of a Plentiful Harvest we cannot hope this will lower the Markett as the Demand is so great abroad, the more we have the more will be sent away—Well the good People are in want. It is a blessing that there is a way to

supply them, and we will not begrudge them a Share of what we can Spare.
We are blessed with *Peace* our Trade flourishes, we desire to be thankful!
True it is the Poor suffer every where but I do believe not in Comparison with
the Poor in England—to say nothing of their Suffrings on the Theatre of
Warr. My ever Honourd Uncle We have in our Congregations a Custom of
above 60 years Standing of having Texts of Scripture apointed for every day
throughout the year. They are call'd the *Daily Words* and *Doctrinal Texts* of
the Brethrens Congregation.[19] They are Chosen every year as you will find by
the following Note which I have coppied from my Book: The daily Words for
this Year are taken out of the Books of the Old Testament. They are the same
which have been made use of in 1789 1790 1792 and 1793. This was Printed in
London 1794—for the Year 1795. The Texts which happen on our Birth days
seem most particular a Word of Exhortation Consolation or Reproof, as it
falls out, to the Party Concern'd. I have look'd out yours belov'd Uncle and
will Transcribe it. The Old Testament text on the 24 of October 1795 is as
follows: In that day shall the Deaf hear the Words of the Book, and the Eyes
of the Blind shall see out of Obscurity, and out of Darkness: Isaiah 29th v. 18.
The Antiphone: Lord, open every heart and Eye, When of thy Grace we tes-
tify. May thy blest Spirit all our Souls inspire, And set each cold and lifeless
heart on Fire. The Words of Jesus in New Testament Text: They that are
whole need not a Physician, but they that are sick. Luke 5th v. 21st. The
Antiphone: Ye that groan beneath Sins Pressure, Come and taste, Peace and
Rest, He's the Source of Pleasure, His Blood, that all healing Ointment,
maketh whole, Flesh and Soul by divine apointment. Oh my Uncle are not
these fine words! Cousin Kitty's Text March 17th 1795: Fear thou not: let not
thine Hands be Slack. Zeph. 3 v. 16. Antiphone: Our poor Endeavour bless,
And crown them with Success. The New Testament Text: Blessed are ye
when men shall revile you, and shall say all maner of Evil against you *falsely*
for *my Sake*. Rejoice and be exceeding glad: for great is your Reward in
Heaven. Matth. 5 v. 11, 12. Antiphone: Those who freely for him will bear
Reproach while here, At last shall in his Glory share. Cousin Betsys text
August 28th 1795. Surely I have behaved and quieted myself, as a Child that
is weaned of his Mother; my Soul is even as a weaned Child. Ps. 132, v. 2.
Antiphone: Therefore I'll humbly Cleave, To my Creator, Who, that my Soul
might live, Assum'd my Nature. New Testament Text: Ask, and ye shall
receive that your Joy may be full: John 16th v. 24th. Antiphone: Ye that feel
quite poor & needy, Come who will, take your fill, All things now are ready.
Cousin *Penry* Powells text July 5th 1795.[20] I have sett watchmen upon thy
walls oh Jerusalem, which shall never hold their Peace day nor Night. Ye that
make Mention of the Lord, keep not Silence, and give him no Rest, till he

establish, and till he make Jerusalem a Praise in the Earth. Isaiah 62 v. 6, 7. Antiphone: May Lord Jesus thine own hand, uncontrould rule in its Border, And be love its sacred Band. New Testament text: Behold I send you forth as sheep in the midst of Wolves: be ye therefore Wise as Serpents, and harmless as Doves. Matth. 10, v. 16. Antiphone: Give us what thine own Mind decrees, and what thy Servants must possess, If they shall serve the[e] with Success. My Text November 12th 1795. The People that walked in darkness have seen a great Light. They that dwell in the Land of the Shaddow of death, upon them hath the Light shined. Isaiah, 9 v. 2. Antiphone: Christ is the Sun of Righteousness, which rises with Resplendent Grace, And doth dispel Sins gloomy Night, That we may share his saving Light. New Testament Text: I will make them to know that I have loved thee Rev. 3, 9. [Antiphone:] With Thanks before his Throne apear, And praise his Name dear Congregation, For every proof and Demonstration, That you his favour People are. These are the Texts which I have coppied off thinking it might give my dear Uncle in particular some Pleasure. You have sent me a very Rich Blessing to this Year. You were in my mind at my entrance into it which with us is very solemn as we spend the last Hours of the old year (with some Intermissions) at Church and allways begin the New with fervent Prayer in which we do not forget to pray for the whole State of the Church Millitant—and indeed all Mankind in general. You will believe on such an Occasion I was not unmindful of my dear Friends especially my beloved Uncle and Cousins. You cannot think much amiss when you supose, very few days pass in which I am absent from you. If you wish to see me you must look for me in a large Room. 8 sisters live with me who Spinn Cotton.[21] I set at the upper end of the Room at a Window fronting the Street a round Table before me, behind me my Bureau with a Closet on the Top, sometimes, indeed most frequent writing at my Desk or again at a small Frame embroidering Sattin for Pincushions, which could I have a good sale for them, would be a handsome income. However they have this year gone off so well that I am quite satisfied. When there comes Strangers I am directly calld to attend them, and must leave the most pressing Bussness to wait upon them, which has been the case more than once since I began this Letter.[22] My dearest Uncle do not forget to pray for your poor Niece that I may become daily more acquainted with my own Sinful Nature and the loving kindness of my Mercyful Saviour. Since I cannot know how short my time may be here below I look on every Letter I write as the last and this makes me write longer Letters than I should do if I had youth on my side and as you dear Uncle are so far advanced in Life, I am continually wishing to receive one more, and again one more Letter from you. Should this come to hand, and you be wearied at its uncommon length give me a Friendly admonition—I will be more concise for the future.

My dear Cousin Kitty most Pathetically asks 2 questions: first wether we shall meet before the Throne of Grace.[23] Dear Kitty I humbly trust we shall. I find very Comfortable proofs in your Letters that you are a *Sincere Believer*. As such I trust we shall be among that number in the Kingdom of Heaven, but wether we shall know each other I imagine no Mortal can tell. I have very frequently had my Meditations on this Subject. Especially as I never had the Happyness to know my dear Pappa, I could and indeed do wish to know him hereafter. My Notions of Heavenly Bliss are so exalted, that I suppose the Heavenly Inhabitants are in such a state of Perfection that one Blessed Spirit is as dear to them as another and if so a peculiar attachment to Relations is not known there—another thing I do believe the Love of Jesus will there take intire Possession, and we shall love our fellow Happy Souls only in him—and that love will [be] so perfect as to admit of no difference. Whatever our Lords dispensations are in Eternity, we are certain they will be intirely agreeable to us. And altho in this Mortality we are so much, perhaps *too* much attach'd to the Creature we shall drop this and every other weakness with our Mortal Garment. I firmly believe that every thing which can render our State in Bliss compleat, will be given us, and if the Knowledge of our Relations and dear Friends was wanting to make it so, it will undoubtedly be granted us. As long as we are creeping here on Earth we are tied and bound to Earth, and its Inhabitants but when once the Curtain is drawn Other Sences present and Obliterate the past—Behold I make all things New saith the Lord.[24] I do assure you notwithstanding I reason *against* our Knowledge of each other in an After State, it very pleasing to *hope* for it and I do hope for it even against Hope. Nay One part of Scripture: The Parable of Dives & Lazarus seem to incourage that Hope. It is Plain Dives knew both Abraham and Lazarus yea he even remembered his Brethren in this World and wish'd they might escape the Torments he suffer'd.[25] Upon the whole where some thing can be said on both Side the Question, I think it is best to leave it to our lord with a Submisive *Thy Will be Done*. Where Families live in Love and Unity their Company and Conversation are Mutual Blessings. We are indebted to our Lords Goodness for such favours in this transitory Life where we often find our Lord is pleasd to give us the advice and assistance of such whom the ties of Blood or Bond of Friendship has united, and w[h]ere such fail he can raise up Strangers to do the Friendly Office. I am a living Wittness to this Truth— But in a State of Perfection we do not require those Helps for the Lord will be All in All, and to All. You observe dear Cousin that it was the Will of the Allmighty that I should come to America. It was many years before I thought so, you Remember my Consent was not ask'd. I was but a Child of Nine Years Old and the Golden Dream which drew me from my Native Country vanish'd when I awakend in a foreign Country Surrounded with Distress. I cannot see that I had any Particular Call to *America* yet since I was brought here—Our dear Saviour whose Mercies are *overall his Works* would not that I should return, or he would not *thrice* have brought our Plan to return to nothing and that during my Mamma's lifetime—Since her decease I might have had an Oppertunity of returning but to whom should the helpless *Maiden* go? I thought I would rather be a *Stranger* yea a Beggar here, than in England. Could I have commanded an Independent Fortune I could then have returnd with *Propriety*—and now I am very far advanced perhaps on the Borders of the Land of Promise. It will make no difference when I cross the Jordan, wether I came thro the Willderness or a nearer Way—wether I go to Heaven from Wales or Lititz, Provided I safely arrive there. True it is that tho I have undergone many Difficulties yet I desire to acknowle[dg]e with thankfulness the Goodness of the Lord in giving me so many Valuable *American Friends*. I have a very large Corrispondance with as many Creditable Persons in Philadelphia and elsewhere as any *one* in my Station can boast of, and if I was in Possession of Thousands could not be treated with more Respect. Among my acquaintances I have Quakers Presbyterians Baptists Methodists Universalists as well as Church People and our own Society. You see Cousin Kitty I wish to be in Charity with *all Men*. I was just thinking I cant Recolect one Roman Catholic on my list and thats rather odd as I was born among them. This puts me in mind to enquire after Miss Gwillim of Abbergavenny who was many years a faithful Corrispondant of mine as likewise my Cousin Catherine Rumsey (Stocker as was) who lived at the same place 20 years agon. I wish you likewise might have it in your Power to enquire after Miss Nancy Vaughn who was living in the Single Sisters Oeconomy at Haverford West, from her I formerly receiv'd sweet Letters but have neglected writing to her some years.[26] Also my dear Kitty thinks to keep the name of Penry—If you are satisfied—I think no state so happy as the *Maiden* state, altho that is not a *general* opinion.[27] Will you not be wearied out before you come to the End of this Letter. I fear you will and yet cannot conclude till I have fill'd my Paper. I was quite vex'd that you was obliged to break off because the Paper would hold no more, I was determind mine should not Confine me Especially as I am writing to 3—yet methinks you three must find [missing] Subject to write me that I am Single. Perhaps your next will be longer I hope it will.

I have never dream'd of you any more than you of me but I have frequently been preparing to cross the Ocean to join you in my Native Country and have felt quite low spirited when I awoke and found it was but a Dream. Often and Often do I ask you to a Dish of tea or Coffee and tell you how very Wellcome I will make you, the Sisters in my Room expressing their wishes to see you all three but unkind Cousin you will not come—well I will be even with you, I wont come when you ask me. Ah my dear! the Fox said the grapes were sower because he could not reach them[28]—just my Case.

And so you were born on Patricks day—what have you to do with the Irish Saint I pray—you have not one drop of Irish blood in your veins I hope.[29] *For your* sake I shall honour the day which I never have done yet—The first day of March is worthy of Honour indeed.[30] I think you might have as well been 16 days older it would not have made any great *ods*. You cannot immagine how the flies torment me. You will observe they make me spoil many words. We have vast Numbers this season. I believe you never saw such Swarms as we have. Your kind Love to our House was receiv'd with uncommon Satisfaction and I am desired to present all our Sisters most Respectful Love to my honourd Uncle and Cousins. My young Folks wish my Cousin Betsy was among them. She I am sure would be highly delighted with such agreeable Set of Companions of her own age. My dear Cousin Betsy I am extreemly obliged to you for your kindness in writing me so Particular—You Cannot be too Particular my love. I am much pleased with your Hand and with your easy Stile a proof of your having receiv'd a good Education and that you Corispond frequently. I was very much pleased that you inform'd your Brother of my Restoration to the Family as I may call it.[31] You have not told me what Busness he follows, whatever it be I wish him Success. When you write him be pleased to give my kind Love to him. I expect as he lives in London he may dispatch my Letter by a London Vessel to you. You mention a dreadful Fire at Wapping. I believe fires are more frequent in England, than here. In Philadelphia in the winter season they have often fires break out, but very seldom more than the house in which it was, is consumed. I am proud of the Tittle you give me of Aunt—you are as dear to me as a Niece can be. I am accustomed to this Honourable tittle of aunt altho I have no tittle to it having neither Sister nor Brother, Yet many dear Spiritual Brethren and Sisters whose Children call me Aunt as natural as tho I really was so. I intend before I finish this Letter to introduce to your Notice some of my Companions who are desireous their Names may be transmitted to my Native Country and my 3 Dear Friends have more than *one* American to talk of. My Room Companions are exceeding kind and loving, they look up to me as to a Mother, they attend and wait upon me, and as I am naturally of a very cheerful Disposition I love young Peoples Company. This they know, and that prevents them from avoiding me as they know they can be innocently cheerful and merry without

giving me umbrage. Before I go any further with this subject let me my dear
Niece return you my hearty thanks for the Trouble you have taken with the
Watch Piece and assure you I will not fail sending you in Return a Piece of
my own Work.[32] Herein I inclose *you* my dear Cousin the Innitials of my
Name done by the same Person who did those you have receiv'd, an adopted
Niece of mine an American born of German Parents one of the first Tuto-
risses in the boarding school at Bethlehem where they have upwards of 90
young Misses from different Parts of the United States and the Danish West
Indies. Her name is Anna Rosina Kliest—Anna Rosel, we call her, Love her
my dear, for her Affection to your Aunt.[33] She will be pleased to receive a
Salutation from you in my Letter. The Texts to your Birth day which I have
wrote will doubtless be very pleasing to you, they are so to me. I hope the
Words will be realized in your Heart. I shall celebrate your coming Birth day
with some of my Companions altho if this Letter comes safe which I most
earnestly wish it may it will not reach you till that day is pass'd. I hope your
Grand Papa will have receiv'd it before his Birth day. I expect I shall be in
Philadelphia then, and Perhaps have wrote another letter to you. If you have
it in your Power to let Miss Gwillim and Mrs Rumsey know of my Wellfare,
and enquire after theirs I should take it very kind. I also wish to hear of
Nancy Vaughn. And now have Patience my Niece I will introduce one after
the other of my Particular Friends to—you will bring them acquainted with
Uncle and Cousin. First, in the Single Sisters house Miss M. Tippet. This
Country Born—her Father an English Man. She is the Directoress of Spiritual Affairs in our House—she has a cousin Sally Tippet in the same Office
in one of our congregations near Bristol.[34] She is a fine woman very much
beloved and respected by us all—and remarkably kind and affectionate to
your Aunt. Miss Peggy Krieger Steward of the House—or the Person who
directs the temporal Affairs. With this Sister I have a great Connexion. I am
her Clerk for the House, I keep the accounts, &c., &c. She is a Real Friend
and Sister to me. She is a German this Country Born.[35] My Room Companions are first Anna Nilson this country (Bethlehem) born, her parents germans a good soul 50 Years of age. Rachel Stohler—German Extraction.
Elisabeth and Marie Barbara Fauesser Swiss extraction. Christina Kiesel—
German—Elisabeth Weller—german Cath. Vetter—French Extraction.
Nancy Hasse born at Bethlehem her Father a German—her Mother a Lon-
doner—very much attachd to the English.[36] These three last my dear Niece,
are from 20 to 22 years of age and desire to claim your Particular Notice—I
chuse to confine my self to my Own Room and the 2 Rulers of the House first
mention'd because as we are near 60 in the House any many of my Particular
Friends among the Number I might fill up my Paper with Names of Persons

to you *unknown*.[37] I will not go out of the House any further than to mention our worthy Bishop and his Lady. His name Huebner—Germans—Friends to your Niece and all the Children of God thro-out the *World*. Mrs Sydrick a Widdow Lady who is my very dear Friend and of my Age[38]—These few— for few they are in comparison desire their Love to my 3 dear Relations—and wish you every Spiritual and Temporal Good.

I believe I mentioned in a former Letter that my Relations in Philadelphia had spent 3 Weeks with me here[39]—Mr Stocker raises in Honour as well as Fortune. He bears an extraordinary Character. Their Regard for me Increases which I am at a loss to know why but certain it [is] they are very tender and affectionate. My Honourd Uncle and Cousins if there be any thing you wish to be inform'd of Concerning my self or the *society* to which I belong, be so kind as to let me know. I will do all in my power to give you Satisfaction. You will doubtless observe my stile is Germanized. The Constant use of the Ger- man Tongue, all our Meetings being in that Language and near 40 Years constant dwelling with Germans has greatly Corrupted my Language. You kindly ascribe my Faults to this. One thing more I had allmost forgott. Our Reverend Brother John Herbst a Native of Germany but who resided some years in England long enough to gain an affection for the English.[40] He rejoices when I hear from my Friends and together with his Lady Wishes my Honourd Uncle & my beloved Cousins Health and Happiness. And Now I think I have said all I can say in one Letter. May it reach your dear Hands fraught with tenderest Love, warmest thanks, and best Wishes. *May you be blest! here and in Eternity.* So wishes so prays—

Your Dutifull Niece
affectionate Cousin
and loving Aunt,
Mary Penry

ALS: Penralley Collection 1363, NLW. Addressed "Mr. Meredith Penry | Struet Brecon | Brecknockshire | South Wales." Endorsed "Received this Letter by | Post September 4th 1795 | Answered it Sept 19 | sent to London | went of[f] | By the General Washington."

1. See Letter 29.
2. MP misdated this letter 1794.
3. See Letter 35, note 5.
4. *"seamd"*: scarred
5. "Picture": see Letter 35, note 4.
6. Thomas Coke (1747–1814), born in Wales, was ordained in the Church of England and became one of John Wesley's most important assistants. He first visited America from November 1784 to June 1785, during which period he traveled to Philadelphia several times and became the first Ameri- can Methodist bishop. Neither Lititz's congregational diary nor its single sisters' diary mentions a

visit to Lititz. MP tried, without success, to contact him during subsequent American visits. See Letters 42, 45, 51, and 57.

7. See Letter 30, note 6.

8. John 21:17; John 14:15.

9. "threatened Insurrection": the Whiskey Rebellion, defeated in fall 1794. See Hogeland, *Whiskey Rebellion*.

10. "some fled . . . no blood was spill'd": some thirteen thousand militiamen from Pennsylvania, Maryland, and Virginia, commanded by president George Washington, marched west to suppress the Whiskey Rebellion in October 1794. When Washington's subordinates, Alexander Hamilton and Henry Lee, arrived in Pittsburgh in November, they found that the insurgents had dispersed and no armed confrontation occurred.

11. For the rumor that Washington's "mother was a niece to the famous General Monk," see the *London Chronicle*, October 17–19, 1775; and Baker, *Early Sketches*, 20, 83.

12. Proverbial: "Gentility without ability is worse than plain beggary." See Ray, *Compleat Collection*, 112.

13. "obedient to *those* that bear Rule over us": MP identifies one reason that Moravians adopted a nonentanglement policy and did not "engage in Politics or Parties." See Letter 2, note 5.

14. "those who will not kiss his Scepter, must bend under his *Rod*": the English divine Thomas Watson used a similar phrase ("such as will not bow to his golden Scepter, shall be broken with his iron Rod") in *Seven Sermons*, 71–72, and *Body of Practical Divinity*, 45.

15. "The Maker . . . learn to *trust*": from Thomas Parnell's 1714 "The Hermit." See *Collected Poems*, 176.

16. On maps in early America, see Brückner, *Geographic Revolution*.

17. A 279-ton ship built in 1792 captained by Jared Goodrich, the *Severn*—carrying Letters 31 and 33 from Meredith Penry—left Bristol for New York in 1794 but was taken by a French frigate and unloaded of persons, cargo, and papers in Brest on September 1. See Williams, *French Assault on American Shipping*, 324.

18. MP wrote to her Welsh relatives during this trip to Philadelphia. See Letter 38, note 2.

19. "*Daily Words* and *Doctrinal Texts* of the Brethrens Congregation": watchwords. See Letter 25, note 5.

20. Penry Powell: brother of Eliza Powell. See Letter 29.

21. MP identifies these women later in this letter.

22. "call'd to attend them": MP served as *fremdendeiner*. See Letter 33, note 7.

23. "wether we shall meet before the Throne of Grace": see Letter 3, note 5.

24. Revelations 21:5.

25. Luke 16:19–31.

26. "Miss Gwillim . . . Catherine Rumsey . . . Nancy Vaughn": see Letter 3, note 7 (for "Miss Gwillim"), Letter 6, note 6 (for "Nancy Vaughn"), and Letter 30, note 10 (for "Catherine Rumsey").

27. "no state so happy as the *Maiden* state": for singleness in Moravian communities, see this volume's introduction.

28. "grapes were sower": in Aesop's Fables, a fox who cannot reach some tasty grapes refuses to admit defeat and instead claims that the grapes are not edible. This is the basis for the modern phrase "sour grapes," meaning the disparagement of something that has proven unattainable.

29. "not one drop of Irish blood": see Letter 48, note 5, for MP's fear of radicals who had recently immigrated from Ireland. Just above, MP seems to disavow any prejudice against Catholics; but for anti-Catholic sentiment in early America, see Beneke, "Catholic Spirit Prevailing in Our Country."

30. "first day of March": St. David's Day, patron saint of Wales.

31. "your Brother": Penry Powell. See Letter 29.

32. "Watch Piece": MP sent a watch piece earlier (Letter 33, note 15); with this letter she sent another made by Anna Rosina Kliest and promises to send one that she herself made.

33. Anna Rosina Kliest (1762–1821) served in the Bethlehem Female Seminary from 1781 to 1805. After her 1805 marriage to John Gambold (Letter 32, note 1), the couple served as missionaries to the Cherokees at Springplace, Georgia. She was called "Anna Rosel," but a different Anna Rosel—Anna Rosina Anders—comforted MP after her mother died (Letter 4).

34. "M. Tippet": see Letter 11, note 3. See also Dresser, "Moravians in Bristol."

35. Regarding Margaret Krieger, see Letter 24, note 4.

36. Five of these women lived out their lives as single sisters: Anna Nielsen (1745–1822), Elizabeth Feisser (1758–1831), Rachel Stohler (1755–1799), Christina Kiesel (1760–1838), and Elizabeth Weller (1774–1809). Stohler returned home to Donegal when she became ill in May 1798. The other three women left Lititz when they married. Barbara Feisser (1766–1806) married the widower Isaac Renatus Harry (1767–1835) in 1795, and the couple moved to Graceham, Maryland, in 1799. Anna (Nancy) Hasse (1774–1855), born at Bethlehem to the German John Christian Hasse (1740–1797) and the English Anna Chase (1743–1786), married J. J. Jundt (1774–1831), who supervised the Lititz single brothers in 1807 and ran the farm that belonged to the Bethlehem girls' school after 1816. Catherine Fetter (1776–1820), who later became an overseer of the girls at Lititz, married bishop Carl Gotthold Reichel (1751–1825) in 1809, after which the couple traveled to Salem, where Reichel had been posted, and later to Europe.

37. At the end of 1794, sixty-six sisters, as well as seventeen big girls and forty-five little girls, lived in Lititz's single sisters' house.

38. Gertrude Peterson (1733–1812), born on Long Island, New York, married Daniel Sydrich in 1774. Peterson and MP were single sisters together in Bethlehem. Later Sydrich moved from Lititz to Bethlehem, where she led the widows' choir. For Huebner, see Letter 19, note 1.

39. See Letter 35, note 3.

40. Johannes Herbst (1735–1812), born in Bavaria, arrived in America in 1786, serving in Lancaster before becoming pastor in Lititz in 1791. He composed the anthem for the dedication of Lititz's new church in August 1787 (see Letter 21, note 7). He was consecrated a bishop in 1811, shortly before he left Lititz for Salem, North Carolina.

🕊 38. TO MEREDITH PENRY, KATHERINE PENRY, AND ELIZA POWELL[1]

October 20, 1795
Philadelphia, Pennsylvania

Philadelphia October 20th 1795

Honourd Uncle and dear Cousins!

Being just at present here in the City of Philadelphia and a Ship belonging to My Cousin Stocker going to Sail tomorrow, I shall just write a few hasty lines to enquire after your Health, and to inform you of mine, which is thro mercy *very good*! may yours be as *good*. Dear Uncle I wrote you a long Letter in the spring, long indeed 2 Sheets of Paper full on all Sides.[2] Your last was dated 20th December past, allmost a twelvemonth past. Times seems very long indeed, that I have not heard from you. I am apt to think many letters on both sides Miscarry, and yet my Letters to you seem to be more fortunate in general than yours to me. I have been these 6 weeks here on a Visit to my only Relations *In America*, and enjoy far more love and tenderness than I deserve! This is an Indisputable Truth. I think to stay 2 or 3 weeks longer, and then to bid farewell forever to the City of Philadelphia at least I think so *now*—for my age and infirmities will hardly permit my taking such a Journey 4 or 5 years hence—Should life be so long lent me, which is a thing I much question. I have 2 acquaintances here, Maiden Ladys of the Name of Powell of Welch extraction, who on Cousin Eliza Powells account, claim kindred with me, and on the stress of this, most Cordially desire their Love to Uncle, Cousin Kitty, and Cousin Eliza and her, Brother *most* Particular.[3] I wish when you write you will not forget to Mention Miss Ann and Patty Powell. I am sensible it will give them Pleasure to receive a Salutation. I have delayed my intended work. In hopes of better or at least more peaceable times. The accounts the Publick Papers give of the Disstresses of the Poor in England are dreadful. If these accounts are not exagerated how heart breaking is the Reflection—that you are in a State of *Starvation*! I pray most fervently that the distructive war you are engaged in may soon End in Peace for the sake of thousands innocent Sufferers—And may you my beloved Uncle and Cousins not have *too* large a Share in the Distresses of *our* Country. My Relations wish you all health and happiness, with the greatest Cordiality and rejoice to hear of your wellfare. I have not seen or heard any thing yet of the Reverend Mr Cooke only that he is in the Country, but what part I know not[4]—I commend myself honourd Uncle to your Blessing and Prayers—and remain with heart felt affection, your ever

Dutiful Niece and loving Cousin
Mary Penry

ALS: Penralley Collection 1366, NLW. Addressed "Mr Meredith Penry | Struet Brecon | Brecknockshire | South Wales | Per Ship | Pennsylvania." Endorsed "Received per Post | December 10th 1795 | Answered it | February 20th 1796."

1. See Letter 29.

2. MP left for Philadelphia on September 6, arriving at Elizabeth Drinker's on September 9. She stayed for two days, socializing with Benjamin Rush, James Logan, and Hannah Sansom, and then moved to Margaret Stocker's. See September 9–11, 1795, Drinker, *Diary*, 1:726–27. She returned to Lititz on November 23, 1795. The last extant letter from MP is dated July 2, 1795.

3. Ann Powell (ca. 1731–1813) and Martha (Patty) Powell (ca. 1741–1827), unmarried Quaker sisters, kept a shop on South Third Street in Philadelphia. They were members of Philadelphia's Quaker Meeting. Other single women lived with the Powells and MP occasionally stayed with them. "her Brother": Penry Powell. See Letter 29.

4. Coke was not in America in 1795; he had visited for a fifth time in 1792–93 and would return for a sixth visit from October 1796 to February 1797.

æ **39. TO ELIZABETH DRINKER**[1]
December 5, 1795
Lititz, Pennsylvania

Lititz December 5th 1795

Ma Tres Chere Amie

I am not pleased with the dedication of this Epistle because it only says: *My very dear Friend.* That *thou* art *one* of my *Dearest* Friends, my heart truly feels, far more than I can express in words, and how happy should I think myself could I once in 6 Months enjoy an Hours Conversation. Yet since it cannot be I must console myself with speaking to you in this dumb Language and waiting *Days* at least if not weeks for an answer. Oh my Friend what a priveledge it is to communicate our thoughts on Paper since a nearer intercourse in denied. Is it a good or bad Sign to grow more tender and affectionate as we grow in years? I find myself more attach'd to my Friends than ever. I do not know when I felt such Pain as when I hastend from you. I dare not think on it, it softens me too much. That night I left you, I sleept at our good Friend Patty Powells and sat off from Philadelphia after 8 O Clock.[2] The company in the Stage was—an Old Frenchman and his Dog Cupidon a gentlewoman named Ferguson a Stranger to me and in Lancaster not known to any one—She had an invisible Companion—a young Lancaster Shop keeper George Moore[3]—and—your Friend Penry—The first day we had fair weather but the wind was high and sharp. I went from the Stage at downings directly to your Daughter Sallys w[h]ere I was receiv'd like your Sister and her Aunt.[4] There I spent a most agreeable Evening. Your good Daughter gave orders to her attendants to make my Breakfast—but I left the House and the Maids fast asleep, as she has doubtless informd you. The next day it raind, we were obliged to leave the Turnpike road in order to reach the Tavern w[h]ere we were to Breakfast, a lane leading to the Tavern was so bad, that fearing we should overset we walk'd thro rain and Dirt a quarter of a Mile—as I was trudging on thro the Dirt, I heard a lamentable outcry behind me, I turnd and saw poor Cupid lying with the hind wheel of the Stage upon his Neck. His Master was jumping about like a Crazy Man crying out O mon Dieu! Mon dieu! O my poor Dog! O my poor Dog! I was indeed sorry for the door Dog and his Master. The Dog was a beautiful Pointer whom he had brought with him from Paris. At the Tavern w[h]ere we breakfasted the French man left us as he was going to another part of the Country so did not see the Wheel which had kill'd his Dog and which he had execrated in his Passion break down. Which happend 7 Miles from Lancaster and we had to stop in the Middle of the road 1½ Mile from any house and there wait an hour and an half till a Chair Wheel could be procured and fix'd on our Axeltree. It raind the whole time as hard as it could pour down—it was quite dark before we reachd Lancaster. I went wett and fatigued allmost to death to my good Friend Polly Roberts who made me a good Dish of Tea and laid me to rest in a comfortable Bed where I reposed and refresh'd my weary Limbs.[5] Next day I went to our Brethrens House and was inform'd on Monday a Stage would come from Lititz in Order to take me home.[6] Monday morning I had the very great Pleasure to embrace some of my dear Companions who came to fetsch me home. With them I sat out towards Evening—When we had allmost reach'd home they tried to conceal me, on the Stage stopping at the Door it was eagerly ask'd wether I was there—my Companions gave no Answer that it might remain doubtful—but I could not contain my joy and cryd out yes God be praised here I am once more returnd to you—In short it was a most affecting Scene, their loving wellcomes and my Satisfaction to see myself among my dear Companions in my sweet azylum of Peace and Love! I have been so fatigued from travelling the Rough Turnpike road that it seemd the Flesh was bruised, and loose from the Bones. Many little affairs required to be brought in order which prevented my writing sooner and indeed My journey has cost me so much money that I must set to work to earn where withal to pay the debts I have contracted. 7 Dollars were given me—and 17 I laid out. My travelling Expences alone was 13 Dollars. I have now bid adieu to Journeys in this World—I rejoice in the Prospect of my last Journey to the Land of Eternal Felicity. *You* my dear Friend, I pray may be continued as long as possible as a Comfort to your dear Husband and Children. As for me I have nothing to bind me to this Life. My Friends whom I leave behind will have reason to rejoice at my deliverance from a frail and infirm Tabernacle— And after a few Years we hope to Meet in the Kingdom of Heaven before the Face of our Loving and beloved Saviour.—Pray give my most Affectionate Salutation to your dear Husband, your kind good Sister—Your dear Billy and my Name sake. Adieu my Friend Our God and Saviour bless you Spiritually and Temporally and grant you the Constant feeling of his peace. Adieu *My dearest Friend*—I remain Sincerely your Affectionate

And faithful

Mary Penry

ALS: Linden Hall Archives. Endorsed "Lititz December 5 1793 | Mary Penry." Jacob Ritter (see Letter 40, note 4) delivered this letter to Drinker. See December 11, 1795, Drinker, *Diary*, 1:759.

1. See Letter 18.
2. MP had returned to Lititz from Philadelphia on November 23, 1795.

3. George Moore partnered with William Henry (ca. 1770–1846) in a Lancaster shop. See 1797 and 1799 Tax Lists, Lancaster Borough Tax Lists, 1750–1812, Microflm Pos. 15–16, LCHS.

4. "your Daughter Sallys": Drinker's daughter, Sarah (Sally) Sandwith Drinker. See Appendix C.

5. "good Friend Polly Roberts": see Letter 17, note 1.

6. "Brethrens House": Lancaster's Moravian church, which contained a worship hall, a parsonage, and a schoolroom, built in 1750. There was no single brothers' house in Lancaster, as there was in Lititz or Bethlehem.

ᥲᵥ 40. TO ELIZABETH DRINKER[1]

February 2, 1796

Lititz, Pennsylvania

Lititz February 2nd 1796

Mon tres Chere Amie

Altho it is but just, that I should write 3 Letters to your one in some measure to atone for past—shall I say Neglect—I don't like the word neither can I apropriate it to myself altho apearences are against me, however that may be, it is chastisement Sufficient not to hear from you. Concerning your Cotton Yarn I cannot find an oppertunity to send any thing except a Letter.[2] I have a few Trifles for you to give your grand Children—But I cannot send them. I was thinking, if you are not Supplied, you can procure Cotton of our Spinning at Philips next door to your Friend Powells—or if you can wait till the Spring, we shall send a quantity of charming Bleach'd Cotton which Boller and Jordan in Race Street has sent to us to spinn, there will be Assortments enough to suit you[3]—As for my part I would serve you herein with all my heart, were it my Power, but no one will take charge of a Small Parcell. I wish you would write me a few lines and give your Letter to your Neighbour Jacob Ritter, to forward to me, I want to hear from you, and how you find your self.[4] May this newly enterr'd year bring you *Health & Happiness* Together with my good Friend Drinker—Your Sister my worthy Friend and Namesake[5]—Your Children—Grand Children and all those you *Love*. I see you Methinks in a thoughtful Posture—are you sometimes thinking on *your M P*

O my Friend how *my* heart melts in Tenderness when I think on you! I dare not enlarge—will only tell you I shall ever remain your Faithful Friend!

Mary Penry

ALS: Linden Hall Archives. Addressed "Mrs | Elizabeth Drinker | Front Street near Race Street | To the care of Mr Jacob Ritter | Philadelphia." Endorsed "Lititz Feb 2 1796 | Mary Penry."

1. See Letter 18.

2. Regarding the single sisters' textile industry, see Appendix D.

3. "Philips next door to your Friend Powells": unidentified. "Boller and Jordan": John Jordan (1770–1845) and Frederick Boller (1767–1802), clerks to Godfrey Haga (1745–1825), purchased his business when he retired in 1793. See Winslow, "John Jordan."

4. Jacob Ritter (1754–1834), a leader of Philadelphia's Moravian community, often facilitated their correspondence. See September 1, 1800, Drinker, *Diary*, 2:1336.

5. "Your Sister my . . . Namesake": Drinker's sister, Mary Sandwith. See Appendix C.

૨ 41. TO MEREDITH PENRY[1]

April 27, 1796

Lititz, Pennsylvania

Lititz April 27th 1796

Beloved and Revered Unkle,

Your Most agreeable Favours of the 19th Sept. A.P. reach'd my hands the 23rd Instant, as I can truely say, to my Inexpressible Joy. I shall in this, indeavour to answer my honourd unkle['s] request, as fully as I possibly can in a Letter. Thankful, if I can in any, the *least thing* afford you any Satisfaction. In your former Letter, which I receiv'd in Philadelphia last October, or November I have forgot which: You wishd to know, wether sending Leather to America, would be of any advantage?[2] Mr Stocker, who understands Commerce as well as any man in Philadelphia bid me tell you—: altho the English Leather, was much prized, the duty upon Importations, was so high, they could not sell it. Unfortunately your Letter arived via New York, the day *after* my Letter was wrote, and the Vessel saild: knowing I could give you no incouragement in this Affair, I was not as thoughtful of writing as I ought to have been—I soon after returnd home, where I found so much Busness, which had lain dormant during my stay in Philadelphia of 11 Weeks, that I was pretty much straightned to recover my lost time[3]—As the Spring aproach'd, I was in Continual hopes of hearing from you—as well as fears, your Letters might be lost. Yet I was determined in my own Mind to write this week. Our Papers are filld with dismal accounts of storms and Tempests—and the *good fortune* of your *Enemies*, in the capture of your Merchant Men.[4] I was just going to enter on a large account of my Sensations on the Receipt of your Letters—but will not detain my unkle with that Subject— but hasten to resolve your queries. First I will begin with *My Church.*[5] We are descendants from *John Huss*, a *Bohemian Divine*, a Learned Pious Man, who lived at the same time with *our Wicklef* and corrisponded with him.[6] In the City of Prague in Hungary he had a fine Church and Colledge, which was much frequented by *English Students*. In the year 1415 the 6th of July, this John Huss seald his Testimony of the Gosple, with Martyrdom, being burnt at the stake at Costnitz in Germany. Huss utterd at the Stake, this remarkable Prophecy: "To day (said he) you roast a *goose* (Huss being the name of *Goose* in the Bohemian Language) but 100 years hence, a *Swan* will arise from my Ashes—him ye shall not *Roast*." This was verrified in the famous *Martin Luther*, who began the Reformation in the year 1517, the 31 of October. After *Huss* was gone, his followers in *Bohemia* and *Moravia*, [were] most cruelly oppress'd, every Method was tried, to compel them to Submit to the Pope and Church of Rome. As the Gosple had been handed down to them, from the *Apostle's times* in a Purity of Manners and Doctrine,—and as their Forefathers *never* had, neither *would* they Embrace the Errors of the Romish Church.—And took up the *Sword*: thus began the *Hussites* warr as it was call'd, which lasted some years.[7] The Major part, strugled chiefly for freedom—and the Cup in the Sacrament, for which reason they were denominated *Calixteners*. From among the multitudes of John Huss's followers, a Comparatively, small number seperated, these put their Sole trust and *Confidence* in the *Lord*, and not in the arm of *Flesh*, these sought a *vital* Religion—the others *Liberty*. These retired from the City into the forests, Settled a Society among them selves, and regulated their Flock after the *Rule* of Scripture. They had a few *Pious Clergy* from among the *Calixteners* with them, but these could not ordain others, and they were justly concernd to have a Regular Succession in their Minestry, to obtain which, it was highly necessary for them, to have a *Bishop*. Not caring nor perhaps *daring*, to apply to the Roman Catholicks, they turnd their eyes to *Stephen* the *Waldensers Bishop*.[8] To him, they sent a deputation. Stephen ordain'd one of the Deputies to a Bishop, and the rest to *Presbyters*. Very soon after this, the poor *Waldensers* underwent the most dreadful Persecution, their *Bishop* Stephen was burnt, and the rest allmost totally destroy'd. The account of this Persecution is extant—and might be compared to the Persecutions of the Primitive Christians under the Heathen Emperors—So great was their number, and so Manifold their Suff'rings. Mean time the little flock of truely Pious Hussites, who after Mature deliberation what *Tittle* they should take, to distinguish themselves alike, from the warrlike *Hussites*, and *Calixteners*, determind to Stille themselves the *United Brethren*.[9] After many Vississitudes, sometimes forced to hide themselves from their *Perscecutors* in Rocks and Caves, in Order to worship God and administer the Sacraments, according to his word, these began to enjoy Liberty of Conscience. Built Churches in Bohemia and Moravia, founded Colledges, Settled Congregations &c. They sent deputies to Doctor Luther, to congratulate and incourage him, in the work of the Reformation, they accompanied this with their *Confession* of Faith. *Luther* receivd the Deputies in much *Love*, highly aproved of their Confession, and gave them the right hand of fellowship.[10] He commended their most excellent Church Discipline, frankly confess'd it was out of his power, to bring his Churches into such order, his People were not so pliable, to be wrought in the form the Brethren had brought theirs. The *warr*, which in the Reign of the Emperor Charles the Fifth, threatned the down fall of the whole Protestant Church, was a trying Time for the *Brethren*[11]—indeed their Suffrings were *Prior* to that *Warr*, for Ferdinand Brother to the Emperor Charles—a very zealous Catholic, was King of Hungary & Boehmia, and try'd by gentle and hard trea[t]ment, to bring his Subjects to Conform to his Faith. Numbers went into Exile, and those that remain'd being chiefly Farmers & the poorer Sorts, keept themselves very quiet, and was Oblidged to content themselves with meeting privately in each others Houses, praying and reading the Bible.

In the Reign of our *good* King Edward the Sixth, a deputation from the *Brethren* came to London brought a Petition and gave in their Confession of Faith[12]—they obtain'd Leave to come to England, their Confession was aproved, and they were acknowledged an *Apostolick* Church, *Elder Sister* to the Protestant Churches. Several came over to England, where they had their own Church and Minestry. *Amos Comenius* the last *Surviving Bishop* who wrote the *History of the Brethrens Church*, which he concludes with such Pathetic Language, that it might well be compared to the Lamentations of Jeremiah, for the destruction of Jerusalem. This Divine Law all the Churches wasted—the Fold Scatterd, and himself as it were left alone—Yet in hopes that the Lord might turn and Visit Zion, and being desireous to keep up the *Succession* of *Bishops*—Consecrated his Sisters Son, the Reverend *Daniel Jablonsky*, who was a Divine in great Repute at the Court of Berlin, and much esteemd by his Royal Master the King of Prusia.[13] On the first of March 1457 the *United Brethren* became a Church, by receiving their Ordination from Stephen the Waldensers Bishop and Martyr—(and who could produce the regular Succession of Bishops from the *Apostles* down to himself) and the 12th of May 1724 was again revived in the following manner: on the before-mentioned 12th of May Five decendants of the Ancient Brethren came to Herrnhuth, the seat of that worthy Pious Nobleman *Count Zinzendorf* and Claim'd his Protection.[14] His Excellence the Count every ready to assist Children of God in distress, most willingly receiv'd these poor Exiles, and gave them permission to settle in his *Domain*. These were followd by manny more, who left all they had, to enjoy Liberty of Conscience. The Count found means to obtain Satisfactory Accounts, of this Ancient Church, her *Doctrine* and *Discipline*—and was at Length assured it was the Will of God that him-self should take the Charge upon him: the more so, as his forefathers were *Exiled Members of this Church*. He was accordingly ordaind a *Bishop* of this Church by the Reverend *Daniel Jablonsky* at *Berlin*, and the *Depositum* of the Ordination was laid upon him—and has been since carefully given to several *Servants* of Christ in our *Church*.[15] *They* receive into their *Fellowship* all the sincere Lovers of Jesus who desire it—without wishing them to quit their own Societies[16]—and as *Members of their Church* those who admire and know how to value, their Excellent Church Discipline, and desire to be in *union* with them. The Apostle of the Reform'd Churches doctor Luthers Reformation is 279 years past, *our* Apostle John Huss, sufferd Martyrdom 381 years past. So that my dear Unkle you see your *Niece* is a *Member* of an ancient Honnourable Church, which claims a *Senior* right to that of the Church of England. You will now wish to know something of the Brethrens *Church Discipline* which I have frequently mention'd. In my discription of our *Congregation Places* you will have an Idea of it. In towns and Cities where we have Churches and Settled Congregations, our People have nothing to distinguish them from other Pious Christians except it be the smallness of their Number—and Simplicity of their Manners.[17] For they are thought but little off, among the *Wise ones* of this world, to whom the Word of the Cross is foolishness—and because, no one can be acknowledged a Member, whose life and Conversation is a Reproach to their calling—and when they are Members, must Submit to a Strickt Scrutiny into their Conduct—and expect Exhortations—or to be disowned, if they offend, unless they acknowl-edge the offence and promise amendment. This, is look'd upon too strickt, and the Vain and the Gay, would be wretched, to keep Company with Sober Folks who do not allow their Members to dance, Play Cards attend the *The-atre* &c. &c. Our *Congregation* places are small *Villages*, w[h]ere none but our own Community live.[18] In Pennsylvania we have 3, Bethlehem Nazareth & Lititz, and in North Carolina 1, Salem. In England there are several, such as Fullneck in Yorkshire—and at Bedford—in Pembrokshire, at Harverford West, and more places I cannot just now recolect—In Ireland there [are] also several such Congregation Places.[19] In such Villages as I observed above, where none but our own Community reside, we have divine Service every Evening, at which either Lessons out of the Bible are read, or a short exhorta-tion given on the Text for the day. We have the Communion every 4 Weeks— We Celebrate all the Holydays your Church observe. On Sunday we pray the Litany, have Sermons as usual in Churches, and our Neighbors some Miles distant, attend the Service on Sun—and Holydays. Our Minesters are fre-quently requested to Christen Children, and to Preach at Funerals, which they seldom refuse, if in their Power to attend, and when it is desired, use the Church of England Ceremonial. Only they do not *Marry* because they make a Point of Conscience, to give into affairs which might give them Trouble, in joining Persons together of whom they have no knowledge—And there are Justices of the Peace quite sufficient, to answer that Purpose, since—whoever will, may in this Country, be married by a Justice. Our Single Men, have a House to themselves w[h]ere they carry on their Respective Trades. Our Married People have their Houses, gardens and every convenience they can Afford. We have one Publick House in our Village, for the entertainment of Travellers and Strangers, indeed this Tavern is vastly different from the usual Publick Houses. No drinking to Excess, Dancing, or gaming is sufferd. We have likewise a very good Shop, with an assortment of every thing suitable for us—and indeed it has as many Customers out of our Circle as in it. The Children of both Sexes are brought by their Parents—They have their daily School, the Boys in the Brethrens, the Girls in the *Sisters* house, w[h]ere they are taught reading writing, English & German, Arithmetic—and whatever else they have Talents for—The Girls are taught the same, together with Sewing Knitting and whatever suits their sex. Our Minesters late & early, exhort Parents to bring up their Children in the Knowledge and fear of the Lord, to assist which, the Children have frequent Meetings, where they receive Instruction and Catechisation—In *Ours* or as we call it—the *Single Sisters*—or the *Sisters House*, we are 56 in Number of different ages, from 15 to Sixty the age of your Niece—who is the Eldest in the House.[20] *Our Rules* are as regular as Clock work. We begin the day with Morning Prayer at Six o'the Clock—In a Pretty Hall intirely addapted to such Meetings, and end the day in the same Manner—We dine in one large dining Hall—we break-fast—drink tea and Sup in our Seperate appartments, w[h]ere 6 or 8 Persons live together—we sleep altogether in a large Hall, each in their *Own* seperate *Bed* and Bedstead. We pay at the rate of 2/6 the week Sterling for Board and Lodging—for which we have daily a good plain Dinner, of Meat Broth—and Such vegetables as are in Season—and our Tea Water for Breakfast and in the Afternoon at 3 O[c]lock, is provided for us.[21] Every appartment in which we Sisters live together, may be calld a little Family of their own. Here we find, each their own Breakfast, Tea or Coffee &c. and in the Afternoon the same. Fire and Candle we find ourselves, each Contributes Weekly a certain Sum—and the overseer in each Room, provides these 2 articles—Our wash-ing is also done in the same way, one or 2 belonging to a Room, wash for the rest—they are paid by the day, and the rest pay by the Piece. We have 2 Looms in our House, in which we can, and have wove very pretty Musslin, both Striped and Plain. Flax and wool, Worsted and Cotton we Spinn a great deal, more particular Cotton.[22] Some of our Sisters do outdoor Work—as gardening, hay making reaping—washing, &c—but only among our own *People* as the Maidens are taken care of as *precious Jewels* and keept out of the way of temptation. Our whole number is about 90. Many of our grown up Girls and Young women, either live with their Parents to assist them in the Family, or live at Service with the Married People. We have likewise Seemstresses and Mantua Makers in our House—and your old *Niece* works Tambour & *Embroidery*, and as yet have never used Spectacles.[23] In our Village we are 300 and some odd Souls—I forgot to tell you that we wash mend and make for the Single Men—and bake their Bread, in our House. Methinks I hear my dear unkle say: have you then no Weddings among you—Yes Sir we have—and the Major Part of our Villagers in *all* our Place Congregations was once Inhabitants of the Respective Choir Houses (as they are Stiled) but we have *No* Courtships.[24] The Parents and our Elders, endeavour as far as human wisdom reaches, to settle all Marriages for the Well doing of each Party, and as there is no Constraint, but the Party can accept, or Refuse the Offer as they please, they cannot complain—and I believe an unhappy Marriage with us, is hardly to be found. Our Married women retain their attachment to their former dwelling and Companions, and educate their Children in the same manner, so that they are frequently days together in our House, when the Mothers are too busy to attend properly to them, the same may be said of the *Fathers*—so that we are in reality *United Brethren* and *Sisters*. My dearest unkle! I never knew the value of your Church till I left it, I have a great Veneration for it—we subscribe with heart and hand, to the Augustan Confession of Faith—out of which your Church has taken her articles.[25] In Philadelphia I was intimately acquainted with the Bishops and Several of the Clergy, and was told that if I chose to partake the Communion in the Church, they had no objection to make[26]—as we have a Church there, and the Holy Sacraments administred every 2 Months—I declined the offer, because it would seem as tho I was either not Satisfied with my own People—or was fond of Novelty—but was I in a place w[h]ere *we* had no settled Minestry—I should have freedom to communicate with your Church, in preference to any other—All our Meetings are keept in the German Language, which is spoken among the Brethren with the greatest Purity—But wherever English are, as in Philadelphia and New York, their worship is in the same Language. Singing, composes a great part of our divine Service, Anthems out of the Bible, and most Beautiful Hyms and Spiritual Songs, accompanied with Instrumental Musick is a most pleasing, as well as edifying part of worship.[27] I have now I think said enough, to give my dear unkle an Insight into our Church—you can if you think proper procure a far more Satisfactory account, if you inquire for the two following Books. The Idea Unitas Fratrum or rather the Idea Fedie Fratrum i.e *The Confession of Faith of the United Brethren* or *Unitas Fratrum* and the History of the Church of the Bretheren by David Cranz—which is to be had at all the Brethrens Chappels in London, Bristol, &c. and which is well worth your Persual.[28] Nancy Vaughn if you desire it, will certainly let you see them, She is a Member of our Church, and was long my good Corispondant.—And Now I proceed to answer my dear unkle his queries concerning *your* Church. There are many *Churches of England*, in I believe every part of the United States. In Philadelphia there are 3. Christ Church, which was built before I came to America—*St. Peters* and *St. Pauls*. The reverend *Doctor* William White is their *Bishop*, he was ordain'd in England shortly before the Warr—I have known him from his Childhood, and whenever I go to Philadelphia the *Doctor* is extreemly Polite, and realy affectionate. I believe he is a good man—but no *Orator*.[29] He has ordain'd several Priests—and last fall, 2 Bishops, he invited me to come to Church, in order as he said, to be a judge w[h]ether there was any material difference between *Our Ceremonial* and theirs—but it raind the whole day—I could not go out. The former Arch Bishop of Canterbury—I think it was *Potter* advised our young Candidates for the Minestry, to apply to the Brethrens Bishops—for Ordination, assuring them, he should be intirely Satisfied—as there was no *other Bishops* then in America—but these young gentry, preferd a *voyage* to England—to *His Grace*, before a Journey of 53 Miles to a *Brother*.[30] However, it was quite well done—for *our* Bishops follow the advice of St. Paul and lay hands suddenly on No Man—We have one *Bishop* at *Bethlehem*, one at *Lititz*, and one at *Salem* in N. Carolina.[31] The Commerce of the United States with foreign Powers is very extensive—*Flour, Corn*, Staves and Heading,[32] Tobacco I believe are the chief Articles, but I must confess, I have so many years been out of the way of *all Commerce* and Shiping, and give so little attention to those affairs, that I can give but a poor account. The Republick of France is at present the *Favourite Ally* and *Our Country—The—Reverse*[33]—The Climate in Pennsylvania is variable, we have frequently in one week—nay in one day such sudden changes, from Heat to cold happens—that you would immagine, you went from Greenland to the West Indies—or from thence to Greenland, these changes often cause Colds, Fevers and many disorders, especially if a Person is not careful of changing their warm Cloathing for Cool. The best way is, suit your dress just to the Season of *the Week* or Day. Our winters differ very much, last winter we had frequent but light *Snows*, and as *much thaw*, only 3 or 4 extreem Cold days. The Month of March, and this Month April, has been so remarkable dry, that we have been very uneasy about the grain. This day 27th we have a fine Rain, for which we desire to be thankful, last Fall we had such Continual and heavy rains, that the Roads were allmost impassable. It is a Misfortune, that some years past, we have such warm days in April—and Sometimes in March, which forwards Vegitation, and while the Buds Plants &c. are tender—a hard frost comes, and kills a great deal of our Fruit, and tender Plants. We have great quantities of Peaches—good Apples and Cherrys—Pears not so Plenty—Apricotts fine Plumbs and Collyflowers grow *not* in comon gardens, Currants Rasberrys and Strawberries plenty—Goosberrys not very plenty, Cranberrys grow Wild. We have fine Water- and Mush Melons, where the Soil is Sandy. Vegetables of all kinds we have in our gardens, Hassle Nuts which grow on Shrubs we have enough—but I never saw any Filberts[34]—Black Wallnuts are Plenty, White, or the so calld English Wallnut is scarce. Such Quantities of Flour is exported, that wheat bears the Price of 3 Spanish Dollars, that is 3 Crowns Sterling. Beef from 4 to 6d the Pound with us—in the City at least 3 times as much. Butter 8d rye 5/. When I was in Philadelphia last fall, Butter was frequently sold at the rate of 2/6 the Pound, and Veal 3 Dollars the loin, Beef from 9d to 1/ and 1/6 Sterling—and fire Wood at the Enormous price of 12 Dollars—or 12 Crowns, your money, the Cord—or load—at the Wharf—besides 1 Dollar ha[u]ling to the dwelling, and 1 Dollar Cutting and piling in the Cellar. So that upon the whole one may rec[k]on 14 or 15 Crowns for the Wood—and 12 Cord, Mrs Stocker said she must lay in for the winter 36£ Sterling for firing in *one* winter. For my part I wonder how People can live in such Cities, for Maids Wages is 6 Shillings the week, and every fashionable extravagence has found its way in to our Cities, that is common in Europe—yet it is none of my Bus'ness how *they* come on—I am thankful for my blessed azylum. I would only wish to make *you* Sensible that I believe upon the *whole*, you can live as well in the *mountains* of *Wales*—as we in our so much prized *America*. Your and my Beloved *Washington*, is a Member of the Church of England. He is a Virginian. *All* his country *Folks* are not so Sensible of his Merrits as we are. His whole aim is to preserve Peace and Tranquility—and all our worthy good Men, are of the same way of thinking—but there are another Party of a Contrary Opinion, who seek to Oppose him—we are now at a Dangerous Crisis—God alone knows how it will turn out.[35] We pray for *Peace*. He has not accepted of a Salary hitherto—being a Man of large fortune and *no* Children. I think I told you in a former Letter, that his Ancestor was our brave *General Monk*[36]—The apointed *Salary* for the President is 25,000 Dollars, and each Member of Congress 6 Dollars the day during their Session—The Senators 1500 Dollars the year, and 2 Dollars the day during their Session. The Members of Congress are 102—13 are for Pennsylvania. The Senate, has 30 Members—2 from Pennsylvania. So much for Politicks.

Will only add: these Gentlemen have the charge of a *Republick Ten times larger than England* and my dear unkle will be a judge of the Reason, why I can give him very little account of former acquaintances who are removed to America, when I tell you, that New York is 130 miles distant from me—Boston 428 Miles, and Carolina near 600. At New York we have a Church, and a Minester, with whom I corrispond. His Spouse came from Yorkshire, and I am God Mother to their Eldest Son.[37] At Salem we have *one Place Congregation*—and Several Churches, but at Boston very few Acquaintances, the Presbyterian is the Dominant Church in New England.

It now remains to answer my dear unkle concerning Mr *Stockers* coming to America. After my Mammas unkle, John Stockers death, his Eldest Son Dudlestone Stocker (who had married a Barbadien Lady) took his Sister Sally, and his 2 Brothers Anthony and John (who were born *after* their Fathers return from a 7 years Slavery at Salle) with him to *Barbadoes* one of the West India Islands[38]—there they were well Educated—and their Brother dying without children they had handsome Fortunes. The two Sons followed Merchandizing, as they had fine Sugar Plantations in the Island, and about the year 48—or 1750 (I have really forgot which)—came over to America. John went to *Rhode Island* and settled there—and dyed Childless—Anthony keept a Store—married extreemly well in Philadelphia, and grew rich very fast—John Clements, his Batchelor unkle, in Bristol, who was Mayor of the City[39]—dying—left his 2 Maiden Sisters, and his Nephew Anthony Stocker his whole Estate. The 2 Maiden Aunts dying shortly after, Anthony was left their *Sole Heir*. He was obliged to go to England, about the time of the American Revolution, in order to settle the affairs of his deceased unkle and Aunts—he took his only Son John Clements Stocker, over with him for Education—and there my Cousin Anthony dyed in the City of Bristol. *Anthony Stocker* was like a Brother to me. And it was my *own fault*, that I did not accept of his generous *offers*, to live intirely with him—and his wife was very tenderly attach'd to me, but my dear Sir—I could not do it—I was happily settled in the Congregation and was assured, whatever benifit I might thereby receive in temporals—was no Compensation, for the Injury My Spiritual Concerns might receive. This refusal produced a Coolness of some years, untill my young Cousin Clem Stocker returnd from England, and a few weeks after, came here to see me![40] We had then an Explanitory Conversation, which removed all heart Burnings, and old Mrs Stocker and my self, being of one age, she being likewise in the *decline* of Life as well as my self. We are Mutually attachd to each Other, in a Strickt Bond of Friendship. Her children look on me, as a Remnant of their Beloved Fathers Family and seem pleased to *see* and hear from me—although they are too much taken up with dress & Fashions, and the amusements of high Life, to find much Satisfaction in the Conversation of an old Maid—yet they think me worthy of their *Notice*. Anthonys Sister *Sally Stocker*, who staid at *Barbadoes*, married rather unfortunate, her Husband took to drinking, spent her whole Estate—and left her with 4 or 5 Children—destitute—Her Brothers provided for her— and after her death—sent for the children and Provided for them—One daughter is married in some part of New England, her name is Jenny Brown, we Corrispond together—but have never met—tho Mrs Stocker has tried various ways, to bring us together, it has hitherto been labour in *Vain*.[41] She is much afflicted with the Palsey, (that is Cousin Jenny)—old Mrs Stocker is a fine hearty Old Lady, and w[h]ere she is known is greatly respected—Her Maiden Name was *Margaret Phillips*—I tell her as she is of Welch descent, she must be related to my Cousin Kitty. Honourd Unkle—this sheet is entirely *yours*. Eliza must read it to you. It is my Intension to do you Pleasure—I have not place here, to say all I would say—shall finish in Cousin Kitty's Letter.

Your dutiful Niece,
Mary Penry

ALS: Penralley Collection 1370, NLW. Marked "No. 1" by Penry, who sent this letter together with two others marked "No. 2" and "No. 3." Addressed "Mr. Meredeth Penry | Struet Brecon | Brecknockshire | South Wales." Endorsed "Rec'd this Letter per Post | July 3 1796 Answered it."

1. See Letter 29.
2. Meredith Penry was a tanner. See Letter 29, note 1.
3. See Letter 38, note 2.
4. "capture of your Merchant Men": between 1793 and 1800, the French seized 2,861 British merchant ships. Harvey, *Collision of Empires*, 124. On July 2, 1796, the Directory issued a decree that made American "neutral vessels"—like British vessels, with whom France was at war—subject to search and seizure.
5. MP's history of the Moravian church follows *The Ancient and Modern History of the Brethren* by David Cranz (London, 1780), deriving the genealogy of the renewed Moravian church from John Hus and the Ancient Brethren. Later historians see this genealogy as contrived and consider the renewed Moravian church as a new entity. See Atwood, "Use of the 'Ancient Unity'"; and Stead and Stead, *Exotic Plant*, 13–22.
6. John Wycliffe (ca. 1325–1384), who translated the Bible into the vernacular, was posthumously declared a heretic at the Council of Constance in 1415. Jan Hus (ca. 1372–1415), too, was condemned by the Council of Constance and burned at the stake on July 6, 1415.
7. "*Hussites* warr": between 1419 and 1434 or 1436, Jan Hus's followers, insisting on the laity's right to drink from the chalice at communion, fought armed conflicts with the Roman Catholic church, which aimed to suppress this practice that, it believed, would disempower the clergy. These Hussites were called Utraquists (after the Latin phrase for communion of both kinds, *sub specie utraque*) or Calixtines (from the word for chalice, *calix*). See Atwood, *Theology*, 76; and Cranz, *Ancient and Modern History*, 19–20.

8. Stephen died at the stake in August 1467. See Cranz, *Ancient and Modern History*, 28–29. Some eighteenth-century historians identified Stephen as the Brethren's first bishop, which modern scholarship disputes. See Atwood, *Theology*, 169.

9. *"United Brethren"*: see Cranz, *Ancient and Modern History*, 23.

10. *"Luther receivd the Deputies"*: according to Cranz, two young Brethren first visited Martin Luther in 1523 and a second deputation visited him in 1524. See also Atwood, *Theology*, 249–51.

11. *"The warr"*: the Hapsburg Charles V invaded the German lands in 1546 and targeted the Brethren. See Cranz, *Ancient and Modern History*, 46–47; Atwood, *Theology*, 268–69.

12. *"depution"*: see Cranz, *Ancient and Modern History*, 51.

13. *"Succesion of Bishops"*: Cranz, *Ancient and Modern History*, 77–82, describes the succession of bishops of the Unity of the Brethren from 1467 to the 1735 ordination of David Nitschmann (1695–1772). For Amos Comenius (1592–1670) and the ordination of Daniel Jablonsky (1660–1741), see ibid., 68–76.

14. *"12th of May 1724"*: the date that five refugees (John Toeltschig, Melchoir Ziesberger, and three named David Nitschmann) arrived at Herrnhut from Bohemia. See Cranz, *Ancient and Modern History*, 105. Other Moravians, who had been at the Berthelsdof estate of Nicholas Ludwig von Zinzendorf (1700–1760) since June 1722, built the village of Herrnhut on these lands. On May 12, 1727, the anniversary of earlier arrival, Zinzendorf led the community to accept a "Brotherly Agreement" that described the Christian discipline under which they agreed to live.

15. *"ordain a Bishop"*: in 1735 Jablonsky consecrated David Nitschmann "bishop of the Moravian Brethren"; in 1735 Jablonsky and Nitschmann ordained Zinzendorf. See Cranz, *Ancient and Modern History*, 82, 197, 211–13.

16. *"without wishing them to quit their own Societies"*: see Letter 2, note 7.

17. *"Congregation Places . . . towns and Cities"*: MP describes two different arrangements. Only Moravians lived in congregation places such as Bethlehem and Lititz. In "towns and Cities," such as New York or Philadelphia, Moravians attended a Moravian church but lived among non-Moravians.

18. *"Congregation places"*: see Gollin, *Moravians in Two Worlds*; and Smaby, *Transformation*.

19. Gracefield (settled 1759) and Gracehill (settled 1765) were congregation places in Ireland.

20. At the end of 1796, MP counted sixty-eight single sisters.

21. Lititz's single sisters' house never featured the communal housekeeping that had organized Bethlehem's choir houses before 1762, so residents paid for room and board.

22. For the single sisters' textile industry, see Appendix D.

23. *"Tambour"*: see Letter 29, note 8.

24. *"we have No Courtships"*: see Peucker, "In the Blue Cabinet," 15.

25. *"Augustan Confession of Faith"*: the Augsburg Confession, composed by Luther and Melanchthon in 1530, which explains the reasons that the Protestant church separated from Rome and articulates its key principles. See Zinzendorf, *Twenty-One Discourses*.

26. *"Communion in the Church"*: that is, at Christ Church, the Episcopal church in Philadelphia, whose bishop, William White, was MP's friend. See below, note 29.

27. Music was central to the Moravian church. See Knouse, *Music of the Moravian Church*.

28. David Cranz, *Alte und neue Brüder-Historie oder kurz gefasste Geschichte der Evangelischen Brüder-Unität* (Barby, 1772), translated by Benjamin Latrobe as *The Ancient and Modern History of the Brethren* (London, 1780); and August Gottlieb Spangenberg, *Idea Fidei Fratrum order Kurzer Begrif der Christlichen Lehre in den evangelischen Brüdergemeinen* (Barby, 1779), translated by Benjamin Latrobe as *An Exposition of the Christian Doctrine, as Taught in the Protestant Church of the United Brethren* (London, 1782).

29. William White (1748–1836), bishop in the United States Episcopal Church. He was chaplain to the Continental Congress from 1777 to 1789 and the second chaplain of the Senate of the United States after 1790. Born in Philadelphia and ordained in London in 1770, he was the rector of Christ Church for fifty-seven years. In the 1790s he lived on Front Street, near MP's cousins, the Stockers.

30. In 1737 Zinzendorf had met John Potter, archbishop of Canterbury, who regarded Moravians as "our brethren, and one Church with our own." See Podmore, *Moravian Church in England*, 210–11.

31. *"our Bishops"*: Johann Andreas Huebner (Letter 19, note 1) in Lititz; Johann Daniel Koehler (1737–1805) in Salem, North Carolina; and Johannes Ettwein (Letter 9, note 2) in Bethlehem.

32. "Staves": thin pieces of wood used to make casks or barrels. "Heading": planking used to make the heads of casks or barrels.

33. MP's horror at the French Revolution leads her to exaggerate, her paranoia fueled by the Federalist newspapers she read. The support that France received from Americans after 1794 was considerably smaller than that received in 1792 or early 1793. See Tagg, *Benjamin Franklin Bache*, 196.

34. "Hassle Nuts . . . Filberts": hazelnuts, of which filberts are a species.

35. "Dangerous Crisis": the controversy over the Jay Treaty, which was ratified only on February 29, 1796. The Jay Treaty resolved issues that had remained since the 1783 Treaty of Paris, which ended the Revolutionary War. One matter at issue, as MP notes in Letter 43, was that the British continued to impress American sailors into British service (Brunsman, *Evil Necessity*). The treaty required Britain to evacuate the Northwest Territory, to cease depredations on American shipping, and to grant the United States trading privileges.

36. "his Ancestor . . . *General Monk*": see Letter 37, note 11.

37. Christoph Gottfried Peter, Moravian minister in New York: see Letter 33, note 13.

38. In March 1715, captain John Stocker's ship with its crew of fifteen were captured and imprisoned at Salé on Morocco's Atlantic coast. Stocker was freed in 1721 and seems to have died in Barbados in July 1729. See Windus, *Journey to Mequinez*, 197; Matar, *British Captives*, 290. Duddleston Stocker (b. 1714) married Susannah Minvielle in Barbados on July 14, 1736. He imported 120 enslaved men and women by 1739. See Faber, *Jews, Slaves, and the Slave Trade*, 98. Regarding Anthony Stocker, who became a Philadelphia merchant, see Appendix C.

39. John Clements was high sheriff of Bristol in 1735 and lord mayor of Bristol in 1752–53.

40. MP refused Anthony Stocker's invitation to live with his family (Letter 7, note 7). "young Cousin . . . here to see me": this occurred in October 1786 (Letter 22).

41. Sarah (Sally) Stocker married George Reece in Barbados on October 8, 1747. They had at least six children: Elizabeth, Margaret, Jane (Jenny), George, Anthony Stocker, and Hannah Clement. Jenny Reece, baptized on December 22, 1753, married George Brown. See Letter 47, note 16.

42. TO KATHERINE PENRY[1]
April 28–30, 1796
Lititz, Pennsylvania

Lititz April 28–30th 1796

Dearest Cousin

I have just finishd a Sheet of Paper, wherin I have endeavour'd to answer My unkles request—as it is intirely relative to things, not so imediately concerning *your* Persons I was selfish enough, to be glad when I had done. My Memory fails me so much, that I am afraid I often repeat a thing to you *more* than *once*, which must beg you to Excuse, as the Conscequence of *Old Age*. My Dearest Kitty—in a former Letter, you express a fear, that you might *disturb* my Peace of Mind thro this (one may Stile new attachment). I have thought a good deal on your observation, and have consulted my heart on the Subject—I cannot say I feel any uneasiness. It is quite Natural I think, for Relations to rejoice in each others Wellfare—and Permit me to say, it proceeds from *Grace*, to feel a *Disintressd* affection. Such I think is *ours*, for each is so well informd of the Others Situation—there can be no Sinister views in our Corrispondance.[2] Our Affection is then a pure an[d] Innoffensive, Yea a laudable affection, a Particle of Divine Love, which God Himself has inkindled in our hearts! and to Meditate on a beloved Friend, draws out the heart to pray for them—We cannot *Pray* unless our hearts is lifted up to the Lord, and the Unction of His Holy Spirit attends it. This, then is a blessing—and for this, Blessing I am indebted to my dearest Unkle and you—*One* observation more, and I've done. When you Write "Your dear unkle sends you his Blessing," I can form the Idea of my Venerable Unkles hand upon my head—and being firmly perswaded—he has *really* and *truely* bless'd me, I truely believe I shall experience the Effects—of *this Parents* Blessings (*I have no other*). I can kiss your Names, at the close of your Letter, knowing *your hands* lay long on the Paper, and seem to realise a Salutation to yourselves. True it is, a Murmering thought, will sometimes arise, at my *Banishment* from *Friends*, and Native Country—yet be not uneasy, it is quickly over, and I obtain my usual Serenity. I must not detain you, any longer on this *Topick*. It will only make us sad, and I want to divert you. The Major *Rice Price*, was the *very* man that saw me in *Lititz!*[3] and I would have given anything, when I found out he knew my Friends, that he had *not* seen me, for I believe I told you, the weather was such I had no thought of seeing the Face of a Stranger, I was busied mending my Stays, and to my knowledged never apeard before a Stranger in so great a *Dishabille*. He lookd at me from head to foot, and seemd to the full as much amazed, as I was confus'd—He recoverd himself however, and pressd me to give him Letters to my Friends, and gave me directions, which he wrote down on Paper, to send to his Lodgings at Lancaster—(which is a town about 8 miles from Lititz). He was a Prisoner on his *Parole*. I have neither seen nor heard, of Mr Cooke, I could allmost be angry with you, for not telling me before, that he was a Relation—a *Welch Woman* in *America*, is very happy to claim a *distant* Relation. I am acquainted with a *Methodist* in *Philadelphia*—a sweet woman. I have wrote post haste, since I receivd yours, to Mrs Stocker, and besought her to inquire of Mrs Haskings, where Dr. Cooke is: being determined to write him, if he has not left the Country.[4] A Letter sent to Mrs Haskings care—will not fail, I immagine. I cannot but reflect on my Sensations, when I shewd him about our *House*, I seemd greatly to wish, a better acquaintance with him—But we met Strangers and so we parted. The Methodists had their Synod, while I was in Philadelphia. I inquired after *Doctor Cooke*, but miss'd seeing him.[5] Mrs Haskings living so far off my Cousin Stockers, and Continual Wett weather, prevented my seeing him. However I was for the first time in my life, at the Methodist Meeting—I heard an Excellent Sermon, that is truth, but the Groaning of the People, during the Minesters long—tho fine Prayer, disturbd me. I could neither satisfactorily *hear* the Prayer nor Pray my Self, as those that kneelt beside me, prayd near as loud as the Minester. The Mrs Haskings I mention'd, is a Relation of Mrs Stockers. Well but only think: I heard a *Welch Sermon* last Fall, when I was at Philadelphia. Mr Morgan Rees a Baptist Minester, preach'd and pray'd *Welch* in the Annabaptist Meeting House, and gave the Substance of his Discourse, afterwards in English—He is a very handsome little Man—has married last winter, one of his own Profession in Philadelphia. All the Clergy (allmost in Philadelphia) and numbers more, went to hear him out of Curiosity I imagine, to hear the *Welch* Language, and indeed nothing else, took *me* there: He spooke the Welch I immagine very fluently, at least the sound was smoother than I expected. He sung and Pray'd in English, but in the Middle of his Prayer, proceeded in *Welch*. When he Explaind to his English Audience, what he had preached to the Welch, he said he had spoke on the Words: *"but we seek a better Country."* He then launch'd into the *Motives* to our seeking a better Country, which was nearly as *temporal* in his Discriptions as Mahomets Paradice. Such as: a good Soil, a good Climate, good Neighbours, &c. &c. He then in part, told us the Miseries—his lately arrived Country Men had fled from—*Despotism* and Taxes, observing: his poor Country Men had been taxd, from the Crown of the head, to the Sole of the Foot: *But* sais he (with a Peculiar Welch accent) if you throw the Cat in the Fire, she'l scamper away, as fast as she can.[6] This was rather laughable—indeed I met with very little edification, in the whole Sermon, except just before he concluded—he gave us a few—words on the better Country in the *World to come*. The good man I was told, receiv'd afterwards an admonition to leave Politics to be discuss'd at the *Coffee House*, and not to do it in the *Pulpit*. There was many of the New Commers there—I am told they intend to settle a Tract of Land by themselves. I was much surprized, to hear that allmost all the Welch, that come over of late years—are Annabaptists.[7] I am realy ashamd that I have wrote you, without acknowledging the receipt of the Gloves you was so kind as to send me, or to return you thanks for them—my letter was seald, and gone, when it struck in my mind—and I told Mrs Stocker, how distressd I was at my forgetfulness, which I beg you to pardon. I live in hopes that the next year, Perhaps the Brethrens Churches will hold a Synod in Germany, when ever they have a General Synod, which is generaly every 6 or 7 years, deputies are sent from the Congregations in America, as well as in England—the Warrs in Germany, has hitherto prevented them, from Meeting together. Should our good Lord grant us Peace, they will certainly have *Synod*, as there has been none these 8 years—that will be an excellent oppertunity for me to send you some little Memorial of my Love.[8] I do *love* your *Cousin Phillips* for your Sake—and for her own, as she undoubtedly deserves my highest *Esteem*, for her kindness to *my Niece* and *Nephew*—and beseech you to let her know, that I am in *gratitude bound* to love her—and your worthy Cousin *Jane Jones*—our *maiden Sister*. What a Happiness it is, in this degenerate Age, to have *Friends* who are lovers of *Jesus*—Do not forgett to give my kind Love, to the worthy *Mr Owen* and his dear Sisters[9]—and my dear Kitty *remember* I am a *Briton* born in *your* Principality, and glory in being a *Briton*. Live and Die my dear, in the *Faith* of the *Church of England*, it is *My Faith*, the *only* saving Faith. We are of the Augustan Confession, as well as *you*, and *we* have *one Lord, one Faith, one Baptism*.[10] My dear Love, *Sects* are not Establishd Churches. *Your* Church— which is more Properly the *English Lutheran, My Church*—and the Church of Rome, are the *only Episcopal* Churches—indeed the *Lutherans* have no *Bishops*—but Superintendants—upon the whole then there are but 3 Episcopal Churches unless the Greek Churches have *Bishops* as I think they have. All those are *Sects* which have gone *out* of their respective folds, and form'd Societies of their own, Such as Quakers, Annabaptists—and numbers, whose names you have never heard, which are to be found in the New World—The Methodists, have their Bishops, but I cannot call it *Legal*—for Mr Wessly had no right to ordain Bishops thats certain[11]—however that is nothing to me, they are very nearly related to your Church, and here, it is not uncommon, for a Methodist Minester to become a Clergyman. The Blacks, have a very pretty Church of their own in Philadelphia. Mrs Stocker took me there one Sunday afternoon, there was a large Congregation of Black Ladies and Gentlemen, according to their *Dress*. Bishop White, read Prayers and Preach'd to them, we 3 was the only *whites* in the Church. They have a Black ordaind Clergyman, his name is Absolom Jones, a very pious Man, who Reads Prayers and Preaches some times; but the Clergy generally officiate on Sundays—It is calld the African Church.[12] Over the gate on a White Marble Slab is ingraved: "The people that sat in darkness have seen a great Light."

On your Birth day, I had some of my Intimates to a Dish of Coffee and Tea, our beloved Sister Mary Tippet, who is our Spiritual *Directress*, was you may depend, one and the Head of the Company.[13] We spoke much about you, and wish'd you many Blessings to your Natal day. This Sister, desires me tell you she takes a Large share in the Welfare of *Maidens*, they being her Peculiar Charge—and further, that it is a real Satisfaction, to hear you are a lover of the Lord Jesus—and She wishes and prays, that you may increase in the *Knowledge* and *Love* of *him*—as well as the *Knowledge* of your *own* utter inability, to think even a good thought—without his Assistance[14]—This Sister is an *American* born, but her Father was from the West of England— she says: if you could assist her, to find out some of her English Friends, it would give her great Pleasure—her Father dy'd when she was an Infant, he was a *young man* when he dy'd, he had a brother about Bristol—one *Tippet* in Kingswood, dyed some years past, his Life was read here, he was a very Pious Man, and the account of his Life, was truely edifying.[15] He was a Member of our Church—and the decease of our Members throughout the world, I may say, is notified, and an account given, of their Lives—*once* you will its very like, read the account of mine, as I have requested my Friends to send it you.[16] *Sister Tippet* has a great Notion the above mention'd Brother, was one of her own Fathers *Brothers*. I am sorry our Unkle Charles daughter is so unkind— He was the only one of my Unkles, I remember—except *unkle Benajmin*, who dy'd before I left England. I can just remember seeing I think, 2 of my unkles at once, at my Mammas house, I think the one was my unkle Thomas—and the other was doubtless your dear Father. I thank you for your kind Invita- tion—was I 30 years younger, who knows what might happen—Now I have given up all Journeys, have taken leave of Philadelphia after a Stay of Eleven Weeks.[17] I am very well when I sit in my Chair, but can bear no fatigue, being very short breathd, owing to my growing fatt—But my spirits are as lively as they was at 30—and my disposition is generally Cheerful—So that my Young Girls are very fond of me.

How long I am to remain in this Vale of Tears is uncertain, very long it cannot be, and I have no Objection, the *sooner* the better. I am *ready* and *I am willing*—When we reach our happy home, it will make no odds wether we sat out from England or *America*. I could *wish* to send you my *Picture*—but its not at my disposal you know—so nothing can be done.[18] How Considerate you are my dear Cousin, in endeavouring to shield me from the Perscecu- tion—of *our*—Shall I say—worthless relations—but seriously *My* Circum- stances and Manner of Life is such—that I could no more assist them, than any other Stranger could and I *never* could encourage a friend of *mine* to come to America, to make a fortune—unless he had a purse full of money. If he comes empty handed, he must serve from 5 to 7 years for his Passage, and *Work like a Slave*—Where *one* makes a fortune, there are *ten* who with tears lament they ever left their Country. I have seen and Spoke with many poor Irish, who have been half distracted, at finding things so vastly different from the discription given them—They are generally Sick, the first year, and then comes time enough for Repentance[19]—You tell me you dont know any of our Family that were Methodist Minesters. The Person who gave me the Infor- mation, was a Surgeon of great emminence in his Profession, named John Lewis. He was long with the Famous Lowther in London. He then serv'd some years in his Profession on Board a Man of Warr, where he became a drunkard—and a man of very loose Principles. He was after this truely awakend—*Join'd* the Brethren, was sent to America to serve in his Profession, wherever it was Necessary. In Bethlehem he was Married, and Sent to *Salem*, in *North Carolina*, as *Doctor* to the Congregation there. Here he came into so much Practice in the Neighbourhood of Salem, and was so Successful in everything he undertook, that he became famous far and near—this brought him into a large Acquaintance—and prov'd his *Ruin*, he took to drinking as bad as Ever—as No admonitions whatsoever had any Effect, he was disownd, and at Length orderd to leave the Congregation. He came back to Pennsylvania—and *here* to Lititz. He had its true, intirely left off drinking, and begd most heartily for leave to stay at Lititz, as he was really concernd for his past Misdemeanors, and it was plain he had left off all strong Liquors, he obtaind forgiveness, and had a House here in the Village fitted up for him and his Wife.[20] He was very weak and Low which moved the Brethren to Compassion, thinking it a Pitty that he should be turnd away, and die among Strangers. Here he lived about 6 weeks, and in that time gave convincing proofs of his Skill—as *My Countryman* I intressd myself in his Affairs—and we have frequently sat together and wept, he at his unfaithfulness, towards our dear Saviour, and I out of Compassion—mean time I soothd and consold him all in my Power—indeed I was commissiond so to do, that the poor Strayd Sheep, might not be destitute of Friends, and there was no One, seemd so near to him, as myself—for he often said it seemd, as tho I was his Relation—He went to Bethlehem with his Wife, to visit her Parents, and dy'd there 2 or 3 days after his arrival—He never believ'd himself in a Consumption, tho it was plain to every one Else. And when I have said: Doctor your Cough distresses me, I fear you are worse than you think yourself—He would say O No I will first strive to regain my strength—and then I know how to get rid of my Cough. Mr Lewis as I observed it was, that shewd me the name of *Penry* in a list of the Methodist Minesters[21]—*Poor Mr Lewis* he might have been of great Service in his profession, but he actually shortned his Days, with the abuse of strong Liquors—When once he had fixd the resolution—*I will drink no more Spirituous Liquors* he keept his word, for he would not touch a drop of wine—and many said his leaving it of[f] so sudden, was his Death—On the 6th of September he left of[f] drinking, and about the 18th of November he dy'd. Our worthy Bishop Hebner and his Lady desire their Cordial Salutations to my Reverd unkle[22]—his Daughter and Grand Children—as does Mrs Stocker and all her Family Consisting of 4 Children—2 are Married, one a Widdow and one a Maiden. She has 2 Grand Children by her Eldest Daughter—now a Widdow, one Grand Child by her 2nd Daughter and 3 by her only Son[23]—The 2 Maidens in Philadelphia, whom I mentiond in my last Letter—Nanny and Patty Powell are of Welch decent—They are Quakers, very sweet and agreeable *women*, and much Respected in the City[24]—they have requested me to tell you, they claim Kindred with Cousin Betsy and her Brother, and desire their kind love to you. I must not forget to tell you—That in our Congregation Places, we allways close the old and enter the New Year at Church—In the first Meeting a thankful Recapitulation is made, of the Blessings receivd in this year. At half after 11 we meet again—and an Exhortation is given on the Words of the day, or last Texts in the year. As soon as the Clock points to 12—or more properly the *watches* which the Brethren carefully *watch*, the trumpets *anounce* the entrance into the New Year—The whole Congregation fall on their *Knees*, and a devout Prayer is offerd up, and most frequently accompanied with many Tears. We pray for all our Congregations and Members—on land or water—on Journeys—or wherever they are—for all our dear Friends and Relations—for the whole Church of Christ throughout the world &c. &c.—I need not tell you I am sure, how earnestly I pray for you! and how happy I am to know—*you* are Members of the Church of Christ—because you are *believers*. You will find in my Letter to my unkle, I trust a Satisfactory account of *my Brethren* and *their Church*—Should any doubts occur, after reading that, and you will let me know—I will endeavor to clear it up. I must introduce a Particular friend of mine to you of the Name of Rosmeyer. Her Maiden name was Evans—her *Fathers Family* was from Denbiegh or Denbeigh I know not how to spell it right—Her father was one of the Principal Gentlemen in Philadelphia and one time Governor of Pennsylvania—Her Relations are at Present in high Stations in the world, but herself by joining the Brethren has given up—*both Riches* and *Grandeur*. Her Spouse a worthy Minester of the Gosple of Christ, was born in the same year as my dear Unkle—and Mrs Rosmeyer is in her 71st year.[25] This worthy Couple—and a Widdow Lady my most intimate friend, are my Next Door Neighbours, and there is none I visit so frequent as these 3 Worthies—The Widdow Lady and my self, were Single Sisters together—then our Intimacy commenced—we are pretty near of an age—her name is *Siedrick*, she is a Minesters Widdow[26]—Mr Rosmeyer and his Spouse—and Mrs Siedrick—desire their *Love* to their *Friends*, worthy Unkle and Cousins—and if any of Mrs Rosmeyers Family, should come to your knowledge which she much questions—it will give her Pleasure, to hear. *N.B.* I always spend the *first of March* with them.[27] My dearest Cousin Kitty, as you not fatigued to death with my Prate—O if I had you with me—how many, many questions I woud ask you—you may in the End be glad, that the Ocean seperates us—Had the air Balloons turnd out better, we might have thought on a Visit, but they are too uncertain—I don't chuse to Venture—We'll soar by *Faith*, as *Scripture Saith*, to *Christ* in *Realms of*

Light—whilst Babels Stones, and *Air Balloons*, can never reach that Height.[28]—
I shall inclose the Texts to your Birth days, to which I have added a few Simple
Lines—as they flowd from my Pen, I am *no Poet*, that you will see—my intentions are better than my Talents—this must plead my Excuse.[29] I do assure you
my living 40 years among none but Germans—hearing—Speaking, this Language constantly has been a great detriment to my Own Language, and I am
very Sensible I make great Misstakes both in Spelling and Wording my Letters,
and the Monysylables I am very apt to *displace*, this, my dear Cousin will I am
sure move you, to pardon the faults I make in writing—for I lived not more
than *half* as long among the English, as I have done among the Germans. I have
wrote *our Niece* a long Letter, I hope she will not take my freedom amiss—Nor
you my dearest Kitty! You conferrd a great Obligation on me in your last Letter
and I can very easily *believe* what you *say*, &c. &c.

I receivd a Letter from Mrs Stocker this morning, she could not give me
any Information respecting the *Crisis* I mention'd—*They* are likewise full of
hopes—and fears—wether the Peaceable Party—or the Other Side—will
gain the Day.[30] You will Perhaps with this Letter, hear the Result—Tho I
cannot tell you. All our Prayers are for Resignation to the Divine Will, being
well assured, that *nothing* can befall us—except he *permits*—and He has
undoubted his wise Ends with everything *that he Permits*—tho we are too
short sighted, to Pennetrate them. *"But Ye my Beloved*, building up yourselves
on your most holy Faith, Praying in the Holy Ghost Keep yourselves in the
Love of God—looking for the Mercy of our Lord Jesus Christ unto Eternal
Life." Saint Jude, 20 and 21 verses.

I remain my Honnourd unkle, and dearest Cousin—Your dutiful Niece
and Sincerely Affectionate Cousin,

Mary Penry

[Enclosure][31]

Extracts from the daily words and Doctrinal Texts of the Brethren's Congregation for the Year 1796.

October the 24th. My beloved, my revered Unkle, my dearest never to be
forgotten Fathers Brother, My only Father—whose blessings are more valuable to me than Gold or Precious Stones, Thou dear Parent—Unkle—
Friend! read the words on the aneversary of your birth. Drawn by lott the
beginning of the year 1795—as is done every Year.[32]

Who is among you, that feareth the Lord, that Obeyeth the Voice of his
Servant, that walketh in darkness and hath no light? let him trust in the
Name of the Lord, and Stay upon his God. Isaiah 30, 10.

> *Antiphone.*
> One view, lord Jesus of thy Passion
> Can make our fainting Spirit glad.

Doctrinal Text
Obey them that have the rule over you & submit yourselves: for they watch
for your Souls, as they that must give account: that they may do it with Joy
and not with Grief: for that is unprofitable for you. Heb. 13, 17.

> [*Antiphone*]
> Let those who have the care of Souls by thee
> Be taught: Thus will their Labours pros'prous be.
>
> When these few lines shall reach my unkle's hand
> May *He* who all things has at *his* Command
> Convey a Blessing to his Heart, and grant
> Health Peace and Happiness. Yea every want
> both Spiritual and Temp'ral—be supplied
> And *nothing* his heart wishes—be deney'd
> Except—of his poor orphan Niece to have the sight
> Dear Unkle—we shall meet in Realms of *Light*!

17th of March 1796
Hearken unto me—O my People, and give ear unto me O my Nation: for a
Law shall proceed from me and I will make my Judgement to rest for a light
of the People. Isaiah. 51, 4.

> *Antiphone*
> Here in thy Presence we appear
> Lord Jesus Christ! thy Word to hear
> Our wandring thoughts & hearts incline
> With thirst t'imbibe thy word divine.

Doctrinal Text
How shall we escape, if we Neglect so great Salvation which at the first began
to be spoken of by the lord and was confirm'd unto us by them that heard
him. Heb, 2, 5.

Antiphone
Grant that I never may despair
Full pardon to obtain
Since Jesus Christ to save my Soul
Upon the Cross was Slain.

My Sister heart—tho with you bound
    In Consanguinity
I have a firmer surer ground
    Which binds me fast to thee
We're One in Jesus such a tye
    Can never be dissolv'd
In him we'll Live, and Constantly
    Cleave to our Souls beloved.
As Virgins *wise* with lamps supplied
    With th' Oil of his rich grace
Our Bridegroom who for us has dy'd
    Will our Weak Faith increase
O may I to the blessed Lord
    And to the *Penry's* name
be no Reproach—but Joy afford
    This is my highest aim.
Receive a tender kiss from me
    Imprinted on these Lines
My dearest Kitty Pennery
    My Spirit with *yours* Joins.

28th of August 1796.
I the Lord have declared, and have saved. Isaiah 23, 12.

Antiphone
Pay due Hommage unto Jesus
Come with thanks before his face
Praise him for his death & bleeding
There he's all our Happiness.

Doctrinal Text
Know that we were not redeem'd with Corruptible things, as Silver and
Gold, from your vain Conversations receiv'd by tradition from your Fathers,
but with the precious blood of Christ, as of a Lamb without blemish and
without spott.

Antiphone
My hearts not mine, not mine,
        Tis thine!
Thou Lamb once Slain
Thy Cross thy Pain
Thy Blood thy Toil
Have claim'd me for they Spoil.

Thou tender Flow'r just opening on the day
What can your Aunt of such importance say
As what above the Scripture texts advise
Consider them, and you'll be truly wise
My precious Love! My dearest lovely Niece!
Such tho unseen I must and shall you prize
Your Letters indicate a Strength of Mind
Which rarely to such tender years is joind
You'[v]e much receivd my Love, the more you owe
To Him—who only can such gifts bestow
Without the unction of his Grace divine
All gifts like Tinsel will a Season shine
but quickly tarnish and their Lustre loose
I trust my Betsy will be *none* of *Those*
who vainly talents to themselves ascribe
Which God and God alone to *us* confide
May you my Precious Niece increase in *grace*
And heavenly Wisdom—till you see his Face.

July the 5th 1796
The entrance of thy Words giveth Light: It giveth understanding unto the
Simple. Ps. 110, 130.

Antiphone
To learn all that, whereby we may
Adorn thy Doctrine every way

[Doctrinal Text]
We have a sure word of Prophecy—whereunto ye do well that we take heed,
as unto a light that Shineth in a dark place, untill the day dawn, and the Day
Star arises in your hearts. 2 Pet. 1, 19.

Antiphone
This leading Star, where it does apear
Revealth Christ our Saviour
Unto the lost—who firmly trust
In him alone forever.

Penry—thou dearly loved, tho unknown Friend
Penry—thy Aunt these lines to thee does send
Heed not, The Measure or the Poesy
Tho Simple—dictated by Love to thee.
Thou Tender branch of *my loved Family*
Frequent in thoughts—in Prayer—Constantly
Upon the Stage of Life you'l soon apear
What is your Part—how will you act my Dear
Will you—with Multitudes the broad way take
Forbid it Lord, for my great Mercy's sake!
O take this youth in thy peculiar care
This is my daily, and my fervent Prayer!
Look at the words above, my dear, tis spoke to you
If you the advice there given will persue
The day Star will arise within your heart
And grace and Wisdom unto you Impart—
take Jesus for your Guide from day to day
And he'll preserve you in the Narrow way
which leads to Life Eternal—There I'll meet
My *Penry Powell*—at our Saviours Feet.

ALS: Penralley Collection 1371 (Letter) and 1368 (Enclosure), NLW. Letter marked "No. 2" by Penry, who sent it together with two others marked "No. 1" and "No. 3." Letter 41 records the address and endorsement.

1. See Letter 29.
2. "it proceeds from *Grace*, to feel a *Disintressd* affection": only the workings of grace enable unworthy creatures to act disinterestedly. See Letter 2, note 2; and for this concept generally, see Gordon, "Glad Passivity."
3. See Letter 30, note 7.
4. In 1785 Martha Potts (1764–1797) married Thomas Haskins (1760–1816), a Methodist minister; the couple moved to Philadelphia in 1789. See Dupuy, "Haskins Family," 64.
5. The Methodists' Annual Conference met on October 5 in Philadelphia, during MP's visit there (September 6–November 23, 1795). Coke was not in America for this meeting. For MP and Coke, see Letter 37, note 6.

6. Morgan John Rhees (1760–1804), born in Glamorganshire, arrived in America in 1794. He married Anne Loxley. Their son, Morgan John Rhees (1802–1853), became a prominent Baptist minister. "told us the Miseries": Rhees was criticized for deluding the Welsh with false promises to entice them to immigrate to America. See Davies, "Very Different Springs," 396.

7. "settle a Tract of Land": in 1796 Rhees purchased a large amount of property, founding the village of Beulah and the township of Cambria, settling there in 1798. See Williams, *Search for Beulah Land*; and Davies, *Transatlantic Brethren*, 216–46.

8. A General Synod had met in Germany in 1789. The next General Synod was in 1801.

9. "*Mr Owen* and his dear Sisters": perhaps Evan Owen (1746–1809) and two unmarried sisters, Mary Owen (d. 1800) and Margaret Owen (1734–1806), who all lived in Brecon. See Brecon St. John's Church Register, PCA.

10. "Augustan Confession": see Letter 41, note 25.

11. MP may refer to Wesley's ordination of Thomas Coke. See Letter 37, note 6.

12. Absalom Jones (1746–1818) founded the congregation of the African Church in Philadelphia in 1792. The church became the African Episcopal Church of St. Thomas in 1794. Jones was ordained as a deacon in 1795 and, in 1804, became the first African American ordained as a priest in the Episcopal church of the United States. For Bishop William White, see Letter 41, note 29.

13. For Mary Tippet, see Letter 11, note 3.

14. "inability . . . without his Assistance": see Letter 2, note 2.

15. Samuel Tippett (1711–1786), a collier from Kingswood. For his memoir, see Dresser, "Moravians in Bristol," 121–27.

16. "an account . . . of their Lives": each Moravian composed a spiritual memoir (*Lebenslauf*), which others completed after their death and which was read at their funeral. Some memoirs were copied and circulated among the global Moravian diasporic communities. For this tradition, see Faull, *Moravian Women's Memoirs*; and McCullough, "Most Memorable Circumstances."

17. See Letter 38.

18. "my *Picture*": see Letter 35, note 4.

19. "serve from 5 to 7 years": indentured servants paid for their passage to America by contracting to labor for an employer for a fixed term of years. See Galson, *White Servitude*; and Wokeck, *Trade in Strangers*. For Irish in early America, see Miller et al., *Irish Immigrants*.

20. Lewis arrived in Lititz on October 19 and left on November 14, 1788, for Bethlehem, where he died days later (Letter 30, note 5). "Lowther": physician William Lowther, famous in London for advertising his antiepileptic powders and drops, published *A Dissertation on the Dropsy* (London, 1771).

21. "list of the Methodist Minesters": see Letter 30, note 6.

22. Johann Andreas Huebner: see Letter 19, note 1.

23. Regarding the Stockers, see Appendix C.

24. For Ann and Patty Powell, see Letter 38, note 3.

25. Maria Evans (1721–1804) married Albrecht Ludolf Russmeyer (1715–1797) in 1754. Only one of their children survived into adulthood. See Letter 46, note 18. The couple labored in Philadelphia, Lancaster, Newport, and New York before retiring to Lititz.

26. For Gertrude Peterson Sydrich, see Letter 37, note 37.

27. "*first of March*": St. David's Day, celebrating the patron saint of Wales.

28. "*Air Balloons*": in January 1793 Jean Pierre Blanchard conducted the United States' first successful manned balloon flight, a forty-five-minute trip across the Delaware River. See Trimble, *High Frontier*, 3–8. These rhymes seem to be MP's own composition.

29. "inclose the Texts . . . a few Simple Lines": printed below as an enclosure.

30. "the Crisis I mention'd": the Jay Treaty. See Letter 41, note 35.

31. The enclosure contains the watchwords for the birthdays of Meredith Penry, Katherine Penry, Eliza Powell, and Penry Powell, copied from *Daily Words and Doctrinal Texts of the Brethren's Congregation, for the Year 1796*, along with poems that MP composed for each.

32. "by lott": Moravians submitted important decisions to the lot. After posing a question, authorities drew slips of paper—one read "yes," one read "no," a third was blank (meaning "wait")—from a lot box. Moravians were confident that the result, far from random, revealed the will of Christ, whom they considered the Chief Elder of the church. See Sommer, "Gambling with God."

ॐ 43. TO ELIZA POWELL[1]
May 1, 1796
Lititz, Pennsylvania

Lititz May the first 1796

My Precious Niece!

How concern'd I was to read of your Disappointments—when the Post Boy call'd, I accused myself of indolence—and that was a Crime—because Such Friends, such dear Friends, ask but a Letter, and ungrateful you to refuse them—you see my dear I plead Guilty, and trust you will most genourously forgive me—and remember, your Aunt is about 60 years of age, that she grows insipid, and sensible of this—is loath to take up the Pen, as she can *never* please herself in *any thing* she writes—but my love, I know your affection—if I may judge by my own feelings, is so tender, you do not mind hand, nor Stile, if it does but come from *me*. I have wrote your dear Grand Papa a Letter apart—and I think have not forgot any thing he expressd a wish to hear. How flattering my dear, is your Grand Papa's saying: he believes me to be a true *Penry*—That I glory in being both a *Penry* and a *Briton*, is certain—a descendant of those brave men, you speak of, do my Love, from time to time, give me some further Information, of my Grand Papa and Mama, for I never heard much of either—Except—their—Misfortunes. I was much pleasd with your little affair of Mr Jenkins. It puts me in Mind of a trick, Mr Stocker plaid his Mamma and me, when I was on a Visit to them. He comes in one day, with care on his Brow—Whats the matter my dear says his Mamma, O Mamma, I saw 2 of your Country Folks in great distress. I wish Cousin Penry, and you would go along with me—Yes to be sure my Son, we'll go, come Cousin, quickly take your hat—and let us be gone. Clemmy Stocker the Rogue, brought us into a street, w[h]ere a Cellar was dug—and shewd us 2 *goats* that had fallen into it,[2] O I could box your Ears, said his Mamma, how could you bring your Cousin and me, here out of Nonsense; he laughd, heartily—neither could *we* refrain. I think my unkles story is worth ten of mine, yet I would tell you that *Jokes* are put on the Welsh in America— yet the Irish, usually was more laughd at, till of late Years, so Many has come to America, and many of them persons of Property, they begin to be more respected. You would be much Surprized, was you to walk the Streets of Philadelphia, to see the Number of Foreigners. Since the Negroes rose, at the French West India Islands, numbers of the Planters came to America, I may say all sorts, Jews and Gentiles, a great many of the so calld People of *Colour*, that is, Molattoes, children of a white Father, and black Mother, You may meet them every where, with Handkerchiefs tyed round the crown of their

Heads, and the ends hanging down behind, large Gold Earrings—rings on their fingers, and dressd mostly in white Muslin.[3] Many, very many of these Islanders—white People, who had thousands—was reduced to live upon Charity. Very many French Familys of note live in Philadelphia—and as you pass the Streets, you scarce hear any other Language but French. They have 2 Chapples, the one lately built, and very Handsome they say—but I never saw the Inside of it.[4] The Universalists have built a large Meeting House, the Famous Mr Winchester who is a baptist and universalist, is their great Apostle—He returnd from England while I was in the City—I went frequently to hear him, He is indeed a fine man, preaches Christ, and him crucified, he has a fine Voice and delivery. I went to see him at his House—he has wrote an answer to *Pains* Age of Reason, which is much admired by all Sincere Christians, but I believe this Zealous Apostles Warrfare, is accomplish'd, and he will soon enter the Joy of his Lord.[5] In the same Pulpit—from whence good Mr Winchester preachd so many Evangelical Sermons—*Priestly* now promulgates his *Deistical notions*.[6] Last Sunday I receivd a Letter from our Minester in Philadelphia,[7] in which among other things he says: "That Priestly Preaches in the Meeting House where Mr Winchester used to exhort, is true enough: and that every Sunday, I hear likewise he has a crouded Auditory. Curiosity has not prompted me, as it has many others, to make one step towards the Place. I am quite contented & thankful, that I find all things I need in my bleeding Saviour, in whom all knowledge & truth is centerd, but that poor Man knowing not Christ himself, nor having felt that Power of His Salvation in his *own* Soul, seeks to lead the Souls of Men to the knowledge of a God, through the Labyrinths of human wisdom and Philosophy. Sure I am neither our Saviour nor His Apostles, had any Occasion in their Sermons to produce such Men as the Heathen Phylosophers—and a *Voltaire*, to prove the Truths they taught. How can the blind lead the blind says *our Redeemer*, will they not both fall into the Ditch,[8] and I find it more and more so in these times. The poor souls who are missled—are to be pitied—I fear they are not a *few*."

I hope my dear Niece—Your Sentiments coincides with this good Brothers!—It is so dark I can hardly see—must pause a little. They have a large Theatre in the City, where Plays are acted once a week, throughout the winter they have a Circus or Amphitheatre, where all manner of tricks are play'd in Horsemanship—they have Fire works, Balls Assemblys—Rope dancing, Concerts Vocal and Instrumental, in short I believe, there is full as much Variety and Extravagance as in the City of London.[9]—And infidellity increases, to the great Concern of all Pious Christians. But let Satan and his Emissaries try all their Strength—Thy Realm Oh Crucified

Redeemer, will last forever—Yes Our Mesiah Reigns in the hearts of *all* His faithful Subjects.

It was a real satisfaction to me, to hear the poor in England receive some Mitigation of their Distress, in the *Donations* of those in Affluence, it is a trait of the English Carector, which even they'r Enemies are forced to acknowledge. The increasing dearness of Provisions with us—unless we shortly have Peace in Europe, will reduce us to the same straits I fear—and we have little prospect of *such* assistance—Our grain has been much injured by the drought, and tho we had a fine Rain the day before yesterday, the cold has increased with the Rain, and we fear the frost has been very hurtful, our Peaches are frozen, (that is the tender Bud) even the hardy Currants in our garden, are froze, Cherries and Apples we fear are in the same State—Such is frequently the Case with us—after a fine growing Season—in *one* night the frost destroys our most Sanguine hopes—The last week we had windows and Doors open, and the heat was really burthensome, to day and yesterday, we have a large Fire, and shiver with Cold when we step out of Doors. Yet we will put our Trust in the Lord, he is our help and our Comfort forever. You will transcribe the lines, I wrote my dear Penry, unless you wish to take yours & your Brothers off from your Grand Papa's and Aunts and send them to him—but, do as you please, my Love. Since writing the above I have just look'd over the *news Papers*—war, war seems the only thing now thought of—Should we be brought into it. Then our Corrispondence will be very precarious—We will hope the best—but as I wrote your Grand Papa, we are in a very Critical Situation—the depredations of the English—on the American Merchant Men, causes heart burnings—and at present we have a Struggle[10]—All honest well meaning men, wish to have Peace preserv'd, whether they will succeed or not, a very Short time will discover. I am pleas'd to see the Church of England Clergy, are thoughtful of the poor Heathen. *Our Brethren* have, and still do, intrest themselves in that Laudible work. We have many florishing Congregations in the English and Danish West India Islands—of poor Blacks—and in Greenland, and North America of Indians.[11] I am sure it will aford you great Satisfaction, to read the History of the Brethren's Church (as I observed before) wrote by *David Cranz*—as well as the *Idea Fidie Fratrum*—Miss Nancy Vaughn, will assuredly lend them to you, if you apply to her in my name—give my love to her—and tell her, I long to hear from her, and her dear Family of Single Sisters, and when I have the Pleasure to hear from her—I will give her an account of Mine, and my Sisters Wellfare.[12] You tell me your dear Grand Papa—often meditates on *me*— from Meditations arise *Prayers*—what a Consolation! Could I now and then, join your Rambles—I fear we should not bring home many Nutts! we should have too much to talk of. You have with propriety, introduced a Lecture on those fine Texts of Scripture I sent you. You have given me a Clue, which I can I think unravel, you believe the *Millennium*—I not only believe it, but think it is at no great *Distance*. Wether I shall be in the Body, when it commences I know not—20 years sooner, or later makes a great Matter at my age—You my dear Niece, may very possible see it in this your Mortal State, You may see our Lord coming in the Clouds—and either be instantly chang'd—or live some years in His *Kingdom* of Peace. The Learn'd Bishop *Newton*, and a German Divine of great Eminence *Bengel* are of oppinion, the years 1836—or 38 will be the happy Period. Others again think the year 1800 is the time—Our blessed Lord tells us, to *Watch* and *Pray*, and to be constantly ready, because we know not *when* he will come. Abundance of Phrophesies have apeard within these few Years[13]—but among them all *three* only have any weight with *me*—that is, its true, not that *these* have propheceyd themselves—they have only attempted to Explain the Propheceys, containd in the Word of God—The German Divine *Bengel* wrote his Dissertation on the Revelations, about the year 1750—Newton later—and the still living Mr *Winchester* about the years 86 and 90.[14]—I forget the dates—it was however wrote in London, from whence he returnd in fall of last year when I was in the City—As for *Brothers*—I will neither plead *for*—nor *against him* but I leave *him* wholly to the Lord![15] *Universalism* gains ground most rapidly—are you a Universalist my *Love*? Shall I say some traits in you[r] last page, seem'd to hint something of the kind—now my dear I will candidly *own*, that *Doctrine* is most pleasing—But at the same time I do not find freedom, to indulge myself in it.[16] I have been told, that if I heartily believed this Doctrine—my love to Jesus, would be more *Intense*—I do not think this Faith would do it—you ask why?—I'll tell you my dear: Can it be possible for the *Soul*, who has receivd Pardon and forgiveness of Sins in the *Blood* of *Jesus*— who is firmly persuaded, He has taken her into His Protection—who has assured her, of a never failing Interest in him—Who has given her, to know that He sufferd Death, yea even Death on the Cross to save *My* poor Soul—Can I love Him with *greater* fervor if I likewise believe—the most wicked of Mankind, have the same—how shall I word it—*Right & Priveledge all mankind have*—that is certain—Iff they will accept it—but shall *their* non-acceptance—render them as happy as *my* acceptance—It *may* be so— but if it be so—will it Increase my Love and Gratitude, I do not see that it will—and if *this Doctrine* be no furtherence to my Increase in true Godliness, why should I struggle for Faith in it—I wish, and hope with my whole Soul—the *Salvation* of all mankind—but I dare go no further. It is no fundamental Article of *Saving* Faith, so I do not feel concernd at having Scruples of

Conscience on that head. The Maker justly claims that World He made—In this the right of Providence in law. "Our Actions uses, nor Controuls our Will—and bids the doubting Sons of Men be Still—what Strange Events can Strike with more Surprize—Than such, as *often meet our wandering Eyes*, Then taught by these—Confess the Allmighty just, and where you can't *unriddle—learn to trust*."[17] Again, I have frequently Sigh'd, that just in this Libertine Age—this Doctrine is so much promulgated, as well in the Pulpit, as with the Pen—As I observed above, I hope, I wish, I pray—*Lord*—if it be according to thy *will*, have *Mercy on all Men*—Amen so be it! I will conclude this Subject, with a Verse of a fine Hymn of *Doctor Luthers*. I do believe if Sinners race, ten thousand times more numerous was, Yet still the Devil has his full—Tis without *Right*, he keeps *one Soul!*[18]

And now my dear—I have next to consider, your fourth Page at Large— You have drawn me Out, my Love into I fear for you, tiresome length—but you must blame yourself for so doing. Again I must tell you, your Doctrine is most agreeable, but is among the Mysteries, we cannot properly find out. As to the *Knowing* of each Other—I have not a doubt but we shall.[19] The first, and Great Object is our *Saviour*, him we shall undoubtedly *know* by the *marks* of those *glorious Wounds*, which procur'd our *Salvation*. I believe we shall distinguish the *Apostles* and *Prophets* of the Lord and *our Primitive Parents, Adam and Eve*, together with *all* those Faithful Servants of the Lord, for whom we had a Veneration here upon Earth—But my dear *Love!* flattering as the Hopes are of *seeing* (to *know*) *you* and *my dear Family* not to go any further at present, I say flattering as these Hopes are—I quickly *loose* them. Pardon me my dear, if I say—grand as your Ideas of Love are Exprest, my Misfortune is: *Mine* are too great, to allow your Modification. *God is Love* from Him, all *Love* proceed—and in *Him* must & will, assuredly *center!* In and thro Him, every Object must *solely*—*be loved*—All His *creatures*, or if you Will—*all Creatures*—will be loved—(remember my dear) *for His Sake*— not for *theirs*, for there is no *Merit* in *the Creature*—everything which renders *us lovely*, is his pure free gift alone[20]—In Heaven is nothing but perfection. In a *State of Perfection* I immagine, one blessed Soul, will be as dear to us as the other—There will be one *grand Family*, every *Member* of which, will Love each other as Children of one Father—and this *Love*, will be perfect. The fond Attachments to friends, and Relations in this Life—will there be general—at least I think so. Here, we judge of Persons and things, very imperfect. There, our Ideas will be just—and we shall undoubtedly be quite satisfied, with our dear Saviours dispensations—tho We here, cannot always understand them. As to Retaining the Remembrance of *Past things*—I know not if this, will be an Addition to our Happiness or Not, our Lord himself is the best Judge. Let us my dear for once suppose—our Peculiar Regard to our Relations—continued *after* this Life—How must then a Parent feel, on seeing a Child—Perhaps an only Child—at our Lords Left Hand! must we not *supose*, it would grieve them? Whereas according to my Opinion, the blessed may, and undoubtedly will feel Compassion—but Sorrow & tears will be done *away*—And if the part we take, in each others Wellfare here—accompany us to the Other World—I do not see why, one Sensation may be suposed, without giving room to *Suppose* the other. Here our fond Attachments, supose a *Merit* in the beloved object, wether Relation or Friend, which we do not find in a Stranger—There, we shall see all the blessed, with a Single Eye, without giving a preference to *Relationship*—So that I apprehend, we shall not feel any Material difference, in our Sensations at the Sight of Parents—than at the sight, of any others of the blessed—This being as I said above no fundamental Article of Faith (as I observed of Universalism) I must leave it. Your System my Love is most delightful to think off—to wish, and to hope for, and I most sincerely do both—Wish and hope—Let us then please ourselves, with this—if Fancy—most agreeable Fancy—It is certainly no Crime—and I very frequently say: after I have seen, and thank'd my *Saviour*—I will look about, for my dear Parents, and my other Connections and Friends. As for Enemies I have none, to my Knowledge, in my humble Sphere, I am not of Consequence enough, to have any. Next I am fond of seeing the Beloved St. John and St. Paul &c. &c. Nor do I in the Least Doubt, my seeing and *knowing*—but alas, not according to my shall I say: benighted Selfish Ideas. You will find I am far from thinking, *Love* will be extinguish'd in the *grave*; No so far from it, I say: *Love* is stronger than *Death*. *Love* and his Sister fair the *Soul*, twin born from Heaven together came—*Love* shall the *universe* controul, when dying Seasons loose their *name*, *Divine abodes* shall own his *Power*, when *Time* and *Death* shall be *no more*.[21] O may *we* learn to Prize, the *Love* of our adored Redeemer! To shame our sins, he blushed in *Blood*, He closed His eyes to show us *God*! Let all the World adore and know, that none but *God*—*Such Love* could shew![22] Undoubtedly We shall in a blest Eternity, have leisure and oppertunity, to see into his *Wisdom* and *Power* which we here are *assured* is *Over all His works*—but during our Pilgrimage in this Vale of Tears, our Calling is to follow Him in *Humility*. Let us not Soar too high, lest we melt our Waxen Wings[23]—We *can* be carried away, by a brilliant *Fancy*, and by looking at the *Glories* loose sight of the *cross*—The great Apostle Paul says: he counted *all* things as Dross, for the Excellency of the Knowledge of Jesus Christ, and adds: "that I may know Him, and the Power of his Resurrection, and the Fellowship of His Suffrings, being made comformable unto *His Death*."[24] See my dear Niece, what Saint Pauls words import, we are to have the Suffering, dying Form, of our Redeemer constantly in View. Which as the Archbishop of Cambray says, is a *Deaths Head*—to our Sinful Affections.[25] *The Glories of God* the Creator of Heaven and Earth is surely not *difficult* to believe—But his *Humiliation*, to have Faith in the God Man—bleeding, dying for mine, and the Whole Worlds Sin—O Stupendious *Love!* here we may say: *Is it possible!* O my Precious *Niece*—this, this, is the *one thing* needful—and I really believe, the great Mystery of Redemption, will be *more* our study in eternity—than the *fiat*—with which, a thousand worlds, could be as easily form'd as *that* was which *we* inhabit. I think I have sufficiently tryd your Patience, I trust my love you will take my freedom not amiss—and let me hear in your next, wether this Doctrine, is agreeable to your Conceptions. I am much pleas'd with your Pertinent Observations— and hope to be favoured, with every *Harmless* flight, of your *Luxuriant* Fancy. You give me in a Mirror, the Portrait of my Self, at your age—and I could not help smiling, at the *Likeness.* Now my *Love* it is time to draw to a Conclusion, Forget not to assure your dear Brother, that he is *Very* dear to me, tell him, to wait on the *Minester* of the Church in Fetter Lane—(The Brethrens Church commonly calld the *Moravian*) give my Respectful Love to *him*—Let Penry tell him, where I live, and give him good advice. If he delivers *this* Message, he will most certainly *gain* a good Friend! His name is *Latrobe.*[26]

My addopted *Niece*, Sister Anna Rosel *Kliest,* I shall send your kind Salutation to—you may depend on her affectionate regards![27] My young Companions request me to present their *Love*, with best wishes for your Spirtual, and Temporal *Wellfare.* W[ere] it Possible we would make you *Wellcome* indeed! Mean while, we shall often speake of—and Pray for you. And on your Birth day, you may represent a Company, of Chosen friends, met together in *Love*, to celebrate Eliza Powells Birth day at a Dish of Tea. Farewell, my Love! May—"The Peace of God which passeth all understanding keep your heart and Mind, in the Knowledge and Love of God—our Saviour Jesus Christ." "And I pray God that your Whole Spirit, Soul and Body, be preserved *blameless* unto the coming of our Lord Jesus Christ!"[28] Amen, Amen!

Ever your Affectionate and *Faithful Aunt,*

Mary Penry

ALS: Penralley Collection 1372, NLW. Marked "No. 3" by Penry, who sent this letter together with two others marked "No. 1" and "No. 2." Letter 41 records the address and endorsement.

1. See Letter 29.
2. *"goats"*: along with druids and harps, mountain goats symbolized Wales in the eighteenth century.

3. The slave revolt in the French colony of Saint-Domingue (Haiti) began in 1791. By 1804, former slaves had founded the Haitian republic.

4. "two Chapples": the first Roman Catholic chapel opened in Philadelphia was St. Joseph's (1733), which many French fleeing Haiti in 1790 joined. The second was St. Mary's (1763), where the first parish school connected to a Catholic church in America was opened in 1782.

5. Elhanan Winchester (1751–1797), born in Brookline, Massachusetts, was the most successful eighteenth-century American Universalist evangelist. A Universalist believes that all individuals will ultimately gain salvation, a topic that MP discussed at length with Eliza Powell and Benjamin Rush (see below and Letter 67). Winchester responded to Thomas Paine's *Age of Reason* (London, 1794) with *Ten Letters Addressed to Mr. Paine* (Boston, 1794). Winchester returned to Philadelphia in August or September 1795; MP was in the city from September 6 to November 23.

6. Joseph Priestley (1733–1804) immigrated to America in 1794 and in 1796 preached in Philadelphia the sermons published as *Discourses Relating to the Evidences of Revealed Religion, Delivering in the Church of the Universalists, at Philadelphia* (Philadelphia, 1796). Many viewed Priestley's Unitarianism as deism or irreligion, but Priestley himself insisted on his piety. See Schofield, *Enlightened Joseph Priestley*, 317–43; and Durey, *Transatlantic Radicals*.

7. "our Minester in Philadelphia": John Meder (1740–1816), the minister in Philadelphia from 1785 to 1799. Before leaving in February 1773 for mission work in Antigua, he served as a tutor at the Fulneck school. In Barbados in 1777 he married Anna Christina Angermann (1741–1804), whose missionary husband had died. Meder later served in New York (1799–1802) and became head of Lititz's girl's school (1802–5). See Jordan, "Biographical Sketch of the Rev. John Meder."

8. Matthew 15:14.

9. "large Theater": in February 1794 Philadelphia's first theater, the "New Theatre" (or Chestnut St. Theater) opened, seating 1,165 patrons. "Amphitheatre": in April 1793 John Bill Ricketts built a large amphitheater in which he performed equestrian shows. He later added a tightrope walker, a juggling acrobat, clowns, singers, and dancers. The venue's success led him to build an amphitheater in New York.

10. "depredations . . . on the American Merchant Men": see Letter 41, note 35.

11. The Moravian church had established missions in the English colony of Jamaica (1754), the Danish West Indies (1732), and Greenland (1733). The Moravian missions in Ohio (Gnadenhütten, Schoenbrunn, and Lichtenau) had been abandoned or destroyed in the 1780s, and the Moravian Indians, after locating in Sandusky, Pilgerruh, and Petquotting, had settled in 1792 at Fairfield, Ontario. A mission on the White River in Indiana began in 1799 (see Letter 59, note 2) and another to the Cherokees in 1805 (see Letter 32, note 1).

12. For these volumes, see Letter 41, note 28; for Anne (Nancy) Vaughn, see Letter 6, note 6.

13. "Abundance of Phrophesies": see Bloch, *Visionary Republic*; and Juster, *Doomsayers*.

14. Johann Albrecht Bengel (1687–1752) published *An Extract of Bengelius's Explanation of the Revelation* (London, 1756); Thomas Newton (1704–1782) published *Dissertations on the Prophecies: Which Have Remarkably Been Fulfilled, and at This Time Are Fulfilling in the World* (London, 1754); and Elhanan Winchester published *A Course of Lectures, on the Prophecies That Remain to Be Fulfilled*, 4 vols. (London, 1789).

15. "Brothers": Richard Brothers (1757–1824), whose writings led to his arrest for treason in 1795, published many prophetic volumes, including *A Revealed Knowledge of the Prophecies and Times. Book the First. Wrote Under the Direction of the Lord God* (London, 1794), a continuation titled *A Revealed Knowledge of the Prophecies and Times . . . Book the Second* (London, 1794), and *Wonderful Prophecies. Being a Dissertation on the Existence, Nature, and Extent of the Prophetic Powers in the Human Mind* (London, 1795).

16. "*Universalism* gains ground": see above, note 5.

17. MP quotes from Thomas Parnell's "The Hermit": see Letter 37, note 15.

18. "I do believe . . . *one Soul*": *Collection of Hymns* (1743), 203. See also Gambold, *Collection of Hymns*, 2:22.

19. "As to the *Knowing* of each Other": see Letter 3, note 5.

20. "everything which renders *us lovely*, is his pure free gift alone": see Letter 2, note 2, and this volume's introduction.

21. *"Love* and his Sister ... *Time* and *Death* shall be *no more"*: a song by Barton Booth (1681–1733), printed in Ramsay, *Tea-Table Miscellany*, 3:218.

22. "To shame our sins ... *Such Love* could shew": Gambold, *Collection of Hymns*, 1:134.

23. "Waxen Wings": the phrase, referring to Icarus, appeared in poems by Alexander Pope and Edward Young, but MP seems not to be quoting from any previous work.

24. Philippians 3:10.

25. "Archbishop of Cambray": François Fénelon (1651–1715).

26. Christian Ignatius Latrobe (1758–1836)—brother of architect Benjamin Henry Latrobe (1764–1820) and son of Reverend Benjamin Latrobe (1728–1786) and Anna Margaretta Antes Latrobe (1728–1794)—was the minister at the Fetter Lane congregation in London. "your dear Brother": Penry Powell. See Letter 29.

27. "Anna Rosel *Kliest"*: see Letter 37, note 33.

28. Philippians 4:7; 1 Thessalonians 5:23.

⤷ 44. TO ELIZABETH DRINKER[1]

August 5, 1796

Lititz, Pennsylvania

Lititz August the 5th 1796

My dear Friend!

Is it not strange, that yours of June 20th 29th should require near 6 weeks to travel between 60 and 70 Miles, but this was the Case, I assure you, it did not come to my hands till the Evening of August 2nd. It receiv'd no Injury during the long Journey, only the flies had pretty much disobliged it—a proof this, that it had rested quietly some time in total forgetfulness—be that as it may, it was truely Wellcome—and I hasten to thank my friend, for this precious testimony of her Friendship. When you reflect—that altho you had wrote, still I had receiv'd no Benifit from it, at the time I sent a few lines inclos'd to Mrs Stocker. Your goodness will pardon (shall I say) intruding upon you with a New Acquaintance—Yet I trust, you will find on trial one worthy of your Esteem, tho more to *outward* apearence a Woman of the World than yourself and Friends—I have said to *outward* apearence—for indeed she far more prefers Godly Company and Conversation; to that, which her Situation and Connections oblige her to keep. And I am certain it is her wish, tho not in her power to be more retired—Her Sister Philips is really a good woman—and they spend many happy hours together.[2] Her sprightly Temper may divert you, and should you both incline to be serious I think you can find Subjects enough for Mutual Edifieation—besides you are both at your Liberty to keep a formal distance—or become Sociable—so much for *that*.

My dear Friend! most readily do I acquit you. I can easily believe writing must be disagreeable to you—And Yet—I am *very* selfish, I really mourn when I have long, very long sometimes, not heard from you! Indeed I am far from the writer I once was, Old Age brings its Infirmities—I feel it—again— I am not my own Mistress in many Respects—Tho it be a very Contracted Sphere, in which I move, Still I have this, and the other little affair to trans- act—and then—my Circumstances—require—Industry. So that taking it alltogether—Writing is a task—yet this being the only Method of Convers- ing with absent Friends—It is renderd most pleasing! Nevertheless I will own to you, that when the talk is wholly on my side, I grow weary of it—when you Receive no Answer in Conversation, the talkative Person must be very insipid! and in Letter writing, *me* that have so few Novelties—that go on in one stated Path—cannot afford much Entertainment, unless Subjects are started which give Scope for animadversions—*Yours* have put it in my Power to *write* in *answer*, or to persue the given Theme—as you shall see directly.

I am thankful with *you*, that you are not *worse*, but I most sincerely wish you were *Better*—I commend your resolution of continuing the prescrib'd Remedies, and am in hopes you will in *Time*—experience the Salutary Effects—for a *work of time* it will be! The Doctor and his Wife desire their kind Love to you—and beseech you not to be discouraged. I have been much pleased with the Perusal of the 5 first Pamphlets of Lectures, which are to form the first Vollume, and which I intend to have bound, but what Course shall I take to obtain the Rest?[3] I have wrote repeatedly to your Neighbour Ritter, and have wrote about 5 weeks agon, to the author, but cannot obtain an Answer.[4] It this Moment comes in my Mind, that (for the first time in my life) I dream'd last Night he was dead, and I saw his Wife and her Mother in great distress. I believe I mention'd to you that those 2 persons seem'd no way suit- able to such a Man—Their Apearence was not very good & their Charectors according to hearsay—very Indifferent. I wish you would enquire wether the Other 2 Vollumes are to be had or Not—that is *occasionally* with my Nephew William's assistance. By the by—you Never mentiond him—nor Molly—nor Aunt Mary—remember them next time.[5] It is indeed a great satisfaction to hear from my Friends in *Poor England*, against whom every Political tongue is sharpen'd. To my Sorrow I see the publick Papers full of the most bitter Invec- tives! The Censor I have read with much Pleasure, as likewise the *latter* part of the Bloody Bouy by the same Author—The first part is too horrid![6] I have a *Welch Niece*—that is my Uncles granddaughter, who writes well, both for hand and Stile, she is near 21, a Girl of good Sense, but she *Soars* above the Starrs—and endeavours to convince *herself* and *Me*—that in the life to come, we shall know and be known to each other—This I do not deny. Yet am not so Sanguine as she is.[7] I imagine when "there is neither Marrying nor giving in Marriage" our Knowledge of each Other will give no Satisfaction to our Connections in this Mortal State or in Other Words: As Children of one Father, we shall love with a Perfect, and *Not* according to the ties of Relationship, imperfect and Straightned *Love*.[8] She seems to have a very Serious turn of Mind, and searches more into heavenly, than Earthly Mysteries. It makes me Smile when I read her Flights, because I see myself—at her age—Still with a Sigh I must Confess—My Searches & Researches, were not so *divine* as hers seem to be. Your Words "We feel in many Respects, as we did, before the Treaty was confirm'd" left a Melancholly impression on my Mind![9] I have been told, that the French Principles of Infidelity gains ground in your City, and that the Church Members were the *most remiss* in attendance on the *worship* of God. I heard this at Lancaster, where I spent a few days lately, at a Friends house—*My* dear Friend, and *your* Friend tho not a *Member* of the Meeting—yet a constant attendant at Friends Meeting—whose friendly *Doors*, are ever open to entertain your Minesters, and whose life & Conversation together with her Husband, is an Honour to your *Society*—this is *Polly Roberts* the Wife of John *Roberts* the Hatter at Lancaster.[10] He will be the Bearer of this, to Nanny Powell who will send it to you!

My Mind was in some Measure agitated, concerning the Treaty and I felt truely thankful that it was confirm'd. Still I have learnd so much in the School of the Holy Spirit, to be still and wait on the Lord since I am assured *Nothing* can befall us without his permission! O might it please him to grant *Peace* to poor bleeding *Europe*, and continue the injoyment of it to us! Altho we certainly have no Merit to intittle us to this Great Blessing!—being I immagine taking all together, not better than those who have, and Still Suffer, all the Distresses of *Warr* and Bloodsheding—

As to what I wrote concerning *Doctor Rush* I have intirely forgot what it was, but I have not forgot to *Love* and *Respect* him and to remember him in my Prayers. When you have an Oppertunity be pleased to present my *love* for it is no *compliment* to him.[11] How kind you are to surpress the triffling Pleasure your Babys receiv'd—in order to keep me from renewing the same at a future day. Pidling it is, as you say, but Nicity is out of the Question. Could I get a Parcell of little Dolls or only Wax faces, I could dress them with more ease to myself, and they would look like something. Nanny and Patty Powell supply me with the most of the Materials for the dress—which are not intirely work'd up.[12] Could I procure Silk Patches, I would make up a parcel of little Pincushions—but having nothing but black and White which must be work'd, to look like any thing—it is too troublesome and takes up too much time. Enough of this Nonsense.

Permit me, with my usual Frankness to ask you: Is it necessary for two such Old Women as you and I, to study the Arangement of our Sentiments in our Free intercourse with each other, provided we write to be understood which I trust we both do? Want of Capacity you *cannot* plead, Neither can you have—I think—any temptation to shine in *orratory* to *me*—so that Pride must be out of the Question—Neither can I see that you are out off the Practice of—if not Epistolatory Corrispondance—Yet you *can* write when you please. I'll tell you what you *can* plead and sorry I am that you *can*. Your own feelings will inform you what that is—which I well know, and *Compasionate*.

Your Quotation, be the author who ever he will prove, he is a very good Moralist or was—for he is undoubtedly at rest in, it is to be hop'd the Kingdom of Peace—In return for your Quotation I will transcribe the Antiphone to the text for the 22nd of August—this year. The text is: They (the Disciples going to Emaus) constrain'd him, saying abide with us, for it is towards Evening. Luke 24, 29. The Antiphone: No farther go to Night but stay—Dear Saviour till the break of Day, Turn in my Lord with me—And in the Morning when I wake—Me under thy protection take—Thus *Day* and *Night* I spend with *Thee*.[13]

This is a fine Ejaculation for every day of our Life—Happy those who ask and obtain such protection against all Outward—and still *more* hurtfull *Indwelling* Enemies. My Love to your other *self*—to your Children Grand Children and Sister Mary—

Your ever faithful

Whilst

Mary Penry

ALS: Linden Hall Archives. Addressed "Mrs | Elizabeth Drinker | Philadelphia | to the care of | Miss Patty Powell." Endorsed "Lititz August 5 1795 | Mary Penry."

1. See Letter 18.

2. "Mrs Stocker": Margaret Stocker. "Her Sister Philips": Rebecca Pyewell Phillips, wife of Margaret Stocker's brother. See Appendix C.

3. "Doctor and his Wife": probably Benjamin Rush and Julia Stockton Rush (1759–1848), given that MP begins by remarking on Drinker's health and sends the doctor's greetings and asks Drinker to do the same. Rush had published three volumes of his *Medical Inquiries and Observations* (1789–94) and a fourth was about to appear. See Rush, *Letters*, 2:780. However, elsewhere MP calls Rush's mother-in-law, Annis Boudinot Stockton, her "dear Friend" (Letter 61), so MP's disparaging remarks about the doctor's wife and mother-in-law may suggest that MP refers instead to Elhanan Winchester, who had published his *Lectures* (Letter 43, note 5). MP described Winchester as "unequally *yoked*" to his wife (Letter 48), and his poor health (he died the following year) could explain MP's dream.

4. "Neighbour Ritter": see Letter 40, note 4.

5. For Drinker's children, William and Mary, and her sister ("Aunt Mary"), see Appendix C.

6. MP bemoans that the public papers criticize Great Britain, and she praises *The Censor* for its pro-British politics. William Cobbett (1763–1835), a British political writer, lived in America from

1792 to 1800 and used his publications to advocate for the Federalist, pro-British cause. His *Censor* ran from March 1796 to March 1797, after which it transformed into the daily *Porcupine's Gazette* until 1800. For Cobbett's conflict with MP's friend Benjamin Rush, see Letter 49, note 11. The second half of Cobbett's 1796 *Bloody Bouy* "trac[es] all the horrors of the French Revolution to their real causes, the licentious Politics and infidel Philosophy of the present Age" (126).

7. "in the life to come, we shall know and be known to each other": see Letter 3, note 5.
8. Matthew 22:30.
9. "the Treaty was confirm'd": Jay Treaty. See Letter 41, note 35.
10. The Robertses lived on Orange Street; see Letter 17, note 1.
11. "*Doctor Rush*": Benjamin Rush. See Letter 27.
12. For Ann and Patty Powell, see Letter 38, note 3.
13. "They . . . with *Thee*": from *Daily Words and Doctrinal Texts of the Brethren's Congregation, for the Year 1796*. For Moravian watchwords, see Letter 25, note 5. August 22 was Elizabeth Drinker's birthday.

෨෨ 45. TO MEREDITH PENRY, KATHERINE PENRY, AND ELIZA POWELL[1]
October 2, 1796
Lititz, Pennsylvania

Lititz October the 2nd 1796

Honourd Uncle dearly Beloved Cousin & Niece!

This time, you will take it not amiss, that I adress myself to my beloved *three in one* Letter.[2] The last time I wrote to each of you a Seperate Sheet, and trust you will say I fully made up the difficiency of my former Lines, the shortness of which you complain off. Your last of February this Year, was wrote as much under a restraint, as the incertainty of Corrispondance in these troublesome times, renders rather Necessary. I repeated to you more than one that a *crisis* was depending—I could not, or Rather chose not, to say what that Crisis was, which is now long—and I will hope fortunately over, it was the Treaty between Great Brittain and America, which you will see in the publick Prints caused Violent Struggles. Our Worthy *President* has verified our fears—and actually *resigned* to the Sorrow of all those, who sincerely love their Country![3] It is not for me, to make out the Conscequencies of this resignation. We must submit to what our dear Lord or *apoints* or *Suffers*; putting our trust in him, who is our best Refuge in time of trouble.

I have delay'd writing some time, in hopes I should have it in my Power to satisfy you, that I had endeavourd, according to your repeated desire, to commence an acquaintance with the Reverend *Doctor Cooke*—hitherto I have not had in my power as he was not near enough, for me to Salute him with a letter, without some trouble, and perhaps expence to him: I have this day wrote to him, as he is expected in Philadelphia this month to the Synod there to be held.[4] Should he come time enough to dispatch this Letter, I shall send it to his care—and open—which may perhaps induce him to send you a Salutation under his own hand.

I am, I may say in daily expectation of a Letter from you. How anxiously have I wish'd my packet has reach'd your dear Hands. The Lock of my Hair had been sometime before prepared to work some little trifle for you—but as more of the same my head can furnish at any time, I hastily inclosed it, wishing most heartily it might arrive safe. I hope my dearest Uncle will be satisfied with the account I gave him, of that Church of which I am thro divine Grace a happy Member![5] I have counted the weeks I expected my Letters would be on the road—and throughout the month of July, scar[c]e a day pass'd; that my spirit did not anticipate the reception of them. I now dream very frequently, that I am with you—and then my first Object is my dear uncle, I look after him, and throw myself into his Paternal Embraces. Still dear Kitty you must not think that this tender attachment is any Injury to my Peace of Mind. Neither can I believe it is criminal to indulge myself in tender Intercourse, with dear & *Pious Friends*. I am sure if it is a crime, my dear Eliza will be very ready to Absolve me. This Fall Miss Ann Powell from Philadelphia was to see me—she desires her best Love to her dear Cousin Elisa—you will not forget my Compliments to good Mr Owen and the Maiden Ladies.[6] On my dear Elisa's Birth day, I was pretty much ingaged in Busness Writing. Yet I did not forget to offer up my Supplications for you—and—your dear Brother—as well on your Natal day as at other times—when the Holy Spirit gives me to interceed—for *you* and my poor frail *self*. As I forgot to send you the Texts on my own Birth day I will now transcribe them: *The Lord will have mercy on Jacob, and will yet choose Israel.* Isaiah 14, 1. [Antiphone:] *We know his boundless love & Grace—enjoy his goodness, care and favour;—He keeps his covenant for ever—can aught exceed his Faithfulness!* The New Testament Text. *The foundation of God standeth sure, having this Seal; the Lord knoweth them that are his and let every one that nameth the name of Christ depart from Iniquity.* 2 Tim. 2, 19. [Antiphone:] *Thou knowst the Congregation—Hath thee for her Foundation—Whate're the world may say;—grant us to cleave for ever To thee our gracious Saviour, May love among us bear the sway.*[7] I think them very weighty and important truths, and wish to be Strengthned—and guided by them! My dear *Cousins Stockers* desire their Love and Compliments to my dear uncle and you, as does my dear Companions—My adopted Niece promised to send me a Letter to inclose to my dear Eliza—but I have not receiv'd it yet.[8] However as its very possible I may write *once* more before winter, I may have one by the next time ready to send you—I beseech you not to forget my best Love to *our* dear Penry when you write, and Pardon my not enlarging much more at present. It falls in my mind that my uncle wish'd to know the price which Land rents at—Here in Pennsylvania Land & Rents are very high but I hear the Back Settlements, offer great advantages to Emigrants, & many of our Country folks come over to lay hold of them. My retired Situation renders me a very poor Judge of these Matters. I will only add that I comend myself to your Prayers and remain honord uncle Your Dutiful Niece, And my dearest Kitty & Eliza, your truely affectionate

Cousin
Mary Penry

P.S. An acquaintance of mine has requested me to desire our dear *Penry* to enquire after a Person, named *John Tune*—the Person who requests to hear of him, is his *Brothers Son*—his name *Samuel Tune*[9]—2 years ago, some Strangers calld at his house, and accidentally hearing his Name, told they had workd for a *Mr John Tune*, that he had a good deal to do about the Shipping on the *Thames*—his proper Busness he has forgot—but is pretty sure this man is his uncle—and he thinks he must be old. Perhaps he has children—

ALS: Penralley Collection 1374, NLW. Addressed "Ship letter | Mr | Meredeth Penry | Struet Brecon | Brecknockshire | S. Wales." Endorsed "Answer'd this Letter | [*illegible*]."

1. See Letter 29.

2. *"three in one"*: a gentle, joking reference to the Trinity, noting that she had sent separate letters to each person previously. See Letters 41–43.

3. "the Treaty": Jay Treaty. See Letter 41, note 35. *"President . . . resigned"*: Philadelphia's *American Daily Advertiser* announced on September 19, 1796, that president George Washington would not seek a third term and printed his farewell address.

4. For MP and Coke, see Letter 37, note 6. Coke arrived in Baltimore in October 1796 for his sixth trip to America to attend the Methodist General Conference; MP expected him to visit Philadelphia.

5. "account . . . of that Church": see Letter 41.

6. For Ann and Patty Powell, see Letter 38, note 3; "Mr Owen and the Maiden Ladies": see Letter 42, note 9.

7. "The Lord . . . the sway": from *Daily Words and Doctrinal Texts of the Brethren's Congregation, for the Year 1796*. For Moravian watchwords, See Letter 25, note 5.

8. The note from Anna Rosina Kliest ("Adopted Niece") was sent on March 10, 1797 (Anna Rosina Kliest to Eliza Powell, November 19, 1796, Penralley Collection 1375, NLW). See Letter 48.

9. For Samuel Tune, Mary Tippet's half-brother, see Letter 11, note 2. He had visited Lititz in August and September 1796.

46. TO MEREDITH PENRY[1]
March 9, 1797
Lititz, Pennsylvania

Lititz March the 9th 1797

Ever Honourd and revered Uncle

I receivd the long wishd for Letters, from Cousin Kitty and my dear Eliza with unspeakable Joy, on Sunday the 26th of February. I had just sat down to Table, but could not think of eating after sight of the Letter, again and again, I kiss'd those names so dear to me, and you may believe they were as often read over. One thing gives me Pain. I dont hear *half enough* of my *dear Uncle*; I want to know a great deal about *you*, what *you say*, and what you *do*. And yet, I cannot expect (or at least ought not) to look for more. Your blessing I receive, I hear of your being in Health; I *should* be satisfied. It came all at once in my Mind, that I can remember seeing my dear uncle at Cathhay;[2] you took me on your knee, and dropt half a guinea in my Bosom, it was either at Christmas or New Year I have forgot which. You may perhaps remember this Circumstance. I feel quite Melancholy, in regard to our Corrispondance. Our hopes of Peace seems intirely vanish'd, the publick Papers, anounce nothing but warr, and Bloodshedding. It is very distressing to hear of the *Thousands* who fall a Sacrifice, to the pride and ambition of their Rulers, and how much *has* Germany Sufferd and how much does that Counry *Still* suffer, it makes my heart ach. As for us in America, the Major part at least, wish to preserve Peace, but our Merchants Suffer much, thro the loss of their Shiping. The French now take, what the English left—How this will end, God knows, but certainly it seems hard, for a Nation that desires to live in Peace with every one, to be dispoild of their Property, by their *good Friends and Allies*.[3] Last Summer, I did not think it worth while to write, as I had little hopes of my Letters coming safe. One thing indeed, prevented me, that was: my wish to have commenced an acquaintance with Mr Cooke before I wrote you. I had a Letter ready to meet him, at his Expected Arrival in Philadelphia in which I had inclosed one to you, which I requested him to forward. The Doctor came into Baltimore, instead of Philadelphia, met their Synod there, and after a very short stay (I believe not more than 2 weeks) saild from *thence* for England—I indeavourd to meet him there, with a letter, but he had left the place, 2 days before my Letter came there.[4] I requested Mrs Stocker, to dispatch my Letter to you as soon as an oppertunity offerd. How *soon* that was in her power I cannot say, she engaged to write a line to *you* in mine. We have had a very cold winter, tho very little Snow our way. The River Deleware was froze over (they roasted an ox upon it) which keept the Shipping back. Indeed the

Americans have lost such a number, they have few left, and do not care to send out many, for fear of loosing them. We have no Ships of Force, to cope with those of other Nations, so that our Trade is without protection. Congress have this Spring, voted a Sum of Money to equip I think 4 Frigates (which is but triffling) for defence.[5] Should we be drawn into a warr, with France the prospect is dark—Yet I should think, the French must be weary. *Now* they have strip'd Germany—and sad alternative, left them nothing but *Starving* or *Tears* according to *their own* words. They must now look after Plunder Elsewhere, England, or America, if it yields food and cash, I suppose they will not hesitate. Our dear Lord preserve us from the so much extolld *freedom* and *Equality*; It is mere *Nonsence*. Those who were the greatest Champions for the delusive Thing, keep what they can get, and suffer their fellow Citizens to Starve.[6]—We must be silent & Patiently wait and see, how long, the Lord will suffer this Scourge of Europe, to drive all before them. You have doubtless an oppertunity of seeing the Newspapers, there you will find that every art is tried, to create Jealousies between us, and England, and to Cement the union with France still closer—however, lately people seem rather *less* Sanguine in their dependance on French fidelity, and are rather loud, in their Murmers on the loss of their Property. An Ambassadour is gone to France, to vindicate our Conduct, in regard to *our Neutrality*, and to Complain of their depridations on our Shipping. We are anxiously looking forward to the Result of his Mission.[7] Their great Victories, both in Germany and Italy, will doubtless make them carry it with a high hand, there is no expectation of their Submi[tt]ing to acknowledge themselves to blame—So that there is no knowing, how long or how short, our Peaceful days may last. Our Worthy Washington has surrenderd. On the 4th Instant our new President, John Adams a native of *New England* entred on his Office. He has been Vice President, as long as our great and good Washington was President, that is these 8 years. He bears a good Charector, time will unfold, what he is, there is no saying anything as yet: There was a great Strugle at his Election, Mr Jefferson had a large Party in his Favour—and is *Vice President*. This latter is a *Virginian*. Mr Adams had but 3 Votes, more than Jefferson.[8] Mr Priestly is in Philadelphia, holds *Lectures*, and preaches *Deism* openly. Publishes pamphlets, full of that Pernicious Doctrine, and is doing all he can, to deprive our Lord and Saviour Jesus Christ—of his *Divinity*, how shocking! what Mischief can this wretched Man do, to the growing generation! it would have been better for him & us, had he been Shipwreck'd on his Voyage to America. *Pain* has publish'd a Scurilous Pamphlet against Washington, which I have read with Indignation; however, *bad* as he is—he has not *sence* enough to do so *much* mischief as *Priestly*.[9] Mr Morgan Rees is *well* married and Settled in Philadelphia. I presume it would be a very good Affront, to hint at his former occupation. I am very indifferent about him, I shall never go to hear him again—I never was more than *twice* in a Baptist Meeting, once at a Funeral, and to hear Mr Rees preach in my Native Tongue[10]—and—if I was not to receive more Edification than I did—in *both* the Sermons; I had far better stay at home; tho the first was preachd by good honest Jenkin Jones (a good natured Simple Soul who gave Offence to neither man woman nor Child) & that is 40 years ago.[11] See my dear uncle how I prate to You, and how little, how very little, do I hear from my beloved uncle in return! forgive me my dear uncle these Complaints. I think it is not acting right, if I do not write *each* of you apart—and I wish to reeive a letter from your *mouth* tho not from your *Hand*. I hope you will dictate to my dear Eliza, and tell her to write in the first *Person*—as I write frequently in my Office— not your dear *uncle* says: but my dear *Niece*, &c. &c.[12] You will understand my meaning. We had a plentiful Harvest last year, but the large Exports keeps up the Price of wheat: It is at present as low, as we can Expect, that is 12/ currency that is 9/ Sterling. Land is rising in Price every Year. The Peace with the Indians is very precarious; The last Papers mention some persons being Murther'd on the Frontiers.[13] You cannot immagine how many Fires there has been. In the States of Georgia, Carolina, New York & Philadelphia, the Citizens has been obliged to Patrol the Streets at Night, together with the Watchmen; and the most of those Fires, has been found out to be conceald, by some wretches who had Evil Designs. A Printer in Philadelphia, with his Wife big with child, and 3 Children, all perish'd in the flames or shortly after, the latter end of January.[14] The Town of Savannah in Georgia, has been thrice set on Fire, and is allmost wholy destroyed.[15] Great Rewards have been offerd, to discover the Perpetrators, but hitherto, nothing has transpired. Scarce a News Paper, but what Informs of such fires. Thus you see my dear uncle, we are in this World, exposed to dangers of every kind, some more some less—and we must be very cautious, of siding with any Party whatever, which is the only way to preserve *our* Peace.[16] And *now* my nearest and dearest Relation on Earth! could I write any thing further, that would please you, I would cheerfully do it, but I think I have said enough for this time. Be pleased to present your Neice's respectful Love to all your dear Friends and Intimates—Particularly your good Mr Owen and his Family—Your worthy Clergyman—altho to me unknown: and tell him: I have a peculiar Veneration for the Clergy of the Church of England—and that I have the Honour to stile the Bishop and Several of the Clergy in Philadelphia *my Friends*— Our good Bishop Hiebner and his Lady, together with our worthy Pastor Mr Herbst and his Lady, desire their Love to my Venerable Uncle.[17] Mr Rosemeyer and his Lady, my Intimate acquaintance here. Himself born in the same year with my dear uncle and his Lady a few years younger, whose Grand Child I had the Honour to Stand Sponsor, a Widdow Lady of my own age, who lives in the Same House, with the Reverend Couple Rosemeyer, and is Likewise my Beloved Friend[18]—*These* request to be introduced to my dear Relations, with tender Love—Mr Rosemeyer has been many years a Clergyman, and much blessed in his care of Souls, but has now these some years past declined the Pulpit, on account of his advanced age. The little Family of Sisters in *my Apartment* must be first mentiond, and then our Large Family in the House who desire their Tender Love—to their Sister Penrys Uncle. Beseeching the Continuance of your Prayers, and Paternal Blessing, I conclude My dear my beloved Uncle! Your Dutiful Niece,

Mary Penry

ALS: Penralley Collection 1378, NLW. Addressed "Mr | Meredeth Penry | Struet | Brecon | Brecknockshire | South Wales | Friendship | London." Endorsed "These letters were received | June 3rd 1797 by the [*illegible*] | Post | Answered July 23rd." Letters 46–48 were sent together.

1. See Letter 29.
2. "Cathhay": Cathay, the central district in Cardiff, Wales.
3. Two French republican armies crossed the Rhine in June 1796, conducting campaigns that penetrated deep into Germany and Austria. These armies were pushed back by the end of 1797. *Porcupine's Gazette*, March 4, 1797, 1, described the "French ships of war and privateers" that were "authorized to seize . . . American vessels destined for or sailing from English ports."
4. For MP's expectation that Coke would visit Philadelphia, rather than Baltimore, see Letter 45, note 4. After the General Conference, Coke and Asbury preached in Virginia, South Carolina, and Georgia. Coke departed for England only in February 1797.
5. The 1794 Naval Act authorized the construction of six frigates. Construction was nearly discontinued after the 1796 Treaty of Tripoli, but work continued on three ships—the *United States*, the *Constellation*, and the *Constitution*—and in 1797 secretary of war James McHenry secured funding to complete these frigates. The *United States* was launched in May 1797, the *Constellation* in September, and the *Constitution* in October.
6. "preserve us from . . . *freedom* and *Equality*": MP was consistently skeptical of the French Republic.
7. "Ambassadour is gone to France": Charles Cotesworth Pinckney (1746–1825), a hero of the Revolutionary War, was appointed minister to France in 1796, but when he presented his credentials in Paris they were refused because of the ongoing XYZ Affair. MP did not yet know this "result."
8. John Adams became president on March 4, 1797, after beating Thomas Jefferson in the 1796 election by a 71–68 vote in the Electoral College.
9. Joseph Priestley traveled from Northumberland to Philadelphia to lecture in 1796 and 1797. See Letter 43, note 6; and Durey, *Transatlantic Radicals*, 191. Paine wrote his *Letter to George Washington* (Philadelphia, 1796)—dated July 30, 1796—from Paris.
10. See Letter 42 for MP's account of hearing Rhees preach.
11. Jenkin Jones (1690–1760) arrived in America from Wales about 1710 and was in Philadelphia by 1725, where he lived and preached until his death.
12. "in my Office": MP often writes letters for others in the first person.
13. "Peace with the Indians": the United States signed the Treaty of Holston with the Cherokees on July 2, 1791, the Treaty of Greenville with the northwestern Indians on August 3, 1795, and a treaty

with the Creeks on June 29, 1796. By February 1797, however, Philadelphia's *Independent Gazetteer* reported that new violence between whites and Indians was "likely once more to involve the frontiers in the horrors of an Indian war" (February 28, 1797), 3.

14. Andrew Brown (1744–1797), who published the *Federal Gazette* (called the *Philadelphia Gazette* after 1793), died eight days after a fire destroyed his printing house on January 27, 1797.

15. A November 1796 fire destroyed 279 houses in Savannah, sparing only 179 residences.

16. "cautious, of siding with any Party": see Letter 2, note 5.

17. "Mr Owen and his Family": see Letter 42, note 9. Regarding Johann Andreas Huebner and Johannes Herbst, see Letter 19, note 1, and Letter 37, note 40.

18. "Grand Child": MP was a sponsor at the baptism of Christian Russmeyer Schropp (1796–1821), son of Maria Russmeyer Schropp (1757–1804) and Christian Schropp (1756–1826). For the Russmeyers, see Letter 42, note 25; for the "Widdow Lady" (Gertrude Peterson Sydrich), see Letter 37, note 37.

✺ 47. TO KATHERINE PENRY[1]

March 10, 1797
Lititz, Pennsylvania

Lititz 10th March 1797

My dear Sister, my Precious Cousin, my Own Kitty *Penry*

You know and can Judge by your own Feelings, what mine must be at the Receipt of a line from your dear Hand. Never tell me, you are not clever at writing—Suposing it were so, it would be quite an Indifferent thing to me, who only Regard the dear Hand that writes, and the Matter it contains, without minding wether the lines, and Letters, are Crooked or straight. I have this winter been often indisposed, and have at present a weakness in my Eyes, which has been a pretty general complaint, this renders writing, rather a Task, and will plead an Excuse for my poor Scribble. I will confess my Weakness, to my dear Cousin, when I read the Account of the sale of Abbersinny.[2] The Tears flowd plentiously from my Eyes! I believe I catch'd the Infection from you my dear—For Myself, is out of the question. God knows my heart, and that I never wish'd to deprive you of a farthing, and a Suspicion which was hinted to me 37 years ago, that your Silence, was owing to your fears of my laying claim to anything in my Fathers Right (This unjust Suspicion) wrung my very heart—at the same time, I could not refrain from *Dispising* those, who thought so mean of *me*.[3] No, I thought, I will rather work my fingers to the *Bone*—and if my h[a]rd Lot should be, to beg my bread, I will ask it of *Strangers*. Pardon this Digression my dear. As every thing has been cleard up to me, you must believe, all such reflections are obliterated. I have lived to see the Children of Mr Adam Tuck, my Mothers Sisters Husband, who cheated her of 500 Pound Sterling, and her Repeating watch, &c. &c., reduced to the lowest distress—which *Drinking* can Occasion—true I was not an *Eye Wittness* of the Fact, but an Intimate Friend of my Mothers was, and she lived to hear it—and we *both* most heartily Commiserated their unhappy Situation.[4] I have lived to see, my Step fathers Estate, intirely gone, from every branch of *his* Family, for whom he had so amply provided, whereas he left *me* nothing—altho 2000£ came from my Mothers family into his—and the Promise of *that*, with a large addition brought *us* from our Native Country.[5] On the Contrary, your Cousin Penry, has never wanted "her needful Food, or Raiment to put on."[6] O happy, thrice happy! those whom the Allmighty takes under his Protection! The Consice account you have given me of your Family, *Convinces* me that *you* are of the number of those *Happy ones.* The Lord is my Portion therefore I lack nothing: be this our *Motto.*[7] You and I my dear Cousin, are in the decline of Life, and can see things in their true light. Our young Niece I imagine, would rejoice in brighter prospects, I can give a pretty good guess, having had the same Mortifications, in Respect to an Independent Fortune. Nevertheless she is bless'd with Talents, a good Education, and That *Lord* whom she seems to wish to live wholly to please, will never leave nor forsake her. I have been drawn out to a greater length, than I intended on this Subject, but I hope your pardon. Believe me, I was glad that I was not within Sight, or hearing, of the Sale of our Grandfathers *Domain*, altho long ago allienated from The Family.[8] It must have been very Cutting to my dear uncle and you, I hope by this time you have overcome that Mortification. Well my dear Kitty, none can deprive us of our Heavenly Patrimony unless we willfully give it up. Let this be our Consolation—and a few years hence, be it Longer or Shorter, we shall bid an eternal adieu to all Sublunary Things—what advantage is it then to us at the Hour of Death, wether we are Princesses or Peasents—Death writes *Vanity* and Vexation of Spirit, on all that is Mortal. The Texts of Scripture to your Birth day the 17th of this Month, are sweetly Consolatory. *The Lord is good unto them that wait for him, unto the Soul that seeketh Him.* Lam 3: 25. Antiphone, *My Soul waiteth on the Lord, and Shall never be ashamed.* New Testament text: *Come unto Me all ye that Labour & are heavy laden, and I will give you rest.* Matth 11. 28. Antiphone: *O Jesus Source of grace, I seek thy loving Face—Upon thy Invitation—With deep humiliation.*[9] That day I shall Commemorate, with asking a party of my Chosen Friends, to drink tea with me; *none* but Maidens! Our dear Eldress, Sister Mary Tippet will be my principal guest, *you* will be the theme of our Conversation—of our Prayers & best wishes. My dear uncle you must Communicate the Texts to his Birth Day, I had not room in my Letter to him. *Speak ye comfortably to Jerusalem, and cry unto her, that her iniquity is pardoned.* Isaiah 40. 2. Antiphone: *Thou must for Thine own sake forgive—It canot be for mine—My power thy pardon to* *receive—My Faith is all divine—A Sinner on mere Mercy cast—Thy Mercy I* *embrace—And gladly own from first to last—That I am sav'd by Grace.* New Testament text. *Grace and Truth came by Jesus Christ.* John 1. 17. Antiphone. *Lord let us be increasing—In Love and Knowledge too.* The Texts to the Anneversary of *my* Birth on the 12th of November next, are as follows: Bless the Lord Oh my Soul, who redeemeth thy Life from destruction, who crowneth Thee with Loving kindness and tender Mercies. Ps 103. [Antiphone:] Lamb of God all praise to thee—Thou hast victory gained—And upon the Cross for me—Endless Bliss obtained. New Testament text. I am the living bread which came down from Heaven; if any man eat of this Bread, he shall live forever. John 6. 51. Antiphone. Grant that continually To live alone for thee—May be my Pleasure.[10] I am sorry your texts allways comes after your day is past. Our English Text Books, comes every year from London. This year we receiv'd them late in the Fall. It is rather Odd, I receive them *from* London and send *back* some transcripts—whereas you could if you pleased, obtain them much sooner. If I could but bring you acquainted with Miss Nancy Vaughn, at Haverford West—I am certain it would be to your Pleasure and Edification.[11] You might then have oppertunities to hear more of the Brethren, and their Labours, among Christians and Heathen—Eliza has the pen of a ready Writer, let her write to Miss Vaughn, and inform her of my Welfare—I would inclose a few lines to her, but am fearful of increasing the Postage—Eliza can tell her it was at *my* Request, and in order to convey my love to her, and her Sisters, who are *mine* since Members of the same Church—Think on it my dear Cousin, let her know that we feel greatly distress'd, at the Suffrings of our dear Brethren and Sisters in Germany, and Particular of our Congregation at Neuwied on the Rhine.[12] I long to hear how she does and her family of Single Sisters. My dearest Kitty you say right that there is a Sympathy in our Manner of thinking—and was you in America, I could venture to say we should dwell under *one roof*—Nevertheless, you are too dear to me (gratifying as would certainly be to have your Company), I cannot be so selfish, as to wish you in *America*. God be thank'd, he is near to all those that call upon him—In England and America, yea in all parts of the Earth. Since you are *not* calld upon to forsake your Friends and Native Country, you can be thankful, and be *one* with me, in our Common Saviour. It requires Grace, to submit to be as it were an *Outcast* from my Fathers House; Altho I have *now* weatherd the Storm, and enjoy a blest repose. I look forward to a blest Eternity, for which it is my daily prayers to be prepared, I have nothing to expect, nor to hope for, in this World, but to hear from my dear Friends and Relations, to hear of their Health and

Wellfare, is the uttmost of my wishes, to feel the Love of my dearest Fathers Brother, and his Family, is the greatest Felicity and this my gracious Saviour has kindly bestowed on me, as a Comfort in Old Age.

I was sorry that I could not give any Satisfaction, to my good Sister Tippet in regard to her Family, as she has great Reason to believe, she has relations at Kingswood near Bristol, but if you have no way to obtain any Information, we must give it up. So likewise in Regard to Mrs Rosemeyer. Her Fathers name was Peter Evans, born at Denbigh in Flintshire.[13] I just now look'd in the Map of England and Wales, which I have under a Glass over my head—and see it is so far from you, I hardly dare hope for any Information. I just mention it, to satisfy the Old Lady. Chance, may perhaps throw it on your way to make enquiry—I am glad Major Price is become so fortunate, I little thought when I saw him here, that I could have been favour'd with any account of my Family, from him, or I should have ask'd some questions, notwithstanding the confusion I was in, at being catch'd in my Dishabille.[14] I wish you could send me a Welch Cheese, that is an article of Luxery to me, who dont see any good Cheese sometimes in twelve months. When I was Last in Philadelphia I saw some the Welch had brought in with them, which was far more esteemd, than either Cheshire or Glocestershire. Imported Cheese sells @ 2/6 and 3/ the Pound that is 2/ and 2/3 Sterling. I dont admire the Cheese made in this Country. But dont be uneasy, I know it is as little in your Power to send me, any thing of that kind, as it is in mine, to send anything to you—yet I will try hard for it, to send you a Piece of my own Needle Work, some time this Summer, by some kind Passenger to London. I wish you would be pleased to give me directions to our dear Penry at London, since I could as then, direct to himself—and could write to him.[15] You have told me nothing of our Cousin in Glocester—my dear your Friends and Intimates, are mine, besure to tell them so—and when you write again, do not forget to mention my Cousin, Stockers Family, it pleases them, and they have been of late very kind and loving to me. They have their Troubles, a Relation of mine, whose Mamma was my dear Mothers first Cousin, came this winter from New Haven in Conecticut, to visit her Aunt Stocker in Philadelphia. There she heard last Month, that her Husband was Shipwreck'd, on the Rocks near the Island of Bermuda. He saved his Life with his Men by swiming, and they were taken up, by an English Man of Warrs boat. Vessel and Cargo, which was wholy Captain George Browns (my Cousins Husbands) Property, intirely lost—and by that means reduced from Affluence—to great Straits—Mrs Brown has lost the use of her Right arm, in the Palsy, and is a very delicate, weakly woman, she buried 3 lovely Boys in one year—she has one Child left, a little girl of 4 years old. Captain Brown is gone to the West Indies, to try to make his fortune there, if he succeeds, he intends to send for his Wife and Child—Meantime, she must be suported by her Aunt, together with her Maid—for she can neither dress nor undress herself.[16] A Melancholly Case this, I have wrote her a Sympathizing Letter, its all I can do. Glad and thankful am I, that *I need not* lie a dead weight on their Hands. My dear Sister Tippet, who has a great Regard for you as a *Maiden*, and my Cousin, wishes you to experience, the Happiness of that State, in an uninterupted Attachment, to that Saviour who being born of a Virgin, has Sanctified our State, and honourd it in a distinguish'd Manner.

> O might we to our gracious Lord—For all His goodness Joy afford—
> Each Virgins care and aim be this—To seek in all things him to please.
> Abide with us on the[e] we call—Jesus thou art our *All* in *All*—
> Let us devoted unto thee—In Soul & Body Hallowed be.
> O Abba Father, thanks and Praise—And Joyful Songs to thee we raise
> That thou thy Son out of Thy Throne—Didst give to be a *Virgins* Son.
> God Holy Ghost we praise thy Name—With Rev'rence we thy Love proclaim
> That overshadowd by thy Pow'r. The *Virgin*—Christ conceivd and bore
> He died for us and thou from thence—Salvation dost to us dispence
> And to the Glory of his Grace, workst in us Fruits of Righteousness
> Fix in our hearts thy blest abode—And make us Temples of our God
> Keep Soul and Body thro thy care—Blameless untill the Lord apear.
> Those who the wondrous deed hast done—Oh Jesu look in Mercy down
> On *us* altho we Sinners be—Void of Angelic Purity.
> Like Mary we with heart and Voice—In thee our Saviour will rejoice
> Since thou has promised in grace—To make our hearts thy dwelling place.[17]

The last lines were I may say wrote in the dark, I am quite ashamed of the writing, tho the Subject is good, I have transcribed these Verses, from some of *our* Hymns. Now my dear Cousin, my paper is allmost fill'd, and in reading it over this Morning, it does not please me at all, its full of Incoherencies—But your Affection will cause you to overlook all faults. I must now take Eliza in hand,[18] she has given me a large field to range in, before I can overtake her, being old, infirm, and forgetful—I shall be no match for her I fear, nevertheless I will *follow* her, thro her Mazes, and endeavour to encourage her to go on with her pleasing Excursions, into the Realms Above. I shall get there *before her* however *In Person*, tho I cannot In Idea keep pace with her. As I presume my letters are read by all three, I have varied my Subjects—what may be lookd for in the one—will by that means be found in the other. Accept here several tender Kisses, which my Lips imprint on this Spott 5, 6, 8—To my dear uncle besure to give the half of them—The Number has arose to 20. Adieu, my dear *Sister*—My beloved *Cousin*—my own *Kitty Penry*—*your own*

Mary Penry

ALS: Penralley Collection 1380, NLW. This letter was sent with Letters 46 and 48. Letter 46 records the address and endorsement.

1. See Letter 29.

2. "Abbersinny": Abersenny, the Penry family estate in the village of Defynnog, about ten miles from Brecon.

3. See this volume's introduction for MP's efforts to recover her "fortune."

4. Martha Stocker (1710–1740), MP's aunt, married Adam Tuck (d. 1742) in 1728. See Settlement on the Marriage of Adam Tuck and Martha Stocker (1728), 568/47, Wiltshire and Swindon History Centre. Two of their daughters, Mary (1734–1778) and Grace (1732–1795), lived outside of Bristol. Six other children, three boys and three girls, died in infancy between 1729 and 1739. See Langley Burrell Church Register, PR/Langley Burrell St Peter/1487/2, Wiltshire and Swindon History Centre; and Sherlock, *Monumental Inscriptions*, 10.

5. "Step fathers Estate": William Attwood's estate. See this volume's introduction.

6. "needful Food, or Raiment to put on": *Collection of Hymns* (1743), 257. See also Matthew 6:25.

7. MP blends Psalm 23:1 and Lamentations 3:24.

8. "Sale of our Grandfathers *Domain*": Abersenny (note 2, above). By the 1770s, Abersenny was owned by the Powell family. See Lloyd, *Historical Memoranda*, 1:186.

9. "*The Lord . . . deep humiliation*": from *Daily Words and Doctrinal Texts of the Brethren's Congregation for the Year 1797*. For Moravian watchwords, see Letter 25, note 5.

10. "*Speak ye . . . my Pleasure*": the watchwords for Meredith Penry's and MP's birthdays.

11. "Nancy Vaughn": see Letter 6, note 6.

12. The Moravian settlement at Neuwied, fifty miles south of Cologne, began in 1750.

13. For Mary Tippet's family in Kingswood, see Letter 42, note 15; for Maria Russmeyer, see Letter 42, note 25.

14. "Major Price": see Letter 30, note 7.

15. "dear Penry": Penry Powell. See Letter 29.

16. For Jane (Jenny) Reese Brown, see Letter 41, note 41. MP's cousin Margaret Stocker was Jane's aunt. In 1790 the New Haven household included George Brown, two white females (his wife and a daughter), and two boys under the age of sixteen. Captain George Brown died in 1800, after which the household contained only the widow Jane Brown and a daughter under age sixteen.

17. MP quotes several hymns from the Litanies of Single Sisters in *Liturgic Hymns of the United Brethren, Revised and Enlarged* (London, 1793).

18. MP means that she is about to write a letter to Eliza; see Letter 48.

⪦ 48. TO ELIZA POWELL[1]
March 10, 1797
Lititz, Pennsylvania

Lititz 10 March 1797

My Precious Niece, my own dear Eliza

I have taken a new Pen, and begin with a Resolution, to write as *fair* as possible, in order to *Immitate* your hand—but you will find I shall not hold out, its not in my Power, to be so precise, and when my heart grows warm with the subject I am upon, I have not time for exactitude—Time was that I wrote (so it was said) a beautiful hand, but 40 years are pass'd since then— and having lived wholly among Germans, accustom'd to hear, read, write and speak that Language constantly—My English tongue has sustain a Material Injury, which will account for the Germanisms, as I may call it, so frequent in my Stile. The Monosylables in particular, I am sensible, are either too frequent, or wrong placed. I am *sensible* of my faults, but cannot *rectify* them, which makes me very diffident in writing, particular to Strangers. Altho I must now and then, as my Office requires, undertake it, such Corrispondance however, being chiefly on Bus'ness, is not difficult.[2] I have its true a large corrispondance, to Philadelphia, and Elsewere, being Friends & Relations mostly, they kindly overlook my Faults, as I trust you my dear will likewise. I was highly diverted at the *sequel* to the Story of the Cat. Wicked Girl, how you mortified me, since I, that am so near sighted, that I can scarce know a person across the street, saw so much (*Prettyness*) in the gentleman— that—had I been 40 years younger—and my Country Man to[o]—I know not wether I should not have *rued* the sight—But tell me my dear—*are you not relations?* Hush—I will not inquire further—perhaps I may be drawn in myself—The *noble* race of *Shenkin*, the line of *Owen Tuder*[3]—(as for the *Train* we'll cut that off). Bless me, I might have ben tempted to undertake a Journey to the City, to claim Kindred, and that would not please my dear uncle. Well, there is a very worthy Country Man of ours, in Philadelphia at least by descent, for he was born in Philadelphia. His name is Richard Price, he is one of the County Commisioners—He was brought up a Quaker, but frequents the Brethren's Church, tho not a member, his wife is a Communicant in our Church.[4] He has built himself a very pretty House in the City, by his Industry and Honesty, he has acquired a Competency, on which they live very comfortable. He is an honest Good man, and so desireous of assisting his poor Country Folks, that I believe the emigrants from Wales find a real Friend in Him. He *seriously* believes, they have withdrawn, from the *iron yoke of Opression*, and gave credit to *every thing* asserted by the gentleman of the

Noble Race of Shenkin. Doubtless these Malcontents, impose greatly on the Americans, and help to widen the breach between us.[5] Within these 2 years, a Pamphlet has been publish'd Monthly—the author of which, does all in his Power to set *Men* and *Things*, in their true light. He seems to have the welfare, of England & America at heart. His works are eagerly read, and have done great Service in opening Peoples Eyes to see their Delusions—*In many respects.* He has both Head and Heart, seems to be both a *politician* and a *Christian*, which we seldom find united in our days. Tho it is his *Misfortune* to be an *English Man*—yet the true Honest Americans, Respect what he says, and Incourage him to proceed—The *others* on the Contrary are ready to tear him to pieces—and I think he is in *Constant Danger.* But He bids them diffiance, and when they give him one blow, he is sure to return the Compliment with two. He has taken the Name of *Peter Porcupine*—his real name is William Cobbett, born in the West of England—and not many years since he left it. His Pamphlet is call'd the *Censor.*[6] You will easily believe, I wish well, to the man who seems to aim at making Truth, Triumph over Falsehood—and to preserve Peace and Union, among ourselves. I have read two excellent pamphlets, in answer to Pains Age of Reason, the one wrote by Mr Winchester, in a Stile comprehensive to the *Meanest* Capacity, the other by the Bishop of Landaff, Bishop Watson a Stile for the *learnd*[7]—and yet I have heard several pious Christians, give Mr Winchester the greatest Preference, being wrote quite Simple, unadorn'd with the Flowers of Rhetoric—it is Convincing without Confusing, yet I must say its a fine Piece, the Bishops, and they realy ought to be bound up together. I look'd into *Brothers* so calld Prophecies, but they were realy to[o] silly, and Illiterate to raise my Curiosity.[8] I wunder how a man so well read as Mr *Hahled* could write in his favour, he must have been infatuated surely.[9] Good Mr Winchester, is gone to his Native Place in New England. His Health is so much impaired, his Misfortunes has been great, his Domestick troubles bear the hardest on him. If ever a man was unequally *yoked*, he is. He is indeed a *Angelic Man* but his Wife is—a fallen Angel—if an Angel she may be calld—she has a *too likely Face.*[10] I have no particular knowledge of the Baptists, Mr Winchesters writings I admire, altho I am not obliged to believe his Doctrine—To be sure Universalism never had a greater, or a better Champion.[11] His Lectures, are I may say anotations on the Holy Scriptures, and in Regard to the Second coming of Christ, the Conversion of the Jews, and the blessed Millenium; He makes one, Prophecy the Key to unfold the other, which explains, and clears up as you read. So that you have a golden Chain of Scripture Texts, strung like Pearls—most pleasing to meditate upon. Priestly & Pain I have mentiond in your Grandpapa's Letter[12]—We find them in this Country, by numbers on the Pinnacle of Honour—I fear on a future day, their Fall will be great. They, have built in the Sand—and are such Master Builders in *their way*, they endeavor to bring every *one* off, from Building upon that *Rock*, which will *break them to Pieces*—unless they repent.—I highly aprove of your Charity towards all Men, it is one of the Tennets of the Church of which you are a Member. Properly Speaking, Mankind are divided into 2 *Classes only*—that is, Christians and those who are No Christians, or if you will, *Believers*—and *Infidles*—Whosoever believeth shall be saved—with its *woeful* Alternative. Of these latter Class, there are divisions, and Subdivisions, tho they are generally under 3 large Tittles, *Jews, Turks*—*Infidels*, under which latter Tit-tle, I suppose the *Heathen* rank, altho I would rather, stile them unbelievers; since the greatest part of them, are more Faithful to their Tradittions, than Christians to the Word & Spirit of God. Are you a Believer in the Lord Jesus, do you Confess with your Tongue, and believe in your Heart, do you suffer his Holy Spirit to lead you into *all Truth*? Then you are a Member of Christ, a Child of God, and an inheritor of the Kingdom of Heaven—The Holy Scriptures tell us: that without Faith it is impossible to please God, and that if we love Him, we shall keep his Commandments—None but such, are Can[di]dates for the Church Militant,[13] altho thieves, and Robbers overleap the bounds, and *thus* get into the Church—Still, th[e]y are not of the first Class. If we are become Children of God, we must Love our *Brethren*, be their outward denomination what it will. The *Sheep* are under the care of the great Shepherd—he knoweth all His Sheep, and they know his Voice, and will follow *none* but Him. How doth my needy Soul rejoice, That by my Faithful Shepherds Choice—My name is certainly inroll'd—Among the Sheep of Christs blest Fold.[14]—Dear Lord, Thou hast (and blessed be Thy Holy Name, art continually carrying on that great Work) Thou hast with Shep-herds faithfulness—Brought many souls to thy blest Fold—Made them partaker of thy Grace—and 'mongst thy followers them enroll'd![15] At the End, there is to be *one Fold* and *one Shepherd*, this our dear Lord says himself, St John 10, 16. How can it be possible for Children of God, if agreed in the fundamental points of Doctrine, (although they may dissent in smaller things) to bear ill will, to each other, they *cannot*. It is not in their *Renew'd Natures*. Here a Barrier is laid, between *Rigour* and unbounded *Liberty*—Believe & Live, if you have Life, Grace will be active—are you a good Tree, you will bring forth good Fruit, a Corrupt Tree, cannot bring forth good Fruit—By their Fruits ye shall know them, Not every one that saith Lord Lord &c.[16] Here my dear you have my opinion of the Church Militant, known *only* to the great Head of his Church, who sees her *Members* under *every Denomination among Christians*. As for the *Stray Sheep* and those who *will not*

Obey the Voice of the great Shepherd or who have *never heard* his Voice in his revealed *Word*, they are partly under his *Long Suffring Mercy*—Or partly under his Displeasure. These, we must leave to him, we can *supose* many things, but we can only trust to what Sacred Scripture inform us—To pity and Pray for all our Fellow Creatures, is our bounden Duty—and if an Opertunity is given us, we are not to refrain with our Council, or reproof as circumstances require. The Rules for our Conduct, in every age and State, are so plainly laid before us, in the Word of God, and his Holy Spirit, explains, and Applies it according to our Several Necessities, that if we attend to that divine Instructor, and observe his Precepts, we shall be led into *all Truth*. And now my love after having cursorily followed your track in the Church Militant, I say *follow'd* for your observations are such, as I perfectly coincide with, therefore need not repeat. Neither have I been, nor am Insensible, to the wonders of divine Love, exemplified in the different Revolutions which paved the Way—for *our ancestors* who were *great Idolaters*, to receive the Glad tidings of the *Gosple*—Neither have I a doubt, but that the present great Revolutions in a Neighbouring Kingdom will, dark as the Apearence is at present, turn out to the Praise & Glory of God, whatever *he does* or *Suffers*, is to answer a good End.[17] Doubtless his Judggements frequently fall upon the Rebelious, but in the midst of Judgement, he remembreth Mercy. He never yet has made Mistakes in his Vast Government! How calm and resigned, is the Soul that puts its whole trust in the Lord. Looking at him, thro every dispensation of his Providence, we know *whatever is is best*.[18] And Now: I quit the Terrestial, and follow you to the Celestial Globe, here I must be very Cautious, and Look for my Guide, The Holy Scriptures who have revealed part of the Glories of the Heavenly Kingdom—and but part, as they tell me: Eye hath not seen, Ear hath not heard, neither has it [e]nterd into the heart of Man, to conceive the Glories[19]—*to be reveald*, also they are not yet *revealed*—In vain then, do I attempt to search them out. Imagination ever on the wing, forms Happiness, and Glories, according to the Wishes, and desires of the Party, from whom she is dispatch'd, and having made great discoveries, returns full of Joy, with a pleasing Account, but when the Question is seriously *Put—are these things so?* she hesitates, she hopes, she fears, she doubts—and with a Sigh Confesses she is *uncertain* if what she saw and heard was the Truth—In all things where the Word of God is our Director, we are safe. It is no Crime to pay a visit, to that Land of Promise, to which we are Travelling, In Idea at least, neither can we think too highly of it. But oh we cannot—as long as we are in this Vale of Tears, have a right Conception of it. Like Christian in Pilgrims Progress, when we attempt to behold the Glories of the Heavenly City, our Hands Tremble, we cannot hold the Perspective

Glass steady.[20] I acquiese in all you alledge, concerning the *Imployment* of the Saints in Bliss, we have good reason to believe it, from the Testimonies in the Word of God. When I sent my Immagination on an Enquiry shall I, can I, with propriety use the Expression, Surely I hope to see and know our Primitive Parents—The beloved Disciple St. John &c. &c. My dear Parents &c. But my knowledge and Love, will have none of the *ties of Nature*—which as I now am *in the Body* is the most pleasing Sensation—that must be given up, and this I still think, altho I console myself, that as all Carnal affections (I mean the affections of Flesh & Blood, not sinful Affections) will be done away, I shall be thoroughly sati[s]fied, yea happy, be the dispensation as it pleases God. If we are permitted to retain the Remembrance of this our Innocent Corrispondance, We will remind each other of it, in the Heavenly Mansions![21]

I will postpone what I have further to say on this Subject, as I shall write again Please God, in May, shall only transcribe the Texts to your—and your dear Brothers birthday,[22] yours is as follows: *Let Integrity and uprightness preserve me for I wait on thee.* Ps 25, 21. [Antiphone:] *The Lord to whom our hearts are known—Cause our whole walk 'fore him to be—His Joy & our Felicity.* [New Testament Text:] *I will, be thou Clean.* Mark, 1.41. [Antiphone:] *The Water flowing from thy side—Which by the Spear was opend wide—Shall be my Bath Thy precious blood—Cleanse me and bring me nigh to God.*—Your dear Brothers: *Out of them shall proceed thanksgiving, and the Voice of them that make merry* Jer. 30, 19. [Antiphone.] *In joyful Hymns of Praise—Like one Man sweetly raise—Voices quite united—With your Liturgic lays—Your Saviour is delighted, He'll with gracious Ear—Your thanksgiving hear—Feel him, he is near.* [New Testament Text:] *Rejoice with me; for I have found my Sheep which was lost.* Luke 15, 6. [Antiphone.] *Now best of Shepherds, ever keep—Thy poor thy little helpless Sheep—Protect it from all Danger.*[23]—Give my tender love to my dear Penry, and do send me his Direction[24]—and my dear Love, excuse this Scrawl, my Eyes are exessive weak to day, I can hardly see to write especially by Candle Light, which I must do, because an Oppertunity offers to send it to the City. Inclosed is a letter from my adopted Niece, which I dare say will please you.[25] Your Cousins Powels in Philadelphia desire their kind love to you, as does my young Companions.[26] I was thinking My Love, we will make an Exchange, you shall come over to America in my Place—and I will go to Brecon—and lay my Bones to rest, in my Native Country. O my dear Aunt you cry—and O my dear *Niece* I say!—Never, never will I in earnest propose—*your* coming to *America!*—People who have Independant Fortunes may live very happy here—But *only* hard working people, can better themselves—and neither *you*, nor I was cut out for that.[27] Indeed *where I am settled* it is very different—but *all* that come to America, have not that good fortune. And now my Precious Niece, I kiss and Embrace you in Spirit *most tenderly.* My dear you will pardon my laying a Small Burthen on you—that is writing *For* your Grandpapa—as well as *off* him—and to Miss Nancy Vaughn, in hopes it may become a pleasure to you, and Introduce you to a Valuable Corrispondant.[28] Adieu my beloved Eliza, I commend you to the Faithful Heart of the loving, and beloved Jesus—and beseech him to bless you, in Spirituals and Temporals, I remain *ever* your affectionate & Faithful Aunt

Marie Penry

You can My dear do as you think proper either write a few Lines in your letter to Me or write a Letter to the Young Lady and inclose it in Mine. It has lain long by me waiting for my writing which I defered—partly on account of Indisposition.

I celebrated Davids Day at Mr Rosemeyers[29]—as I do indeed every year. I had a Leek and some Green Branches pin'd to my Window Curtain by my Young Companions who frequently wish you were with them.—I shall write in 6 or 8 weeks again—as I seem not to have half answered your Letter.[30]

ALS: Penralley Collection 1379, NLW. This letter was sent with Letters 46 and 47. Letter 46 records the address and endorsement.

1. See Letter 29.

2. MP served as the clerk in the single sisters' house in Lititz.

3. *"noble* race of *Shenkin",* the line of *Owen Tuder":* both the surname Shenkin and Owen Tudor (ca. 1600–1641), a Welsh courtier and the grandfather of Henry VII, were familiar symbols for Wales. The phrase "noble race of Shenkin" became popular from a song in Frederick Reynolds's *Folly as It Flies* (London, 1797).

4. "wife is a Communicant in our Church": Anne King (1741–1825) joined the Moravian church in 1759, marrying Ezekiel Worrell in 1760. Three of their children survived into adulthood: Susanna (b. 1761), Ezekiel (b. 1764), and Joseph (b. 1766). In 1791, after Worrell's death, she married Richard Price, a widower who was a Quaker.

5. "these Malcontents": MP disdained the radicals who, denouncing an oppressive British government, immigrated to America, where they expected to find a land of republican liberty. The radicals' account of British tyranny, MP contends, exacerbated tensions between Americans and Britons.

6. For Cobbett's *Censor,* see note Letter 44, note 6.

7. Elhanan Winchester, *Ten Letters Addressed to Mr. Paine, in Answer to His Pamphlet, Entitled The Age of Reason: Containing Some Clear and Satisfying Evidences of the Truth of Divine Revelation* (Boston, 1795); Richard Watson (Bishop of Landaff), *An Apology for the Bible in a Series of Letters, Addressed to Thomas Paine, Author of a Book Entitled, The Age of Reason, Part the Second, Being an Investigation of True and of Fabulous Theology* (London, 1796).

8. "*Brothers . . . Prophecies":* see Letter 43, note 15.

9. Nathaniel Brassey Halhed (1751–1830)—most famous for translating the Hindu legal code into English (*A Code of Gentoo Laws,* 1776) while employed by the East India Company—published *Two Letters . . . on the Present Confinement of Richard Brothers in a Private Mad-House* (London, 1795) and defended Brothers in the House of Commons, which led to Halhed's resignation from that body in 1795.

10. "unequally *yoked*": Winchester's fifth wife, Mary Knowles, was known as a "desperate fury" whom he "loved with a doating fondness proportioned to the madness of her temper." See *Christian Telescope* 1, no. 51 (July 23, 1825): 203. Winchester died in Hartford, Connecticut, on April 18, 1797, shortly after MP wrote this letter.

11. "Universalism": see Letter 43, note 5.

12. See Letter 46.

13. "Church Militant": Christians who fight as soldiers of Christ against the devil and sin. Just below, MP contends that soldiers of Christ exist in every Christian denomination and only God knows who these soldiers are.

14. "How doth . . . Christs blest Fold": *Collection of Hymns* (1789), 274.

15. "Thou hast . . . them enroll'd!": Ibid., 152.

16. Matthew 7:16, 21.

17. "Revolutions in a Neighbouring Kingdom": the French Revolution. For MP's millenarianism, see this volume's introduction.

18. "*whatever is is best*": Alexander Pope. See Letter 33, note 8.

19. 1 Corinthians 2:9.

20. In John Bunyan's *Pilgrim's Progress* (1678), the Pilgrims attempt to view the "Celestial City" through a "Perspective-Glass" (122).

21. "Remembrance of this our Innocent Corrispondance": see Letter 3, note 5.

22. Eliza Powell's birthday was August 28, Penry Powell's July 5.

23. "*Let Integrity . . . all Danger*": from *Daily Words and Doctrinal Texts of the Brethren's Congregation for the Year 1797*. For Moravian watchwords see Letter 25, note 5.

24. "my dear Penry": Penry Powell. See Letter 29.

25. MP had mentioned this letter (Kliest to Powell, NLW) in Letter 45.

26. For Ann and Patty Powell, see Letter 38, note 3.

27. MP was skeptical about immigrants' high hopes for their lives in America. See this volume's introduction.

28. For Anne (Nancy) Vaughn, see Letter 6, note 6.

29. "Davids Day": March 1, celebrating the patron saint of Wales. Regarding the Russmeyers, see Letter 42, note 25.

30. These two paragraphs in MP's handwriting appear on the reverse of Anna Rosina Kliest's letter to Eliza Powell, sent along with this letter.

ᔕ 49. TO ELIZABETH DRINKER[1]

April 2, 1797
Lititz, Pennsylvania

Lititz April 2nd 1797

My beloved Friend!

I sat down to answer your Wellcome, *truely wellcome* lines, which I receivd late last Evening, but alas, I know not when or how it will reach your hands! as I cannot make Use of Post, on account of the Expence, I have no *certain* method in my Corrispondance, which is very frequently a Concern to me.—I cannot impose a Tax, on my Friends for my poor letters, neither can I well afford, to pay for theirs—Yet if *you* would favour me more frequently I would not grudge paying for them. I wish I had a Friend, of power Sufficient to frank my Letters.[2] This winter has been remarkable for Cold—and *Colds*, we have had a great *many*—and very little Snow, which renderd the Roads allmost impassable as it quickly melted, and became litterally Mud. The 2nd week in November I went to Lancaster to spend a few days with our Friends Grace Parr—and *Polly Roberts* both being *Friends* (altho I believe you do not know the last mention'd) I stile them *ours*—She is a sweet woman. Her Husband is a Hatter, *gaius mine Host*, not only to *your* travelling Friend, but to your Friend Penry.[3] She has an oposite Neighbor, a Presbyterian, a Charming woman and my dear Friend—When we all meet—we are Members of *one Fold*, thou Outwardly of different Callings, but this Circumstance is no restraint upon us, we are *one* in Christ. What a heavenly *Virtue* is Charity! I returnd home the 2nd of December much indisposd, and was 6 weeks confined to the House with the Influenza.[4] I cannot complain that the Season was *Melancholy*, although very little out of our Circle, was to be heard or seen. I have no want of *Society* within our own Walls—and can *chuse* my Companions as suites myself. My Cousin Stocker and I corrisponded more frequent, than *last winter*, untill *Dorsch* died, which put a *Period* to our *Freedom* in sending Letters. We hardly know now how to act.—Boller and Jordan have such a Multiplicity of Bus'ness on their Hands, that Letters lie at their House *Weeks*—before they are sent to me—or to my Friends.[5] I receivd for Instance last Night a Letter from Mrs Stocker, dated the 8th of March, and 16 days ago a Neighboring waggon was down, and loaded it at their House, and I surely believe the Letter lay there—and was forgotten. There cannot be a finer Station, as all the Waggons our way have dealings with them—But they are ever in haste to quit the town, and this causes the omissions I complain of—I am in daily expectation of a Neighbours going down with his waggon, which Oppertunity I shall gladly embrace—but cannot please my self with hopes of Letters in Return—unless they be there ready—and are not forgotten. In the month of February, I received Letters from my *Welch Friends* very agreeable—My good Old Uncle was at the date of their Letters 6th October a:p in good Health. Two Passages in their Letters are worthy of *note*. The one is to this purport: "*Those* who have Emigrated from *Wales* lately, were not much aproved of by the Sober part of the Nation, this we tell you that you may not conceive a bad Opinion of your Country folks—and Imagine we all resemble *those*—God turn their Hearts, and put it *not* in their power to do you (the Americans) an Injury."— "Every thing is very Quiet at Birmingham, since P—stly left it—we hear of no more Riots there."[6]—They have had they say a glorious Harvest and Stile themselves a *highly favourd Nation*. And such I think them!

I have never saw—nor heard P—stly but that He is a *Deist* and glories in his Infidelity promulgating his Pernicious doctrine to the Uttmost of his

Power—is a Melancholy truth. A Lady in Lancaster told me, she had heard him and his oratory was such—there was scarce a Possibility to withstand him—Had this *wretch* been drownd in the *ocean* on his Passage hither it would have been for the Benifit of thousands who swallow the Poison with avidity. Only look at the advertisements of his works, the tittles evince his Apostacy. And what is the *Infidellity he writes against* and what are his tennets? according to which, he calls praying to the Lord Jesus, the crime of *Idolatry*?[7] O my Soul come thou not in his Councils! Let me join with the Disciples of the blessed Jesus and say Lord wither shall I go? Thou *only* hast words of Eternal Life!

> My Song shall bless the Lord of all,
>   My praise ascend to his abode;
> Thee Savior by that Name I call,
>   The great *supreme*, the Mighty *God*!
>
> Without begining or decline,
>   Object of Faith, and not of Sense
> Eternal Ages saw him shine,
>   He Shines eternal Ages hence:
>
> As much when in the Manger laid,
>   Allmighty ruler of the sky;
> As when the Six days work he made,
>   Fill'd all the Morning Starrs with Joy;
>
> Of all the Crowns *Jehovah* wears,
>   Salvation is his dearest Claim;
> That gracious sound well pleas'd he hears,
>   And owns *Immanuel* for his name.
>
> A cheerful confidence I feel,
>   The Object of my Faith I see;
> My bosom glows with heavenly Zeal;
>   To *worship* him who dy'd for me!
>
> As man, he pities my Complaint,
>   His pow'r and Truth are all divine;
> He will not fail he cannot *faint*.
>   Salvations sure, and must be mine.[8]

Pardon this, I will not say (Rhapsody) because such are my Sober and fixd thoughts of my God and Saviour.[9] May what you Mention in regard to peace be a true Phrophecy altho the last papers indicate no peaceable disposition in the French, either to England *or* America—(bless me I write false, every other word allmost). You Mention P.P. I own I think *well* of him, altho he is blunt, and sometimes as you observe *worse*, however that which fix'd his Charector with me, as a *Man of Principle* is the Later Part of the bloody Bouy, in which he derives all the *Excesses* committed by the French, from the right source whence all Crimes committed among so calld Christians—unquestionably proceed, that is Irreligion—the Infidelity they unhappily adopted, made them—*Brutes* not only Savages but *Brutes*! Its very true, he is frequently *rude* in his Satire—but when he reasons, it is with calmness and precision— He seems to be a fast Friend to the Constitution, and a Zealous advocate for Religion; altho he professes he is not as he Ought to be—I think he is serviceable, to Open the Eyes of those who was so frenchified as to Praise every thing done or Said by them, and I think his Retaliating on the French and their adulators, is Tit-for-tat—how have they abused the English—He is a *dreadnought*.[10] However, I would not be in his Coat for any thing—for he creates himself many Enemies—and they may one day wreak their Revenge on him—[11]

God be thank'd neither You nor I, have any Active part to perform in these Affairs; to pray for Peace *frequent*, and *fervent*, is our Calling.—I am Still wishing and hoping to see the Books—I think I mentiond to you so long ago—If they are pack'd up and sent to Boller with a Charge to send them carefully to me—an Oppertunity may shortly offer. Tommy Say's Trance[12]— I very much covet seeing—And now my dear *Friend* how do you do? I think frequently on you—in particular when a *Silent* hearer of *this* and the *Other Case* which I *quietly* think somewhat resembling your Complaints. A few days ago I accidentally heard an Observation made, which I treasured up in my Mind as it was a Consolation to me on your Account. It was this—Many things are mention'd under different names as peculiar *Disorders*, which are only *Conscequences* of the *Chief* ailment—So that people may depend, whatever Molifies the Chief disorder, cannot be Injurious on the whole. You will perhaps wonder at my mentioning this, but I really think so much on you, I catch at every thing I hear when I am thought wholly inatentive to what is said. I am very desir[ou]s of hearing from you as often as you convieniently can—and when a considerable time elapses without a Letter I imagine you are too poorly to write. I hope your Thumb will be well by the time you receive this.[13]—I did not indeed know the Hand which wrote the Superscription, and hastily broke it open—as soon as I saw the dear Subscribers name

I threw aside my Cousins Letter, and gave yours the Preference; my Sisters observing that said: Oh that Letter is from the Sister of your heart, without doubt—(they know you by that tittle). I told them it was so—I am much Obliged to my Nephew for his assistance. Apropo tell him I have a Rocking Chair now as well as my good William and that I find it Convenient and useful for a little exercise. It is lucky that I yesterday began to write. I this minute hear of a Neighbour going to town—tho I had many things to say, must break off abruptly—*My* Love to all that are near and dear to you—ever Yours

M Penry

ALS: Linden Hall Archives. Addressed "Mrs | Elizabeth Drinker | Philadelphia | To the care of | Mrs Stocker." Endorsed "Lititz April 2 1797 | Mary Penry." Margaret Stocker delivered this letter on April 20, 1797. See Drinker, *Diary*, 2:909.

1. See Letter 18.

2. To "frank" a letter was to send it by public conveyance free of expense.

3. "*gaius mine Host*": Romans 16:23. Grace Parr (ca. 1740–1814), born Grace Peel in Lancaster, married William Dowell (d. 1768) and, later, William Parr (d. 1786). She was a wealthy widow with no children during the years that MP visited Lancaster and stayed with her at what is now 141 North Prince Street. For Benjamin West's portrait of Grace Peel, see Cooper and Minardi, *Paint, Pattern, and People*, xiv. Polly Roberts and her husband, a hatter, lived in Lancaster (see Letter 17, note 1) and, like Drinker, were Quakers ("*Friends*").

4. The single sisters' diary does not indicate this trip to Lancaster during November 1796.

5. "Dorsch": Friedrich Doersch had begun to carry letters between Lancaster to Philadelphia in 1782. See Hocker, *Genealogical Data*, 163. The "Widow Dersch" rented a house from MP's friend John Roberts in Lancaster. See United States Direct Tax of 1798, Microfilm 372, Roll 6, LCHS. "Boller and Jordan": see Letter 40, note 3.

6. MP's uncle was warning against the Welsh radicals who, with English, Irish, and Scots radicals, emigrated in great numbers in these years. See Letter 48, where MP discusses "these Malcontents"; and Durey, *Transatlantic Radicals*. "Birmingham . . . Riots": in July 1791, rioters in Birmingham, England, attacked religious dissenters, setting fire to the home of Joseph Priestley, who blamed the government for encouraging the rioters. Priestley left England for America in April 1793.

7. As a Unitarian, Priestley denied the divinity of Christ. He believed, however, that the resurrection was the "central miracle" of Christianity precisely because "God chose to accomplish it with a man who was like other men in all respects." He believed that his Unitarianism or "rational Christianity" was a necessary antidote to deism. See Garrett, "Priestley's Religion," 7. MP was thinking of titles such as *A General View of the Arguments for the Unity of God; and Against the Divinity and Pre-Existence of Christ*, first published in Birmingham in 1783 but reissued in Philadelphia in 1794 and 1796; and *Observations on the Increase of Infidelity* (Northumberland, 1795).

8. "Jehovah Jesus," one of William Cowper's Olney Hymns, published in 1779. See Cowper, *Poems*, 165.

9. "Rhapsody": an expression that was inspired, irrational, enthusiastic, or uncontrolled—hence MP contrasts it with "Sober and fixd thoughts."

10. "P.P.": Peter Porcupine, alias of the British political writer William Cobbett, who wrote the "bloody Bouy" (Letter 44, note 6). "*dreadnought*": a powerful ship or engine.

11. Cobbett fled America in 1800 after a court issued a judgment of $8,000 against him in a libel suit initiated by Benjamin Rush. Cobbett had ridiculed Rush's treatment—bleeding—for yellow fever. See Myrsiades, *Law and Medicine*.

12. Either *A True and Wonderful Account of Mr. Thomas Say, of Philadelphia, While in a Trance* (Philadelphia, 1792) or *A Short Compilation of the Extraordinary Life and Writings of Thomas Say* (Philadelphia, 1796).

13. In 1796 and early 1797, Drinker suffered from pains in her right side, stomach ailments, and pains in her face and mouth from her gums and teeth. See Drinker, *Diary*, 2:813, 815, 823, 834, 843. Furthermore, she had sliced open her left hand. See February 3, 1797, Drinker, *Diary*, 2:886.

50. TO ELIZABETH DRINKER[1]

May 6, 1797
Lititz, Pennsylvania

Lititz May 6th 1797

My Friend!

Accept of a few hasty lines to inquire after *your* and your dear Families Health—and to assure you of my unalterable *love*. The bearer of this my intimate Friend of many years Standing, will be a living Letter; and answer all you wish to know of me; The Widdow Sydrick, who lived many Years with her Husband in your City, where he was Minester of the Brethren's Church, comes Once more to visit her Old Friends—Very fain would she have had *me* with her—but I cannot—travelling is too Expensive; I was quite Sick of my last Journey *there* on that very Account. Mrs Nitschman who goes with her is an agreeable woman, Sister to our Worthy Jacob Van Vleck at Bethlehem.[2] I beg leave to recomend them to your friendly Notice.

Our Friend Pemberton gives me hopes of seeing her here this Summer,[3] could you come or give me hopes of coming, I would enjoy *those* hopes, but alas your weak State of Health forbid those pleasing Ideas. I cannot write you as fully as I wish because I have been prevented writing till allmost too late— Pardon therefore the abruptness of this—My Friend the bearer will make up for my deficiencies. My Love to your good Spouse Sister Son William and all the rest of your dear Family[4]—I remain ever yours

Mary Penry

ALS: Linden Hall Archives. Addressed "Mrs | Elizabeth Drinker | Philadelphia | To the care of | Mrs Sydrick." Endorsed "Lititz May 6 1797 | Mary Penry." Gertrude Peterson Sydrich (1733–1812) and Mary Van Vleck Nitschmann (1757–1831) delivered this letter on May 13.

1. See Letter 18.
2. For Sydrich, see Letter 37, note 37. On June 2 Drinker sent a letter and "sundries" back to MP via Sydrich. See May 13, 19, June 2, 1797, Drinker, *Diary*, 2:917, 919, 924. "Worthy Jacob Van Vleck": Jacob Van Vleck (1751–1831), whose sister Mary (1757–1831) was the widow of Immanual Nitschmann (1736–1790).

3. Likely Phebe Lewis Morton Pemberton (1738–1812), regarding whom see Letter 20, note 4.
4. For the Drinker family, see Appendix C.

🦢 51. TO MEREDITH PENRY, KATHERINE PENRY, AND ELIZA POWELL[1]
November 11, 1797
Lititz, Pennsylvania

Lititz November the 11th 1797

Honourd Uncle! my dear Cousin and beloved Niece!

This is the third time, that I have wrote you this Year, and have not had the Satisfaction of hearing from you since April last, which Letter was dated in February. I am extreemly anxious to hear from you, my dearest uncles advanced Age makes me Aprehensive that every Letter from him will be the last! Nor is there any Reason to prevent your thinking the same of *me* I imagine. As much as I felt troubled, at the Enemys landing so near you, so you have had your fears for me, on account of the Contagius disorder which raged in Philadelphia and other Sea Ports on our Continent.[2] My Relations all left the City. My Cousin Nancy Potts, Mrs Stockers eldest, widow Daughter had taken the fever, was carried from her Bed to the Carriage, and by easy Journeys in which she mended visibly as she travelld, brought to a healthy part of the Country where she recoverd. Cousin Polly Millar and her Husband was on their Return from the Sea Shore w[h]ere she had been for her Health, they were met by a Gentleman who inform'd them the disorder had broke out in the Next house to theirs, they staid but one Night in town, and went to lodgings in the Country. Cousin Peggy Stocker went with her Sister & Brother in Law Mrs Stocker Her Son Clemy with his Family and Cousin Nancy with her two Children went to a Place calld Potts Grove where Clemy's wifes Family Live.[3] On the 16th of August she wrote me a Melancholy Account of the Situation of her Family every one advising her to fly for her Life, and 2 Servants and her Daughter sick, she believed with the Malignant Fever. I was kept in a Cruel uncertainty till the 16th of September, when I received a Letter from her with an account of Cousin Nancys Recovery, and all their Healths—Ive not heard one word from them Since—now near 2 Months but Hoping (as every one are returning Home) Our Family will do the same. I have wrote her, and shall inclose this, to her care. The City has been left allmost destitute of Inhabitants, it is suposed that 2 thirds fled from the dreadful disorder—The Poor have Sufferd greatly, alltho every thing has been done to Mitigate their Suff'rings, that was possible. *Death* has taken the larger Part of that Class, out of this Vale of Tears altho many of the best Citizens has been taken off likewise, among whom we Number 6 Physicians. The Disorder was judg'd to be full as bad, if not worse than it was 4 years agon, and the Mortality it is thought would have been greater, had not the Inhabitants left the City by times and in such Numbers. Poor Philadelphia, it is to be feard the *sudden* Return as one may call it, of this dreadful Disorder after only 4 years Respite, will be a great injury to its Increase, and especially make Strangers rather avoid than seek, this really before the disorder florishing City!

In our Little Village we are blest with a wholsome pure air [and] have, taking all together been remarkable healthy, we burried 2 Old Men who dyed in the Appoplexy, the one a Reverend Clergyman of my dear uncles age, the other a Batchelor not much younger.[4] Heartily and truely do I rejoice to hear that Mutinies Rebelions &c. are overcome and a Spirit of just Subordination to the Excellent Laws and Constitu[t]ion of the British Realm takes place of the so calld Freedom and Equality under which Mistaken Notions so many bands of *Slaves* and *Free Booters*, have made a *New appeerence*[5]—How long *we* may Peaceably enjoy those blessings which our good Lord bestows on us in America I know not. *Many* fear it will not be of Long Continuance. We must rely solely upon him who alone can protect us, and hope the best.

I hear nothing of Mr Coke. I have not, and it seems shall not see him[6]—O my dearest uncle could I but this Moment throw myself into Your Paternal Arms! But I give up my Will to that Lord who has thought best that I should spend my days in America, and you yours in your Native Country! How does my dear Nephew do? why don't he write to me himself.[7] How does my dear Kitty, my Eliza, your good Friends Owens, Our Relations at a distance—have you heard from nancy Vaughn? what is become of my Cousin Kitty Rumsey (Stocker as was) and her daughter who lived at Abergavenny—is Miss Gwillim many years my faithfull Corrispondant Still living—I think hardly, for she must be very old.[8] Well I will now conclude. It is the Eve of my Birth Day tomorrow I shall be 62 years of age—I am certain of your Remembrance, and that you would gladly ask me to a Dish of Tea if I could come. Adieu my ever Revered Parent, My dearest Cousin My beloved Eliza my dear Penry Powell—I remain ever your—*Dutiful Niece* and affectionate Cousin

Mary Penry

ALS: Penralley Collection 1381, NLW. Addressed "Mr | Merideth Penry | Struet Brecon | Brecknockshire | South Wales | Per the Clothier." Stamped "Liverpool Ship." Endorsed "Received this Letter | per January 7th 1798 | Answered it | per April | 23rd 1798."

1. See Letter 29.

2. "Enemys landing so near you": In 1797, a French invasion regiment of 1,400 troops sailed with orders to destroy Bristol. Weather conditions forced the fleet to land at Fishguard Bay in southwestern Wales on February 22. The invaders surrendered on February 25. "Contagius disorder": the yellow fever, which had visited Philadelphia in 1793, returned in the summer of 1797. See Letter 32, note 5.

3. "Relations all left the City . . . Potts Grove": on August 20, 1797, John Henry Hobart reported that "the Stockers . . . are gone to Potts Grove." See *Correspondence*, 287–88. In 1761 the ironmaster John Potts (1710–1768) laid out a town called Pottsgrove (in 1815 renamed Pottsville). James Potts, the deceased husband of Ann Stocker, was one of John Potts's thirteen children; John Clement Stocker's wife was one of John Potts's grandchildren. See Appendix C.

4. Albrecht Russmeyer (see Letter 42, note 25) died on July 4, and single brother John George Stark (1718–1797) on August 30.

5. "*Free Booters*": marauders or pillagers. Earlier in 1797, two mutinies—the Spithead (April–May) and the Nore (May–June)—had occurred on Royal Navy ships.

6. Thomas Coke had returned to Great Britain in February 1797 to preside over the Irish Methodist Conference that summer, but he was back in America when MP wrote this letter. For MP and Coke, see Letter 37, note 6.

7. "dear Nephew": Penry Powell. See Letter 29.

8. "Friends Owens": see Letter 42, note 9. "Miss Gwillim": see Letter 3, note 7. "nancy Vaughn": see Letter 6, note 6. "Kitty Rumsey": see Letter 30, note 10.

৯৺ 52. TO ELIZABETH DRINKER[1]

March 22, 1798
Lititz, Pennsylvania

Lititz March 22nd 1798

My dearest Friend!

Your truely acceptable Letter rejoiced me it is true—but I was coverd with confusion, at the Intimation that you had not heard from me, of the *return* of our Friend Sydrick.[2] Not trusting my own memory I ran to her, to enquire if she could remember my having wrote, and acknowledged my *Obligations*. She convinced me, by putting me in mind of the Message she commisiond me to deliver to you, of *thanks* for your kind entertainment, which she had received at your house, and which I read to her out of my Letter to *you*. This is some *ease* to my own Mind, and clears me of the Sin of Ingratitude—Yet my Friend, since nothing of the kind reachd your Hand—how good your heart must be, to pass over such an aparent Slight.

Well my dear, I acknowledge your condescention has effectualy roused me out of the Indolence I seem to be lost in—Can I hear the friend of my heart, wish to hear from me and shall I refuse her that, what she Stiles a pleasure— Yet let me in Parenthesis observe that if I knew how to send my Letters, otherwise than with the Post—I should write more frequent—Mr Simons the Jew in Lancaster, has kindly offer'd to send my Letters Post free to his Daughter, the widdow Cohen next door to Nanny Powell, but—here I am fearful of intruding too much—Mrs Cohen sends Letters to me, when left with her Neighbour Powell. As for Boller, he has the best will in the World to oblige—but the multiplicity of Bus'ness, causes him to forget triffling Letters.[3] And yet it is vexatious, that tho I write but *seldom* the *few* I write should not *all* come to hand. Most certainly the first Letter I wrote you after our Friend Sydricks return has miscarried. Your good Natured sweet Sally Downings Visit here—was the next to a Visit from yourself—She has partley engaged to be here again this spring, with her Daughter.[4] I shall see, wether she keeps her word, according as *that* turns out, our Corrispondance—*may* become more frequent. And do you immagine my dear, that any subject can be *more* agreeable to me than *your* Family, doubly dear to me for their sakes, as well as yours. Your loving, jealous expression: Very well Polly Penry, pleased me better than the greatest compliment—for under these words, were couch'd an affection—better felt than described! not easily overlook'd by a feeling heart. You ask me how long since I went to A.B School—since 1747 or 48 I cannot justly determine, either in my 12th or 13 Year, but I believe in my 12th. I came to America in the year 1744.[5] Our Acquaintance has been near 50 years! and during the years interviening, between my going to Bethlehem—and paying you a Visit at your House in Water Street, How often, have I lamented my *departed* Friend![6] But you are given me as from the dead, and I will not dwell on the Years of mourning for my loss. When I was last in the City Abby Griffiths sent word she should be glad to see me. I am sorry now, that I did not call on her[7]—as it was a Silly Backwardness on my side, which prevented me. Think my dear (if we take it for granted) that we shall know each other in the Life to come. How rejoiced our good Anthony will be to see one after the other, arrive in the Regions of bliss.[8] It is making a large stride from Heaven to Earth, but I must write to my Friends just what's uppermost—and having about half an Hour ago read the German Paper, in which the French preperations for landing in England is described: I must confess my heart feels quite depress'd—Since that Scourge of Europe has hitherto been Successful, we cannot pretend to judge, what further Message of desolation their armies may have.[9] We hear many Reports, but little that we can depend upon. P.P's Gazette we duely receive— and I believe, he is an honest, tho very blunt English Man, and I cannot say I approve every thing he says, tho he very often makes me laugh, and I really felt my self hurt, when he abused our worthy Friend.[10] The Murther and Robery, is very frequent in our Neighbourhood, there is now a Case depending at Harrisburg, for a Murther committed about 10 Miles from us—A

Brother in Law with the foreknowledge, and according to the wish of his Wicked Wife, hired a parcell of Irish Villains, to kill her 2 Brothers, who were Single, in order to inherrit their Estate, the one is all killd, the other escaped.[11] We are allmost afraid to go to Lancaster at least on Foot. Impiety seems to gain ground every where, according to the Papers, your City abounds with *every kind* of Sinful *Pastimes*, and up in the Country Libertinism of *every kind*! prevails—Melancholy times these—and *we* likewise may as well expect a Visitation, as those parts of Europe, who have sufferd the Scourge already. O my Friend what changes We have lived to see, and God knows what awaits. Nevertheless we will put our Trust in the Lord, who will *Reign* in spight of all his Enemies. All their endeavors to dethrone *Our King* is *vain*, and they will find it so to their *confusion*. I wish you would give me some small insight into the Politicks of the times. You may depend I was greatly concerned in the Contested Election—because I *feard*, the *one*, and respected the other—Your Vermont Lion, has greatly divertd me—altho it makes but a poor Apearance in the *circle* he moves in.[12]—You ask me wether I have heard from my Friends across the Atlantic, I had that Pleasure last April—and October, the last dated August the 12th my good Old uncle wrote a most Affectionate, and truely Pious Letter, laments Priestlys sad falling off, and observes his Tennets were too common among the Presbyterians. But said God can bring order out of Confusion—He says the refuse of Brittain leave that Island for America, and that alltho they were glad to get rid of them, he feard they would create us much Trouble![13] the good Man prays most devoutly that the Lord would protect us. His Daughter my Cousin Kitty Penry and his Grand daughter (my *Welch Niece*) Eliza Powell writes very sweet Letters and express themselves happy and Loyal Subjects to the best of Kings. Well my dear Friend what shall I say further? I hope you will not be visited with the Yellow Fever next summer, but in Mercy be preserv'd from that dreadful Calamity.[14] We have had a very Sickly time throughout the Winter, a disorder very much resembling the Influenza has gone thro our Whole House. I was confined 3 weeks, a Violent Cough with a smart Fever was my Complaint, and the most of us had the same disorder, others again, had a sore Throat with a gathering, which broke, and the discharge of Matter, was amazing: it was the same with those of us who had the Cough, we realy believed we had a boil in our Head, the Pain and discharge was so violent. The disorder seems now over. We had 12 Children Innoculated for the small Pox, and they all did extremely well under our good Doctors Care, which we were the more thankful for, as the Disorder has been very fatal to the Children, and Adults in Lancaster, and the Country round about us.[15] The day before yesterday a Son of one Thomas Barton (a Printer, lately from Philadelphia) at Lancaster ran from his Fathers door, to get up behind a loaded Waggon, his foot slip'd as he was Climbing up, he fell, the Waggon Wheel went over his Neck, and killd him instantaniously. What a shock for the poor Parents![16] I could relate several incidents so Melancholy, that I will not wound your Feelings by repeating them. I shall send this [to] Patty Powells care, inclosed to Mrs Stocker—If you could Point [out a] Person more suitable, Particularly some friend in Lancaster, I would do [missing]. Our Friend Sydrick, desires her kind Love to you, and your whole Family! Mine to your other Self—my truely respected Friend, and tell him: Old as I am, I would cheerfully take a *much* longer Journey, to enjoy your Company and Conversation—were the state of my Finances such, that I could afford it.[17]—Yet a few Years, and all complaints of that Nature will cease—and we shall meet never to part.—

My kind Love to your Son William my Nephew! to my *sweet* Sally Downing, to Nancy, Polly, Your little Grand Children &c. Now my good dear Aunt Mary—*You* who has renderd the usual despised State of Old Maids—a worthy honourable State by *your Carriage* in that *Solitary Path*, in which I walk with so much Content, accept of my tenderest Love[18]—*We* Maidens will Love & Respect each other—and not think those worthy our displeasure who affect to look down on us with *Compassion*! Adieu my Beloved—Ever your faithful

Mary Penry

ALS: Linden Hall Archives. Addressed "Mrs | Elizabeth Drinker | Philadelphia | To the care | of Mrs Stocker." Endorsed "Lititz March 22 1798 | Mary Penry." This letter reached Drinker on April 4; another letter with drawings arrived the next month. See April 4, May 26, 1798, Drinker, *Diary*, 2:1018, 1038.

1. See Letter 18.

2. Drinker did hear from MP after Gertrude Peterson Sydrich, who had visited with Drinker (see Letter 50, note 2), returned to Lititz (August 16, 1797, Drinker, *Diary*, 2:953). MP here replies to a letter that Drinker wrote on March 2, 1798 (Drinker, *Diary*, 2:1008).

3. "Mr Simons the Jew in Lancaster": Joseph Simon (1712–1804), an important Lancaster merchant. In 1779 his daughter, Belle or Belah (d. 1824), married Solomon Myers Cohen (1744–1796), and the couple lived in Philadelphia. For Ann and Patty Powell, see Letter 38, note 3. For "Boller," see Letter 40, note 3.

4. For Sally Drinker Downing, Elizabeth Drinker's eldest child, see Appendix C.

5. "A.B School": Anthony Benezet (1713–1784), an important Quaker abolitionist, taught MP, along with the young Elizabeth Sandwith (later Drinker) and Hannah Callender (later Sansom).

6. The Drinkers lived at Water Street for ten years (1762–71) after their marriage, moving in March 1771 to Front Street.

7. Abigail Powell (1735–1797)—likely a schoolmate of MP and Drinker—had married William Griffitts (1724–1762) in 1752 and had four children. She had died on November 16, 1797.

8. "good Anthony": Anthony Benezet, MP's and Elizabeth Drinker's teacher, had died in 1784.

9. In October 1797, the Directory placed Napoleon at the head of the army to plan an invasion of England. More than 225,000 regulars and militiamen mobilized in Britain to oppose the invasion. In

May, a few months after MP's letter, Napoleon redirected his energies against Egypt and Austria, and an invasion of Britain did not occur.

10. "worthy Friend": Benjamin Rush. Cobbett's *Gazette* replaced his *Censor* in 1797. For this controversy, see Letter 49, note 11.

11. John Hauer hired four recent Irish immigrants to murder his wife's brothers, Peter and Francis Shitz, who had inherited a large estate from their father. Francis Shitz was killed on December 28, 1797, and a grand jury issued its indictment in March. See *Correct Account of the Trials*.

12. "Contested Election": the 1796 presidential election between John Adams and Thomas Jefferson. "Vermont Lion": Matthew Lyon (1749–1822), a Democratic-Republican congressman, represented Vermont from 1797 to 1801. *Porcupine's Gazette* followed Lyon's career, especially in February 1798 when he spit on congressman Roger Griswold, in response to which Griswold beat him with a wooden cane. For "the filthy affair, of Lyon," see *Porcupine's Gazette*, February 15, 1798, 2. Lyon strongly criticized president Adams in the press and was the first person tried for violating the Alien and Sedition Acts. Found guilty and jailed, Lyon became in November 1798 the only person elected to Congress from jail.

13. "refuse of Brittain leave that Island for America": see Letter 49, note 6.

14. The yellow fever, which had struck Philadelphia in 1793 and 1797, would return in 1798. See Letter 32, note 5.

15. Smallpox inoculations began in America in 1721. Philadelphia experienced some ten smallpox outbreaks during the eighteenth century, with about five hundred people dying in 1759 and about three hundred in 1773. Elizabeth Drinker inoculated five of her children. See Dine, "Diaries and Doctors."

16. Thomas Barton, in partnership with Gotlobb Jungmann, printed German and English texts in Lancaster.

17. A few months later MP traveled to Philadelphia with funds from a visitor from Baltimore. See Letter 55, note 6. She left Lititz on June 16, lodged with Margaret Stocker, attended services at the Moravian church on Race Street, and visited Elizabeth Drinker frequently (Drinker, *Diary*, 2:1047–53), arriving back in Lititz on July 22, 1798.

18. For the Drinker family, see Appendix C.

ᕤ᪲ 53. TO MEREDITH PENRY[1]

November 17, 1798

Lititz, Pennsylvania

Lititz November the 17th 1798

Ever dear and Honourd Uncle

Your dear Letter dated the 22nd of April I receiv'd the first week in November, to my unspeakable Joy. Oh my dear Uncle, how precious is every Word which proceed from your Lips, as dictated to our dear Eliza, I only think it *too little*. I could read by the *Hour* letters from you, and read them over and over again, kissing your dear Name with such warmth of Affection that I think you must be sensible of it. I am delighted to find you are in good Spirits—at least was so, when your last was wrote—and I hope this will find you the same. As for your being a Soldier I doubt not your *Courage* but the day is too far spent, Evening draws near, and with it the time of *Rest* and yet to the very last we are called upon to fight Manfully against the *world* the *Flesh* and the *Devil* in which warrfare we are more than Conquerors thro Him that loved *us*. Since last Fall times are greatly chang'd with us in Political Matters. The French have too soon for their own Interest discoverd themselves. Our Envoys Dispatches being made publick (sorely against the will of *their* Friends among *us*) has rous'd America in *general* (altho it is to be feard they have a *strong* party here) and the warrlike preparations has intimidated the directory, who are now creeping upon all fours to bite us privately— and I very much fear, that we shall have something resembling the Irish Rebelion in America.[2] Last week General Washington arrived at Philadelphia. The Troops went out to meet him, and he left his Carriage and exercised *himself* the Soldiery.[3] We hear he Conven'd all the Staff Officers, and it is suposed they have Matters of importance to transact, which is conducted with the greatest Secrecy—undoubtedly against our Internal Enemies who have their Envoy at Paris, a Man who is a disgrace to the Name of *Logan*, whose Father & Grandfather were Men of Strickt Honour and Probity, and very eminent Citizens of Pennsylvania. I drank tea with Mr Logan at an acquaintance['s] House—when he was a suspected Person and his Countenance was very dark and gloomy. His Father Mr William Logan was a dear Friend of my Mothers, and the Name of his Grand Father is still held in Veneration by the Indians. I was in Philadelphia when he went off, 2 days before I was in his Company, when he apeard in a great Flutter. Boats were sent off after him, but the Vessel was saild—and now this Man will do more Mischief than 50 Letters![4] Yet our Lord *can* confound the devices of our Enemies. You will Easily believe me dear Uncle, when I tell you it does my heart good, to hear the Tone so much changd in Regard to England, which is now spoke of with Respect.[5] And at my Relations house last Summer, a Gentleman was so obliging as to play on the Violins and Sing: *Rule Britania, Britania rule the Waves* &c. This Minute I have had Porcupines Gazette of the 10th of November put into my hands, from which I will transcribe the following Lines. "Now is the Crisis advancing. The abandon'd faction devoted to France, have long been conspiring, and their Conspiracy is at last brought near to an explosion. I have not the least doubt but they have fifty thousand men provided with Arms in Pennsylvania alone. If vigorous Measures are not taken, if the provisional Army is not raised without delay, a civil *warr*, or a Surrender of Independence is not at more than a twelve months distance— The Partizans of France are linked together in one Chain from Georgia to New Hampshire. The Seditious Impudence of the Democratic Societies has given Place to the dark and Silent System of organiz'd Treason & massacre, imported by united Irishmen, the Horrors of which may be learnt, not by viewing that Kingdom during the late Rebellion, but by attending to the discoveries that have been made, by reading the Intentions of the Conspirators, if their Plans had been attended with Success, all the innumerable Miseries to which the Proprietors of Ireland were doom'd by the Shear[es]'s and their blood thirsty gaing at this moment are intended for the Proprietors in this Country."[6] This is a Shocking Picture—and with such, our News Papers are fill'd, may our good Lord avert the threatned Storm. *We* can do nothing further, than set down quietly and pray fervently to our good Lord for Protection—we are sure that without his permission, no Evil can befal us, and if he in his divine wisdom shall see fitting to visit us with warr, as well as Pestilence, we must humbly Sumbit, being assured all things shall work for our good in the end. We hear many different Stories about Admiral Nelson and Buonaparte. The last account was the latter had beaten the former, and taken 7 Ships of the Line and that Nelson in a fitt of dispair at being Conquerd, had blown his own brains out. Accounts before these, mention Buonaparte's defeat and made Prisoner to Nelson.[7] I wish we could here the Truth. I should very much like to hear a little News from you, altho I think Cobet is very Punctual with his News from England, yet as the French landed so near you I earnestly wish'd to hear some Perticulars.[8] Glad I am, that there is *Religion* in England and your account of the thanksgiving day in Pembrokshire gave me indeed great Satisfaction. Is then the Prince of *Wales* grown any better as he grows in years, may God of his Infinite Mercy spare your good Old King many Years, since the charactor we have of the Prince of Wales is but indiferent, you know better than I do if he deserves it.[9] I have been told that Atheistical and Deistical writings were much out of Fashion in England, and that several of the Nobility had turnd such authors out of their Libraries. A good Sign this of better times, we are drawing to the Close of the 18th Century and some wise men insist, that it will end on the 31 December 1799—which is reasoning above my Comprehension, true it is we shall write 1800 on the first of *January* following—but still the Century will not close till the 31 of December following.[10] I suppose this way of Reasoning is *Logic* a part of Science I am a Stranger to [and] shall therefore—If my Life is spared thus long, end the 18th and begin the 19th Century as the rest of Christians do and let the *Logicians* (if they so chuse) date a year beyond me. Were we as certain of the Comencement of the Blessed Milenium as we are of the 19th Century it would be worth living to see—but at the present Situation of the World, altho these times *may* be preparatory to it, they seem not calculated to an Entrance into Peace and Harmony, for since my Rem[em]brance, we have never had more tempestous times, than since the French Revolution. By & by, in the Lords good Time, the raging waves will be still'd, and his Spirit will openly as it ever has privately, rule in the hearts of Men, and the Present evil will produce much good. I last Summer read the Preface to Sewell's history of the Quakers, wherin he quotes part of a Prophecy of Arch Bishop *Usher*, in which he observes that in all former Perscecutions of the Christians, the most *emminent* were selected, but that the *Next* Perscecution would fall on the Nominal Christians, the very worst of those who bore the Name, would be the greatest Sufferers, and the Number would be comparatively small, of *real* and *true* Christians, that would suffer in the Perscecution he foresaw in our days.[11] And I believe he foresaw right—For how Many thousands have fallen in France and in those Countries under their Dominion, and the most of those have *not* Sufferd on a *Religious* account. I hope the next Century will bring about more pleasing Revolutions than the last 10 years of this for our Lord will reign Sole Lord, and his Enemys will be his Footstool.[12] We my dear uncle shall be gatherd to our Fathers ere long, and quit this tempestous Sea of Life and Perhaps ere long, be Eye Wittnesses when the Earth will be coverd with Righteousness as the Waters Cover the Sea, for when we are once with him an hundred years will be like so many Moments. The World is grown Old in Sin and Iniquity, the whole Creation pant for a change, and that change is fast aproaching, Divine and Prophane writers agree in this Point, that all Nature expects a total Revolution, all things are working to this end, the wicked are the Instruments of Gods Wrath against Infidellity, and numbers are cut down, that incumberd the Earth, Many are laid low in the Dust, who lifted up their Impious Hands and Pens against the most high. Where are Chesterfield, Rousseau, Voltaire, the Old king of Prusia &c. &c. They are gone, and their Names held in abhorence by many who were once their Disciples. That poor wretch Pain, drags on a mi[s]erable Existence at Paris, and gets his bread by vilifying his Creator, and is such a mean Despicable Apostate, that even the admirers of his tennets despise the Man— Priestly is sunk as much in disgrace, as he once was in favour.[13] Such is the end of these men and such will be the end of all those *enemies* of our Lord, who are still living in Rebellion against their Creator. In England such wretches has been, and very Possibly still are in Numbers. Nevertheless our Blessed Lord has worthy Champions in his Cause. Perhaps more in Number, than in any Part of Europe of the same bulk, and they will be indued with Strength from above, to stem the Torrent of Infidelity. It is like a Balsam pourd out, to hear it so frequently mention'd that in England, there is a Place for Refuge for Religion, and for her Votaries. *Amen Amen!*

My dearest uncle you will be weary of Perusing my Chitt Chatt and yet I cannot leave off as long as I have space for writing. You wish to know wether I have a good Voice, alas no! I have no Voice for Singing, but a delicate Ear for

Musick, altho I never learnd to Play on any Instrument except the Guitar, and that not worth mentioning. When I was young I had a Strong inclination for Music, but my Step Father being a Quaker, he would not suffer me to learn Music.[14] I took to drawing of my own Accord, without any teaching, and could make a tolerable hand in painting Flowers and Birds in Water Coulours, but I have left that off some years.[15] Altho I continue to embroider Pockett Books and Pin cushions on Black and White Sattin, and to this day have never used Spectacles. Last Monday I enterd my 64th Year. My Spirit often visited you on that day, and felt very much disposed to take a walk with my dear Uncle. I have obtain'd leave to send you my Picture which was drawn in my 22nd Year.[16] In the Spring I shall send it to Mr Thomas Compston in Philadelphia who is the agent for the Welch Society, and has engaged to send it safe. It has been very much injured when the British were in Philadelphia. Mrs Stocker had left the City and those who log'd in her House tore off the Frame of the Picture which was very handsome, this together with smoke and Dust has almost Ruin'd it. Nevertheless Mrs Stocker would not part with it to any one but you. If I could afford it, I would far rather send you a Miniature likeness of myself as I *now* look—but who knows what I may be enabled to do. *One* will be sent either large or small. The Welch Society of which I gave you a description increase greatly and were it not for the fatal Pestelential Fever I should have heard more of them.[17] From the Begining of August to the End of October, we had scarce any Communication with the City. I shall send my Packet to Mr Compston to forward to you—but you will be pleased to direct your letters Still to the care of Mr Stocker—who has requested me whenever I write you to give his Cordial Salutation as does his Mamma and Spouse—In July his Lady presented him with a little Daughter which was a great Joy to them. He has 2 Sons Anthony, and John Clements and 2 Daughters Patty Rutter—and Anna. His ladys Maiden name was Rutter—a Son and daughter he has Burried. Mrs Stockers Youngest Daughter Peggy, is shortly to be married to a Scotch Merchant, a very Sober Young Gentleman, named Alexander Miller whose Brother John is Married to her Sister Polly.[18] Their Parents are both living in Edenborrough Scotland (I believe Ive not spelt the word right). They are all in high Life. Mr Stocker bears an Extraordinary Charactor. He is indeed an Excellent good Citizen. He is now a Member of the Assembly, and might fill the first Offices, if he would incline to serve but being a Man of an Independent fortune, he prefers ease to Toil—For—whatever is committed to his charge is faithfully taken care off. As one of the the Directors of the Bank he is so trusty, that on the least alarm in the City either by Night or day, he is one of the first at the Bank with his Musquet. To sum up all: he is an Obedient Son, an Affectionate

Husband, a tender Father, a faithful Brother—a good Churchman—and—for—a—Gentleman—a Religious man—He is extreemly well satisfied with me, since he thinks me no disgrace to the Family—of the Stockers—and my dearest Uncle—I hope not to the Penrys whose name I bear—

We have last week lost a most Emminent Clergyman, who departed to the Joy of his Lord at Bethlehem in his 52nd year. He was a man of uncomm[on] talents both in the Minestry and care of Souls—He lived 6 years with us at Lititz, and *all* lament our Loss which is his great gain!—he left a disconsolate Widdow but no children.[19] As I am prevented by several interviening obstacles from writing much to my Cousin & Niece they must share in my dear Uncles Epistle. Our Bishop and his Lady Mr Herbst and his Spouse request their Love to the dear Old Man.[20] One of my Intimate Friends to whom I communicated your Letter, said it was well worth drinking a glass of wine to your Health which was done accordingly, and you may be sure I pleg'd him with a right good will—altho I am not used to, nor fond of any kind of spiritous Liquors. Our Family request their best Love to you—be pleased to give my kind Love to all your Friends and Intimates, in Particular to Mr Owen and his Family. I thought on you on your birth day and wishd to be *one* hour with you! It is not in my Power to send you the texts for the next year untill they come over from England, which is generally in the Spring.[21] And now my dear uncle recomending myself to your Prayers as my second Parent I bid you adieu for this year—wishing you a happy close of the old & entrance into the New, and that the coming year, you may be bless'd with Health and every Spiritual and Temporal Comfort. So prays your ever Dutiful Niece

Mary Penry

P.S. I cannot refrain transcribing the closing Lines of a Piece in the Gazette for the 12th Instant:

"The ways of God are inscrutable but allways Just. Never was there a Nation so ill treated as Great Britain. The foulest Calumnies ever engenderd by Envy and Malice have been heaped on her without Measure. A thousand times has her Fall been foretold, A Thousand times have her Enemies Revelled in the hope of hearing her last Groan. In spite of all this she is now greater than ever. The fate of the world hangs on the Sceptre of her King."[22]

To the last Strophe your Niece cannot assent. The fate of England and the whole World depends on the Will of her Creator and preserver—and if she does not throw off her Allegiance to him, he will protet her with his Mighty Arm, and not England alone but all who put their trust in him—In every Kingdom People & Nation.

ALS: Penralley Collection 1383, NLW. Addressed to "Mr | Meredith Penry | Struet Brecon | Brecknockshire | South Wales." Endorsed "Received January the 25th 1799." This letter was sent with Letters 54 and 55.

1. See Letter 29.

2. "Envoys Dispatches being made publick": the XYZ Affair. On March 20, 1798, President John Adams turned over to Congress evidence that French officials had mistreated American peace commissioners. These dispatches, when leaked in April, caused a political firestorm. Federalists pushed for war, which Adams resisted, but on July 7, 1798, Congress annulled the 1778 Treaty of Alliance. See McKitrick and Elkins, *Age of Federalism*, 588. The Irish Rebellion of 1798, an uprising by Irish republicans against British rule in Ireland, lasted from May to September.

3. The Senate approved President John Adams's nomination of former president George Washington as lieutenant general and commander in chief of the United States army in July 1798. Washington, who accepted the appointment reluctantly, arrived in Philadelphia on November 10, 1798.

4. "disgrace to the Name of *Logan*": George Logan (1753–1821), the son of William Logan and grandson of James Logan. See Letter 7, note 3. After receiving a medical degree from the University of Edinburgh in 1779, he returned to America and served as a Pennsylvania representative in the 1780s and 1790s and as a senator from 1801 to 1807. In 1798 he went to Paris to negotiate peace with the French to settle the Quasi-War. Federalists denounced his activities and passed a statute that made it a crime for individual citizens to interfere in a dispute between the United States and a foreign country. See Tolles, "Unofficial Ambassador."

5. "England . . . now spoke of with Respect": see Letter 46.

6. MP omitted several sentences in copying these lines from *Porcupine's Gazette*, November 10, 1798, 3.

7. Neither report was true. Admiral Horatio Nelson (1758–1805) spent the summer of 1798 hunting the French in the Mediterranean and was injured, but not mortally, at the Battle of the Nile (August 1–3, 1798).

8. "the French landed so near you": see Letter 51, note 2.

9. "good Old King": George III (1738–1820). George Augustus Frederick, Prince of Wales (1762–1830), was known for his extravagant lifestyle. He married Princess Caroline of Brunswick (1768–1821) in 1795 but the couple formally separated in 1796, and his various mistresses, before and after marriage, were well-known on both sides of the Atlantic.

10. A week earlier *Porcupine's Gazette*, November 12, 1798, 2, calculated the end of the eighteenth century: "We must of course wait until the end of the year 1800, before we can say 93,600 weeks have expired, or 18 centuries have ended." Later MP contends that the eighteenth century ends on December 31, 1799. See Letter 56, note 18.

11. The preface to Sewel's *History of the Rise, Increase, and Progress of the Christian People Called Quakers* quotes the prophecy of archbishop James Ussher (1581–1656) that a future "dreadful persecution" would target "the formal christian" rather than "the most eminent and spiritual ministers and christians" (ix).

12. Luke 20:43.

13. MP mentions Philip Dormer Stanhope, 4th Earl of Chesterfield (1694–1773), Jean-Jacques Rousseau (1712–1778), Voltaire (François-Marie Arouet) (1694–1778), and Frederick the Great of Prussia (1712–1786), all Enlightenment figures who seemed, to the devout such as herself, irreligious heretics. Thomas Paine fled to France in 1792 and remained there, occasionally imprisoned, until 1802, when he returned to America. See Letter 63, note 10. He had published *The Age of Reason* in 1794. In 1798, Joseph Priestley became identified publicly as a "friend of France" when Federalists published his private correspondence. Cobbett's *Porcupine's Gazette*, August 20, 1798, gleefully announced "Priestley Completely Detected" and urged President John Adams to deport him. See Graham, "Joseph Priestley in America," 224–25.

14. "my Step Father": William Attwood. See this volume's introduction.

15. "tolerable hand in painting": MP sent drawings to Elizabeth Drinker. See Letters 20 and 52.

16. "my Picture": see Letter 35, note 4.

17. "The Welch Society of which I gave you a description": perhaps in a lost letter.

18. For the children of John Clement Stocker, and for others of the Stocker family mentioned here, see Appendix C.

19. John Augustus Klingsohr (1746–1798) led the church in Lititz from 1784 to 1790. He left Lititz in 1790 to become head pastor at Bethlehem. He had married Anna Elizabeth Mack (d. 1835) in 1784.

20. "Our Bishop and his Lady Mr Herbst and his Spouse": Johann Andreas Huebner and Johannes Herbst. See Letter 19, note 1; and Letter 37, note 40.

21. "Mr Owen and his Family": see Letter 42, note 9. "texts for the next year": Moravian watchwords. See Letter 25, note 5.

22. These lines are from *Porcupine's Gazette*, November 12, 1798, 3.

ઌ 54. TO KATHERINE PENRY[1]

November 17, 1798

Lititz, Pennsylvania

Lititz 17th November 1798

My dear Cousin Kitty

I am extreemly Sorry that the oppertunity I now Embrace to write you, has been offerd me at so Short, a Notice that I fear, I shall neither be satisfactory to you, or myself. I cannot enter into a detail of the many hindrances which interviend whilest writing to my uncle, the badness of the writing the Incoherence of the stile, will convince you, I could not write at my ease. To my Uncle I have wrote on Politics and to you my dear Kitty, I shall enter into Family Affairs.[2] I immagine the Miss Elizabeth Penry you mention, must have been a Daughter of our Grandfathers Brother, I have frequently heard my Mamma speake of that Family with great affection, and she told me, Miss Sally Penry was my God Mother, and I was to have been calld after her, but my Papa would have me call'd Mary.[3] According to her discription, they lived in affluence, and *ours* was reduced—no wonder they lookd Cool on us. "See how the Doves to new built Houses run, And cautiously the ruin'd Towers shun, Happy are those who have a Friend in deed—But they *more* happy are who none does need."[4]—Well, you and I have lived to see many rise and Fall, and being in a state of mediocrity ourselves we cannot fall from any great Heigth however, so much the better for us! the more we grow in Years, the less we shall be affected with those Vississtudes, and I really think it is a great weakness to lament at the loss of Fortune, when we enjoy all the Necessaries of Life. It is the *Intrinsic* Worth, which make us Noble, and a *Noble* mind, looks down with Compassion on those favourites of Fortune, in an humble Confidence, that since their Misfortunes were not the fruits of their own

Irregularities, they are upon a par with those, who ride in their Coach and Six, who are very often in themselves of *very* small importance. As for our Uncle Charle's daughter, I wonder how she can think herself above either of us—I think her understanding must be weak indeed. Nevertheless, I would advise you to write once more to her, and inform her of the disintressd corrispondance we have—my dear was you to ask any favours—(unless indeed Necessity constraind you) I would be the last to advise you to it.[5] Poor dear Cousin Kitty, how disagreeable it must be to your high Spirit, to see some of your own Connections Slight—and others—shall I say be a disgrace to you. It is so mortifying this last Circumstance, that it reconciles me in some measure, to my *Exile* from my Native Country. I do not like to say much on the Subject, but be assured I think often on it—and altho in so large a Family as *ours*, it cannot be expected *every* Member of it will turn out well, yet it is vexatious to see, and hear of their Bad Conduct. Poor Mrs Stocker has but 2 Brothers, and one of them is a perfect Vagabond a poor dirty drunken Fellow, whom they must maintain, to keep him out of the Work House, and this is a great Trouble to the whole Family, and they would *Transport* him if they could.[6] When I first came to Philadelphia there was a poor drunken Fellow, one *Ned Penly* and my Schoolmates would sometimes call him my uncle, as the Name had some semblance with mine[7]—Oh how have I cried for vexation and wish'd him at Jericho. He has been dead and gone, many years, yet I still remember how ill I could bear such Jokes. But now, I think I am become more Passive, I have learnd to *know myself*—and that among the *children of God* I am one of the *meanest*, that when I close my eyes to this world, all *Rank*, and *Family Pride* is at an end, and In the Kingdom of Heaven, the *poor* of this world I fear, will be more *numerous* than the *wealthy* and the *noble*. O my Cousin, blessed are the meek for they shall Inherrit the Earth![8] I wish I had less Pride, and more Meekness—I beg you will present my best Love and Respect to all your Friends, and those of *our* Relations, to whom it may be any pleasure to think on the Poor Exile from America. I think we are very fortunate with our Corrispondance, considering these critical times, very few of your Letters have miscarried and I believe not one of Mine. I wrote you last Spring a large Packett, which I hope you have long had in Hands. I should have wrote you much Sooner, had not our Corrispondance with the Sea Ports been Stopd by the Fatal Pestilential Fever, which raged in Philadelphia, New York, Boston and in short in most of the Ports in the United States, a very trying Circumstance this, even for us, on account of our work as we Spin great quantities of Cotton for New York, and could not send any there, which we felt very severely.[9] Cash I think never was scarcer, a general Stagnation of Busness, and every thing dear. Wheat is now a Dollar and a half our Currency, that is 7/6 Sterling—Butter 9d. Sterling, good tea from 7/6 to 15/, Lump Sugar 2/ and Muscovada or Brown Sugar 1/ the Pound, *all Sterling*. Beef is here in the Country 4d a Pound by the Quarter, and Veal 3d in the City, tea Sugar & Coffee is Cheaper, but Meat and Grain, butter &c. is double that Price. Land is greatly fallen in Price and House Rent in Philadelphia for Numbers have left the City, and retired back in the Country. Last year the Fever carried off about 4 thousand, and this year about 5 thousand in Phila-delphia alone—and it has keept on so late this year, that it is greatly to be fear'd the Houses could not be well cleans'd before the Citizens returnd, and will very likely breake out again. Poor Philadelphia will be ruin'd thro this sore Visitation; when we remember that 50 thousand left the City, and yet the Number of deaths were so great, we may call the Disorder by its proper Name the *Plague* tho every one is loath to pronounce that dreadful Word.[10] The years 1793 97 and 98 I suppose on a Moderate Computation, has carried of[f] 15 thousand!—It is even now wisperd, that Numbers die daily, but they are burried in the Night, and it is keept as privately as Possible, that the Country People may not keep away from bringing their Produce to the Mar-kets—The Flux has been very fatal in the Country, but none dyed of the Fever in the Country, but those who were infected before they left the City, and some recoverd, as soon as they came into a Pure Air—Altho those were a very small Number. My Cousin writes me, that her daughters Husbands Partner, catch'd the Infection at a Tavern, by sleeping in a Bed in which a Person had dyed in the disorder. He went to a Gentlemans House, in which the Young Lady he was engaged to be married to, was, with her Mother, and was taken Sick, the Family immediately left the House, all but the 2 Ladies who closed his Eyes—and were obliged themselves to lay him in the Coffin, and even to Screw it, not one Creature could they get, for Love or Money to perform that Office. People forsake their nearest and dearest Friends, and leave them to Perish, so great is their Terror—Oh the Distress of Hundreds during these last 3 Months is unspeakable. Hitherto none of my Relations have been afflicted with the disorder, they fled from the devoted City as Mr Stocker express'd himself in a Letter to me[11]—and they have been graciously Preserv'd. The Philadelphians have now resolved to have a Canal thro the City, in hopes that will be of Service, God knows best[12]—hitherto these Visitations have not had much Effect on their Morals, they ascribe the disor-der to Natural Causes, and when it is over they quickly forget their fears. We in our large Family enjoy our Healths and are cheerful and Happy—Could I but accompany this Letter and only spend one 24 hours with you I think, I could be satisfied. When the Luft (german I protest, only think) *air* Balloon is brought to such Perfection that it can be Steered as a Ship, then I will try to pay you a visit.[13] I must now think of my Eliza, and conclude my letter to you, my dear Cousin, with this *Side* or Eliza will be sick of Disapointment— adieu my beloved Cousin *ever ever* your Sincerely Affectionate Cousin

Mary Penry

Kiss my dear uncle for me

ALS: Penralley Collection 1382, NLW. This letter was sent with Letters 53 and 55. Letter 53 records the address and endorsement.

1. See Letter 29.
2. See Letter 53.
3. "Miss Sally Penry": see Letter 3, note 7.
4. MP joins two couplets from different poems printed in various miscellanies. In Tapner's *School-Master's Repository*, both poems are titled "Friendship" (195, 209).
5. "disintressd corrispondance": MP advises her cousin to assure the Penrys that their correspondence is not motivated by financial interest.
6. "perfect Vagabond a poor dirty drunken Fellow": Thomas Phillips. See Appendix C.
7. "one *Ned Penly*": Edward Penly, who obtained a marriage license in 1745 and was listed on the 1756 Philadelphia tax list (occupation unknown), was a beneficiary of William Attwood's will. See Last Will and Testament, Register of Wills Office.
8. Matthew 5:5.
9. For the single sisters' textile industry, see Appendix D.
10. "the Fever": yellow fever. See Letter 32, note 5.
11. "devoted City": accursed city. "Devoted" means "set aside for destruction," as in the story of Jericho (Joshua 6:15–27). In eighteenth-century editions of the King James Bible, the chapter title of Deuteronomy 20 was "What Cities must be devoted."
12. "Canal thro the City": in August 1798, Jacob Hiltzheimer mentioned a "canal from Norriton, near Schuylkill, to the neighborhood of Philadelphia, to bring the water into the city, for the great benefit of its health." See *Extracts*, 3:259.
13. "*air* Balloon": see Letter 42, note 28.

❧ 55. TO ELIZA POWELL[1]
November 17, 1798
Lititz, Pennsylvania

17 November 1798

My dearest Niece

Your dear lines was most acceptable to me, but would have been far more so, if they had not been so *concise*. True you had to write for three Persons, but my love, look over my Letters, you will find I generally write 3 times as much again. And only think how disapointed I must be to see you write so large, as to fill your Paper, and my pleasure is at an End in a few Minutes. I know not what to ascribe it to. All my Corrispondants insist upon long Letters from me, and they generally write Short ones. You have been a very good Girl, and have formerly wrote longer letters which gives me hopes you will make me amends, for the Lilliputian Letters, of the last & this Fall. I hope you receivd my Letters of Last Spring, in which I acknowledged the receipt of your Pretty Present of the Ribbon with many Thanks—I likewise paid the Tribute of sincere condolence with you, on the decease of your dear Brother—whom *you* Still Remember—and *I* have not forgot.[2] I am an answer in debt to your Former Letter, at Least an answer to a Momentous Question, which I must again beg your leave to postpone, as I am really too much hurried to give it due Reflection—and this time I would rather, if Possible, entertain you with something New. Last Spring a Lady from Baltimore (a Sea Port above 100 Miles from here) came to Spend a few weeks at Lititz. She is a Person of Family, and ample Fortune, but unhappily Married to a worthless Frenchman who for some Misdemenor, fell into the hands of Justice—and she with her only Child a girl of 13 came hither till the town talk had subsided.[3] She Spent 10 Days here, I was her constant Companion and at taking leave, she made me a handsome Present; her Bounty enabled me to pay a Visit to my Relations in Philadelphia where I spent 4 weeks, extremly agreeable.[4] I never was receiv'd with *more* affection—and I must quickly inform you that we have found out the Identical Mr Powell [(]you related the anecdote of the—[*illegible*] Small Cloaths) was Grandfather or great Grand Father to the 2 Miss Powells in Philadelphia. So my dear I congratulate you to the Relationship to 2 worthy Old Maids—They are not Rich, they keep a Shop, but they are esteemd and Respected by the best in the City.[5] So that tho the advantage is nothing to you nor me, yet Relations of such Charactors, are well worth claiming—and I advise you my Eliza to write a Pretty letter to them—*longer* than that to Miss Kliest—since they are Relations, give them a Simple account of your Fathers Family, and Misfortunes, and a modest account of your present Situation, as in Confidence—Yet without descending to Meaness, or to ask Favours—I am *very* sure it will be extremely agreeable to them—and can do no harm if it does no good. You must Direct to Miss Ann Powell who is the Eldest, her sisters name is Patty—Your Letter must be addressd to both—but the direction to the Eldest—As they are Strickt Quakers, the more simple your Stile is, the more agreeable it will be—take particular care to avoid unnecessary Complements, write plain, and affectionate, that will *take* with them—and perhaps when I am gone, you may have a Friend in America. You must request them to favour you with an answer, Consult with your Grand Papa and Aunt about this Matter. During my stay in Philadelphia, the Festival of Independence was celebrated, which is the 4th of July. It was a grand Show, and very Martial. The Americans have been roused to Indignation, by the treatment their Envoys had receivd from the French Directory, and the American Army was *forming*, several Companies of Volunteers, both Horse & Foot with the American Standard Flying, all the Gentlemen with black Cockades, and the most of them in Regimentals, Blue turnd up with white, or pale yellow, made a most Noble apearence, but the Prospect of *Warr* affected me to tears![6] They Paraded thro the chief streets with drums and Trumpets, and their Beautiful Colours flying, The Spread Eagle the 13 Starrs and Stripes—this was the 4th of July—and a Few Weeks after the City was desolate & deserted—Many hundreds, who were Joyful Spectators, and numbers, who acted their *Parts* in the festivity of that day, in the short space of a Few Weeks, were cut off in the midst of their Strength and years—young Hearty People was the chief Objects of the Pestilential Fever. And yet, alarming as the disorder is, the Fever of Sedition, is worse, for it is allways better to fall into the Hands of God than into the Hands of Man—and I fear this last mentiond Fever is the point of breaking out. Numbers, numbers, have taken the Infection—nor have we any Refuge but in our God & Saviour. For your and my Consolation, permit me to transcribe a Paragraph from a Favourite author who speaking of Confidence in God says as follows:

"Nor is it less our duty to trust in thee, O Allmighty Saviour of Sinners, who savest us not by Bow, nor by Sword, nor by Battle, nor by Horses, nor by Horsemen, nor by Might and Power but by thy Blood which thou didst shed, and by thy Spirit which thou pourest down. Surely shall one say: In the Lord have I righteousness and strength. For he shall be enabled to disern all other grounds of Trust to be but arms of Flesh—but Lies and Vanities—but Spiders Webs—and perishing gourds—but those foundations that shall be overflown with a Flood; whilst He that puts his trust in the Lord shall be safe, and shall inherrit his Holy Mountain.

"Though his distinguish'd Priveledges should be like those of Capernaum that was exalted up into Heaven, He confides not in the Temple of the Lord, but in the Lord of the Temple—Though He could boast an Illustrious Descent from the Venerable Abraham, or claim Kindred, according to the flesh, with Jesus Christ himself, He would not on that account think himself intitled to the divine Regard—Though he should find much worldly Substance; He will not say to Gold, thou art my Hope, nor to fine Gold, thou art my Confidence, as though the Allmighty would esteem his Riches; or as though they could be profitable, in the day of his wrath. Though He should equal Heman in the deepness of his Exercise, and Paul in the abundance of

Revelation, He would not reckon it expedient for him to glory. Though for the Cause of Christ he should even pour his blood, Yet by the Blood of the Lamb would He overcome; yet in the Blood of the Lamb (and not his own) would he wash His Robes, and make them White. Tho his Gifts should be eminent, His Knowledge clear, and extensive, tho in the sweetness of his natural Temper he should be like a Moses; and a Paul in the blamlessness of his Life touching the Righteousness of the Law, tho his profession were ever so strickt, and his Reputation ever so fair in a word, tho he should shed many Tears, pour many Prayers, endure many Hardships, make many Vows, form many Resolutions, and exert the most Vigerous endeavours in working out his own salvation: yet all these things he counts but Loss and Dung that He ma[y] win Christ, and be found in him. Though the saving Grace of God should be implanted in his heart, He is not Strong in the Grace that is in himself, but in the Grace that is in Christ Jesus! His justifying Merit is the alone ground of his Confidence, for the pardon of his Guilt; His Sanctifying Spirit, for vanquishing the Powers of his inbred Corruption. All other Confidences he rejects, because the Lord hath rejected them. No tempest shall be able to batter down his Walls, his foundation shall *never* be razed, his Confidence shall *never* be rooted out of his Tabernacle but shall have a recompence of Reward. O Blessed is the Man that trusteth in the Lord, and whose *Hope* the Lord is: for he shall be as a Tree planted by the Waters, and that spreadeth out her Roots by the River, and shall not see when *Heat* cometh but her leaf shall be green; and shall not be *careful* in the year of drought, neither shall cease from yielding Fruit." William McEwen, on the Types &c. page 339.[7]

It is a Peculiar Pleasure to my *Young Companions* to be particularly mention'd by my Eliza and they all request the most affectionate Salutation to you. I am in hopes my Letter to Nancy Vaughn will pave a way for your Corrispondance[8]—Oh how ardently do I wish to procure an Azylum for you—if you should survive your Grand Papa and Aunt! With my Picture which (unless the troubles in America should increase) I have some hopes of sending you some trifle of my Work—I have nothing to bequeath you my love at my decease but my Watch, which being at present, but 2 years old, I trust will not be superanu[a]ted when it reaches your Hands altho I should live 10 years longer.[9] I wish you a happy entrance into the coming year both Spiritually and temporally. Give your *Old Aunts* Love to your *Young* Companions and tell them the *Old World* is far better than the *New*. I have experienced the truth. It is in your own Power to live godly in Christ Jesus—where he has Placed you—and you are as near your Heavenly Home in Great Britain as in America. I *know* I am in that part of the *World*, and in that State of Life unto which it hath pleased God to *call me*. It was not *my* Choice but *his* Direction and I humbly Submit—I remain my Sweet Love your ever Affectionate Aunt

Mary Penry

Give your dear Grandpa a kiss in my Name.

ALS: Penralley Collection 1382, NLW. This letter was sent with Letters 53 and 54. Letter 53 records the address and endorsement.

1. See Letter 29.

2. "decease of your dear Brother": Penry Powell (see Letter 29) died on January 30, 1797. No spring 1798 letter from MP to her Welsh relatives survives.

3. "Lady from Baltimore": perhaps the wife of "Dennis Pease" (see Letter 56, note 8), a captain living in Baltimore in 1799 who had sailed under a French passport. *Porcupine's Gazette* identified him as a "French agent" in 1798.

4. MP left for Philadelphia on June 16 and returned to Lititz on July 2, 1798.

5. For Ann and Patty Powell, see Letter 38, note 3.

6. "treatment their Envoys had receivd": the XYZ Affair. See Letter 53, note 2.

7. Despite the specificity of MP's reference, the quoted lines did not appear in any edition of the text known as "McEwen on the Types": *Grace and Truth; or, The Glory and Fulness of the Redeemer Displayed. In an Attempt to Explain, Illustrate, and Enforce the Most Remarkable Types, Figures, and Allegories of the Old Testament* (Edinburgh, 1763). The passage is from William McEwen's *Select Set of Essays, Doctrinal and Practical*, 2 vols. (Edinburgh, 1767), 2:74–79.

8. For Anne (Nancy) Vaughn, see Letter 6, note 6.

9. "my Picture": see Letter 35, note 4. Margaret Stocker sent the watch after MP died. See Letter 69, note 13.

⁊❧ 56. TO ELIZABETH DRINKER[1]

December 19, 1799

Lititz, Pennsylvania

Lititz December 19th 1799

My Friend!

Before I received yours I had in my Mind to write you and inquire after your Wellfare, as well as inform you of mine. When our Shop keeper returnd from the City, about ten days ago, he told me he had tea & Sugar for me, which would come up with his goods.[2] Being no way used to such Presents, I could not believe it intended for me, but suposed it was for my Friend Rusmeyer, directed to my Care—Soon after I receivd your Letter which cleard up the whole affair—and I return you my Sincere thanks for your *Kind remembrance*. Perhaps it was the more acceptable as times go &c. &c. &c. I have a mind for once to send you a Journal of the last summer at least the Part

I acted in it but in order to account for the chief Occurrence, I must take you back at least a year and a half if you have patience to accompany me in my Retrogate motion—Or have I already informd you of it. Like the most Old people I frequently tell a Story twice over. Well to the point. A very pressing invitation which I receivd from a Gentleman and Lady (to whom I shewd our House) inclined me to take a Journey to Baltimore, as they genourously offerd to bear my Expenses[3]—Yet being Intire Strangers I would not go there without an Inquiry. Having a Corrispondance with a Mrs Rogers a Worthy Member of the Methodist Church a Grand Daughter of Mr Celius as we calld him, but whose name is spelt Hesilus, if you Remember he was a Limner in our time when we were girls,[4] well, I requested Mrs Rogers to inform me wether it would be prudent to accept the invitation—She wrote me to come by all Means and she would make me welcome—gave me directions who to inquire after w[h]ere the stage put up that I might directly be under Protection. One of our Brethren having Bus'ness at Baltimore I sat out with him to Lancaster the first of June—having previously receivd Recom[en] datory Letters from Mrs Stocker and Mr Alexander Millar—to Mr Ireland and Mr Grundy 2 Merchants at Baltimore.[5] Monday the 2d of June at noon we reachd York town where I had a real Satisfaction with several of your Friends—None of *your Public Friends* could be better receivd or more Hospitably entertaind—than *your Friend* was—2 Nights I sleept at Timothy Kircks at their Pressing desire, even to the Concern of our own People who allmost took umbrage at my prefering Strangers to them, however that was quickly over—I calld upon that dear Man Herman Updegraff, and we had a short, but intresting Conversation which I trust was blessd to us both—I likewise was in Company with Friend Hamilton who tho a Nobleman a Man of Erudition, and every way a *Gentleman* is as plain and simple in apearence as one of your Preachers[6]—on the 4th after Dinner we sat out for Baltimore, where we arrived early in the afternoon of the 5th. I enquired and was shewn to the House of Mrs Rogers Friend—she herself being with her Family at her Country Seat, as she inform'd me in her Letter. When I came to Mr Kents warehouse and told my Name I felt very much confus'd finding he had no knowledge of me—I shew'd him Mrs Roger's Letter. He immediately became extreem friendly, said his Wife was certainly prepard by Mrs Rogers to receive me, and sent his Nephew with me to his dwelling House where Mrs Kent gave me a very Cordial reception[7]—Mrs Kent is a good Woman but rather Stiff—a very Strickt Methodist—and a Mother in *their* I[sr]ael, a Sweet good Man a Minester of the Name of Lisle was resident in the house. They *would* not inform Mrs Rogers of my arrival till the 3rd day mean time I sent my Recom[en]datory Letters as directed. On the 7 Mrs Rogers sent her

Carriage to bring me to Greenwood and receivd me as tho I were her own Sister—Mean time Mr Ireland and Mr Grundy was sending all about to inquire for me, and at length a note from the first reach'd me, and peremptorily demanded my Person—which I promised to obey on Monday—Sunday I went with Mrs Rogers to Methodist Meeting—Monday Morning to *Pace's* who were the Persons that had requested my Company[8]—I was received by them with Open Arms and my Apartment prepared as for a Person of Distinction, but Mr and Mrs Ireland, would not permit me to go there to Stay— The Charactor of the Woman (before Marriage) altho now unexceptionable His being a French Man their Family Roman Catholic &c. and I, a Stranger, chose rather to Submit to those whose judgement was better than mine (and in all apearence very much against my own Interests) made an excuse as the Lady expected every hour to be confined, it would be improper for me to be there—they aquiesed in my determination but it was Ob[v]ious they were not pleased—and so your Friend had to bear her own Expences. Upon the whole I had an agreeable Sejour at Baltimore of near 3 Weeks, was very Politely entertaind, and might if I had consented made a permanent Abode there[9]—*not as a Wife*, but a companion to a Lady of Fortune who made me the most advantageous Offers. These Offers are nothing to me they are not New—nor are they flattering to One whose heart and Mind is Steadily Fixed to continue "in the *way of Life unto Which it hath pleased God to call her.*"[10] I returnd in Company of a Gentleman and Lady who brought a Little Girl to our Boarding School,[11] I was taken ill the day after my Return home, and that was a painful disorder a Bilious Cholic which I thought would bring me to the Haven of eternal Bliss, but our dear Lord saw I was not ripe for that Happiness, and restord me to my usual State of Health.[12] At Baltimore I became acquainted with a Swedenborger and find they do not believe in Resurection of the Body[13]—His description of the Joys of Heaven was rather in the Stile of the Alcoran—a wish after a fine Flower—a Tree &c. will be there. Momently gratified I told him my Creed was very short comprised in the four following lines, "Tis Heaven on Earth to taste *his* Love (i.e. Jesus) To feel His Quickning *Grace*, And *All the Heaven* I ask above, Is, *but to see His Face.*"[14] They have Strange Notions those Swedenburgers. This Gentleman gave me 3 Pamphlets which are very Pretty.[15] The one on Influx teaches the same Doctrine held by *all true Christians.* The Influx or Inward Work of the Holy Spirit in the Human Heart which according to its Sacred Influence being more or Less draws us nearer our God—Or leaves us at a Distance from him—the other piece is a Short Account of the Life of Emanuel Swedenburg—the 3d a Poem by one of his Disciples being an Invitation to the New Jerusalem which their Sect are Building. And now I supose you are

Weary of following me from one Subject to the Other at such a distance from home to which I will hasten, but first make an Excursion to Philadelphia and rejoice with you at the Addition made your Family by the little *Sandwith* and my hearty Prayer is that he may prove an Honour to the Name, as a Christian and good Citizen—if he is *one* he will be the other thats past a Doubt[16]—My poor dear Cousin Peggy Millar has not been so fortunate. Poor dear Soul what must she had suffered Corporally and Mentally! The Lord has given her a quiet Resignation to his Will yet I doubt not she will long feel distress'd for the loss of her Sweet Babe.[17]

We are now hastning to the close of this Century—for so I take it to be, having Seen a Book printed near 300 Years past, in which the year of the World the Olympiad, the Roman Consul the Jewish aeria &c. &c. are all noted down and it is there proved beyond a doubt (in my Opinion) that a Mistake was made in the dates after the birth of Christ, and according to this Author (a German Lutheran Minester) on the 25 of this Month 1800 Years are *past* since the Birth of Christ and on the 31 the 18th Century is past and over.[18] This Last Year has been very Remarkable both in Church & State that is taking the Words in an Extensive point of View altho in American no great Revolution has been Effected in either. Yet the Prince of darkness has been at work in the Children of disobedience both Spiritually and Temporally. *Even We* in our narrow Circle have experienced more of his Machinations than all the Years put together that I have lived among the Brethren. The detested French Principles and those Infamous Atheistical and Deistical Writings, which abound every where in the German Language, have found their way among us, and been hurtful to some of *our careless ones*, we dismisd them after, trying in Vain, to bring them to true *Reason*, but their Influence on the Minds of some unsettled youth among us, has been like a slow Poison, however we do not despair of their Recovery—should they Contrary to our Hopes not recover, we must dismiss them also which is a great cause of Grief and Sorrow.[19] As for Political Affairs we cannot at the present Crisis be I think too careful of our Words, wether Epistolatory or Verbal. Yet we know each others mind sufficiently, and I believe we are of *one* Sentiment. I often wish for an Hours Conversation with you—but what signifies wishing—If wishes were Horses, you know what Conscequence would follow. I forgot to tell you that we have a pretty little Boarding School in our House, of 8 fine Girls, the youngest is from Baltimore and not quite seven Years of age.[20] Numerous applications have been made and are still making, but as we cannot increase our Number for want of Teachers, every one must wait for a Vacancy for which reason, a list of the Applications is keept, and according to the time they have applied, they must be admitted. I have heard this Fall from my Uncle in Wales but the date was old, last February[21]—They are well or was well then, and enjoy'd Peace and Competence—But it is time to relieve you and my self and hasten to conclude. My Occupations at this time of year, are so many and various they will not admit a detail. After the Holy days are past, I hope to gain some Liesure hours, which I wish for truely, and then I shall think on my dear little Nieces your Grand daughters—My kind Love to Parents and Children, to your Spouse and Sister Mary.[22] And accept of a tender Embrace from your ever Faithful Friend unto Death

Mary Penry

ALS: Linden Hall Archives. Addressed "Mrs | Elizabeth Drinker | at Mr Henry Drinker Seniors | Merchant | Philadelphia." Endorsed "Lititz December 19 1799 | Mary Penry."

1. See Letter 18.

2. "Shop keeper": Samuel Grosch (1768–1850), who took over the Lititz store from John Becker (1722–1804).

3. "Journey to Baltimore": the Lititz single sisters' diary notes that MP returned from Baltimore on June 29, 1799, with Kitty DeWitt (see below, note 11).

4. Rebecca Young Woodward (1756–1818) married Philip Rogers (1749–1836) in 1776. Their estate, Greenwood, was northeast of Baltimore. She was the eldest daughter of Henry Woodward (1733–1761) and Mary Young Woodward (1735–1820), who had married in 1755. The widowed Mary Young Woodward married John Hesselius (1728–1778), the son of the painter Gustavus Hesselius (1682–1755), in 1763.

5. "Mrs Stocker and Mr Alexander Millar": Margaret Stocker and her son-in-law. See Appendix C. "Mr Ireland and Mr Grundy": George Grundy (1755–1825) and Edward Ireland (1736–1816), who was married to Mary Cheeseman Ireland (1746–1805). Two of the Irelands' children had died before MP's visit; a third, Elizabeth (1774–1840), had married Judge Zebulon Hollingsworth (1762–1824) in 1790.

6. "our own People": members of the York Moravian congregation were concerned that MP was staying with a non-Moravian, Timothy Kirk (1749–1829); Herman Updegraff (1738–1811) became the father-in-law of MP's friend Caleb Cope when John Cope (1763–1803) married Mary Updegraff (1760–1831) in 1786. "Friend Hamilton": unidentified. "as one of your Preachers": Quaker simplicity in dress.

7. "Mrs Rogers Friend . . . Mr Kents": Emanuel and Eleanor Kent were married in Baltimore in 1788. The Methodist Kent was a tea merchant. See Andrews, *Methodists and Revolutionary America*, 181.

8. Perhaps "Dennis Pease." See Letter 55, note 3.

9. "Sejour": stay (French).

10. "*way of Life unto Which it hath pleased God to call her*": from the Anglican church catechism.

11. "Little Girl": Thomas and Elizabeth DeWitt brought their daughter, Catherine (Kitty) DeWitt, from Baltimore in 1799. On December 24, 1799, MP noted in the Lititz single sisters' diary that Kitty DeWitt "kept the melody wonderfully well" when she sang hymns. DeWitt's father left her a piano forte when he died in 1807.

12. "Bilious Cholic": severe pain in the upper abdomen, usually caused by gallstones.

13. Emanuel Swedenborg (1688–1772), Swedish theologian and mystic, whose *Heaven and Its Wonders and Hell from Things Heard and Seen*, published in Latin in 1758, offered an account of how individuals live on after the death of the body.

14. MP quotes from Isaac Watts, "Felicity Above," in *Horæ Lyricæ*, 9.

15. "3 Pamphlets": probably Swedenborg's *A Theosophic Lucubration on the Nature of Influx, as It Respects the Communication and Operations of Soul and Body* (London, 1772), *A Short Account of the Honourable Emanuel Swedenborg, and His Theological Writings* (Baltimore, 1792), and Joseph Proud's *Jehovah's Mercy Made Known to All Mankind in These Last Days . . . as Now Manifested by His Messenger and Scribe, the Honourable Emanuel Swedenborg. A Poem* (London, 1789).

16. "the Addition": Sarah (Sally) Drinker Downing gave birth to her fifth child. See Appendix C.

17. Margaret Stocker's daughter, Peggy Miller, lost her first baby. She died after giving birth to a second in 1801. See Appendix C.

18. "a Book printed near 300 Years past": unidentified. Elizabeth Drinker noted that "they are ringing and firing out the old year, according to the old ridiculous custom—and as some say the old Century: M. Penry tills me in her letter that she is of that opinion, and gives her reason for her belief." See December 31, 1799, *Diary*, 2:1252. Earlier, MP contended that the eighteenth century would not end until the close of 1800. See Letter 53, note 10.

19. "we dismisd them": individuals who received the *consilium abuendi* (Latin: advice to leave) were required to remove themselves from Moravian communities.

20. At the end of 1799, MP listed eight girls in the boarding school: Margaretta Marvell, Sarah Scheafer, Sally Kapp, Amelia Steinman, Nancy Steiner, Anna Maria Henry, Matilda McCallister, and Kitty De Witt. Beck, in *Century and Three-Quarters*, 24, identifies the boarding school girls during these early years.

21. February 1799. Meredith Penry died in May 1799.

22. See Appendix C.

57. TO MEREDITH PENRY, KATHERINE PENRY, AND ELIZA POWELL[1]

May 23, 1800

Lititz, Pennsylvania

Lititz May 23rd 1800

Honourd Uncle, dearest Cousin, and beloved Niece!

I am indeed ashamed to confess: that almost a year has past, since I wrote you, and your last was dated in February 1799. God knows what changes you have undergone since then. I am allways afraid that the next Letters, will bring me an Account of my dear Uncles departure to eternal bliss.[2] Nevertheless I will hope the best, and that these lines will safely reach your hands—and what is more, that I shall receive Letters with your dear name subscribed. You will doubtless wonder at my great Neglect, Indeed I had many things to prevent me, early in the Spring I went to Baltimore, a fine Town in Maryland about 90 Miles from hence.[3] After an agreeable Stay there of three weeks, I came home and was soon after taken very ill of a Bilious Fever, and kept my bed some time. After my Recovery the Yellow Fever broke out in Philadelphia and New York, and all Intercourse with the Sea Ports was at a Stand—It was not till November that the Corrispondance was again opend.[4] Throughout the Winter I heard of no Vessel being up for England. In November my youngest Cousin Peggy Millar was deliverd of a dead Child, after Suffring beyond description.[5] In January Her Spouse a Scotch Gentleman Mr Alexander Millar, wrote me in both their Names, requesting me to come and spend a few weeks with them, alledging this season was better for me to come, than the Summer, on account of the dreaded Fever. On the 9th of February I went to Philadelphia and staid 8 weeks among my Friends there, very much to my Satisfaction altho I was laid up half of the Time with a Bad Cold.[6] In the Passion Week I returnd home, as I could not give up the Solemn *Celebration* of those blessed days among *my own* People. On your Birth day my dear Kitty, Mrs Stocker and I, talkd much of you, and wish'd for your Company to a dish of Tea. While I was in Town the Solemn Funeral Orations—and Processions in Honour of the Immortal Washington, was Celebrated or held, but my Cousin Peggy and my self were too weak and indisposed, to see or hear any thing, altho we were honourd with Tickets. America has indeed sustaind an Irreparable Loss in Washington.[7] Yet I cannot but congratulate *him*, on the great change for his *Eternal Wellfare*. He was in years, he could not act as he wishd—He had many Enemies, and they were the *worst* of Men yet too powerful for him to overcome—He saw a Party Spirit dividing his beloved Country, and for-saw—Pehaps the Evils which threaten us—He is gone to rest before that Evil day—May I be permitted to do the same! The Minds of people here, are in a great Fermentation concerning the Election of a new President—the time of the Present being nearly elapsed—Jefferson has a powerful Party—but the true Federalists do not aprove of him, and the *quiet* in the Land, do not expect peaceable times, if he should be chose to fill that office.[8] It is generally believed he is too great a Friend to France, for the Wellfare of America, how true this is I cannot pretend to say, time will shew wether he is better or worse than Report makes him—as I am Confident God—and not Chance—is the director of our Affairs, I can only beg him to order things according to his blessed will—wether he prepares a Scourge to Cor-rect us, or a Protector of our Civil and Religious Liberties.[9] You have doubt-less heard that William Cobbet (alias Porcupine) has left the State of Pennsylvania, on account of a Law Suit which was depending between him, and a Valueable *Friend of Mine* Doctor Rush, for a Libel[10]—Cobbet was Cast, and fined a Sum Sufficient to ruin Him, if he had not Powerful Friends who helpd him upon his Feet again—It is thought by the most impartial, that the fine was too severe—but poor Cobbet sufferd *more* for his being such a *thorough English Man* than for his Crime. He has now dip'd his Pen in Gall, and knows no bounds in Retaliating on doctor Rush the Injury he suposes done him. I sincerely Pity the Doctor, who is so worthy a Man, so

Sincere a Christian, and such a Phylanthropist, that he would *fly* to the Assistance of his bitterest Enemy—His Sons it is, who have forced their Father to sue Cobbit for Pleasentries, which he in a Vein of Levity wrote concerning him—and now being provoked he publishes the most bitter *Truths* (For Cobbit is no Liar) his very Enemies acknowledge that—This does the Docter more Injury, than the former Pasquils. When I was last in the City, the docter calld several times to see me—and his Conversation was most Edyfying—Pity so good a Man should be brought before the World like a Spectacle! I believe could he recal what he has done, he would gladly give up half his Estate. On the first of March I thought to have great Pleasure among my Country folks in Philadelphia[11]—but it snowd the whole day, I could not Stirr out of the house—I was however honourd by the President of the Welch Society Mr Samuel Merideth, the Son of Rees Merideth, with a piece of Kidd from their Table—I was likewise presented with the Societies Copperplate, which I have Glaz'd in my apartment. It is a beautiful Piece, represents the Mountains of Wales at a distance—a Ship has just reachd the Shore of America, the People are landed, Women with their Spinning Wheels, Men with Packages, great rolls of Welch Flannel lie on the Ground, a fine Figure of a woman advances, with an Infant in her Arms, and a group of Children round her. Hospitality holds out her hand, to wellcome the Mother and her Children, and points to 2 Figures Agriculture and Plenty—in One Corner is the Welch Harp, and in the other— The—Goat—at the Top of the Piece is an Eagle feeding its young—Standing on a Globe with a Label surrounding it with the Words: *Cherish the Virtueous Stranger.*[12] See my dear Uncle what an Honour it is, to be a Welch Woman, and the daughter of a Welchman! Yesterday—I had the honour of a Visit from an august Personage, the *Prince of Wales*—a Mr Llewellin a Native of Carolina, whose father came from Wales [as] a Child—Nevertheless he stiles himself of a Noble Family, the Llewellyns were formerly Princes, which made me give him that Tittle, poor Man, his Principality is very small. He married a Widdow in Lancaster—(8 miles from Lititz) who keeps a large shop, of which he is in Right of his Wife—the—*Prin—ci—pal.* I believe he brought nothing to her, but his Person, and a pretty common Education—however he bears the Charactor of an honest and industrous Man[13]—He beg'd me to present his Compliments to you, he knows very little of his Fathers Country, yet is proud of his Family and desent—

I have no way of sending my Pourtrait to you, and indeed it has been so ill used when the English were in Possession of Philadelphia I am ashamed to send it you;[14] Neither is this a time to send anything of Value, the sea swarms with Pirates of all Nations. I saw in a late News Paper, that Bishop Coke was arrived at New York. I hope he will go to Philadelphia, both there, and in Baltimore, he will hear of *me*. Mrs Stocker will do all in her power to see and speak with him, if he comes to Philadelphia, and I left in the Hands of a Methodist Lady in Baltimore, a concise account of our Family—so that I have some hopes of hearing from him now.[15] Will you ever Honourd Uncle, once more dictate a Letter to your poor Niece—and will you my beloved Eliza write for your Grandpapa—and will you my dearest Kity *Penry* write to your *own* Cousin, and pardon her long silence. I have dreamd of Late much of being at Brecon—but awake I shall never be there, unless in Idea, you know not how often I silently wander about looking for your dwelling—Oh you who have so many Relations within call, can have no conception of my feelings, who can be Years without seeing *one*. I have taken my farewell of Philadelphia. Old Age and Infirmities render long Journeys too fatiguing. Indeed my heart seemd as tho it would break, when I took leave of Mr Stocker and his Family, they were extreemly kind to me indeed; made me Presents of several little articles of cloathing—Tea and Sugar—and seem to regard me as a Relation they are proud of presenting to their Friends. They speake of *you* with so much tenderness, that it binds me more closely to them—Old Mrs Stocker, the Widdow of my dear Cousin Anthony Stocker, is to me as an own Sister. She is very happy in her Children and Grandchildren! *Remember* herself and all the Family desire their Love to my dear *Clover Leaf*. Our Cousins Powells, were quite charmd with Eliza's Letter, and have promised as soon as they can get Sight of an Old Family Bible, which is at present in Possession of a Relation of thiers who is out of his Head—they will then write you at Large—They call me their Cousin for Eliza's sake, and believe undoubtedly that *you* are related, but this *Bible* must be searchd into, and it is 30 or 40 miles from where they live—their Love attends you.[16] Our Worthy Bishop has been extreemly ill—He is yet in such a state of extreem weakness, that we cannot look upon him as out of Danger.[17] In Philadelphia they dread the return of the Yellow Fever, and are as it w[e]re on the Wing, ready for flight, it is a most lamentable Situation, and a great loss to people in Busness, to shut up their houses att least 4 Months in the year, and pay exhorbitants rents, for apartments in the Country.[18] I no longer enjoy a good State of health, my Constitution was never Strong, and it is now still weaker; I think my *house* has so many *Chinks* that I can Spy day light shining thro', the dawn of that eternal day, which I hope will e'er long breake on my *Soul*! Give my very kind Love to *any* and *every* of our Relations you hold worthy to claim Kindred with—To good Mr Owens and his Family, and all your good Friends and Acquaintances Our Family in the House of Maidens, desire their Love to their Sister Penrys Friends.[19] Do write me a long Letter, of every thing worth Notice, I want to know how the poor blind harper does—our Glocester and London Cousins, and every thing proper for me to know. I kiss and embrace you my dear Uncle as tho my arms were round your Neck! My Kitty—My Elisa—my Arms are Stretch'd out to infold you—adieu adieu Bless—and Love—your Dutiful Niece

And ever affectionate *cousin*

Mary Penry

ALS: Penralley Collection 1390, NLW. Addressed "Mr Meredith Penry | Struet Brecon | Brecknockshire | S. Wales." Endorsed "Received | August 2nd 1800 | Answered | October 3rd 1800."

1. See Letter 29.

2. "almost a year has past": no 1799 letter to her Welsh relatives survives. MP did not know that Meredith Penry had died on May 6, 1799.

3. "went to Baltimore": MP describes this trip in Letter 56.

4. Yellow fever revisited Philadelphia and New York in 1799. See Letter 32, note 5.

5. See Letter 56, note 17.

6. MP left on February 9 for Philadelphia, where she stayed with Margaret Stocker and Alexander Miller. She met frequently with Drinker, who gave her money before she returned to Lititz. See *Diary*, 2:1275–88.

7. Washington died on December 14, 1799, at age sixty-seven. For the Washington's birthday speeches and procession in Philadelphia in 1800 during MP's visit, see Kahler, *Long Farewell*, 30–35; February 21, 1800, Drinker, *Diary*, 2:1276–77.

8. "*quiet* in the Land": Psalm 35:20. Those with "peaceable consciences" identified with this term, as MP may have found in Sewel's *History of the Quakers*, which she read. See Letter 53, note 11.

9. In the election of 1800, Thomas Jefferson defeated president John Adams, winning an Electoral College victory of 73–65. Jefferson became the third president of the United States on March 4, 1801.

10. "Libel": for this controversy, see Letter 49, note 11.

11. "first of March": St. David's Day, honoring the patron saint of Wales.

12. Samuel Meredith served as the president of the Welsh Society of Philadelphia, organized in 1798, until 1816. John James Barralet engraved its copperplate, which is recorded in Stauffer and Fielding, *American Engravers*, 23. A drawing (perhaps draft) of this composition, mistitled "Immigrants Arriving in America," appears in Raley, "John James Barralet," 23.

13. "Mr Llewellin": in 1799 Matthew Lewellen (1775–1802) married the widow Maria Dickert Gill (1766–1806) and opened a store with her father, the gunsmith Jacob Dickert (1740–1822).

14. "my Pourtrait": see Letter 35, note 4.

15. For MP and Coke, see Letter 37, note 6. Coke arrived in Philadelphia in April 1800 and departed for England in May.

16. For Ann and Patty Powell, see Letter 38, note 3.

17. Johann Andreas Huebner (see Letter 19, note 1) recovered and left Lititz for the Synod of 1801 (see Letter 60, note 17).

18. See Letter 32, note 5.

19. "Mr Owens and his Family": see Letter 42, note 9.

ॐ 58. TO BENJAMIN RUSH[1]
June 26, 1800
Lititz, Pennsylvania

Lititz June 26th 1800

My invaluable Friend!

I return you my Sincere thanks for the 2 Boxes of Pills, which I presented in your name to 2 particular Friends of mine, who with me have a prediliction for whatever comes from you, and whose praise of its good Effects I hear with delight. As for myself I am in so relaxd a habit of Body, that I have little Occasion for Medicines of that kind. I find wine moderately drank, that is: a half Gill a day, to be my best Medicine. I have given up, my favourite beverage Tea, and instead of that, at our usual time of drinking tea, I take a bit of Bread—dry—and half a glass of wine which I find a great Service to me.[2]

I would not for the World be instrumental in disturbing your Peace of Mind by bringing to your Recolection what you wish to forget. Nevertheless permit me with that Freedom which your obliging Epithet has given me—to tell you—that all you suffer is the Natural Conscequence of your *not* being of the World[3]—The World sais our Blessed Lord loveth its own, Ye are not of the World &c.[4] Your Charactor—Your Life & Conversation claim from her that Respect, she is obliged to pay *such* Charactors. But true Genuine Love looks to the Heart tis there and only there a Consanguinity (permit me to use the Expression) exists. A person who is satisfied with your Medical Skill, with the Talents our Lord has bestowed on you—who admire you as a Gentleman of Honour & Strickt Probity, will be very apt to Mortify you by indeavouring to cast Reflections upon you. And let it not pain you my dear Sir it is all for your good. In the little Circle in which I move, I have my Mortifications also—and that I look on as Blessings. It keeps me humble and shall such a poor little insignificant require such abasement O Sir, Consider the Sphere *you* move in, and ask your own heart wether it be wholesome or not. Pardon me my dear Sir! I do sometimes think you are a *Nicodemus*. He bore a good Charactor. Joseph of Arimathea the same, they believ'd in Jesus but not openly profess'd—for fear of the Jews.[5]—The *World* look upon you with a half averted Eye. They suspect you are one of Our Lords Disciples— and the Enemy makes use of his Instruments—for fear such a dangerous Man might have too much influence. He wishes to lower you because he thinks it his own Intrest is Concern'd. Our Lord suffers it for your Benifit—and to wean you of[f] from all Sublunary persuits and draw you into a Closer union with himself—To give you Courage (not to lay his Sacred Body in a Tomb, or to purchase Spices to embalm it. But to take him into your heart to Live in

Him, as he in you.)[6] I will not inlarge. Pardon my freedom who am and while life lasts shall continue your *unchangeable* Friend, Obliged Servant

And affectionate *Sister*

Mary Penry

On perusing your Letter again, I blame myself for Enlarging on what you are yourself convinced of—but during my writing I had only your perscecutions and their Intent in *view*, once more then let me request forgiveness for my freedom.

ALS: Rush Family Papers, Correspondence, Box 13:50, Library Company of Philadelphia. Addressed "Doctor | Benjamin Rush | Philadelphia | To the care of | Mrs Stocker." Endorsed "Mary Penry | June 1800."

1. See Letter 27.
2. "half a glass of wine": for MP's liking for wine, see also Letters 64 and 67.
3. "all you suffer": Rush's quarrel with Cobbett. See Letter 49, note 11.
4. John 15:18.
5. John 3:1–2, 12:42, and 19:38.
6. John 19:40.

ᘒᕫ 59. TO JAMES BIRKBY[1]

October 1800

Lititz, Pennsylvania

I came this morning from Lancaster and brought the Ladle and Cash with me with the Receit all which I transmit with Sister Kluge[2]—have not time to write but—Shall I hope atone for it by a long Letter with next oppertunity. I have been 2 weeks at Lancaster and missd the oppertunity of writing[3]—I wish ever[y]thing may be tasteful that this Ladle is used for—Love Love to my *truely beloved Brother Birkby* and *Sister Hannah*

Received of Mr Hall[4]

3 Dollars	1.2.6	
2 quarter ditto	3.9	
Copper	3	
Sum	£1.6.6	

ALS: PP BiJ, Folder 2, MAB.

1. James Birkby (1732–1803), the Moravian pastor in New York and in Staten Island from 1784 to 1799, married Hannah Brook in 1768. When his wife died in 1799, Birkby returned to Bethlehem, where his niece Hannah Fearnley (1771–1823)—the "Sister Hannah" mentioned in this letter—cared for him.

2. On October 3, 1800, Anna Maria Ranck (1772–1820) married John Peter Kluge (1768–1849), who had worked for a decade among Surinam's Arawak Indians. Before leaving for mission work in Indiana, the couple stopped in Bethlehem, carrying MP's letter and ladle. See Gipson, *Moravian Mission on White River*.

3. MP spent two weeks in Lancaster in the fall of 1800. See Letter 60, note 3.

4. "Mr Hall": David Hall (1767–1814), a silversmith in Lancaster. See Gerstell, *Silversmiths of Lancaster*, 45–55.

ᴥ 60. TO ELIZABETH DRINKER[1]

April 3, 1801

Lititz, Pennsylvania

Lititz April 3rd 1801

Dear Friend

Your truely kind Letter dated the 10th Instant came to my hands as a most wellcome present on the 24 of the same month. I was realy quite amazed to hear that you have receivd no letter from me since May last, I cannot take upon me to say I am certain I wrote you more than twice since—but I am pretty sure I did—I have been very unfortunate last year with my Corrispondance.[2] Several Letters I wrote during the Summer and Fall were never deliverd. 3 I am ashured of those I wrote to Mrs Stocker, she never receiv'd and I have greater cause on that account to suppose mine to you met with the same fate. I have the last year met with many things, which if communicated just as they happend, might be entertaining to a Friend who takes [a] kind part in what befal us, but after the circumstances are past and as it were forgotten the Relation is no longer pleasing. Last Spring I was 3 Weeks at Harrisburg with 2 of our Boarders and in the fall 14 days with our Friend Grace Parr.[3] *If you* were settled at Lancaster—Oh what happy Hours might I not spend with you—and your to me truely *Dear* Family—But thats out of sight as Mrs Stocker says: at least in this world. In the Life to Come we shall meet without being fatigued with travelling or fearing the Expences incident thereto. *We* my dear Frends according to our time of Life may look forward to a more Speedy Meeting in the Kingdom of Heaven—than to our Meeting again on Earth—My Resolution is taken not to come to your City again, unless I could do it with less Expence to my Friends—and Old Persons and Children are allways best Home. You are no traveller—I have no hopes of your Coming our Way or I would say I would meet you at Lancaster and bring you to my little Apartment and Oh how much should I rejoice to see and Converse with you—but be still my heart; all these Wishes and desires are Vain—look only forewards to the Completion of every Sanctified Wish and Holy desire in the Kingdom of Christ! I seem indeed to have every year less and less share in the Affairs of the World. *Politics*, as an Englishwoman I once thought very proper to reason upon—alltho without any greater power to alter, than by taking thought as our Lord says to make one Hair black or white[4]—or add a Cubit to my Stature—I am now sick of it—I have very lately smarted for a few silly expressions in which I betray'd too great a Love for my Native Country. The Speaker of the Senate or Assembly I know not which—but his Name is: Weaver thought proper to take great offence,[5] notwithstanding at the same time I acknowledged the great obligations I shall ever think myself under to the Country who has edducated and Supported me to Old Age—I am no Hypocrite, surely I can love and Honour America, and yet be pardond for my Regard to my Native Country, which notwithstanding I do not even wish to rule over America. May they only be sufferd to live as a Nation and I will add—may they prosper—without *Detriment* to America—Surely there can be no real Offence in such Sentiments. But We are all lookd upon with an Evil Eye because we are faithful to our Rulers declare ourselves of no *Party* attend to no Civic Festivals &c.[6] This Gentleman was pleased to say I was such a Sensible woman I could instill bad Principles into the boarders. Now as to my Understanding, if ever I had any, I betray'd a total want of it at the first conversation—and supposing I were a Sensible Woman, my Politics would be of no detriment to our Boarders since the Children hear no manner of Conversations on the Subject, and they among themselves are not sufferd to have anything to do with it, as long as they are with us—for it is very likely their Parents may not all think alike and if they were allow'd to converse on such things, they might dispute and Quarrel together. So Mr Weavers fears have no foundation. *We* must submit says the Apostle to every Ordinance of Man for the Lord sake[7]—*We* look on the present times as Critical—and dangerous—*We* are call'd to watch and Pray—not to *resist*. *We* must submit to whatever the Lord suffers. Be it fair weather or Storms, we must go thro—but He leads and guides his poor Feeble Children. That is our Consolation he sais: In this world ye have trouble—but be of good cheer, I have overcome the World.[8] This my Friends is the result of my Meditations on the present aspect of our Political Affairs. *Great* indeed are the Changes We have seen since We went to good Master Benezets school,[9] and the sky thickens more and more frequent and more aweful are the Claps as the Storm gathers over us, wether it will be dispersed by a Wind of the Lord or weather it will descend in Showers God only knows—to him we must alone look for refuge. Did you my Friends feel any thing of the Earthquakes we have so frequently been visited with this Winter? On the 20th of November between 5 and 6 in the Morning we had the first Shock—which was tremendous indeed! It could be compard to nothing better than a Cannon fired right under us—attended with a loud rumbling and a tremor of the whole Earth—but not a *reeling*—or it might have had dreadful Effects indeed. 8 days together we had 1 2 3 sometimes 4 Shocks but none so hard as the two first. In December January February and March we have had sometimes louder sometimes more gentle schocks.[10] I can assure you my Nerves were so affected that the least Noise brought me in a tremor. The unusual appearance of the Hemisphere which allways foreboded the Earthquake sets one in painful Expectation of what may happen before the shock is felt—At present the Sky looks as usual, and we have had high winds, which give us hope we shall be favourd with a Respite from those aweful Shocks. We are at present in the heart affecting Meditation on the great Occurrences of the Passion Week in which we find our true Pasture—We wish to recal every Scene of that Grand Transaction and in spirit to attend our Suffring Lord throughout the Whole—

Last week our Children had their Examination and many from Lancaster who have girls in our Boarding school came here to see and hear what improvement their Children have made. They were examind in Spelling reading and writing German and English—Arithmetic Grammar Geography Music Sewing knitting Tambour and embroidery or Satin Stich as I believe you call it more properly.[11] I inclose one of the themes which one of our boarders of 8 years of Age pronunced, with ease and Energy—on her Favourite branch of Learning Music in which she bids fair to be a proficient.[12] Its so scribled I fear you will scarce be able to read it. The Parents were extreemly gratified, and were moved to tears at the Piety which was visible in their Music and Singing. In our Boarding School we have 14—and 14 or 16 of our own Children (girls) among whom we have some, I may say Angelic Voices. Tho you dont hold with Singing, yet I know you can read without offence a theme in praise of Music. Our Boarders had besides the inclosed one theme, "Thoughts in the Season of Lent"—and putting our Trust in God.—In German the Girls, had a very pretty Dialogue which they conducted with ease and Freedom—the one Party inquired into the Reformation, and from thence Naturally into the beginning of the Brethrens Church, and receivd concise and Satisfactory answers from the other party. The Word Party here, you know means only a part of the whole—The very name of Party in a Political Sence is disagreeable.[13] You tell me our Friend Hannah

Sansom is gone to rest, happy she is, after having gone thro her share of trouble, is her Husband living or did he go before her? She lived to see her Children settled in the world, and then had leave to *Retire*. Is Friend Swett still living? If she is please to give my love to her.[14] Is our good Sister *Mary* still hearty and active in good Works, how does my dear Nephew—still weakly, or recoverd both *Health* and *Strength*? my tender Love to him[15]—to all your Daughters, Polly and Sally in particular as best known to me. A Friend was here some time agon of the name of Lambert, with him I sent you Salutations in abundance, he would fain have had me write but I told him the time was too short, I could not write a short Letter to you.[16] I am at present troubled with a Cold and cough which is no ways agreeable to a writer. I can not keep my hand steady for Coughing and Wattering of my Eyes. Let me hear from you soon—and as far as you can or chuse—let me hear how affairs go on—in Church and State—you have Both with you—I live more under an *Eclesiastical* than Civil Government. So can only speak of the former. Two of our Bishops saild in October and November last for Germany to attend the General Synod of the Unitus Fratrum which is to Commence at Herrnhuth the first of June—One of those Bishops was from Carolina the other from Lititz[17]—We have had no General Synod these 9 Years—and look forwards with impatience to the *Result*—which we shall hardly receive till very late this Year. A Country Man of mine Philip Howell—who is a Misionary among the Negroes in the West Indies, wrote me a Letter from Bethlehem just before he sat out for New York in order to sail for his destin'd Post.[18] He writes that in the *highly favourd* Island *England* it was heart refreshing to see Minesters of all denominations unite together like Brethren in the Cause of Christ and taking sweet Council together how they might proclaim the glad tidings of Salvation both to Christians and Heathen—That the number of true believers increases—That it was a Season of Trials, a time of *Prayers* and *Supplication* and a *time of Blessings*. This is some Consolation since a Mighty Host are gatherd against them! God knows what distress they may be in by this. We have lately received a Diary of our Congregations in Ireland during the time of their greatest troubles.[19] It drew tears from our Eyes, both of Praise and thanksgiving as well as Sympathy, they had but *one* (among their numerous Congregations) a young Man Son to one of their Members who joind the United Irishmen. And he was pardoned by the Magistracy because of his Youth and Inexperience. This Spring our People will begin a Mission among the Wabash Indians who have invited them, a Minester and his Wife, with a few Families of Christian Indians were to set out after Easter. This Minester has been some Years a Misionary among the Arrawach Indians near Surinam. Last Fall he came here—obtain a Helpmate out of our

House, they went from here to the Indian Congregation at Muskingum w[h]ere they Spent the winter and as I observed before next week they are to proceed to the *Wabasch*.[20]

Your Old Friend has began Housekeeping which you will say is rather late in the day. Last November I removed into a little Room to myself—the furnishing of which together with fire and Candle were unusual Expences and bore a little Heavy. I have now I hope allmost done with burning my Money—as my Country Man still'd paying for wood[21]—but my furniture must be bought by degrees, such as a looking Glass & Carpet, the Latter to save washing my room often &c. &c. How pleased I should be to entertain you in my little Apartment, it is just 10 feet Square—I was in hopes of getting a Floor Cloth such as we formerly used—But Mrs Stocker tells me the Price is so high, that its out of sight—for my Purse—and I must do with out it— that's all.

Now my dear Friends I have wrote a great deal to very little purpose—if it diverts you I obtain my Wish—I wish my Nephew would write some pretty little agreeable Piece—that in the general dearth for Books with me—would be a favour. I take no News paper. I now and then get a few sent me, but sparingly: see no Magazine.[22] Such Periodical Papers are frequently both Instructive and amusing and I could get the loan of them if they could be brought up and sent back with less trouble. I have not work'd one Sti[t]ch of Satin Work this Winter—But hope this Summer to perform my Promise to my Nephew—The beginning of next Month (God willing) I think to visit Bethlehem—having been long requested to come—and after my return my first thoughts will be to fullfill my Obligations to Mr Wm Drinker and Mr Josiah Hughs—Without any Sinister Views on the *Old Bachelor* or the *young one*.[23]

Adieu my beloved Friend! *Sister of my Heart!* Adieu—ever your faithful

M. Penry

Not knowing how circumstances may be with my Cousin Peggy Millar I inclose to you my Letter to Mrs Stocker. If Peggy is safe in Bed, then you will be kind enough to send it [to] Mrs Stocker; But should matters turn out as we *fear* that either Child or Mother—or Perhaps both loose their Lives— Mrs Stocker will have no Inclination to read Letters.[24] In that case please to keep it by you to a more Suitable time. I send it [to] you open that you may peruse the other 2 Themes—You are Wellcome to read the Letter. I have nothing that I would wish to conceal from You—before you deliver it, please to Seal it with a Wafer—but Let not the impression of the Seal be too plain, as my Seal is allways the Initials of my Name—And I do not wish them to know I had sent it open—M: P

As matters turn out, You may destroy it for I must write in a different Stile suposing the worst should happen.

ALS: Linden Hall Archives. Endorsed "Lititz April 3 1801 | Mary Penry." Drinker received this letter on April 8 and her diary quotes MP's account of the earthquake. See *Diary*, 2:1399.

1. See Letter 18.

2. Caleb Cope carried Drinker's letter with news of Hannah Callender Sansom's death to Lititz. See March 9, 1801, *Diary*, 2:1392. No May 1800 letter to Drinker survives.

3. MP left for Harrisburg on July 13, 1800, with Matilda McCallister and Anna Maria Henry, whose parents lived there. The group returned to Lititz on August 1. Years later, Anna Maria Henry Smith (1788–1858)—she had married Thomas Smith (1773–1846), a Federalist congressman—remembered that MP "invited me to vesper" every Saturday "in her neat little apartment, where a lay sister attended to her wants and kept everything in perfect order." See Smith, "Communication from a Former Scholar." The Lititz single sisters' diary does not record MP's fall trip to Lancaster. For Grace Parr, see Letter 49, note 3.

4. Matthew 5:36.

5. Isaac Weaver (1756–1830), Speaker of the Pennsylvania Assembly from 1800 to 1803, had served in the House since 1797. He later became state treasurer.

6. "we are faithful to our Rulers declare ourselves of no *Party*": for the Moravians' nonentanglement policy, see Letter 2, note 5.

7. 1 Peter 2:13.

8. John 16:33.

9. "good Master Benezets school": see Letter 52, note 5.

10. On November 22, 1800, the *Lancaster Journal* noted "several alarming Earthquakes" in recent days.

11. "Tambour": see Letter 29, note 8. "Satin Stich": a long, straight embroidery stitch that appears like satin.

12. Eliza Jacobs Haldeman recalled that while at the Lititz Boarding School she "delivered a speech on 'Church Music'" at the public examinations. See Haldeman, "Seventy-Seven Years Ago." MP included this speech, "On Church [Music]," in this letter to Drinker.

13. "The very name of Party in a Political Sence is disagreeable": see Letter 2, note 5.

14. Hannah Callender Sansom died on March 9. Her husband lived for more than two decades. See Letter 18, note 5. "Friend Swett": Susannah Siddon Swett (d. 1807) married Benjamin Swett (d. 1774) in 1760. Benjamin Swett's daughter, Ann, had been Henry Drinker's first wife. The Drinkers cared for Susannah Swett late in her life.

15. "still weakly": William Drinker had contracted tuberculosis.

16. "Lambert": unidentified, probably a Quaker ("Friend").

17. "General Synod": held in Herrnhut in 1801. Bishops John Daniel Koehler (1737–1805) of North Carolina and Johann Andreas Huebner (see Letter 19, note 1) of Lititz attended. Neither returned to America.

18. Philip Howell (1758–1803). His memoir appears in *Periodical Accounts*, 18:65–72.

19. Moravian congregations had been established in Dublin (1750), Ballinderry (1755), Kilwarlin (1755), Gracefield (1759), and Gracehill (1765), the last two being "*Congregation Places*" (Letter 41). See Stead and Stead, *Exotic Plant*, 77.

20. "Minester and his Wife": John Peter Kluge and Anna Maria Ranck Kluge. See Letter 59, note 2.

21. "still'd paying for wood": MP's countryman called (or "styled") paying for firewood "burning . . . Money."

22. "I take no News paper": MP does report news and quotes from newspapers frequently in her letters.

23. William Drinker, Elizabeth Drinker's unmarried son, was at this time thirty-four years old. Josiah Hughes joined the Library Company on April 5, 1787.

24. Drinker recorded Peggy Miller's death on April 10. Drinker followed MP's instructions and kept the letter to Margaret Stocker—but sent it in July after receiving Letter 62. See April 10, July 11, 1801, Drinker, *Diary*, 2:1400, 1426.

ᶿᴗ 61. TO BENJAMIN RUSH[1]

April 25, 1801

Lititz, Pennsylvania

Lititz April 25 1801

Dear Sir

Your truely affectionate—and let me add heart affecting Letter of the 11th Instant, did not reach me till the 22nd. I could not earlier acknowledge your goodness my mind was too unselteld. Notwithstanding I dreaded the Conscequence as I believe many more did. Hope was still left—What shall I say—I cannot dare not find fault with our dear Lords dispensations—whatever he does: *Is Right*. I have Lost my darling Cousin—but she has gaind Eternal Life.[2] I can upon no account Lament her Loss—that is: when I meditate on the blessed Change she has made—but I sincerely Sympathize with her Mourning Mother, her disconsolate Husband—Brother, Sisters &c. Oh my dear Sir the thought of *their* distress, is allmost too much for me. I have been frequently tempted to wish my dear Peggy could have found the Single State *most Proper* for her Situation. 2 Years and 1 Quarter she has been a Wife and during that time she has sufferd a great deal—what she certainly might have avoided—having had such an excellent Husband—makes the reflection still more Painful—for his anxiety was proportionable to his Love so that the Happiness they mutually enjoy'd in that short space, hardly atoned for the Pains of mind and Body each respectively went thro—Yet let me not murmer our Lord foreknew it would be to their Mutual Benifit. I must confess my weakness, believing as I firmly do that no Doctor can save a Person from Death when the Lord thinks proper to call them. Still I could not help feeling a very painful sensation on reading your favour to find: you sir was call'd in—*when she was past Your Assistance!* I hope her other friends will not recolect this. If they should it will cause them much Pain—at the same time I adore the Goodness of our Lord who wisely orderd—that altho you could no longer be of Service to the *Mortal* part—you should inquire into the Situation of her *Soul*—administer healing Balm—and have the inexpressible Satisfaction to be assured of its efficasy. And I am comfortably assured you have not been wanting in aplying your Cordial advice to her distress'd Family. Happy are they who have *such* faithful Friends whose endeavours to *Mitigate the Pains* of those *Wounds* they *cannot cure* deserve the most grateful acknowledgment. I was greatly refreshd at the account you gave me of the Triumphant ascention of my dear Friend—your worthy Mother[3]— Oh might I soon meet her and my dearest *Peggy* where no further Seperation can afflict us—here my dear Sir Permit me to conclude myself—*ever* your Sincerely obliged Friend & faithful Sister

Mary Penry

ALS: Rush Family Papers, Correspondence, Box 13:51, Library Company of Philadelphia. Addressed "Doctor | Benjamin Rush | Philadelphia." Endorsed "M Penry."

   1. See Letter 27.

   2. Peggy Miller, Margaret Stocker's daughter, had died on April 10. See Letter 60, note 24.

   3. "worthy Mother": Rush's mother-in-law, the poet Annis Boudinot Stockton (1736–1801), died on February 6.

ತ⁀ 62. TO ELIZABETH DRINKER[1]

June 14–22, 1801

Lititz, Pennsylvania

Lititz June 14th 1801

Tres Chere Amie

   I wonder wether my Friend received my Packet (as I may stile it) with a Letter inclosed to Mrs Stocker, and wether that Letter—*could* with propriety be Sent to her. My fears were just—my dear Peggy was a Martyr to the Married State. Doctor Rush wrote me of her decease on the same day, altho it did not reach me till ten days after.[2] I wrote to the Doctor to Mrs Stocker and Mr Alexander Millar about the middle of April, but have not heard one word from any one of the Family Since. Out of Respect to their grief I thought I would wait in Silence till Mrs Stocker wrote to me, but to day I sat down and wrote a few lines for I begin to be very uneasy. Peggy Stocker is in Years—her Brother Philip's Situation distressd her much and now her daughters death I fear will quite overset her, she is in years has very strong feelings I am really much concernd at the obstinate Silence which is observed.[3]

This indeed I very well know, the young ones never trouble themselves with writing to me—and should Mrs Stocker be removed I shall not expect to hear from them, but Mrs Stocker has ever been a faithful Corrispondant—her Silence alarms me. If you can give me any Information concerning the family I shall take it very kind.

The beginning of May I made a Journey to Bethlehem w[h]ere I spent near 3 Weeks much to my Satisfaction, It is allways a peculiar Pleasure to see the Place w[h]ere I spent the first Years of my Life in the Brethrens Congregation and w[h]ere I have many Old Friends.[4] It is indeed a most delightful Place for the Situation and most agreeable Society—one is sure of meeting with there. Yet I must own Lititz suits for my age and turn of mind—better—We are more quiet and not overun with Strangers as they are. Their Extensive Boarding School draws Numbers, Parents and Relations with Children bringing them to the school, and taking them Home.[5] Our Little Boarding School is now 18 in Number—and more we cannot take, till a Vacancy happens, we have every Week allmost fresh Applications. We have been hitherto very fortunate in having among our Children none whom we could not keep with us. They are in general Pliable and good naturd—and not Corrupted in their manners. Last week a Friend was here who has a daughter at your boarding school—It must be a very pretty Institution—God be praised, that we have some Seminaries where Youth are instructed in true Religion. Never was such Institutions more Necessary than Now in this falsely call'd Enlightened Age of Reason—I procured the loan of Robinsons Account of the Illuminati.[6] I read it with astonishment, it was now clear to me, what those Enlightned pieces w[e]re, which our venerable Synods have so frequent and so Seriously warned our Congregations against—and forbid their Members the reading of those pamphlets. In Germany they were in more Danger than here, or in England, altho I am told a German Bookseller in Lancaster has imported Numbers of those baneful Writings.[7] I wish they may not circulate.

We are now in very Critical time. I believe the Hour of Temptation has long since began—I wish it were at an End. We are comforted with hopes that when things are at the worst, we may hope a Change—I should think it cannot be much worse with the Church of Christ—For what dreadful fallings off have I lived to see—Surely surely, it must have reach'd its height. Oh may the Lord turn and Visit his Zion and heal her breaches!—

Not one perswasion among Christians in our days, but what lament the falling off of their Members—It is quite disstressing to think of it!—Our Church—exhibits dreadful Examples of this Truth, which make the faithful Members mourn and lament in the Stile of Jermiah the Prophet.[8] Yet why should I entertain my Friend with such disagreeable Topics—a Recent exhibition of that kind, fills my heart with grief & has drawn these Meditations from my Pen!

I trust my dear Friend will not retaliate my long Silence, but will let me hear from her shortly—I humbly trust my gracious Saviour will preserve me in these Latter days of trouble from falling off from the Faith. True it is, neither Age nor Situation can Secure me—Nothing but an humble Faith in him who alone can Preserve me—is my Security. He is my Refuge and Rock of Defence[9]—As long as the Lord preserves me in this frame of heart and mind I *demand* your Friendship, as a fellow Heir with yourself, of the Kingdom of Christ. My Kind Love to your dear Husband Aunt Mary My Nephew William and all and every Member of your dear Family not forgetting friend Sweat.[10] Adieu my beloved Betsy!

Ever Yours in the best of Bonds
Mary Penry

Yesterday was 8 days that I began this letter. The following day my dear Mrs Stocker and Mr Alexander Millar Surprized me with an unexpected Visit: It is past discripton what I felt![11] Peggy Millar had ever been my darling Cousin, and her death had cost me numberless tears. The sight of the Mother and Husband, awakend all my feelings—It was the same with them—so that the first hours of intercourse were devoted to—fruitless Grief—However Music "which has charms to soften Rocks" soothed our Melancholy[12]—and knowing Mr Millars extreem fondness for Music, I procured him as much gratification as possible and they spent 2 agreeable days with me. I should have given Mrs Stocker this Letter for you, but unfortunately I had not seald it and she requested to have it given to her Open. This I had my reasons for not doing so was fain to make an Excuse. She has begd me to request you will give her the Letter I sent to your care as she wishes to have the Themes the Children repeated at their Examination.[13] You will be pleased to answer this her Request as soon as you convieniently can.

I shall keep this Letter ready to send perhaps somebody from Philadelphia may be among some of our Visitants, with whom I can send it. The heat is today so great—I am scarce able to form a Letter, will therefore not enlarge, at present Adieu my Love ever yours.

M Penry

ALS: Linden Hall Archives. Addressed "Mrs | Elizabeth Drinker | Mr Henry Drinkers, Senior | Philadelphia." Endorsed "Lititz June 14, 1801 | Mary Penry." Drinker received this letter on July 9, 1801. See Drinker, *Diary*, 2:1425.

1. See Letter 18.

2. See Letter 61 for MP's reply to Rush.

3. "her Brother Philip's Situation": Thomas Phillips. See Letter 54, note 6. "daughters death": see Letter 60, note 24.

4. "Journey to Bethlehem": along with four other single sisters, MP left for Bethlehem on May 8 and returned to Lititz on May 29, 1801.

5. "Extensive Boarding School": the Bethlehem girls' school first admitted non-Moravian students as boarders in 1785. In 1801 it had sixty-seven students, eleven of them children from the congregation and fifty-six children from "different places." See Lists Concerning Enrollments, MAB; and Haller, *Early Moravian Education*, 13–32.

6. In 1798 a third edition of John Robison's *Proofs of a Conspiracy Against All the Religions and Governments of Europe, Carried On in the Secret Meetings of Free-Masons, Illuminati and Reading Societies* appeared in Philadelphia.

7. "German Bookseller in Lancaster": either Christian Jacob Hütter (1771–1849), whose 1801 almanac advertised eight thousand books for sale, or Johann Albrecht (1745–1806), another active German-language printer in Lancaster. The prominent German bookseller in Lancaster, Ludwig Laumann (1725–1797), had died in 1797. See Arndt and Eck, *First Century of German Language Printing*, 2:1223, and Wellenreuther, *Citizens in a Strange Land*, 11–48.

8. "Stile of Jermiah the Prophet": in the genre of the jeremiad, an author laments and denounces the degenerate state of society's morals and prophesizes its collapse in the near future.

9. Psalm 94:22.

10. "friend Sweat": see Letter 60, note 14.

11. The Lititz single sisters' diary indicates that these visitors arrived on June 22, 1801.

12. Loose quotation of the opening lines of William Congreve's 1697 play *The Mourning Bride*. See *Complete Plays of William Congreve*, 326.

13. "Letter I sent to your care": see Letter 60, note 24.

🐦 63. TO ELIZABETH DRINKER[1]

August 30–31, 1801

Lititz, Pennsylvania

Lititz August 30th 1801

Ma tres Chere amie!

I wonder wether my Pennance is allmost at an End, if not, it were generous in you to let me know how many weeks or months more it is to last, and in how many Letters I am to Atone for my past Silence. I have wrote 3 very long Letters since I have had the pleasure of one line from you, was you displeasd that I sent you our Childrens Exercise, and that I troubled you with the Packet to my Cousin with (restrictions) which she afterwards wish'd to see, and which in my last I requested you to send her.[2] I will answer myself the first question—you was not displeas'd with the Specimens I sent you and I know that you have *in Idea* more than once wrote me in answer to that—and the other 2 Letters I wrote you.

As we have lately had several Visitants from your City with whom I could have sent Letters if I had had them ready, I find my self this afternoon so at Leisure that I am determined to converse an Hour with my Friend, in hopes an oppertunity may serve to send it you. The last I wrote you was shortly after I had the pleasure of seeing Mrs Stocker and Sandy Miller here. This day week Mr Miller was here on his return from Baltimore wither he had taken *Maria Potts* on a visit to some of her acquaintance there.[3] He returnd home alone. He muchd wish'd to take me to Town with him, but I am determined to go no more unless expressly sent for, and as that seems very unlikely it should ever happen again—*a long farewel* to Philadelphia.

Poor Mr Miller is extreemly low Spirited when with me. It seems I recal his dear Peggy to his Remembrance—I pity him and revere his Sensibility.[4] I wish most heartily the time which the Laws of Decency has apointed, were over, and he had a *good* Wife a *good* One he deserves for he is a good Man. And so Domestic that he will be unhappy untill he has a Companion to share his Joys and Sorrows. I have been told one is allready made out for him—but I think at least 6 Months, they might suspend their Judgement. This I know: my dear Peggy often said if the Allmighty took her from him, she wish'd not that he might remain a Widdower longer than decency required. And I join in the Wish!

And how does all your Family do, small and great? perhaps you may be out of town. Yet I supose letters can be sent you, and if you send a Letter to my Cousin Nanny Powells they can send it me with the assistance of their Neighbour Cohen. Next week I shall go to spend a few days in Lancaster.[5] And what will you say when [I] tell you the IN*famous* Timothy Matlock has scraped an acquaintance with me on the footing of old Schoolmates. As we have nothing to do with Political Squables we must be civil to *all*. I have seen his Canary Birds and his choice flowers and they are doubtless as *fine*—and as *Pretty* as any mans—and I can give them due Praise.[6] Johny Roberts and his wife are extreemly intimate there, they live just *oposite*.[7] It would be very silly in me to refuse conversing on indifferent Subjects, with one who never injured me. My Sensations are indeed vastly different in his Company to what they are among my friends—still he is not my *enemy* and if he were—we are Required to love our *Enemies* &c. &c. &c. *Hamilton* the Printer and Matlock has been ingaged in a paper warr sometime.[8] What Timothy writes I know not for I read no *Demo's* paper—But Hamilton is very severe upon him—If all be true what Hamilton writes, I shall not be proud of his *Civility* (I had almost wrote Friendship)—which at present is out of sight. I wish to hear your opinion of the case and how far you think I may Venture on this I could almost say forbidden Ground—believe me my friend I do not look on this or that opinion in Politics but *French Principles*—which is the *greatest* Irreligion is my *greatest* Terror. I do believe no true and Sincere Christian can join with that party—as Poulson in his Almanac observes in his quotation from The Works of King, I think its intitled *Signs of the Times*.[9] I wish I could draw you in to write me [a] long Letter, and inform me what you are about in the City. Our Country News Papers begin to murmer concerning a great man—his *displacing* Several, and his sending for the *Notorius Paine*, has given great umbrage it seems[10]—as for Paine he is such a *Sot* I don't think him Capable of doing much Mischief. The Snake in the Grass is a greater object of terror to me than an Open Enemy—And the *Illuminati* are more dreadful than an Army of 10 thousand Soldiers. Like Miners in the Earth they work in Secret and Effect Revolutions before we are aware. That such dextrous Miners are among us I have not a *Doubt*—may Our Mercyful Lord and Saviour *Counter Mine* them if it be his blessed Will, or endue us with Stedfastness and Patience in whatever Suffrings & trials may await us! Amen—Amen. Monday August 31. Yesterday I wrote the forgoing but a violent pain in my head constraind me to lay down my Pen. In the forenoon I was busy with my Account Books, and since Dinner I have been waiting on Strangers till just past 5 O Clock and one of our Visitants Mr Richard Renshaw has ingaged to take care of this if I send it to Lancaster.[11] Which I shall do tomorrow if Possible.

And now my dear what shall I say farther. I hardly know what to write unless you give me a theme; one thing I must tell you, I hear of the loss of one Friend after the other (the Misfortune attending Old Age) and that creates an ardent wish in me to retire from a World in which I shall by and by, have no Connection. Be it so! I trust to meet my Friends above, never to be seperated more—As for you my dear you have so many ties in Children and Grand Children that I must heartily pray with them, that both you and your dear Spouse may be spared many Years as a Comfort to them and each other. The evening shades prevail—adieu till tomorrow.

I just now hear one of our Stages will go to Lancaster at 6 in the Morning for which reason I must close my Letter this Evening. Please to give my very kind Love to my good Friend your Husband, To my good Nephew William, to Aunt Mary Sally Nancy Polly and Henry[12]—with their Spouses and Children as you chance to see them to Friend Pemberton and all who think worth while to ask after me. Oh could I have the Pleasure of your Company a few Hours in my little Apartment—how happy should I think myself, perhaps ere long we may meet in a Building not made with hands, Eternal in the Heavens. Adieu. Beloved Friend of my heart ever yours in the Bonds of Sincere Friendship—

Mary Penry

ALS: Linden Hall Archives. Endorsed "Lititz August 30 1801 | Mary Penry."

1. See Letter 18.

2. See Letters 60 (which enclosed the "Childrens Exercise") and 62.

3. "Mrs Stocker . . . Sandy Miller . . . *Maria Potts*": Margaret Stocker; her son-in-law, Alexander Miller; and Miller's niece and Stocker's granddaughter, Maria Potts. See Appendix C.

4. "revere his Sensibility": see Letter 22, note 3.

5. For Ann and Patty Powell, see Letter 38, note 3. Their Philadelphia shop was next to the Cohen residence. See Letter 52, note 3. MP left for Lancaster on September 11 and returned to Lititz on September 28, 1801.

6. Timothy Matlack (1730–1829), born in New Jersey, settled with his family in 1745 in Philadelphia, where he attended the Friends School. He lived in Lancaster from 1778 to 1817. "Canary Birds": an increasingly common house bird. See Goldsmith, *History of the Earth*, 5:339. MP's politics were very different from the radical Matlack's, so she is boasting here that she has been civil to him. Matlack lived on the southwest corner of Orange and Jefferson Streets, at what is now 222 East Orange Street. See Landis, "Col. Timothy Matlack."

7. For the Robertses, see Letter 17, note 1. John Roberts's hat shop was on Orange Street.

8. William Hamilton left Philadelphia for Lancaster in 1794, establishing his print shop on West King Street. His *Lancaster Journal*, co-founded with Henry Willcocks, became Lancaster's most influential Federalist newspaper. In 1799 William and Robert Dickson, along with William's wife, Mary, founded a rival paper, the Jeffersonian *Lancaster Intelligencer and Weekly Advertiser*.

9. Edward King's *Remarks on the Signs of the Times* (London, 1798), republished in Philadelphia in 1800, was advertised in Poulson's *Town and County Almanac*. The particular quotation has not been located.

10. "great man . . . the *Notorius Paine*": shortly after his March 1801 inauguration, Thomas Jefferson invited the controversial Thomas Paine to return to America. Paine accepted the invitation and returned in October 1802. By the end of his first term, Jefferson had displaced nearly 50 percent of all Federalists employed in the federal civil service. See Prince, "Passing of the Aristocracy."

11. Richard Renshaw (1772–1835), who married Mary Johnston in September 1801, became a Philadelphia lawyer.

12. For the Drinker family, see Appendix C.

ᎧᏴ 64. TO KATHERINE PENRY AND ELIZA POWELL[1]

October 23, 1801

Lititz, Pennsylvania

Lititz October 23rd 1801

My dear Cousins Kitty Penry and Eliza Powell

You have every Reason to think me *Culpably* indiff[er]ent to the Ties of nature, in thus long neglecting to write, but indeed my dear Cousins I feel very sensibly the Infirmities of Old Age. Writing once such a Pleasure becomes a Task. Next Month I shall be 66 years of Age, let this plead some Excuse— mean time rest ashured that Letters from *you* are some of the greatest Comforts I can injoy. Your 2 dear Letters of July and October was handed to me at *Bethlehem* last May where I spent 3 weeks among my Old Friends and former Companions very agreeably and having taken a final Leave.[2] I have lost this Spring a darling Cousin, Mrs Stockers youngest Child, the Wife of Mr Alexander James Miller a Merchant from Edinburg in Scottland. She died in Childbed on the Ninth day after the delivery of a dead Child, on the 11th of April. She was a fine woman, and bore a most excellent Charactor. She had not been a wife 3 years, her first Child was born dead as well as the last. The Husband Mother and whole Family have been inconsoleable for their Loss.[3] Mrs Stocker & Mr Miller came to visit me in the month of June in order to recover their Health which grief had greatly impaird. I have been myself a real Mourner for my Cousin Peggy but our Loss is her gain so we must be resigned. I did not receive the first Letters you wrote after my dear Uncles decease.[4] It would have been cruel to wish him much longer in this Vale of Tears, yet I felt much grieved that we have lost him. So it is whoever lives to Old Age generally survive the most of their dear Connections. I should be glad to hear how you are settled since his death, and wether you enjoy the *Conv[en]iences* of Life which is just what I enjoy but *no superfluities*. You tell me Pride finds its way among you. Alas in this County it is worse. Atheism—Deism and the whole train of Ills, which are the Conscequences of Irreligion rule in America. Party Spirit is at an Alarming Heigth. God knows to what lengths that will lead us: Many Serious People are aprehensive the so calld United States will disunite—and that, may bring on a civil Warr in the midst of our Own fears.[5] I sincerely rejoice in *Private* that great Britain has hitherto been successful—but I dare not openly betray my Satisfaction for there is such a Spirit of Bitterness, among the so call'd Democrats, that if their Power was equal to their Will— the English *Name* would be expung'd. However the Lord reigneth, him they cannot dethrone, nor can they overpower those who are under his Protection. The invasion of England has been much talkd off, and certain success expected—my answer to one who exhultingly told me how Credible it was, that by this time the Conquest of England was Completed, I replied: Holy Scripture advised him that girded the Sword *on*, not to rejoice like him that put it *off*. What *may* happen is to be sure uncertain but you can say with the Royal Psalmist: *Hitherto hath the Lord help'd us*.[6] My heart is wounded to read of the Blood and Slaughter of our fellow Creatures and to think on the Lamentations of the Widdows and Orphans. I assuredly believe we live in the later days indeed, and I fear it is but the beginning of Troubles. I hope I shall rest in

Peace before the Worst days commence. We are certainly not sufficiently thankful for the good we have injoyd and the Peace and quiet we have Possess'd, when all Europe allmost, and in short 3 parts of the Globe out of 4 has experienced the Miseries of Warr—Pestilence—or Famine.

True our Cities have been visisted by a Malignant Fever and some thousands have been taken off in it; but the survi[v]ors seemd very soon to have forgot the Chastisement, as they are still in Peace & Plenty they think little of the Evil day.[7]

Have you not heard from Miss Vaughn of Haverfordwest.[8] I most sincerely wish I could bring you acquainted, but as she is not much younger than myself perhaps she finds writing too great a Task. I have put off Writing indeed some time in hopes of sending you a Minuature Likeness of your Cousin Penry when she was 19 years of age—a good Friend of mine who has a great Genius, and has taken to drawing in Water Coulours, came this Summer to visit his Sister who is a Tutorriss in our Boarding School[9]—This Young Man was so kind as to Copy a small Piece from the Large Picture my Mamma had drawn when as I observd above I was 19 years of Age. The Piece when finish'd would Lie under a Shilling. If I can but get it safe to your Hands I shall be quite Happy. We have a Boarding School in our House, consisting of 20 young Ladies from different parts of the United States who are instructed in Reading and Writing both German and English, plain Work & Knitting, Tambour and Sattin Stich, Music and drawing Arithmetic Grammer Geography and the Use of the Globes, but not Dancing[10]—We began This Institution about 4 years agon at the repeated Request of Parents who earnestly wish'd us to take the charge of their children upon us—chiefly they say that the children may have Religion and Piety early instilld in their tender hearts, which they cannot meet with in other Schools—we have children of various Religious Denominations.[11] They constantly attend our Meetings and together with our own Children are Instructed in the fundamental Articles of the Christian Faith according to the Augsburg Confession which the Brethrens, and the Church of England subscribe too.[12] At Bethlehem they have near 100 Boarders—and among them many, from the West Indies whose Parents send them there with a Proper Conveyance and leave them 5 or 6 years according to their Age and their good Pleasure.[13] We have not had *one* Instance of their being unhappy among us—It allways costs them Floods of tears when they leave us. Children whose Morals have been corrupted before they came we will *not* admit—and if we have been *deceived* in the Childs Charactor, we send them back—in this we are *strickt*, as one Corrupted Child may do the others the greatest Injury. Both here and at Bethlehem, a Clergyman is the Inspector.[14] But the Tuition of the Children is solely confided to the Single Sisters. Ours, Board and Lodge and have their Schools in our House. At Bethlehem they have 2 houses close to the Sisters House. In one of which the Inspector and his Lady spend the greatest part of the day. Ours is but in its Infancy, we cannot as yet afford to build—besides wasching mending and making, finding Bed and Beding for a larger number—we find hitherto Impracticable—We have 4 Tutorisses, of our own Children, we have near 30 day Scholars, who acording to their Talents learn the *same* as the Boarders—This number, added to the Boarders amounts to 50 from 6, to 14 years of Age. As soon as a Vacancy happens that a young lady her School time being over, returns home, the one who has been longest on the List of Candidates—supplies her place. Our Inspector has more on the list than we have Boarders—you would be amazed what Numbers apply— and we are constraind to refuse for want of Room—for we are upwards of 40 Single Sisters in our House beside the Boarders. I have endeavourd to entertain you a little with an account of *our* affairs. Old as I am, I am still thought capable to hold the Office of Clerk, in our House. And I desire to spend and be spent in the Service of the *Virgin Choir*.[15] You have given me an account of your Price Current—I will now tell you the Price Current of what I must purchase. A loaf of Bread made of Middlings, weighing 4 [pounds] before its Baked costs 1/ Currency about 9d Sterling—Butter the Pound 9d sterling— Loaf Sugar about 17 pence Sterling, Tea, good 12/ Currency, 8/ Sterling— Coffee 18 pence Sterling—Wine I cannot afford,[16] Spirits I never drink, Water I have gratis, Fire Wood I purchased for this Winter cost me at least 30/ Sterling—Candles 13 pence the pound Sterling—Cheese is too dear for me because—I can do without—Shoes and Stockings I compute the one at about 8/ the other 4/ Sterling the Pair—Pink Ribbon which the Single Sisters con[s]tanly wear, as the Married wear Blue, and the Widdows white,[17] cost about 9 pence the yard your Money—sometimes more—sometimes less. Linnens are so high—that we have taken to wear Coarse Musslin, Sheets, and Shifts—Cottons are reasonable from 3/9 to 7/6 sterling according to the Quality—fine White Musslin we wear in Summer being a neat and cheap dress, and dark Cottons in Winter—Shifts are very little worn for upper garments. My underpetticoats are made of *our* own Country—*Welch Flannel*. An undercoat of Yellow Flannel costs me 12/ currency—before tis made up—3 yards at 4/—beside the binding. Have I not wrote quite in the Old Maids stile—well that is acting quite in Charactor. And *now* my dear and ever dear Cousins permit me to close this Long Epistle and to request you to write me a long Letter in Answer. Mrs Stocker, who took your Letters with her when she was to see me—together with her Family, desire their best love to you. I have not heard from the Miss Powels this 8 months—otherwise than sending their Love—for they cannot abide writing which I am sorry for—their Love I am sure is tender—but Quakers as they are—do not Corrispond much with Church People.[18] My Young Companions thank you, for your Salutation and return it—with best wishes for your Spiritual and Eternal Happiness. In which I fervently join and remain ever your affectionate *Cousin*

Mary Penry

My best Love and Respects to *all* that hear this Letter and ask after me—You must send me their beloved Names.

ALS: Penralley Collection 1391, NLW. Addressed to "Miss Katherine Penry | Struet Brecon | Brecknock Shire | South Wales." Endorsed "Recieved this | Letter per | Post Sunday | 6th of December | 1801."

1. See Letter 29.
2. MP left for Bethlehem on May 8 and returned to Lititz on May 29, 1801.
3. "died in Childbed . . . their Loss": see Letter 60, note 24.
4. Meredith Penry had died on May 6, 1799.
5. "civil Warr": talk of disunion and civil war was common during the 1800 presidential election. Although at his 1801 inaugural address Jefferson tried to put the election strife behind by announcing that "we are all Republicans—we are all Federalists," serious divisions persisted.
6. 1 Kings 20:11; 1 Samuel 7:12.
7. Regarding yellow fever, see Letter 32, note 5.
8. Anne (Nancy) Vaughn had died on April 3, 1798, at Haverfordwest. See Letter 6, note 6.
9. For this miniature and the "great Genius" (George Fetter), see Letter 35, note 4.
10. "Tambour and Sattin Stich": see Letter 60, note 11.
11. "This Institution": historians typically state that the Lititz girls' boarding school began in 1794, when Margaretta (Peggy) Marvell arrived from Baltimore. Since here MP notes that the school commenced in 1797 ("4 years agon"), contemporaries may have dated its beginnings differently. There were eight girls in the boarding school at the close of 1799, and thirteen at the close of 1800. See Handler, *Linden Hall*, 36–38; and Haller, *Early Moravian Education*, 89–93.
12. "Augsburg Confession": see Letter 41, note 25.
13. "West Indies": see Bancroft, "Maria Beaumont." Bethlehem's girl's school had 67 students in 1801. See Lists Concerning Enrollments, 1790–1828, FemSem 255.1, MAB.
14. "a Clergyman is the Inspector": Johannes Herbst (See Letter 37, note 40) led the Lititz girls' school after Johann Andreas Huebner left for the Synod of 1801 (see Letter 60, note 17).
15. An echo of 2 Corinthians 12:15. For the Moravians and singleness, see this volume's introduction.
16. "Wine I cannot afford": for MP's liking for wine, see also Letters 58 and 67.
17. "Ribbon": see Sommer, "Fashion Passion," 87.
18. For Ann and Patty Powell, see Letter 38, note 3.

❧ 65. TO BENJAMIN RUSH[1]

January 23, 1802
Lititz, Pennsylvania

Extract of a Letter from Mary Penry Lititz

"I have been much indisposed with Shortness of breath & had one
night & 2 days a severe Cramp in my breast which I really thought
would put a period to all my infirmaties—I most heartily wishd for
some of good Dr Rush's pills which your Sister Peggy & myself have
found of great service[2]—I have great reason to believe the spasms in my
breast are chiefly owing to flattulency and I wish you would be kind to
speak to Dr. Rush about it and ask him if he would be so kind as to send
me something to relieve me—for I can neither go up or down stairs
without losing my breath nay if I exert myself ever so little I am almost
breathless—I have no great appetite, that gives me no concern as long
as I have no qualms & my bowels are in no way obstructed—On
account of the rash in my eyebrows which is sometimes very disagreeable I intend next week to be cuppd in preference to Bleeding."[3]

Mrs Stocker sends her love to Dr. Rush & if he will please comply with the
above she knows of an opportunity for Lititz on Monday morning early if the
doctor will be good enough to send the Medicine down.

Copy (unknown hand): Rush Family Papers, Correspondence, Box 13:43, Library Company of
Philadelphia. Addressed "Doctor Rush." Endorsed "Ordered [*illegible*] | January 23, 1802."
Internal evidence suggests MP sent this account of her condition to Margaret Stocker's sister-
in-law, Rebecca Pyewell Phillips.

1. See Letter 27.
2. "Sister Peggy": Margaret Stocker.
3. "rash in my eyebrows": see Letter 24, note 5.

ૐ 66. TO ELIZABETH DRINKER[1]

February 6–8, 1802

Lititz, Pennsylvania

Lititz February 6–8th 1802

Dearly beloved Friend

Your truely acceptable lines to the care of Caleb Cope came safe to my hands about 2 weeks ago.[2] I should have wrote very shortly upon the Reception of it, but was incapable of so doing, having been pretty much indisposed with a disorder in my Bowels which has been like an Epedemic Fever, as allmost every one has had it old & young.[3] It is a very grievous complaint when attended with great pain, which the most experience. I was favour'd, for I had very little pain, but was excessively weakend, so much that I could scarce stand on my Feet. During this period I received your Letter and now feel able (willing I allways am) to write you. In the first place [I] must observe we had very little winter till within these few days, the weather is very severe. We have had a great deal of Sickness among us, which we are apt to think is in some measure owing to the drought, the Springs are so low, the water is bad and unwholesome. We have had no deaths since last September except 2 Children with these 2 weeks—of—2—and 3 years old.[4] The children in general have been very sickly. The Measels are all around us—but have not yet reach'd our little Village, and we wish we may be spared till more favourable weather, for many of our Boaders as well as near 50 in Lititz has not had them. The Papers speak very confidentially of annihilating the small Pox by means of the Vaccine Pox, could there be a preventative found out for the Measels it would be a great Blessing.[5] As you observe just as a thought Strikes me I must put it to paper be it in order or otherwise—You will remember: a Frenchman has given out, his having found the Longitude—In one of the Philadelphia Papers, there is a piece which makes a jest of the suposed discovery—and observes that if any one wish'd to know what perpetual Motion was they would find it, at a certain Stand in the Market where an Old woman sat whose Tongue was in *Perpetual Motion*.[6] I repeated this drollery to a Friend, who took it in a Litteral Sence i.e. that the famous discovery proved upon examination to be nothing more or Less, than the poor old Woman Tongue—and related it to a Third person as a fact! I do not know when I have had more diversion than this mistake gave me for as I am not the author of the *Discovery*—the woman be she whom she will, can not blame me—If this little digression raises a smile you will put up with it. A Mr Downing was here *yesterday* (when I wrote the above), sorry I was that my Letter was not ready, it would have been a fine oppertunity to have sent it. I think to send it to Caleb Cope who seems to have a regard for me—Do you know Caleb? He is a great Orator for the Federalists, and I fancy rather too free with his political Principles. It does no good and is only making Enemies of those, who if you leave them at peace would be friends with you. Such is my Situation in regard to Mattlack as I am only a *hearer*. He is very friendly—and indeed it is the same with Caleb—I never contradict him and he is ever in a good Humour—But I have often wonderd whether, if Caleb and Mattlack was to meet (which they avoid as much as possible) wether their disputes would not terminate in a *pitch'd Battle*![7] I canot endure disputation be it on Politics or Religion—The *heart* must be *convinced*! and what Mortal can effect that? As long as the Bible is in our hands, and that be our Sure Guide, we can leave all Vain disputations to those who have not learn'd, in the school of the Holy Spirit—what is truth. Our Carnal Reasonings will not be of much service and may sometimes be only *casting of Pearls*.[8] I have this Winter been most delightfully imployed in Reading a Treatise Intitl'd The Wisdom of God displayd in the Bible wrote by a German Divine of great Erudition 2 Volumes Quarto.[9] It was not Wrote for You my Friend nor for me—who believe the Word of God but to open if Possible the Eyes of those who have been Stumbled by reading those pieces full of Comments to the dishonor of the Bible, with which Europe abounded in the years 87 to 96 and 97.[10] From the first Chapter of Genesis to the last of the Revelations he has display'd not human Wisdom but an Inspiration of the Holy Spirit—in answering every Possible cavil which men I had almost added and *Demons* have brought up. Although as I observed above, I am convinced of the Truth and Validity of this Divine Book, yet I must own it gave me a heart felt Satisfaction to find every thing, even what sometimes apeard rather Mysterious or Shall I venture to say *Trivial* accounted for in the most sublime manner and all and every Chapter and verse placed in such a point of *view* as demands *Respect*. If any Particular Passage should come in your mind and you will let me know I will endeavour to give you the authors opinion. Last week I received Winchesters Lectures which Mrs Stocker sent me.[11] I look forward to the perusal with Pleasure.

You ask wether we have a Library. I cannot say that we have, its true our Minesters have allways a Colection of good Books which every Member is wellcome to read but they are all on Divinity. There is a small begining made to a Circulating Library of History and Voyages, but I am no subscriber, I cannot afford it! I do not supose such a mixture of good and bad as Cobbets works are, would be admitted.[12] Our Boarders are not permitted to keep any

Novels during their Stay with us. They have books fitt for Children, and Young Persons, History, the Spectators—Guardian &c.[13] When they are from under our Tuition—they are to do as their Friends think proper, Our care is then at an end. I am as fond of Reading as ever but I have left off inquiring after Books. Only now and then my Curiosity rises when I read of new Publications—at present I shoud like to read the death of Cain as I have the death of Able—and the Welch Prophecy of Beulah I believe it is calld—I seem to be at present more fond of Prophecy than any other Subject.[14] And yet as there is so small a proba[bi]lity of my living to see the Accomplishment of many more prophecies it is silly in me don't you think so? to trouble my head about it. We are surely poor Creatures, allways looking for food out of doors, when we have plenty *within* offerd us gratis!

My dear Friend I am greatly obligd for you[r] Solicitude concerning my living Alone but I will give you a discription of my Situation which I am certain will make you easy in that Respect. I am Alone only as much as I please. I sleep in the large Hall with the rest of the Family.[15] I rise when I think proper which generally [is] at 7 O Clock when I come down I find a Warm Room. I pay one Shilling the Week to the Sister who makes my Fire in the Morning and brings me Wood and Water, makes my Bed and cleans my room every Saterday. Throughout the day I keep up my fire, and put my Room in order my self. Toward evening I let my fire go out and spend my Evening sometimes in one room sometimes in another but never in my Room unless I have something particular to do. My Room is front exactly 10 Feet Square, one Window with 25 panes of Glass. I have 2 tables, My Desk with a Closet on top—3 Chairs of my Own, and 2 borrowed ones a very small Looking Glass &c. I find my own fire and Candle furniture &c. But I pay no rent for the Apartment, and here I set wishing I had you at my Side. Mr Downing was pleas'd with the Old Maids room, it is very likely you would be pleasd to[o] if you saw it—but as Mrs Stocker says: I fear, *Thats out of Sight!*

I wish you would be good as to let your Neighbor Alexander Miller know, that the Parcell with the Books came safe on Friday last, but not a line have I receiv'd since the 24th of December last—My Nephew William I dare say will be kind enough to tell Mr Miller this[16]—and that my Lancaster Friends send so often to the Post Office to inquire for Letters without success, that I am really ashamed—and must leave off inquiring.[17]

You must know, Mr Miller has inform'd me, he should write by the Post, and pay the postage in Town—desiring me to write by the same Conveyance but—I receive no Letters—and shall at last not know what to think. Mr Miller has hitherto behaved so kind and affectionate to me that I cannot

Judge hard of him but am apt to doubt wether sufficient care is taken of such Letters as are post paid in Philadelphia. The parcel I mention'd was the *Lectures*—they came in a country Waggon and I supose the Letters lie at Bollers Still.[18]

I very very often wish we could converse a few Hours together, were it but once in a Month, but it cannot be. It is some consolation to hear from you, and more to read what you have wrote but many things cannot be so well expressd with the Pen as Verbally. When we shall both be arrived at our Eternal home I do hope we shall meet more frequent, than we have done in this Vale of Tears! I am grievd at your *complaints* but *we* cannot expect to grow more hearty with our Years—but quite the Reverse—Still as you observe *You* have been greatly Favour'd! Your Children are settled happily— your grand children aford you much pleasure—You and your Spouse grow old together and When the time comes, that you are called hence—You [will at last] be made willing to leave this Subl[unary] for a dwelling in *Heaven*.

I am a very poor scribe at the best—but by Candle light I am still Worse, which must plead an Excuse for this Scrawl. How does our good Aunt Mary do—My Nephew and the rest of your dear Family, I *inquire* in order to introduce a Salutation to each of them—For your last gave me an Account of their Wellfare. Mr Downing has promised to perswade your Daughter Sally to pay us a Visit. He tells me she has daughter at Westown—I should like very much to see that place[19]—We go on in our little Circle as usual—We do not wish to exceed the number of 20 Boarders tho we are Continually requested to take more Children. We cannot make place for more—and are grieved to refuse them. I must now relieve you and my self from this tiresome Epistle— My best Love to your other *Self*—and to any Friend who thinks it worth while to inquire after me—

I supose when this Letters is Seald many things wil fall in my mind that I could have wishd to communicate. Yet I have wrote enough for this time— Adieu my best beloved *Friend*, accept of a tender kiss just here—which I give the *paper*—you see I have blotted it with my Lips! Once more adieu—Your ever Faithful and affectionate

Mary Penry

I read—and burnt the piece you sent me—I think my self very happy that I see and hear so little of such Pieces—as you observe—when we were Girls— we had no Notion that Mankind could Possibly be so *depraved*. I have been inform'd pamphlets in the most Blasphemous Stile—circulate in Philadelphia. Kyrie Eleison![20]

ALS: Linden Hall Archives. Addressed "Mrs | Elizabeth Drinker | Mr Henry Drinkers— Senior | Philadelphia." Endorsed "Lititz Feb 6 1802 | Mary Penry." Drinker received this letter on March 17, 1802. See Drinker, *Diary*, 2:1500.

1. See Letter 18.

2. Caleb Cope: see Letter 25, note 3.

3. "indisposed with a disorder": see Letter 65.

4. Johanna Lichtenthaler (nearly three years old) died on January 23, and Carl Phillips (nearly two years old) on February 4.

5. Philadelphia newspapers printed a letter from Dr. Benjamin Waterhouse, author of *A Prospect of Exterminating the Small-Pox* (Boston, 1800), reporting that "every person . . . inoculated with the Kine pox matter, resisted the small pox." See *Poulson's American Daily Advertiser*, January 21, 1802, 2; *Philadelphia Gazette*, January 21, 1802, 2.

6. Lewis DuPre announced in the *Philadelphia Gazette* that he had discovered "the principles of the *perfect motion* (vulgarly called PERPETUAL *motion*)." Congress rejected DuPre's petition for a patent after congressman Samuel Latham Mitchell, a physician, stated that perpetual motion "was contrary to the physical laws of matter." See *Philadelphia Gazette*, January 13, 1802, 3.

7. "Caleb and Mattlack": for Caleb Cope, see above, note 2. For Matlack, see Letter 63, note 6.

8. Matthew 7:6.

9. MP notes in this letter that church members could borrow books from the minister's collection. Johannes Herbst's copy of Daniel Joachim Köppen, *Die Bibel, ein Werk der göttlichen Weisheit* (Leipzig, 1788) survives at Moravian Men's Seminary Collection, Moravian College.

10. "those pieces": published writings that denigrated scriptures. Moravian authorities "forbid their Members the reading of those pamphlets" (Letter 62).

11. "Winchesters Lectures": Elhanan Winchester's *Course of Lectures, on the Prophecies That Remain to Be Fulfilled*, published in four volumes in London (1789) was reprinted in America as two volumes in Connecticut (1794) and New Hampshire (1800).

12. For the "Library," see above, note 9. For Cobbett, see Letter 44, note 6.

13. MP's disdain toward novels is commonplace. See Kerber, *Women of the Republic*, 235–64. "Spectators": Joseph Addison's and Richard Steele's *Spectator* essays (1711–12). "Guardian": Joseph Addison's periodical (1714).

14. Mary Collier's 1761 translation of Salomon Gessner's *Death of Abel* (1758) was reprinted frequently in Great Britain and America before 1800. *The Death of Cain in Five Books; After the Manner of The Death of Abel. By a Lady* was first published in 1789. "Welch Prophecy of Beulah": unidentified.

15. "living Alone": MP had recently obtained "a little Room to myself" (Letter 60), a space in which to work but not sleep. See also Letter 41.

16. "Mr Miller": the widower of Margaret (Peggy) Stocker. "Nephew William": Elizabeth Drinker's eldest son. See Appendix C.

17. "Post Office": Lancaster's first post office opened in 1789. See Hecht, "Pennsylvania Postal History," 422.

18. "pay the postage in Town . . . post paid": see this volume's introduction. "Bollers": see Letter 40, note 3.

19. "daughter at Westown": Westtown opened in 1799, matriculating forty children from Quaker families. Elizabeth Downing, Elizabeth Drinker's granddaughter, attended Westtown School from April 1801 to November 1803; one of her samplers appears in Brooks, *Threads of Useful Learning*, 150–51.

20. "Kyrie Eleison": "Lord, have mercy" (Greek).

🦢 67. TO BENJAMIN RUSH[1]
March 11, 1802
Lititz, Pennsylvania

Lititz March 11 1802

My Worthy and highly esteemed Friend and *Brother*

Your Favour did not reach my hands till the 4th of March. The Pills I had receivd 4 weeks before the Directions. I am extreemly obliged to you for this and the many proofs of your kindness to such a poor Insignificant!

You advise me to 2 things, which are impracticable—Good Wine and Exercise in a Carriage. Cold Water thanks to the Lord for that truely great Blessing is Plenty and I make a plentiful use of it. I bathe in water from the Pump, which proceeds from a fine Spring allmost *all over* every Morning, throughout the Winter and once in the week sitt up to my knees in fresh water—which I find braces my Nerves and prevents Rhe[u]matic Pains, with which I was much afflicted before I used the Cold Bath. It is now 3 years since I began the bath in Summer and continued throughout the coldest weather. Very often Icicles hang to my hair.

Since then I believe few are less troubled with coughs or Colds, and if a Pain sieze me in Arm or Leg, repeated bathing the Part afflicted with cold water makes a Cure in a few hours time. But the difficulty of Respiration is my greatest complaint—and that I supose incident to my age—From my Birth I have ever been short breath'd, and Old Age increases it, growing very Fatt and using very little exercise, undoubtedly must be hurtful—but what cant be cured must be indured! The time aproaches, when I shall breathe freely in a better Atmosphere and shall be able to move without Pain or Trouble.

I drink very little water throughout the winter—3 small Cups of Coffee in the Morning, every day Soup is *one* part of our Dinner. Tea at 2 OClock in the Affternoon and very often at 7 OClock tea for Supper. This is a constant and daily practice, which it seems to me I cannot well do with out—they stile me a Tea-ist. *That* is my Old Wine—and Cordial. But when I am very weak and low, it is amazing how a glass of good Wine strengthens me—but not having made a practice of it, it seldom comes in my mind to wish for it.[2] In the days of my Youth, the best of Madeira wine was at my Command. Now I am old I can do very well without it. My dear Friend, a contented Mind is a very great Blessing. This it has pleased our mercyful Lord to grant me. He has withheld no *good thing* from me. I only have reason to pray for a grateful heart. I Wish dear Doctor! that it were possible to *hope* we might *once* see you here. Oh with what Pleasure should I bid you wellcome—but I dare not indulge the most distant *Hope*! Alas it is in Vain to think of it. I am reading the Lectures, and I read them with Pleasure. But I am grievd at heart at being Inform'd that the Doctrine of Universal Salvation has a most pernicious Effect on Numbers who heartily Embrace it, many I am told so far relax in their Moral Duties till at length they become *Atheists*.[3] I cannot but maintain my opinion the doctrine should from the begining been more private! what service is it to the Profane to tell them they should at last be saved alltho they spent their Lives in the worst manner—such persons swallow it with avidity and grow more careless—and more hardend. As for Believers—They undoubtedly have allways wish'd the Salvation of all Men, if consistent with our Lords Will, yet wether they were perswaded it would happen, or left in doubt—the Resignation to the Will of God will allways preserve them from murmuring at his dispensations—they certainly "must believe the Allmighty just, and where they cant unriddle, *learn to trust*."[4] Pardon me this digression dear Doctor. I own I am not *quite* a Convert to the Doctrine—although I most heartily wish it may be true!—Before the Halcyon days come, Mr Winchester has given us such a fine Discription of, We have days, and perhaps years of trouble to go thro, and we find ourselves still in the Vale of Tears. It is true if we had not the blessed Promises to cheer us, we might be heartless, yet it is so absolutely Necessary for us to be humble that I look upon it as the greatest Blessing, day by day, to feel myself a poor dependant being, begging to be fed with the Crumbs which fall from the Masters Table! Pray for us Brethren says the great Apostle to the Gentiles, Pray for *us* my dear Friend, let us pray for each other in *this hour of temptation which is come* upon the Earth—our adversary knows very well his time is short—and is the more indefatigueable—

And now my dear Friend I come incouraged by your Condecension with a Request that you will be so kind as to give your advice to a poor Handmaid of Jesus! She is a person of such experience in taking care of our growing up Girls to which as the *chief point* I must in adition bear my testimony: She is namely a Sincere Believer, and in her walk and Conversation an examplary Sister—fain, very fain would we detain her a few years here below, because *such* persons as my Friend is, are alas! not so plenty among us, as they were 20 or 30 years agon. Our Doctor has done all he can for her but it seems to her he does not rightly comprehend her disorder.[5] He fears (for he, and all her Friends would fain have her spared a few years longer) I say he fears she is Consumptive! If any thing could give us hopes of recovery it is this: she has very little expectoration. She is a Sempstress but uses freely Exercise, is extreemly brisk and active, cheerful and bears up amazingly under all her Complaints. She has requested me to ask wether you think it is worth while to attempt a Cure—and has so much Confidence in you that she says if any man can help her: It must be Doctor Rush: she frequently says: She would rather wish to be disolved and be with Christ but that she has no freedom to pray for it—and she only wishes for so much assistance as will inable her to fullfill the Duties of her calling. I requested her to State her Case, which she has done in German, the translation of which is inclosed. I am in hopes as the Season of the Year advances Oppertunities will be found, to send up any thing to her. My good Mrs Stocker I am certain will indeavour to assist us. We must act with Precaution, for our doctor might be griev'd if he knew she ask'd advice elsewhere. If sent to me, there is no harm done: our doctor knows—my Preference—and thinks it quite Natural as I am an English woman. I have taken the Pills these 8 days and find some relief, but I find flattulency is the greatest Affliction I have to complain off, when my Stomach is empty I feel best, but as soon as I swallow one Dish of Coffee I am directly puft up and have such a disagreeable rolling, and Noise in my Bowels as makes me quite Sick. This I believe is the Cause of those Storms as I call them which has several times brought me very near death—namely a most violent Pain between my Shoulders and thro my Breast for which our Doctor gave me twice an Emetic.[6] This last winter a few drops of Mint Oil gave me ease after a Racking pain of 2 nights and a day. I gave some of the Pills (for the Breast) to my friend, but they increased the soreness. She took of them 3 days, and we would not venture any further. And now I believe the good Doctor will be pleas'd if I conclude this lengthy Epistle! which for your Sake I will presently. Only give me leave to wish *you* and *your Spouse* and *Children* Health and Happiness in this World—and in the World to come *Life ever-lasting*—amen, amen!

I remain your *Faithful Friend, Sister* and Obliged Servant

Mary Penry

[Insertion][7]

In December 1799 a rash came out over my whole body but did not continue long, and I felt pretty well after it was over—In the month of February following I was afflicted with pains in my Limbs and a Slow Fever which brought on a voilent Pain in my Breast pretty high up, on the left side attended with a *dry* Hectic Cough and now and then spitting of Blood for which bleeding has been of great Service to me. Last spring I was much better, but throughout the whole Summer I was afflicted with a Slow Fever and Violent Head ach together with a pain at my Breast. This winter the pain or rather soreness in my Breast is very afflicting and some times stickes between the shoulders that I feel quite stiff as it were, keeping my self warm and a little perspiration seems to give me some ease. The least cold I take throws out an Eruption of red pimples with a very disagreeable Itching more especially on the Breast. These some weeks past I have been much troubled with a Lax, but as that has been a general Complaint with us this winter I do not reflect upon it. I have been long very *irregular*—gennerally 6 or 8 weeks—I am in my 26th year. My appetite has been better this winter than the Last.

ALS: Rush Family Papers, Correspondence, Box 13:49, 52, Library Company of Philadelphia. Addressed "Dr Benjamin Rush | Philadelphia." Endorsed "Mary Penry." Insertion endorsed "Mary Penry's friend | vs: Blisters | &c. | March 23 1802."

1. See Letter 27.
2. "glass of good Wine": for MP's liking for wine, see also Letters 58 and 64.
3. "Lectures": Elhanan Winchester's collected *Course of Lectures, on the Prophecies That Remain to Be Fulfilled*, which MP reported receiving in Letter 66. "Doctrine of Universal Salvation": see Letter 43, note 5.
4. From Thomas Parnell's "The Hermit": see Letter 37, note 15.
5. "Our Doctor": Gottfried Heinrich Thumhardt (1745–1819), born in Germany, joined the Moravian church in 1775 and served as a missionary and doctor at St. Thomas. He arrived in Lititz in 1792. "examplary Sister": Catherine Fetter. See Letter 37, note 36.
6. "Emetic": a substance that produces vomiting.
7. See note 5, above. MP translated from German the "case" of Catherine Fetter.

?? 68. TO KATHERINE PENRY[1]

July 10, 1802
Lititz, Pennsylvania

Lititz 10 July 1802

Dear and ever dear Cousin Kitty

A twelvemonth and indeed 3 months in adition, have elaps'd, since I saw a line from you. I was just on a *farewell* visit at Bethlehem the greatest part of the Month of May last year. There, I had the pleasure to receive 2 letters from you and my beloved Niece, wether I answerd them or not, remains a doubt with me.[2] If I have not, impute it not to want of affection. If I know my own *heart*, love tenderness, desire to hear from you, and an affectionate Sympathy in all your concerns, is as deeply engraved *therein* as ever. But my dear Old Age with its Concomitant Infirmities, has made writing, once my delight, a real *Task*, which like the Children I am very dilatory in performing. Among the Infirmities mention'd above, frequent ailments which bear hard on the Aged, is not one of the least impediments to an *agreeable* Corrispondance— But I will not tire your Patience with my Valetudinarian Complaints.—

I have near 2 years had a small apartment to myself, from which when deep in Meditation I frequently absent myself[3]—cross the Atlantic, and join *you* in my Native Country, but alas I cannot find you, not having the least Conception of the place of your abode—nor can I represent Persons my Eyes never beheld. Nevertheless I seem to have an Ideal Gratification in thinking *on* you, and conversing *with* you, *wherever* my fancy places you. I am more fortunate in regard to my Mr Stockers family, when I make my Ideal excursions, if I do not find them in one place, I know where to find them in another. All this you will very justly stile *small talk*, neither diverting nor Improving. I confess it, and will try to start a different Subject. Yet what shall I in my retired Situation find out pleasing to my Friends! I cannot promise! Indeed, True love, and gratitude, constrain me to call upon your attention, to a Melancholy Scene—I have lost a darling Cousin, who departed this life last April was twelvemonth. It was my dear Mrs Miller, formerly Miss Stocker, the Youngest Daughter of my dear Mrs Stocker![4] She was so aimable in *every* Station of Life—no wonder our grief for *our Loss* has not yet subsided! Her dear Mamma I fear will never get over it. Yet she with tears, acknowledges that every dispensation of divine Providence is right—and prays for more Resignation to the divine Will. I often think it is a Misfortune, to attain to Old Age, because we Outlive Many dear and Valuable Friends. Our greatest Consolation is the hope, we shall soon follow them. And My dear uncle, who seemd like a Second Father has left me behind—altho at his age it would have been very selfish indeed, to have wish'd him a much longer Continuance in this Vale of Tears. Yet that fault your Cousin Penry has been guilty of— She prayd fervently for his Life—but whatever is—*is best*.[5] As for my own part, I seem hastning down the Hill of Life and can in all proba[bi]lity Write but few Letters more to my dear Relations on the other Side [of] the Atlantic. You will be prepard for the tidings (as it cannot be expected to be at a distance) and I trust none of my Friends will *wish* me to outlive my self—a State of Life the *most* Melancholy—and which I am constantly praying *may not be my Misfortune.*

At Length *you* have the Blessing of Peace restord to you, which has given me great Satisfaction. Europe has Sufferd innumerable Calamities—may She now have a little Respite—Wether *America*, may be sufferd to injoy her present Tranquility any length of time is doubtful—The public Prints are full of Prognostics on the aproaching Settlement of the *French* at *Louisanna*.[6] I will not break my head or heart about it, on my own account, I hope to be at *Rest* in my grave, before it comes to the worst, yet I very much Pity the rising Generation, they may experience what *we* are threatned with. It seems to me, that all things tend to the great Period—when time shall be no *More!*[7] The

Infidelity of the present age, is more allarming to me than anything else that
I hear off. I have never—nor will I, while I keep my Senses, read any thing
contrary to our most Holy Faith—But I hear and see enough to Convince
me—there never was a time, that Infidelity was so bold, and contemning all
things Sacred so general as the Present. Nevertheless our Lord still has his
Thousands who have not bowed the *knee* to *Baal*[8]—this I firmly believe.

I read very little of what is wrote in defence of Religion, because it is very
seldom unmixed with Quotations from the Writings of its Adversaries,
which is too Schocking for me—But last week a friend in Philadelphia, sent
me a Book whose tittle is Christian Phylosophy, wrote by Viscissimus Knox
a Clergyman of the Episcopal Church—in England. I admire it much, and
wish it may be productive of that good the author wishes, and seems capable
off inculcating.[9]

It is some Consolation, that none of my Conections (that I am acquainted
with) or my Friends are among the Class of Infidels—Place men—or Democrats. The difference between *Federalists* and those *last* mention'd, are sufficiently described in the Public Prints, of which you doubtless see extracts, for
every thing of moment crosses the Attlantic. Parties are sometimes Storm-
ing, sometimes becalm'd—the state of all Republican Governments. Neither
is the Calm very Salutary or of Long Duration.

If we knew rightly to prize the Blessings we injoy, the United States would
be the happiest Nation in Christendom, but Peace and Plenty has introduced
Licentiousness and what will be the Conscequence time will discover. I very
much long to hear how you go on—My *Mother Country*, and *America* my
affectionate Nurse claim an allmost equal share in my heart, and best wishes.
The Blessings of returning Peace, will I hope be felt and injoy'd with *you*, may
you improve those Blessings by a grateful Attention to your Spiritual and
temporal Affairs. I address *you* in the name of the Whole nation, you will
easily comprehend. We have the Prospect of a fine Harvest if the Rains which
we have at present, are not a hurt to the Harvest which is now Begining.
Wether the transportation of Flour, may not be impeded as some think it
will, Will not be hurtful to our Farmers and Merchants I know not. At present grain is cheap to the Joy of the poor who must buy their Bread. Indeed we
have no cause of complaint—all the Necessaries of Life are Plenty, and
Labour is *well* paid. You have told me that in Your Country the Industrous
Poor, could live, and I have not a doubt, but honest poor, will find the means
of suport everywhere. True it is, there is a vast odds between the Continent
of *America* and an Island so populous as Great Brittain. Here numbers are
constantly moving further Back, and settling vast tracts of Land, which
with you is impracticable—We indeed every year take numbers off your

hands, and Many of those whom you are glad to part with, which by the by, do not turn out the best—and Many move away to the back woods, whom *we* can spare.

Hitherto we may say we have been favour with Health, at present we hear nothing of the Yellow Fever in any of our Cities. In some part owing to the Vigilence of the Magestrates, who are very Strickt in causing Suspected Ships to perform quarentine.[10]

Innoculation of the Kine Pox, has now obtain an allmost general approbation. In our little Village it has been successfully administred.[11] This Spring upwards of 70 Children and adults have had the Measels, and thro Mercy we lost not one. We are here at Lititz healthy and Industrous, and Happy in the Love of Christ and fellowship with each other. We are in daily expectation of a *Bishop* from Germany together with his Lady, and several others. Our Bishop who resided at Bethlehem dyed last December in a very advanced age.[12] We are likewise in expectation of a Minester and his Wife, from *Yorkshire* for our church at New York. His name is *Holms*.[13] Our Boarding School which is keept in our House, goes on *Well*. We teach Reading, Writing, Arithmetic, Grammer, Geography, History, Astronomy, Composition, Music—drawing, Embroidery Tambour, plain work, and knitting.[14]—We have at present 23 young Ladies, who lodge and board, and are (as I said before) Instructed in our House, from 9 to 14 years of Age, not a Week passes without fresh Aplications, which are noted down, and when *one* leaves us, another comes. 2 years is the General Rule for their Stay—some continue longer. Your Cousin Penry is too *Old* to take an active share in this Institution—one of the chief Tutorisses is my particular Favourite, her Name is Sally Fetter, to her I shall bequeath the Office, of informing you of my demise, not doubting she will Survive me, for she is not older than our dear Eliza.[15]

And Now my dear I have only to add: that you will with this, receive a Miniature of your Cousin Penry, concerning which, I have to Observe: the Hair is too dark, and the Temples too Strait—but its a wonder that it is so well executed as it has been taken from my Picture, which had the disadvantage of a Cap, which intirely conceald my hair—and the Artist being a Stranger to the dress I wore at 19 Years of Age. A likeness it is—tho not the most Perfect—yet I have not a doubt it will be acceptable.[16] My dear Mrs Stocker who is more than a Sister to me—in every Respect—will take upon herself the trouble of transmitting this Packet to you. As she has requestd whenever I wrote you, I should make hers and her dear Familys love acceptable to you, I take this oppertunity to present you, with the love of Mrs Stocker, her son my dear and affectionate Cousin Mr Clements Stocker—his

Lady Mrs Stocker, my Cousin Nancy Potts and Mrs Miller, the first a Widow Lady with 2 fine Children a Son and a Daughter, the first promising fair, to become one of our first merchants, the other a *Belle* who is at present a young lady of great Sence, and deservedly *admird.* Mrs Miller has but one Child of her own, a sweet Boy—Mr Stocker has 4 fine Children—2 Sons and 2 Daughters, his Eldest Son is in a Counting house in the City, the Youngest at Colledge. My Cousin Nancys Son I hear will shortly sail for the East Indies. *One* more, the Widower of my dearest Cousin Peggy, Mr Alexander Miller, Brother to my Cousin Pollys Spouse, is a dear good Friend of mine.[17] I entertain the Sincerest Affection for him, and beg leave to introduce him in the Number of my *Conections*—My dear Mrs Stockers Brother, Mr Philips and his Lady are among my *worthys,* as such I recomend them to you.[18] And now my dear Cousin Kitty I must Conclude or our dear Eliza, will be jealous, adieu my dear dear Kitty, do let me hear from you soon—Ever yours whilst

Mary Penry

My Love and Compliments to all *your* worthys as if named—You must specify them to me, as I have done *mine.*

ALS: Penralley Collection 1392, NLW. Endorsed "Received this Letter | by Post September |16th 1802 | Answered it | October 3rd." This letter was sent with Letter 69.

1. See Letter 29.

2. MP left for Bethlehem on May 8 and returned to Lititz on May 29, 1801. She had written her cousins in October 1801. See Letter 64.

3. "small apartment": see Letter 66, note 15.

4. "Cousin, who departed this life": Margaret (Peggy) Stocker Miller. See Letter 60, note 24.

5. "whatever is—*is best*": see Letter 48, note 18.

6. The Louisiana Purchase would occur in April 1803, but in May 1802 Philadelphia newspapers reported that Napoleon would re-settle the French at New Orleans, which he obtained from Spain in 1800. See *Philadelphia Gazette,* May 27, 1802; and *Gazette of the United States,* June 23, 1802.

7. "the great Period": for MP's millenarianism, see this volume's introduction.

8. 1 Kings 19:18.

9. Elizabeth Drinker sent Vicesimus Knox's *Christian Philosophy; or, An Attempt to Display the Evidence and Excellence of Revealed Religion* (London, 1795). See June 14, 1802, Drinker, *Diary,* 2:1524.

10. "Yellow Fever": the yellow fever revisited Philadelphia later in 1802. In October, Benjamin Rush advised Elizabeth Drinker that "it would be very improper for our family to return, as there was several ill not far from us." See Elizabeth Drinker to Henry Drinker, October 21, 1802, Cope Evans Family Papers, 1683–2012, MC.1242, Special Collections, Haverford College Library.

11. For smallpox inoculations, see Letter 52.

12. Johannes Ettwein (see Letter 9, note 2) died on January 2, 1802. In July, bishop Georg Heinrich Loskiel (1740–1814) arrived in Bethlehem to oversee all Moravian congregations in Pennsylvania and adjoining areas. Loskiel's *Geschichte der Mission der Evanglischen Bruder unter den Indianern in Nordamerika* (Leipzig, 1789) was translated as *History of the Moravian Mission Among the North American Indians* (London, 1794) by Christian Ignatius Latrobe.

13. John Beck Holmes (1767–1843), a teacher at the Fulneck school from 1791 to 1799 and pastor of the Moravian congregation at Yorkshire, had been announced as the new minister in New York but never assumed that position. See Stocker, *History of the Moravian Church*, 196.

14. "Tambour": see Letter 29, note 8. "Boarding School": see Letter 56, note 20.

15. Salome (Sally) Fetter (1778–1861) taught both at the girls' school in Lititz (1799–1808) and in Salem, North Carolina (1809–18). In 1819 she married the widower Eberhard Freytag (1764–1846). See Myers, *Century of Moravian Sisters*, 186–89.

16. For this miniature, see Letter 64.

17. See Appendix C for "my Cousin Nancy Potts" (Anna Stocker Potts), "Mrs Miller" (Mary Stocker Miller), "Mr Stocker" (John Clement Stocker), "Cousin Nancys Son" (Andrew Potts, who would die in St. Thomas: see Letter 71, note 2), and "the Widower" (Alexander Miller, whose wife had died in 1801).

18. "Mr Philips and his Lady": John and Rebecca Pyewell Phillips (see Appendix C).

৯৬ 69. TO ELIZA POWELL[1]

July 10, 1802
Lititz, Pennsylvania

Lititz 10th July 1802

My dearest Niece

I have chatted such a length of time with your good Aunt, that I fear you will stand but a poor Chance.[2] I am for this day pretty nearly exhausted, for my love I have not your Resources, Old Age they say is sometimes Loquacious, but not always agreeable—and now I think of it—how comes it my dear, that you have contracted your Letters so remarkably? Formerly a Sheet of Paper wrote down quite to the edge and hardly a Margin left, was the form of your Letters—now half a Sheet must content me—and *very little* of former important *Topics! here* I have given myself a Slap in the face—but let it pass. I *was* at your *age*, what *you* are *now* in full Strength and Vigour of Mind—*Now* I am an Antidiluvian allmost, consider my love, your *turn* is to entertain me—I have indeed often thought of the Topic you laid before me for discussion, and which I never seriously replied to, that was if I rightly Remember the *Perseverance* of Saints.[3] It is an Intricate question and seems out of my Sphere to determine on. The Apostle advises us to look unto Jesus not only as the Author, but finisher of our Faith, and I aprehend our greatest danger proceeds from Neglect of this advise.[4] Our will to act right or wrong is I believe in our own power— yet if we submit our will to *Him* he can and undoubtedly will incline us, to wish, and will what is best pleasing in his Sight. Our Perseverance than depends on our will—but it must be a Sanctified will—a will under obedience to him—Thy Will—not mine be done is the Prayer of a Believer. You seem to hesitate wether a Person who forsakes the Lord was ever truly Converted, and

I am myself doubtful wether such a person, dug his Foundation deep enough, or wether it was in Sand. I have lived to see many Instances of Persons who as you stile it, and very Justly, have fallen off from the Faith, yet I cannot but say, notwithstanding apeerences was fair, during their State of Grace, still, there was a nameless something wanting, which made me fear for them—a certain levity which now and then, betrayd itself; and that solid dependance on our Lord and holy fear to grieve him, so absolutely Necessary to such poor frail beings as we are, was wanting. These observations my love will confirm you in the doubt wether such who have fallen, were in a real State of Grace. Such who have in true Contrition, returnd to the Lord have confess'd their fall was oweing to an Indulgence of little Frailties as they stild them, which pavd the way for greater—let you and I my love beware of these quicksands!

The Parable of the Prodigal Son, is a fine example of our Lords mercy to poor Backsliders as Scripture stiles them.[5] We read a great Number of comfortable texts in Holy Writ in which such are incouraged to *return*. Indeed we were all of us Strayd Sheep! But my love let us not search into our Lords dealings with Backsliders and apostates—as we humbly trust *we* shall not add to their Number—

Will this answer do for you, or will you seek to make yourself unhappy, "by making distant Evils present by Reflection, and fretting at what which never may befal you."[6]

Here in our Back Counties there are wonderful Relations of Awaknings when Thousands are converted in a few days.[7] I dare not condemn what I do not understand but its a very strange Phenomenon, time will discover wether the work is of God! It were greatly to be wish'd that the Lord might visit his Zion and repair her breaches, Vital Religion seems to be at a very low ebb, yet I sincerely believe the Lord is carrying on his Work in Stillness, and He only knows his true worshipers, they certainly exceed Our Conception. All things work together for good, tho we are too short sighted to see it—nor is it Necessary, if we only believe his Power and his *Love*.

I wish instead of with Pen and Ink, I could converse with you in Person an hour or so—yet I do not wish you in America neither—unless you had an Independant fortune. We shall meet I trust in the Kingdom of Heaven—and according to your System (which I do not gainsay) have sweet Conferences together, more Perfect and Intelligible I hope than in this State, or it would not be so desirable an acquisition.[8] My beloved Eliza I represent you something as I was at your age—a little Romantic, I read your Flights with delight—why am I to hear no more of them, have I not treated them with due Respect—or do you think the Price Current of your Markets more agreeable—let me hear the *one*, without excluding the other.

Are you a great Reader, which are your Favourite authors, have you too much Sence to read *Novels*, have you a taste for Milton, and Youngs Night thoughts? have you read Popes Works—the Spectator, and such old Fashiond books which I still remember with Respect?[9] How does all our Friends who *Deserve* your Notice? Have you not heard from Haverford West?[10] See my love I give you Subjects to inlarge on, and shall expect a long answer. There are 2 little Ladies, here in the Boarding School—first Cousins—Nancy and Elisa Jacobs, descendants from Welch Families, Miss Nancy from both Father and Mother side—Miss Eliza of the Fathers side only. With these 2 young Ladies I celebrated St Davids day the first of March, with a dish of tea.[11] Since then another young Lady came, of the name of Weaver.[12] Her Father is a german, her Mothers Maiden Name was Willis, The Grand Parents came from Wales—these 3 young Ladies desire their Compliments to my Welch Niece. The first Tutoriss Miss Sally Fetter, a great Favourite of Mine, a most deserving Person, and one of our Single Sisters—as all the Tutorisses are—desires her kind Love to you—When *she* writes to you—she will do it to inform you, the Hand that writes this will never more use the Pen! It is very Possible this is the last Letter to you, should it be so you will cheerfully submit to the Lords will—and surely think I have lived long enough. Miss Fetter will perform an Executors part, and Transmit the Watch to you—which is all your poor Aunt has to bequeath you.[13] Now dont be melancholy—alltho it is very probably this *may* be the last Letter, still it is Possible you may receive Several. I cannot say I am certain, yet it behoves persons of my age to be in daily expectation of the great Change, and that *I am*, which Occassions my writing in this Stile. I must begin another Subject in order to withdraw your Mind from the gloom, which the foregoing has very likely overcast it. Do you never hear from my Uncle Charles Daughter. He was the only *one* of my Fathers Brothers, whom I can perfectly remember. Your Silence in Regard to our Family at Large, I take very kind—as you have hinted—many of them are beneath your Notice—But if you have anything agreeable to relate it seems it would be pleasing to me to hear—however you are under no Constraint, you have understanding sufficient to write a Letter without the Incumbrance of Family Affairs. I pray to God none may take it in their Head to Cross the Seas while I live—*You* know who I mean. Scarce a *Family* in the small Circle of my Acquaintance, but who have to lament the depravity of some of the Branches, therefore we can console ourselves with the Reflection *ours* is not Singular. I am sure the Recolection of my Family Both Father and Mothers side has ever made me wish—If I could not be an *Honour* to them, I might at least be no *Disgrace* to the Name of *Penry*—or *Stocker*—but *we* cannot help it, if others Value it *not*—The time aproaches when it will be said of the *Best* of Mankind "How lov'd, how valued *once*, avails thee not, To whom related, or by whom begot—A heap of Dust alone remains of *Thee*, Tis all thou art, and all the Proud shall be."[14] *Yet—no—*forbid it *Faith* and *Hope* we have Immortal Souls! Ever our garment of *Dust* shall once be changd to a glorious and Heavenly Body. The word *all* shall Sygnifie all our Corruptions shall be Buried in Dust—and all our Vanity totally extinct—It apears to me that what I observed at the Beginning of my Letter—you would stand a poor chance is verified—and I think you have found it so. This seems not calculated to give you much Pleasure, yet my love you must take it as it is—I never copy my letters, or perhaps this would have been more Correct, on Reading it over, I am very far from being Satisfied! And Since I am become too dull for my sprightly Eliza—adieu! Ever Ever your Sincerely Affectionate Aunt—

Mary Penry

ALS: Penralley Collection 1392, NLW. This letter was sent with Letter 68, which records the address and endorsement.

1. See Letter 29.

2. "chatted such a length of time with your good Aunt": MP is referring here to Letter 68.

3. "the *Perseverance* of Saints": the doctrine that individuals who are regenerated cannot fall from God's grace.

4. Hebrews 12:2.

5. Luke 15:11–32.

6. A 1782 edition of the *Letters of Abelard to Heloise* quotes Seneca's Epistle 13 in similar language: "How void of reason are men . . . to make distant evils present by reflection" (96).

7. "Relations of Awaknings": Francis Asbury and other Methodists preached to enormous crowds during the Second Great Awakening. A March 1802 meeting in Mecklenberg, North Carolina, drew five thousand people, while another that year in Cane Ridge, Kentucky, drew twenty thousand.

8. "We shall meet I trust in the Kingdom of Heaven": see Letter 3, note 5.

9. MP conforms to typical eighteenth-century taste, dismissing "novels" as frivolous or immoral and praising edifying literature such as John Milton's *Paradise Lost* (1667, 1674), Edward Young's *Night Thoughts* (1742–45), Alexander Pope's poetry, and Joseph Addison's and Richard Steele's *Spectator* essays (1711–12). See Letter 66, note 13.

10. "Haverford West": Haverfordwest. See Letter 6, note 4.

11. Nancy and Eliza Jacobs entered the Lititz girls' school in 1801. This "dish of tea" was the tradition of vespers. Eliza Jacobs recorded that she and her cousin Nancy "had the pleasure of taking tea with Miss Penry" (March 1, 1802, Diary, 1801–3, Linden Hall Archives), and decades later she recalled that MP invited students of Welsh descent to her room on St. David's Day, "where she had a little feast spread in honor of the occasions . . . She always had a bouquet of imitation leeks, made out of green silk, which she pinned on their breasts." MP would play Alexander Pope's poem "Vital Spark of Heavenly Flame," which had been set as a hymn, on the piano. See Haldeman, "Seventy-Seven Years Ago."

12. "name of Weaver": on May 19, 1802, a Mr. Weaver from Virginia had delivered his daughter Helena and his niece Elizabeth to the boarding school.

13. "Sally Fetter": see Letter 68, note 15. "the Watch": the Stockers sent MP's silver watch to a Bristol merchant, Thomas Daniel, who transferred it to Katherine Penry. See Thomas Daniel to Katherine Penry, February 6, 1806, Penralley Collection 1403, NLW.

14. MP likely encountered these lines (from Alexander Pope's 1717 "Elegy to the Memory of an Unfortunate Lady") in James Hervey's "Meditations Among the Tombs," which, like MP, replaced the word "honour'd" with "valu'd" (*Meditations and Contemplations*, 1:33).

70. TO GEORG HEINRICH LOSKIEL[1]
September 28, 1802
Lititz, Pennsylvania

Lititz September 28th 1802

Reverend and dearly beloved Brother!

I should not have ventured to intrude on your precious time, but the inclosed Translation gives me so fair an oppertunity for a few lines—I cannot possibly resist the Temptation.[2] I *Wish* (by any means thought best) that my poor Country Men might obtain a few Crumbs of that Food prepared for the Nourishment (according to the wish of the Philanthropic author) *prepared* for *every Heart.*

Upwards of 30 Years have elapsed since my translations have ceased, there being no great Occasion for it where the German Language is so generally understood. And I was not in a Situation to do it Gratis &c.[3]

I have frequently felt a very strong desire to translate detachd Pieces that more Particuarly affected my own heart. But I have hitherto been restraind by prudence. In the first Place I was truely sensible My Ideas were not Sufficiently Sanctified, and might injure rather than explain the Idea of the author; neither do I at present think myself Capable! Altho with the deepest humility—Permit me to the honour of our dear Lord, to acknowledge— within this few *weeks* and *Days* He has done great things for my *Soul!* Glory be to his Holy Name!

The German Divine's express their thoughts with so much energy, a Single Phrase often Says more than *lines* in English. Your Language is so rich so powerful We cannot attain to it. Do we only translate those Sentences— what are Pauses with you, are breaks with us—which require to be suply'd with words Consonant to the Subject. And—can I make up the defficiency— I think not—An attempt has been made, which I lay before you—Imperfect as it is. It has been a most pleasing employment—Which shall be persued or laid asside—as you think proper!

Commending myself to your Prayers as a poor feeble Sheep of the Fold under your Care—I beg leave to subscribe Myself—Your grateful, and Sincerely affectionate Sister

Mary Penry

ALS: PHC, Letters from Lititz, 1800–1804, MAB. Addressed "The | Reverend Brother | Loskiel." Endorsed "Received."

    1. Bishop Georg Heinrich Loskiel arrived in America in 1802 (Letter 68, note 739).

    2. "inclosed Translation": unlocated.

    3. During the 1760s, MP translated German materials into English. Daniel Sydrich, also in Lititz, translated English materials into German. See Daniel Sydrich to Joseph Powell, March 5, 1770, PP PJos 1, MAB.

 71. TO KATHERINE PENRY[1]

September 29, 1803

Lititz, Pennsylvania

Lititz St Michaels day 29 September 1803

Dear ever dear Cousin Kitty Penry!

Your long wishd for and most wellcome letter dated October—1802 I receivd the 24 of September, also 11 Months after date. Indeed I allmost feard my dear Cousin was gone before me to the Realms of bliss—which I hope will not be the case. I wrote you when at Philadelphia, where I spent the winter in the House of Mourning, my Cousin Nancy being inconsolable for the loss of her only son a fine hopeful Youth in his 21 Year.[2] They sent for me to assist in consoling her. I know not but she would have continued in that Melancholy Situation, had she not been roused by the aparent danger of her only surviving Child, a Young Lady *every way* accomplishd in Person and mind. Miss Maria Potts was so much afflicted at the death of her Brother, and her Mamma's grief, that she seemd to me like a fine flower withering on the stalk. She who had been accustomd to enjoy all the Gayeties of Life, now keept Close to her Chamber, at least she did not go out of the House for 3 months: at last a pain in the side, and a Hectic fever gave the Allarm, and Mrs Potts has been travelling with her daughter all the Spring, and spent the best part of the Season at a bath to drink the Salutary Waters &c. On their way they calld to see me—I was very fearful Maria would not recover, but they write me word she has perfectly regaind her Health. The dreadful Pestilential

Fever, having again been the Scourge of New York, and several Sea port towns, quite late in the Season (that is in September) has made its apearence in Philadelphia.[3] Most of the rich, have left the City, although the weather coming on very cool seems to give hopes its progress will shortly be stop'd. Mr Alex: Miller wrote me how and w[h]ere our Conections had disposed of themselves, and thus set my heart at ease on their Account. But alas my dear Cousin how is my mind agitated at this Moment, on the danger impending—or perhaps now realized in England or Wales, or both! It seems as tho your implacable Enemies, were desireous to *swallow* you intirely! When I take up the News paper—I long to hear, yet dread to read! The tremendous preperations making to destroy you, the discontents in Ireland, the want of unanimity in your leading Men &c. &c. is deplorable[4]—My greatest Comfort is in the Reflection: England has ever been an azylum for the opress'd and perscecuted on a Religious account! How many thousands are those, who day and night Surround the throne of grace with fervent Prayer, and yet my dear I can place no *confidence* in all this, because I verily believe we live in the last days, when tribulations shall *increase*—and Sorrow and Trouble of all kinds will come on the Christians in the *first place*.[5] But may we be inabled to say and *Pray: Thy will be done!* Our gracious lord will not lay on us a Burthen greater than we can bear, to him I comit my dear Native Land, and my still dearer Conections! The Tyrants reign will once have an *End*—and you and I my dear Cousin, may very shortly be taken from this *Vale* of tears, and transplantd to the Kingdom of heaven! Even those who are *not* the best Friends to England, shudder at her dangerous Situation and by no means wish her downfall, being very Sensible—That such a Conquest, would only pave the way for more attempts of the same kind—*and we*, may have more cause to deplore, than rejoice thereat. Think how anxious I shall be to hear from you, and O pray do your best, to give me some information—I think Liverpool would be the best place to convey letters to for America. I know there is more arrivals from thence, than any part of the Kingdom. I am glad my Picture such as it is, has reachd your hands[6]—2 very great Faults (if not observd in a former Letter)—I must mention—first my Hair is a light Chesnut—(what is not turnd grey)—secondly my temples are not *strait* as the drawing you have is—and 3rdly I had at that time of Life in which my Picture was drawn that was in my 20th year a remarkable lively *Eye*—neither is the drapery like *my* dress which was more gay and *open*, but you will say what nonsense is this—it is a Resemblance—tho a very faint [one] and that is sufficient. That I hear of your Illness after recovery, is quite agreeable to me, and your valuable Life will I humbly hope, be preservd for our dear Eliza's sake—

you seem to be her prop and Stay, may you continue so these many years to come—If you find a good Husband for her, I should not be sorry, a Single woman of her age seems somehow so unprotected in the midst of the World![7] I never experienced *this* because in my twentieth year I came to live among a House, full of Maidens, and have continued among them ever since. But I hope and believe my dear Niece, will never wish to change her State, unless she met with an *Honest* good Industrous Man—I would rather hear she took an Industrus tradesman or Mechanic, than a poor *Gentleman*. Of *this* Class our Family has exibited *many*—and according to the Vulgar saying Gentility without ability is—you know—what—*we* have dearly paid for the Experience of this Coarse but true saying![8] Most truely do I rejoice that you are suported by kind Providence, that tho in a state of mediocrity—you are content. I am sometimes curious to know: in *what manner* you contrive to suport yourselves—I sometimes fancy you take in Lodgers, if it be not too delicate to your feelings, should be glad to hear—but if you had rather be silent on that subject I submit. We are certainly more under a restraint in a Letter than we should be in conversation, since we cannot be sure of Letters coming safe to the party addressed. I still continue Scribe, and Book keeper, my Eyes still hold good without Spectacles. My dear Mrs Stocker, and her Son and Daughters often assist me with Cash and cloathing, so that I have every Necessary of Life.[9] I can earn very little now with my needle, being grown weak & infirm, but I will not say one word more, that I may not cast a gloom on your Spirits. I dare not reflect on the *Possible* distress these lines *may* find you in! I consider every thing attendant on that *scourge warr*, such as *taxes, scarcity of Provision*—I dare not proceed—it makes me shudder. *Frequent* and *Earnest* are my Supplications at the throne of Grace—*all that is in my Power!* I am Certain my dear Relations in *America*, wish my dear Relations in *Wales*, every Blessing, Spiritual and temporal, and have desired their Kind Salutations whenever I write. I could say a great deal about them, but delicasy restrains my Pen as these letters are to be sent them, together with yours for their Perusal—Mrs Stocker and I have no secrets between us, she is to me as a Sister, she loves to read our Corrispondance, and she is left at Liberty to read them alone, or communicate them to her Children as prudence dictates! All my Friends here desire their tender love to you, as *Maidens* you'r both intitelld to our tenderest regards. My kind love to those dear Friends with you who are kind enough to be pleas'd with my scribble. Tell them I glory in being a *Penry* and a Welch woman! but with the deepest Humility let me rather glory in the Lord! that I have been brought to know him, and to experience the Efficasy of his precious Blood. My Prayers for my dear Connections and their Friends, and my beloved Country at large, you may depend are frequent, more Especially at the present Crisis. *The Lord save & protect you!* I beseech you when oppertunity presents, give my kind love to *our* Cousin Philips, and tell her I feel a tender regard for her. All your worthies are included in my Salutations, tho not named. I seem still to Miss my revered Uncle, and yet it would be cruel to wish him still in this Vale of Tears. Happy are the dead that die in the Lord!

Mr Alexander Miller (whose first wife was my dear ever to be rememberd Cousin Peggy Stocker) was married last winter to a very aimable Young Lady[10]—the Families, that is his Brother John the worthy Husband of my Cousin Polly—formerly Stocker. His Brother William who has a sweet English Lady to his Spouse, Mrs Stocker, Her Brother and his Lady—Son and grand children together with her son my beloved Cousin Stocker his Lady and their Children Constitute—one Family of Love—my Cousin Nancy Potts and her aimable Daughter Miss Maria Potts you will take for granted is included in the same *Bond*.[11] Your—

Mary Penry

ALS: Penralley Collection 1393, NLW. Addressed "Miss Catherine Penry | Struet Brecon | South Wales | Care of Mr Phillips No. 16 Shore | Ditch | London | Monticello." Endorsed "This Letter | came to hands | December 31 1803 | Answered | this Letter | January 7th | 1804." This letter was sent with Letter 72.

1. See Letter 29.

2. "the loss of her only son": Andrew Potts, who visited Lititz in 1794. See Letter 35, note 3; and Appendix C. MP left for Philadelphia on November 15, 1802, and returned to Lititz on March 11, 1803. No letter from Philadelphia to her Welsh relatives survives. As usual, MP visited with Elizabeth Drinker. See Drinker, *Diary*, 2:1593, 1596, 3:1632.

3. The yellow fever revisited New York and Philadelphia in 1803. See Letter 32, note 5.

4. The Peace of Amiens ended on May 18, 1803, when Britain declared war on France. Napoleon renewed plans to invade Britain, establishing an Irish Legion to foster rebellion against England by the end of August. Fears in Britain were intense. Some 350,000 men answered the government's call for volunteers. See Philp, *Resisting Napoleon*.

5. For MP's millenarianism, see this volume's introduction.

6. "my Picture": see Letter 35, note 4.

7. "Single woman": for MP's concerns for single women, see this volume's introduction.

8. "Gentility without ability": see Letter 37, note 12.

9. "every Necessary of Life": for MP's financial circumstances, see the volume's introduction.

10. "Young Lady": Anna Maria Bass (1775–1853) became Alexander Miller's second wife on November 25, 1802.

11. For these members of the extended Stocker family, see Appendix C.

ᵶ❦ 72. TO ELIZA POWELL[1]
September 29–October 15, 1803
Lititz, Pennsylvania

Ever dear, yea ever dear Niece, *Eliza Powel.*

Allmost I have transgressd the Bounds mark'd with 2 Crosses w[h]ere my Letter to your Aunt should end, and yours begin.[2] I hope this once you will find me impartial, and you will with [all due] humility confess that its paying you a Compliment at your Aunts Expence—however since both Letters is as much at the service of the *one* as the other, I trust each will be satisfied. Having said enough to your Aunt of my Melancholy Sensations to convince you I have a heart truely affected with *your* troubles, I shall not repeat what is already on Paper, but assuming a more lively stile, endeavour to answer you in kind; but first let me in parenthesis observe—(The chilling thought: God only knows their present Situation, then perhaps my cheerful Sallies, may be ill timed). These reflections allmost stop my Pen—yet by the time this comes to hand, the Sun of Peace and happiness *may* break thro the cloud, and shine on you in full Splendour. Yes my dear, I confess I was *not* satisfied with your short Letters. I sometimes fancied you was weary of the Task, and made haste to close your Letter. I confess indeed I have not wrote these 2 years past, either so full, or so often, as formerly, for which failing, old age and its attendant Infirmities must plead an Excuse. It is from you my love, I am to receive the *subject* as in former Epistles, and my task is to expatiate thereon. A fertile Genius like yours, can never be at loss, it is therefore from my niece, who *now* is what I *once* was, I expect entertainment. First let me ask you what Multiplicity of Bus'ness you have on hand. Your dear Aunts ill Health, I give you full Credit for, as that doubtless ingaged the chief of your time, a dejection of Spirits is not National with the Welch, how came you by it? (But let me wisper in your Ear, I am often in the *Cellar* and often on the Top of the House, but my mother was an English woman, I supose thats the reason.)[3] That you are not pleas'd with your own Letters, is all owing to Pride, my dear. I am Old, yet never wrote a letter to my own Satisfaction, all owing to pride depend upon it. We dispise our own Productions and why—because they are not *faultless*, and we aim at Perfection, which we shall *never* attain to in this Life in no shape whatever, also not in *Writing*: you may then supose your Compliments are quite lost on me, knowing them to be unmerrited—and only proceeding from a Partial Tenderness, which is very apt to Magnify the Qualities of the Object belov'd, beyond their real worth. Tho I stiled myself an Antidiluvian, were it true that I lived before the flood, there is 10 Chances to one against me that I should have seen the tower of Babel, I should doubtless have perish'd in the flood, since there was but 8 persons in the Ark, and all of them Married.[4] To have been *one* of Abrahams Household, would have rather been my *Choice*, to have observ'd How frequent he receivd visits from our Lord, and to have admired his Faith, but old Japhet was my Grandfather, and yours to[o] my Love—from whom nothing particular is Mentiond except the People who descended from Him, but here I am too fast. *Noahs* prophecy is too remarkable to be past over: *Japhet* shall dwell in the Tents of *Shem*. We are ingrafted true in the true Olive, who were branches of the Wild Olive—We are *now* in the Tents of *Shem*, and O May the time soon come, that the Jews, the Natural Branches, who were cut off, may be again ingrafted in their *own olive*.[5] The present Babel Builders are 10 times worse, than those who built the Tower, those had ignorance to plead— But in our days—nothing but Satanical wickedness rules in the hearts of the Illuminati. I have read Robeson History of their Rise and progress, and I am convinced they are true Subjects and Instruments of Satan—and I will never, while I have my reason, read or listen to their impious tennets.[6] That you are a great Reader I am convinced of by your Stile, and am very much pleased that you are not fond of Novels, how many fine Peices come out in England. Read but the Evangelical Magazine, which is a composition capable to *amuse* and *instruct* the *Christian* of every Denomination.[7] In oposition to the Builders of a *worse* than Babel, let me set up the Builders of Zion—the Church of Christ, who are at present indefatigeable in *your* Country, in *this*, in *Germany* and *all parts of Christendom*. It is with unfeigned satisfaction I can observe how plainly we see Persons of all perswasions, reaching the hand to each other, and uniting to spread the Gosple of Christ, throughout the World— Read Dr. Hawies accounts of the Industry, of the pious of all Denominations, and the Blessings attending their Exertions.[8] Last winter at Philadelphia I was greatly edified in the Company and Conversation of several Pious Persons among the Presbyterians;[9] It is well known, how rigid they were formerly, but now the Partition wall is breaking down, and it is not inquired, what Denomination you are off, but wether you are a Lover of the Lord Jesus—This my Love is the best *News* I can inform you about, nothing doubting it will be most agreeable to you to hear. We have had a Sickly Spring, and summer; I believe greatly owning to the extreem Drouth. In our House we have had no illness to confine us to our Beds, but all around us, People have been afflicted with the Flux, which carried off Numbers of Children. We have had no fruit, Frost and drouth has destroyd our Cheries Applies &c. but if we have bread & Provinder for the Cattle, we will be thankful. The 2 young Ladies who celebrated Davids day with me, anno 1802 have compleated their Education and are returnd to their Friends.[10] The boarding school in our

House, continues in great Repute, and so many Applications are made, that a House is now building solely for the Boarding school as we have not place in our House for more than 27 or 28—our Present number.[11] Miss Fetter the first Tutoriss and the Friend I mentiond, having heard what you have wrote concerning her, desires her kind [Love to you] and thinks her Letter as you say: will not be very wellcome. I am quite easy about it; [*missing*] Eliza knows: having lived so many years among Old, and Elderly People, *our* and your Beloved [*missing*] Father and Uncle, and your dear Aunt, to wittness the Infirmities of Age, and not to Lament a Grandpapa of 80 odd, and an aunt near 70 to any immoderate degree.[12] W[e]re the distance not so great how much larger might our Corrispondance be, how many things might we communicate to each other! The 2 Miss Powels in whose Company I spent many Hours last winter greatly to our mutual Satisfaction, tho they know not of my writing I can venture to say: their Love attends you *both*[13]—they speak of you as of dear Relations—but my dear they are strickt Quakers, and I believe at present there are no set of People so bigoted as they are, now that Believers of all Classes draw close together in Brotherly Love, They keep aloof, and seem not to wish to be social with any out of their own Pale—To me whom they Regard as a Relation, and too Old to be any Acquisition to them, they behave in the most Friendly Terms—But after my decease you will hear no more of them, nor of my Relations here, that you may be certain—your Situation in Life is too Mediocre to attract the attention of Persons in Affluence, and as for my self I expect should I survive Old Mrs Stocker to be *Buried* with her![14] I have *so* much *sense* as *to expect it*—as it is the Natural Consequence— and the way of the World! My dearest Love, my Eliza! Set your heart and Affections upon things above—all is vanity and vexation of Spirit, except that proceeds from Religion! Faith in Christ, Love to him, Childlike dependance on him looking in Faith constantly unto *Jesus* the Author and Finisher of it—can alone cause a Happy Life and Tranquil Death.[15] I sincerely Compasionate my poor uncle Williams Wife, tho by this time I supose she is gone, may she have a happy Exit—our poor Relations—worthless as they are, are objects of my prayers. To me they cannot aply for pecuniar[y] Assistance, they must work for their Living as I have done these 47 years, and still continue to do it at 68 years of Age. I am not ashamed of Poverty when not coupled with disgrace! As I intend writing again this fall or if the Shiping should be stopd, early in the spring I will conclude my long and unentertaining Scribble, my love to those dear Parents whose children you inform me were transplanted to the Kingdom of Heaven, tell them I think we ought not to lament Children—for Oh how many Trials and troubles have they Escapd, which we have Suffer'd—Adieu My *niece* my beloved Eliza and my dear Cousin *Kitty Penry*, ever untill death your sincerely Affectionate Aunt and Cousin

Mary Penry

When we meet above we shall recognize each other in perfect bliss without al[l]oy—and I my Eliza, shall with Joy acknowledge *Thee*.[16]

Excuse my Blunders—I am so accustomd to the German Language, that sometimes I can scarce write English—

15 October. My Letter is still with me, I have no opper[tunity] to send it to Philadelphia as my Friends have all left the City on account of the fever[17]— No accounts but of the terrific [*missing*] of the French. In what anxiety I spend my time, wishing yet fearing to hear from my dear Country.

ALS: Penralley Collection 1393, NLW. This letter was sent with Letter 71, which records the address and endorsement.

1. See Letter 29.
2. MP writes this letter and the previous one on one sheet of paper, separating her two letters with "2 Crosses."
3. MP is saying that she derives her variable temperament, sometimes in high spirits and sometimes down in the dumps, from her mixed English and Welsh parentage.
4. "8 persons in the Ark": 1 Peter 3:20.
5. Genesis 9:27. MP's reference to "the Tents of *Shem*" suggests that, like the Jews, Christians have been scattered from their true home, which others occupy—and MP looks forward to the Jews' return, since this is a sign of the end-time when Christians will be reunited with their Savior.
6. "Robeson History": see Letter 62, note 6.
7. The *Evangelical Magazine* began publication in London in July 1793.
8. "Dr. Hawies accounts": probably Thomas Haweis's *Essays on the Evidence, Characteristic Doctrines, and Influence of Christianity* (Bath, 1790). For Haweis (1734–1820) and the Moravians, see Mason, *Moravian Church*, 75–76.
9. MP left for Philadelphia on November 15, 1802, and returned to Lititz on March 11, 1803.
10. "2 young Ladies": Nancy and Eliza Jacobs. See Letter 69, note 11.
11. "a House is now building": an addition to the boarding school (*Anstalt*) was dedicated on August 26, 1804.
12. MP assigned Sally Fetter the task of informing her Welsh relatives of her death (the letter that "will not be very wellcome"; see Letter 68).
13. For Ann and Patty Powell, see Letter 38, note 3.
14. MP expects that she will be forgotten by her American relatives as soon as Margaret Stocker dies.
15. Hebrews 12:2.
16. MP seems to have finally embraced her niece's belief that "it is Possible after this Life to know Those in heaven who was dear to one on Earth" (Letter 5). See Letter 3, note 5.
17. "the fever": yellow fever. See Letter 32, note 5.

❧ 73. TO [MARGARET STOCKER][1]

January 21, 1804
Lititz, Pennsylvania

I've closed the old and entered the new year with peaceful sensations. In the
first moments of the new year, a fervent prayer was offered us before the throne
of grace, first for our congregations and all its divisions, then for all our congregations in America, and in the parts of the globe—for our missionaries,
and their different folds—for the whole church militant[2]—for the missions of
the servants of God *out* of our circle—for magistrates, and finally for all conditions of mankind,—nor did our ministers forget poor old England!—you will
easily conceive my own petitions. I went from one friend to another and
begged the Lord to bless them as I laid their names at his feet. I can only add,
that I wished you and every one of your dear family a happy year.

Printed Copy: Poulson's *American Daily Advertiser* 33 (May 23, 1804): 3. This letter is embedded in MP's death notice.

  1. For Margaret Stocker, see Appendix C.
  2. "church militant": see Letter 48, note 13.

❧ 74. TO MARGARET STOCKER[1]

May 8, 1804
Lititz, Pennsylvania

this is the 8 of may I receivd your letter and Kind present I have been very ill
my disorder has made rapid strids how long I may Languish under this
oppression of my breast my good lord knows best may he give me patience
and support me until the End I am in his Hands he knows best the right hour
to him I leave itt—I dare not write much my nerves are so extreem weak—
When I think its Possible this may be my last to you The feelings of Love &
Thanks—and Thanks quite overcomes me—Please to give my love to good
Dr Rush and all and Every other friend adieu.[2]

                                                                Mary Penry

Copy: Margaret Stocker to Katherine Penry, May 30, 1804, Penralley Collection 1399, NLW.
This letter is embedded in Stocker's letter to Katherine Penry.

  1. See Letter 73.
  2. "good Dr Rush": Benjamin Rush. See Letter 27.

Departed the 17th of May 1804

Our late Single Sister *Mary Penry* left behind the following written account of her earthly journey:

I was born on the 12th of November 1735 in Abergavenny in the principality of Wales in Great Britain. My father was Hughgonius Penry a surgeon there, and my mother was Maria born Stocker. Both my parents belonged to the Anglican Church and were by their perception devout people. My father achieved a reputation as a talented and honorable man in his profession, especially in the field of anatomy. He did not enjoy good fortune in his earthly affairs, however, and my mother was also taken advantage of, cheated out of what was rightfully hers by disloyal guardians.[1] And so they both lived in desperate and worrisome circumstances.

During the first years of their marriage they lived in a building full of Catholics, among them a Knight of Malta.[2] He was very friendly toward my parents, and attempted every which way to convince them to convert to Catholicism. He saw that my father remained steadfast and could not be persuaded otherwise. But this Maltese Knight did have some hope of making my mother a compatriot in his faith. But concerning me, he was determined to succeed. Even in the first hours of my life, he had already dedicated me and my life to the Virgin Mary, that I shouldn't stay in the world, rather live in a cloister. I mention this, since what he envisioned was indeed realized in part, albeit in a very different way.

In the year 1744 my father passed away, and my mother moved with me to Bristol. She was taken in by her relatives as a widow and was well cared for. It wasn't long before she received an invitation from a relative of her mother to come to America. This woman had already been living in America for many years and didn't have any children of her own.[3] Because of this, she promised

---

1. MP's baptism is recorded on November 1, 1735 (OS), in Abergavenny St. Mary's Church Register, PCA. See this volume's introduction; and Letter 9.

2. "Knight of Malta": a Roman Catholic lay religious order, whose motto is *Tuitio fidei et obsequium pauperum* (Defense of the [Catholic] faith and assistance to the poor).

3. MP's father died in 1740. The "relative of her mother" in America was Ann Stocker Attwood, who died in 1747.

to look after us as her own. We accepted this offer happily. We arrived in Philadelphia on the 16th of September 1744. We were received warmly by our relative and her husband, Mr. Attwood, a wealthy merchant in the city.[4] It soon became all too apparent that she was deceived. What she had first sensed became reality of misery and despair. This Mr. Attwood was a terrible person, someone who had little concern for either God or his fellow man. But nonetheless in 1747, a year after his wife had died, he had cajoled my mother so much, she did in fact marry him, albeit of necessity.[5] From this date forward our true despair began, for on a daily basis he threatened to kill my mother.

What I had to endure during this period is indescribable. It wasn't just the matter of seeing my mother in such distress, which wore heavily on me, I also was in danger, enduring temptations and the snares of the world. At the same time, a deep sense of my own depravity was awoken in me, and I thought I was losing my sanity. I would gladly have died 1000 times over, if I had known with certainty that I would be saved. I turned to our precious God, asking Him for guidance and care. I was saved by Him.

In the year 1754 I came to the Brethren's church for the first time. Late Br. Rogers's witness found an immediate opening into my heart.[6] I am amazed how the Savior would care about me, especially at a time when I was not in the right frame of mind. As a matter of fact, I rejected any feelings toward Him and His wounds. I trembled when I heard of these things and considered them blasphemous. I found the members very kind-hearted, and I wanted to become like them. Of course, any real change to my heart was unthinkable. Despite this, the Good Shepherd tended to me with indescribable fidelity. The 2nd of March 1755 was the great day when the Savior appeared before my heart in His martyr image, and revealed to me His nail wound to my eternal blessing. This impression has stayed with me despite all the external and internal changes I have experienced over the years. Dear Brother Haidt, who was in Philadelphia at that time, remarked with joy that my soul had just begun to live.[7] But he also feared that the bright spark that

---

4. For William Attwood, the "wealthy merchant," see this volume's introduction.

5. "of necessity": Mary Attwood gave birth to a child, Elisabeth, on January 20, 1751; the marriage took place two months later (not in 1747). Elisabeth Attwood died on September 26, 1758, not yet eight years old.

6. "Brethren's church": the Moravian church in Philadelphia, founded in 1742. Jacob Rogers (1715–1779), ordained in the Church of England in 1737, joined the Moravian church at Bedford in 1741 and came to America in 1752, serving in Philadelphia. He married Anna Mary Parsons in 1756, and the two left for North Carolina in 1758. When his wife died in 1759, he returned to Philadelphia. He left for England in 1762, supervising a new Moravian congregation at Bath, and died in 1779.

7. Johann Valentine Haidt arrived in Philadelphia in June 1754 and preached regularly until he left for Bethlehem in September 1755. See Nelson, *John Valentine Haidt*, 94.

now glowed in me might be extinguished, if I remain among the distractions of the world. Therefore he explained to me the ways of the Brethren's Church and beliefs, especially the Sisters' House in Bethlehem. What I heard excited me so much that I wanted to become a member of this group.

On January 25th of 1756 I was accepted into the congregation at Philadelphia. It was only a few months later, after making many requests to move to Bethlehem, was I given permission to do so. On August 13th of the following year I became a participant in the body and blood of the Savior in Holy Communion for the first time.[8] It's difficult to describe the joyous feeling I felt.

In 1760 the Lord decided to call my mother home to be with Him.[9] On June 3, 1762, I arrived in Lititz. Here the dear Savior taught me the hard way for the well-being of my poor heart. This allowed me to see my inherent depravity even more. But I still was not cured. Because I rejected admitting to my true nature, and tried to help myself by my own means, I only slipped deeper into despair. I continued on in this sad state until the Savior granted me the grace to reveal my entire former journey of faith to our then Choir Helper, Sister Maria Magdalena, in an open and truthful manner.[10] Even so it was difficult to recognize myself as such a totally lacking sinner.

At the first communion of the Single Sisters Choir in Lititz on the 28th of August 1764 my bloodied man of sorrows smiled upon me with grace. I'll always remember this moment and will kiss His punctured hands and feet when I come to Him. I promised from then on to serve Him faithfully with all my strength as a single sister, where and how He deems appropriate.

August 14 of 1765 I was blessed to be admitted to the hourly prayer watch.[11] On the 13th of November of that same year I entered the class of Helpers. The time I spent praying with them was a true blessing for my heart. On the 23rd of October 1768 along with 2 other Sisters I became an Acolyte during a Synod held here [in Lititz].[12] So as I look back now upon my life's long

8. MP and her mother were received into the Philadelphia congregation on January 25, 1756. MP left for Bethlehem on June 16, 1756, and took communion there on August 13, 1757, marking her acceptance as a full member of the Moravian church.

9. Mary Attwood died on September 21, 1760. The following day Johann Valentin Haidt conducted her burial service.

10. "Sister Maria Magdalena": Maria Magdalena Augustine (see Letter 9, note 7), the spiritual leader of the single sisters in Lititz.

11. "hourly prayer group": beginning in 1727 and continuing for one hundred years, the Moravian church conducted an unbroken prayer, achieved by assigning individuals particular hours they would spend in devotion.

12. "Acolyte": an honor recognizing lifetime commitment to service to the church. Acolytes assisted the pastor in distributing elements of Holy Communion. A Provincial Synod occurred at Lititz from October 20 to 23, 1768.

journey, and consider to what extent the Savior guided me with patience, grace and favor, I can only wonder and am lost in my thoughts.

To this point written by herself. The Single Sisters add the following:

We can attest that our late Sister served our Choir and House tirelessly and faithfully in several ways according to her many strengths, even up to a few days before her end. She served as financial bookkeeper, a room supervisor, and attendant to visitors.[13] Her heart concerned for the sake of the Savior and particularly for all the Choir's dealings, and her dignified manner toward everyone, were proof of her faith. During all these years of difficulty, it was clear to everyone by her whole demeanor, how much her heart was attached to the Savior. It was also obvious the Savior's martyrdom and death had taken root in her. If she became aware her relationship with the Savior had faltered, she could not rest until she was comforted and received forgiveness from Him.

For some years now one noticed a decline in her strength; nonetheless, she gladly continued to serve where she could. Otherwise she remained healthy throughout until winter last, when she began to weaken. She complained of chest pain, which increased over time despite several medications. At the past Choir Festival she participated in the many gatherings.[14] She could not thank her Savior enough for being so merciful on that day, especially during the Holy Communion of the choir when, according to her own words, she felt heavenly; it would be her last. On the 5th of May, she was taken to the infirmary. The chest pains and congestion increased and caused great anxiety, especially the first eight days. But in her hour of need she turned to her Savior. Her heartfelt prayers were answered as the Savior took away her fear. It was in such a state of happy and innocent childlike courage she saw the end of her days here. It even made her sad, if someone told her the end might not be so near after all. Two days before her departure it did in fact seem as if she would recover. On the 16th she endured such a strong attack on the chest, it seemed to her and us that her end was near. She spent the night in a very weak state. It came to pass on the 17th at 9 in the morning, and with blessing of the congregation and her choir she gently fell asleep—68 years, 6 months and 4 days.

> Enjoy, O dearly purchased soul,
> Your election by grace with delight;

---

13. "attendant to visitors": MP served as *fremdendeiner*. See Letter 33, note 7.
14. "Choir Festival": the single sisters' Festival Day is May 4.

Soar up from this earthly cavity
Into the wedding hall with jubilee;
Throw yourself at the feet of your Bridegroom
Who has entrusted himself to you on earth;
Let your tears of love and joy flow
For your hard-earned mercy.

Join in with all the redeemed,
Assembled around the throne of the Lamb
And sing the song that will resound forever
In honor of the Son of God and Son of Men.
We, who down here are longing
To soon be at home with the Lord,
Until then we will look forward
With sinners' tears to our redemption.

[German original]
Unsre selige Schwester Maria Penry hat von ihrem Gang durch diese Zeit
folgende Nachricht hinterlassen:

Ich bin geboren den 12. November 1735 zu Abergavenny im Fürstenthum
Wales in Großbritannien. Mein Vater, Hughgonius Penry, war Chirurgus
daselbst und meine Mutter Maria, geborne Stocker. Diese meine beyden
Eltern waren von der Englischen Kirche und nach ihrer Erkenntniß religiöse
Leute. Mein Vater hatte den Ruhm, daß er in seinem Metier geschickt und
besonders in der Anatomie sehr erfahren gewesen. Er hatte aber kein Glück
in der Welt, und meiner Mutter untreue Vormünder brachten sie um alle das
Ihrige, so daß sie beyde in sehr kümmerlichen Umständen waren.

Die ersten Jahre ihrer Ehe hielten sie sich in einem Hause auf, wo lauter
Catholicken wohnten, worunter sich auch ein Maltheser-Ritter befand.
Dieser bezeugte sich eine große Freundschaft gegen meine lieben Eltern und
that sein möglichstes sie zu bereden, zur catholischen Religion überzugehen.
Meinen Vater fand er unbeweglich; von meiner Mutter aber hatte er *einige*
Hoffnung und bey mir blieb ihm kein Zweifel, denn er devovirte [devotirte]
mich in den ersten Stunden meines Lebens der Jungfrau Maria und
betheuerte, daß ich nicht in der Welt bleiben, sondern mich in ein Kloster
begeben würde. Ich erwehne dieses darum, weil es zum Theil eingetroffen,
wie wohl ganz anders als der gute Mann es meynte.

Anno 1744 ging mein Vater aus der Zeit, und meine Mutter zog mit mir
nach Bristol, wo sie als Witwe unter ihren Verwandten sehr wohl besorgt

wurde. Nicht lange darauf bekam meine Mutter eine Invitation nach America, wo eine Verwandte ihrer Mutter schon viele Jahre wohnte, und da selbige keine Kinder hatte, versprach sie *uns* an Kindes statt anzunehmen. Diese Invitation wurde mit Freuden angenommen, und wir kamen am 16. September 1744 in Philadelphia an, wurden sehr liebreich von unsrer Verwandtin und ihrem Mann William Attwood (einem reichen Kaufmann dieser Stadt), empfangen. Hier sahe meine Mutter bald ein, wie sehr sie sich betrogen und daß sie aus einer vermeynten in eine wirkliche Noth und Jammer versezt war, denn gedachter Attwood war ein Bösewicht, der weder nach Gott noch Menschen was fragte. Jedoch brachte er es 1747 durch seine Schmeicheley bey meiner Mutter soweit (nachdem seine Frau bereits vor einem Jahr gestorben), daß sie ihn wiewol aus Noth gedrungen heurathete. Nun ging unsre Noth von neuem an, denn fast täglich drohte er meiner Mutter, das Leben zu nehmen. Was ich in dieser Zeit für Jammer ausstund, ist nicht zu beschreiben, denn nicht alleine die Noth meiner Mutter drückte mich, sondern ich kam auch in Gefahr, durch Versuchungen und Strike zu Fall zu gerathen. Zugleich fing mein Verderben an, recht in mir aufzuwachen, so daß ich öfters dachte, ich würde von Sinnen kommen, und 1000mal wäre ich lieber gestorben, wenn ich nur versichert gewesen wäre, daß ich selig würde. Ich wandte mich dann zum lieben Gott und bat ihn um Bewahrung, und er erhörte mich.

1754 kam ich zum ersten Mal in die Brüderkirche und wurde unter des seligen Br. Roger's Zeugniß gleich ergriffen. Es ist mir zum Erstaunen, wie sich der treue Heiland mit mir einlassen konnte zu einer Zeit, da ich nicht nur ganz unbekümmert gewesen, sondern sogar eine Wiedrigkeit gegen Ihn und Seine Wunden fühlte, so daß ich zitterte etwas davon nennen zu hören, weil mir das alles gotteslästerlich vorkam. Ich kriegte aber die Geschwister lieb und wünschte so zu werden wie sie. An eine Herzensänderung war aber gar nicht zu denken. Der gute Hirte ging mir aber mit unbeschreiblicher Treue immer nach. Den 2. Merz 1755 war der große Tag, da mir der Heiland vors Herz trat und mich meine ewige Gnadenwahl in seinen Nägelmal erblicken ließ. Der Eindruck hiervon ist mir bey allen Abwechselungen immer geblieben. Der liebe Bruder Haidt war damals in Philadelphia und sahe mit Freuden, daß ich nun anfing zu leben, befürchtete aber, daß der Funke wieder bey mir verlöschen möchte, wenn ich in der Welt bliebe; erzehlte mir daher manches die Brüdergemeine betreffende, besonders von dem Schwestern-Hause in Bethlehem, welches ein Verlangen zur Gemeine in mir erregte.

Den 25. Januar 1756 wurde ich in Philadelphia in die Gemeine aufgenommen und etliche Monate darauf bekam ich auf mein anhaltendes Bitten Erlaubniß zur Gemeine in Bethlehem und am 13. August folgendes Jahres hatte ich die Gnade, ein Mitgenoß am Leib und Blute des Herrn im Heiligen Abendmahl zu werden. Wie mir dabey zu Muthe gewesen, kann ich nicht beschreiben. 1760 gefiel es dem Heiland, meine liebe Mutter zu sich zu nehmen. Den 3. Juny 1762 kam ich nach Litiz. Hier führte mich der liebe Heiland in eine heilsame Schule für mein armes Herz; er deckte mir mein Grundverderben noch mehr auf, so daß ich's recht innewurde, ich sey noch nicht curirt. Weil ich mich aber dieser Selbsterkenntniß wiedersezte und mir selbst zu helfen suchte, so gerieth ich in große Noth. In dieser Verlegenheit ging ich so lange hin, bis mir der liebe Heiland die Gnade schenkte, ganz offenherzig und grade mit unsrer damaligen lieben Chorarbeiterin, Schw. Maria Magdalena, über meinen ganzen bisherigen Gang auszureden. Es hielt aber sehr schwer, mich als eine arme Sünderin zu erkennen, als woran es mir hauptsächlich fehlte.

Den 28. August 1764 bey unsrem ersten Chor-Abendmahle kriegte ich einen gnädigen Gnadenblick von meinem blutigen Martermann, der mir noch unvergessen ist und auch dafür werde ich, wenn ich zu ihm komme, seine durchbohrten Hände und Füße küssen. Ich verband mich nun aufs Neue, Ihm in dem Stande einer ledigen Schwester aus allen Kräften zu dienen, wo und wie es Ihm gefällt.

Den 14. August 1765 hatte ich die Gnade in die Stunden-Beter-Gesellschaft admittirt zu werden, und am 13. November kam ich unter die Helfer. Meine Gebetsstunden haben mir manches für mein armes Herze ausgetragen. Den 23. October 1768 wurde ich nebst noch 2 Schwestern bey Gelegenheit eines hier gehaltenen Synodi zur Acoluthie angenommen.

Wenn ich nun meinen ganzen Gang überlege und bedenke, mit welcher Geduld und Gnade und Huld Er mich geführt hat, so verliert sich mein Denken darüber.

So weit ihre eigene Worte. Die ledigen Schwestern thun noch hinzu:

Wir müssen unsrer selige Schwester das Zeugniß geben, daß sie in unserm Chor und Hause nach ihrem Vermögen, besonders als Rechnungs-Führerin, Stuben-Aufseherin, Fremden-Dienerin und überhaupt wo sie konnte, mit unvermüdeter Treue diente (bis wenige Tage vor ihrem Ende). Ihr teilnehmendes Herz an der ganzen Sache des Heilands, besonders aber an allen Vorkommenheiten in unserm Chore und sowie auch ihr aufrichtiges Betragen gegen jedermann, erwarb ihr eine durchgängige Legitimation. Bei allen schweren Vorkommenheiten in den vielen Jahren war aus allem zu merken, wie sehr ihr Herz am Heiland hinge und daß der *Eindruck* von *Seiner Marter und Tod* tiefen Grund bey ihr gefaßt hatte. Und wenn sie etwa merkte, daß etwas zwischen ihr und dem Heiland war, so konnte sie sich nicht beruhigen, bis sie Trost und Vergebung *von ihm* empfing.

Seit etlichen Jahren bemerkte man ein starke Abnahme ihrer Kräfte, dem ohnerachtet diente sie noch, wo sie konnte mit Vergnügen. Übrigens genoß sie immer eine sehr gute Gesundheit bis den letzten Winter, da sie anfing zu kränkeln und über Beschwerden auf der Brust zu klagen, welches aller angewandter Mittel ohngeachtet immer mehr zunahm. An unserm Chorfeste wohnte sie bey aller Schwachheit noch allen Versammlungen bey. Sie konnte dem lieben Heiland nicht genug danken, daß er ihr an dem Tage so gnädig gewesen, besonders bey dem Chor-Abendmahl, das lezte welches sie hienieden genoß, wobey ihr nach ihrem eigenen Geständniß himmlisch wohl war. Am 5. zog sie ganz auf die Krankenstube. Die Beschwerden auf der Brust nahmen immer mehr zu und die großen Beklemmungen verursachten ihr besonders die ersten 8 Tage manches ängstliche Stunden, womit sie sich aber auch zum Heiland wendete und ihn so lange bat, bis er ihr auch die Ängstlichkeit wegnahm, so daß sie in den letzten Tagen mit kindlich frohem Muthe und großer Freudigkeit ihrem Ende entgegen sehen konnte und es sie ordentlich betrübte, wenn man ihr sagte, es könnte noch lange währen. Es schien auch in den lezten 2 Tagen, als ob sie sich wieder erholen könnte. Am 16. abends aber überfiel sie eine solche Beklemmung, daß sie und wir vermuthen konnten, daß ihr Ende nahe wäre. Sie verbrachte die Nacht hindurch in großer Schwachheit, u. am 17. vormittags in der 9. Stunde trat der selige Moment ein, da sie sanft und selig unter dem Segen der Gemeine und ihres Chores entschlief—ihres Alters 68 Jahre, 6 Monate und 4 Tage.

Genieß nun theur' erkaufte Seele
Mit Freuden deine Gnadenwahl;
Schwing aus der irdnen Leibeshöle
Dich jauchzend in den Hochzeitssaal;
Leg deinem Bräutgam Dich zu Füßen,
Der hier Sich dir vertrauet hat;
Laß Lieb's u. Freuden-thränen fließen
Für die dir saur' erworbnen Gnad.

Stimm ein mit den Erlösten allen,
Versammlet um des Lammes Thron,
Ins Lied, das ewig wird erschallen
Zu Ehr'n dem Gott's und Menschensohn.
Wir, die wir uns alhier noch sehnen,
Bald bey dem Herrn daheim zu seyn,

Woll'n bis dahin mit Sünderthränen
Uns unserer Erlösung freu'n.

Copy: Women's Memoirs, M–Z, Moravian Church Museum and Archives. This document, written in German, has been translated and transcribed by Edward Quinter. A second and identical contemporary copy also exists in the Moravian Church Museum and Archives in Lititz.[15] The *Gemeinnachtrichen* (1805 Bei. VII, Moravian Archives) included another version of this memoir, which eliminated details (some names and details about William Attwood's cruelties) and omitted the verses at the end.

---

15. Dr. Jeffrey Gemmell, director of Music Ministries at the Lititz Moravian Congregation, discovered this copy, which is joined to the memoir of David Tannenberg (1728–1804), who died two days after MP. This document has been housed in a glass case in the Lititz Museum with other Tannenberg items.

Mary Attwood was born the 5th of July 1715, at a Village call'd White Church in Sommersetshire, the South of England, and bred up to the English Church.[1] Her Father was Joseph Stocker the Son of John Stocker Colonel of a Regiment of Horse and her Mother Mary the Daughter of Thomas Warren Commodore of a Squadron in the Reign of King William the third.[2] At the Age of 4 Years She lost her Mother, who Died in a Confident Relyance on the Meritori[o]us Death and Suff'rings of her Redeemer. After her Mothers Death, She was taken under the Care of her Grandmother till her Father Marrying again She return'd home But was Soon after Sent to a Boarding School for Education where she Remain'd near two years. As her Father was very Solicitous to bring up his children in the fear of the Lord he made it his chief Reason for living in the Country, in order to keep them the better from the evil of the World and Endeavoured to the best of his Knowledge to Instruct them in the Principles of true Religion early to put their trust in God and to apply to him Alone in every Need which had a happy Effect on his Heart and Supported her as She often Said, under many Trials. A little before his Departure out of this Life he Sent for his Wife and Children to give them his Blessing, to this his Daughter in Perticular Said the Lord Should be her Portion which would be an Everlasting Benefit to her but what he would leave her was merely temporal and Transitory, concluding, these my eyes shall behold my Saviour and not anothers, by his Death he has Purchased my Salvation, In Confidence of which I Shut my eyes to this World being assured I shall open them in his Kingdom, &c. After his Death which happen'd in her Thirtenth Year, She came with her Step Mother to live in Bristol.[3] In October 1730 she was Married to Hugh Penry a Doctor with whom she liv'd happily 10 Years and had 2 Daughters, the Eldest lived but

---

1. "English Church": Anglican church.

2. For commodore Thomas Warren, see Letter 9, note 3.

3. Joseph Stocker's will, written on November 9, 1727, was probated on November 4, 1734. See Last Will and Testament, PROB 11/668/30, NAK. He seems to have died in 1728 or 1729. Mary Stocker was the sole executor of her father's will and was to inherit all her father's real and personal estate when she turned twenty-one or when she married, if "such marriage be with the consent of either of my Trustees." This clause was used to disinherit Mary Stocker. Crisp, *Abstracts*, 89, misprints Mary Penry's name as "Mary Pears."

two months the other is now in the Single Sisters House in Bethlehem.[4] In the Year 1740 Her Husband dyed and left her in Strait Circumstances. Her having Married Without the Consent of her Guardians occasion'd the Forfieture of all her Father had left Her, By which account She accepted the Invitation of a Distant Relation of her Mothers Setled in Philadelphia who together with her Husband had writ for her to come over and live with them Promising at the Same time to Provide for her and her Daughter as their own children they themselves having none. In September 1744 she arriv'd in Philadelphia. Her Relation dying soon after her arival she was married to the Widdower William Attwood a Merchant by whom she had one Daughter, who in her seventh year went happily home to our Saviour and is interr'd in the Brethren's Burying Ground in Philadelphia.[5] Having a very Unhappy Life with this Husband it made her often seriously reflect on the many calls she had Receiv'd in her Heart from our Saviour for she was never Dead tho' she too often as she used to say suppress'd her Convictions. Her Daughter being awakned at that time and keeping to the Brethren's church prov'd a fresh occassion to her for Reflection, having given her a strickt Education it Surprized her much, to find her Seeking after something more Solid then what she had taught her. Notwithstanding She gave her free liberty to follow the Biass of her Inclination, However fearing she might be deluded she invited Some Brethren and Sisters to her house to find out thereby if they were really children of God or not—being convinced of this she Imediately Respected and loved them yet without testifying any desire of being in any Conexion with them nor yet did she come to the Church till after her Husbands Death when she was truly awaken'd under the Ministry of Brother Haidt. It was some Time before she could believe our Saviour would accept of her as a Sinner and that she must come to him just as she was and receive Pardon and Mercy *Gratis* till at length finding by Experience all attempts to help her self were fruitless she came on her knees to the Friend of Sinners and begd for Grace obtaind her Desire and found Pardon and Peace and a Blessed Rest for her Heart which remain'd Uninterrupted till her Faith was lost in Fruition.

In the Year 1756 She was Receiv'd in the Congregation on the 25th of January, and what added to her Joy at the Same time with her Daughter. In April 1758 she was Partaker of the Holy Sacrament to her lasting Blessing. When she felt any Perticular Blessing she was usually Silent and as She

---

4. Mary Stocker married Hugh Penry on October 3, 1730. MP ("the other") had moved to Bethlehem in June 1756.

5. For the widowed Mary Stocker Penry's "Relation" in Philadelphia, for William Attwood, and for their daughter, Elisabeth Attwood, see this volume's introduction.

express'd it, would keep the Treasure lock'd in her Heart fearing she might otherwise talk it away. When I feel uneasy She used to Say then I tell it my Sisters am a Sinner over it and beg them to assist me with their Prayers. But when my Saviour draws near my poor Heart it is too Precious to talk much off, I'd rather in Stillness Meditate his Boundless Love to his poor Creature which draws me deeper into him. For several years together by Prayers and tears she beg'd for Leave to live in the Congregation but could not obtain her fervent wish. To be more United to the People of our Saviour She mov'd near the Brethren's House in Philadelphia and had the Satisfaction the last 4 years of her Life to live in one House with Sister Parsons whom she tenderly Lov'd and where Company and Conversation was thro' our Saviours grace a real Blessing to her.[6] They came together Regularly once a Year to Visit the Congregation in Bethlehem and their children and She never Return'd without a Blessing for her Heart—The last time She came was in May this year Her Heart was quite melted at the Grace bestow'd upon her, She was a Guest at the Single Sisters Love Feast on their Choir Festival and could not enough express her Satisfaction over it. She went to Nazareth and Visited her choir there and was for the first time in their Liturgy & returned with a Melted Heart and flowing eyes.[7] She Said She never felt so Happy in all her Life, it was to her as tho' she was a little Child on the mothers knee (so She Still'd the Congregation). As she happen'd to be here at a time when many went home whenever she heard the Trumpetts blow she would sit and with Silent tears accompany the Sound and afterwards repeat some Verse by which one could Plainly discern her desire of soon following. At her going from Bethlehem she had much Conversation with her Daughter the result whereoff was "I am fully Satisfy'd you my dear are Happy and so am I. I now return to Philadelphia and there attend my Saviours will either to bring me here to his Congregation or to translate me to his Church above."

Copy (in MP's hand): MC Phila I.192, MAB.

6. "Sister Parsons": Hannah Parsons (1699–1773), the widow of William Parsons (1701–1757), who founded Easton, Pennsylvania. Hostile to Moravians, Parsons separated from his wife when she associated with the Moravian church in Philadelphia, to which she was admitted as a communicant in 1751. In 1769 Hannah Parsons moved to Bethlehem's widows' house.

7. Mary Attwood "visit[ed] the widows" on May 1, 1760. See Diary of the Nazareth Congregation, MAB.

APPENDIX C: THE STOCKER AND DRINKER FAMILIES

Penry's correspondence frequently mentions two women and their families: Margaret Stocker and Elizabeth Drinker.

The Stocker and Phillips Families[1]

Margaret Stocker (1737–1821), with whom MP stayed during most of her visits to Philadelphia, was her closest friend and confidant for twenty-five years. She was born Margaret Phillips, one of three children of John Phillips (1702–1762), the son of a Welsh curate, and Anna Phillips (1706–1748). In 1754 she married MP's cousin Anthony Stocker (1730–1778), who had arrived in Philadelphia several years earlier and established a store on Water Street. He became one of the largest West Indies importers in Philadelphia, partnering in 1770 with Thomas Wharton (later the commonwealth of Pennsylvania's first governor).[2] Anthony Stocker died in 1778 in England. MP's letters often mention the Stockers' children and grandchildren:

1. Anna (Nancy) Stocker (1756–1821), who married James Potts (1752–1788) in 1778. They had three children:
   a. Anthony Stocker Potts (1779–1785).
   b. Andrew Potts (1780–1803), who died of yellow fever in St. Thomas.
   c. Maria Potts (d. 1823), who married George Poe (1778–1864) in 1808.
2. Mary (Polly) Stocker (1757–1846), who married John Miller (1760–1836). They had one child:
   a. Clement Stocker Miller (1790–1841).
3. John Clement Stocker (1760–1813), who married Mary Katherine Potts Rutter (1762–1821) in 1782. He was a city alderman (1795–1811), an original trustee of the Mutual Assurance Society, and director of the Bank of Pennsylvania. They had four children:
   a. Anthony Stocker (1782–1832), who married Elizabeth Clark in 1815.
   b. John Clement Stocker (1786–1833), who married Caroline DeTousard in 1808.

---

1. See Clark, *Record of the Inscriptions*, 150–51, 155–58; Townsend, "Phillips Bible Record."
2. Anthony Stocker to Aaron Lopez, August 15, 1770, in *Commerce of Rhode Island*, 342.

    c.   Martha (Patty) Rutter Stocker (1789–1868), who married Robert Morton Lewis in 1815.

    d.   Anna Maria Stocker (1798–1879), who married Lawrence Lewis in 1817.

4.   Margaret (Peggy) Stocker (1771–1801), who married Alexander J. Miller (1769–1838). Peggy died in childbirth in 1801 (see Letters 60–64).

John and Alexander Miller, whom the sisters Polly and Peggy married, were brothers. They had a third brother, William Miller (1766–1841), who was married to Rachel McLong.

Margaret Stocker had two brothers. One was John Phillips (1739–1806), who married Rebecca Pyewell Phillips (1741–1820) in 1766. Their first child—a daughter, Margaret, born in 1767—lived only eight weeks. Their son, William Phillips (1771–1845), married Anna Smith (1774–1856) in 1799, and the couple had ten children, including three born during MP's lifetime:

1.   John Smith Phillips (1800–1876).
2.   Elizabeth Phillips (1801–1868).
3.   Camilla Phillips (1803–1887).

Her other brother, Thomas Phillips, never married. Penry describes him as a "Vagabond a poor dirty drunken Fellow" whom his family had to maintain (Letter 54).

The Drinker Family[3]

Elizabeth Drinker (1735–1807), with whom Penry had attended Anthony Benezet's school in Philadelphia in the 1740s, was a devoted diarist and for twenty years Penry's faithful correspondent. Born Elizabeth Sandwith, she married the Quaker merchant Henry Drinker (1734–1809) in 1761. Elizabeth and Henry Drinker had five children who survived into adulthood:

1.   Sarah (Sally) Sandwith Drinker (1761–1807), who married Jacob Downing in 1787. They had five children:
    a.   Elizabeth Downing (1789–1882).
    b.   Mary Drinker Downing (1792–1879).

---

3. Drinker, *Diary*.

      c.   Henry Downing (1795–1854).

      d.   Sarah Sandwith Downing (1797–1843).

      e.   Sandwith Drinker Downing (1799–1847).

2.   Ann (Nancy) Drinker (1764–1830), who married John Skyrin in 1791.

3.   William Drinker (1767–1821), who remained unmarried.

4.   Henry Sandwith Drinker (1770–1824), who married Hannah Smith in 1794.

5.   Mary Drinker (1774–1856), who married Samuel Rhoads in 1796.

Penry often sends greetings to Elizabeth Drinker's older sister, Mary Sandwith (1732–1815), who remained unmarried and left most of her estate to Drinker's children and grandchildren.

Mary Penry served as clerk for the Lititz single sisters' industries, whose customers included prominent families. Edward Shippen sent his son Joseph Shippen, then the colony's secretary, the "Cotton, which Miss Penry at Leiditz (the daughter of Old Attwood's Cousen) has got Spun as fine as She possibly could.... You will see ... that the work of Spinning, and carding &c could not deserve less money."[1] Sarah Bache, Benjamin Franklin's daughter, also resorted to Lititz for cotton when the Revolutionary War disrupted Bethlehem's economy. "The Lady Abbess" in Lititz, she wrote, is "an acquaintance of mine (who Papa will know by the name of Polly Pennery she inquired much about him and desired her best respects when I wrote)."[2]

Many financial accounts related to the single sisters' textile industry survive (see figure 4), as do the eight business letters listed below. In the letter reproduced here, MP describes why the single sisters made products to order rather than keeping an inventory of finished goods.

To Mary Shippen, January 25, 1771 (Linden Hall Archives)
To Edward Shippen, August 26, 1771 (Linden Hall Archives)
To Mary Shippen, January 10, 1772 (Linden Hall Archives)
To Mary Shippen, February 22, 1772 (Linden Hall Archives)
To Mary Shippen, April 10, 1772 (Linden Hall Archives)
To Mary Shippen, August 26, 1774 (Dreer Collection, Box 21, Folder 46, HSP)
To Edward Shippen, October 17, 1774 (reproduced below)
To John Ettwein, [1794] (Letters from Lititz, 1790–1799, LG: VIII, MAB)

---

1. Edward Shippen to Joseph Shippen, May 2, 1771, Edward Shippen Letters and Papers, 1727–1781, Mss.B.Sh62, American Philosophical Society.
2. Sarah Bache to William Temple Franklin, September 16, 1779, *Papers of Benjamin Franklin*, 30:351.

ह्ळ TO EDWARD SHIPPEN

October 17, 1774

Lititz, Pennsylvania

Mr. Shippen

Sir:

Yesterday I received your favour, and have the Pleasure to send your stockings with this—They cost 12/. We beg Mr. Shippen would not take it amiss that we have detained him so long, I can assure you Sir, it has been a real concern to us. We meet with so much difficulty to get the wool combed and dyed that it hinders us greatly. For we never keep worsted stockings ready knitt, because every one chuses rather to bespeak them as it suits them. And some chuse one couleur, some another.[3] If Mr. Shippen fancy's this couleur we have a pound of combed worsted ready. If you had rather have them mixed, be pleased to let me know, and we will do our endevour to serve you. The under sheriff refused to take the stockings he had expressly bespoke, and we had some trouble to dispose of them, as the gentleman had them knit in a Peculiar Way, according to his own fancy, which made them almost unsaleable.[4] Be pleased to present my compliments to Mrs. Shippen, and Miss Patty Gray, with many thanks for their kind remembrances,—which includes me.[5]

Sir, your Obliged Friend and humble servant,

Mary Penry

Typed Copy: PP MEL 19, MAB.

---

3. The Lititz single sisters undertook work mostly on order; they did not stock finished items for customers.

4. See Mary Penry to Mary Shippen, August 26, 1774, Dreer Collection, Box 21:46, HSP.

5. Mary Shippen (see Letter 16, note 1); Martha (Patty) Gray (1713–1794) was Mary Shippen's cousin.

BIBLIOGRAPHY

PRIMARY SOURCES

Archival Materials

American Philosophical Society, Philadelphia, Pennsylvania.
Beinecke Rare Book and Manuscript Library, Yale University, New Haven, Connecticut.
David M. Rubenstein Rare Book and Manuscript Library, Duke University, Durham, North Carolina.
Hagley Museum and Library, Wilmington, Delaware.
Historical Society of Pennsylvania, Philadelphia, Pennsylvania.
Jacobsburg Historical Society, Belfast, Pennsylvania.
Lancaster County Historical Society, Lancaster, Pennsylvania.
Library Company of Philadelphia, Philadelphia, Pennsylvania.
Library of Congress, Washington, DC.
Linden Hall Archives, Lititz, Pennsylvania.
Moravian Archives, Bethlehem, Pennsylvania.

Diaries
Diary of the Bethlehem Congregation, 1755–1806. 28 vols. BethCong 14–41.
Diary of the Single Sisters' Choir at Bethlehem, 1748–66. BethSS 1–2.
Diary of the Lititz Congregation, 1762–1804. LitCong 12–53.
Diary of the Single Sisters' Choir at Lititz, 1762–1805. 5 vols. Lit SS 1–5.
Diary of the [first] Philadelphia Congregation, 1753–67. MC Phila I.7–8, 192.
Diary of the [first] Philadelphia Congregation, 1754–60. PhA IV.
Diary of the Lancaster Congregation, 1760–1806.
Diary of the [first] New York Congregation, 1757–65.
Diary of the Nazareth Congregation.

Membership Catalogs
Catalogs of the Single Sisters and Girls in Bethlehem, 1754–60. BethSS 26.
Catalog of the Single Sisters Choir and Girls at Bethlehem, 1760–1839. BethSS 24.
Catalogs of the Congregation at Lititz, 1759–65. Box: LC II.
Catalogs of the Single Sisters in Lititz, 1762–1826. Lit SS, 8–19.
Catalog of Northern Congregations [including Lititz], 1768. Box: Catalogs, Town and Country Congregations.
Catalogs of the Congregation at Philadelphia, 1742–1965. MC Phila I, 513–47.
Catalog of Moravians, Friends, and Children Deceased in Philadelphia, 1744–68. MC Phila I.514.
Catalogs of the Congregation at Lancaster, 1765–1804. Box: Catalogs, Western Region of PA and MD.
Catalogs of the Congregation at Nazareth, 1745–1823. Box: Nazareth Catalogs I.
Catalogs of the Congregation at Nazareth, 1783–1816. Box: Nazareth Catalogs II.
Catalogs of the Congregation at Hebron. Boxes: LeA, LeB.

Church Registers

Church Register of the Moravian Congregation at Bethlehem, 1742–1801. 2 vols. ChReg 10–11.

Church Register of the Moravian Congregation at Lititz, 1765–1800. ChReg 75.

Church Register of the [first] Moravian Congregation at Philadelphia, 1743–1822. ChReg 107.

Church Register of the Moravian Congregation at Nazareth, 1742–1861. ChReg 82.

Church Register of the Moravian Congregation at Hebron, 1748–1869. ChReg 77.

Church Register of the Moravian Congregation at Lancaster, 1743–1821. ChReg 64.

Church Register and History of the Moravian Society at Carroll's Manor in Maryland, 1763–78. ChReg 19.

Financial Materials

Ledger of the Store at Bethlehem, 1768–75 (Ledger C). BethStore 102.

Journal of the Single Sisters' Choir at Bethlehem, 1762–66 (Journal A). BethSS 42.

Ledger of the Single Sisters' Choir at Bethlehem, 1762–64 (Ledger A). Beth SS 50.

Accounts of the Single Sisters' Choir at Lititz, 1767–84. Box: LC VII.

Accounts of the Single Sisters' Choir at Lititz, 1779–99. Box: Lititz, Accounts of the Choirs, 1769–1824.

Moravian Archives, Southern Province, Winston-Salem, North Carolina.

Moravian Church Archives, Muswell Hill, London, UK.

Moravian Church Museum and Archives, Lititz, Pennsylvania.

Accounts of the Single Sisters' Choir in Lititz, 1765–1804. Box: Early Financial Accounts, Single Sisters.

Catalogs of the Congregation in Lititz, 1762–1815.

Catalogs of the Single Sisters in Lititz, 1764–1811.

Moravian College, Bethlehem, Pennsylvania.

National Archives, Kew, UK.

National Library of Wales, Aberystwyth, Wales, UK.

Penralley Collection, on deposit from the Rhayader Museum and Gallery (CARAD), Rhayader, Powys, Wales.

Powys County Archives, Llandrindod Wells, Wales, UK.

Quaker Meeting Records, Haverford, Pennsylvania.

Register of Wills Office, Philadelphia, Pennsylvania.

Special Collections, Arts and Social Sciences Library, University of Bristol, Bristol, UK.

Special Collections, Haverford College Library, Haverford, Pennsylvania.

William Penn Charter School Archives, Haverford, Pennsylvania.

Wiltshire and Swindon History Centre, Chippenham, UK.

Winterthur Library, Winterthur, Delaware.

Printed Sources

Adams, Abigail. *Abigail Adams: Letters.* Edited by Edith Gelles. New York: Library of America, 2016.

Bunyan, John. *The Pilgrim's Progress.* Edited by Roger Sharrock. Oxford, UK: Clarendon Press, 1960.

Burr, Esther Edwards. *The Journal of Esther Edwards Burr, 1754–1757.* Edited by Carol F. Karlsen and Laurie Crumpacker. New Haven, CT: Yale University Press, 1984.

Butler, William. *Arithmetical Questions on a New Plan . . . Intended to Answer the Double Purpose of Arithmetical Instruction and Miscellaneous Information . . . Designed for the Use of Young Ladies.* 2nd ed. London, 1795.

Calvin, John. *Institutes of the Christian Religion.* Edinburgh, 1863.

Clark, Emily, ed. *Voices from an Early American Convent: Marie Madeleine Hachard and the New Orleans Ursulines, 1727–1760.* Baton Rouge: Louisiana State University Press, 2009.

Cobbett, William. *The Bloody Bouy, Thrown Out as a Warning to the Political Pilots of All Nations.* Philadelphia, 1796.

A Collection of Hymns, with Several Translations from the Hymn-Book of the Moravian Brethren. 2nd ed. London, 1743.

A Collection of Hymns for the Use of the Protestant Church of the United Brethren. London, 1789.

Commerce of Rhode Island, 1726–1800: Volume 1, 1726–1774. In *Collections of the Massachusetts Historical Society.* Boston: Massachusetts Historical Society, 1914.

Congreve, William. *The Complete Plays of William Congreve.* Edited by Herbert Davis. Chicago: University of Chicago Press, 1967.

Cooper, Mary. *The Diary of Mary Cooper: Life on a Long Island Farm, 1768–1773.* Edited by Field Horne. Oyster Bay, NY: Oyster Bay Historical Society, 1981.

A Correct Account of the Trials of C. McManus, J. Hauer, E. Hauer, P. Donagan, F. Cox, and Others, at Harrisburgh, June Oyer and Terminer, 1798, for the Murder of F. Shitz. Harrisburg, PA, 1798.

Cowles, Julia. *The Diaries of Julia Cowles: A Connecticut Record, 1797–1803.* Edited by Laura Hadley Moseley. New Haven, CT: Yale University Press, 1931.

Cowper, William. *The Poems of William Cowper: Volume 1, 1748–1782.* Edited by John D. Baird and Charles Ryskamp. Oxford, UK: Clarendon Press, 1980.

Cranz, David. *The Ancient and Modern History of the Brethren.* London, 1780.

The Daily Words and Doctrinal Texts of the Brethren's Congregation, for the Year 1795. London, 1794.

The Daily Words and Doctrinal Texts of the Brethren's Congregation, for the Year 1796. London, 1795.

The Daily Words and Doctrinal Texts of the Brethren's Congregation for the Year 1797. London, 1796.

Defoe, Daniel. *The True-Born Englishman and Other Writings.* Edited by P. N. Furbank and W. R. Owens. New York: Penguin, 1997.

Drinker, Elizabeth. *The Diary of Elizabeth Drinker.* Edited by Elaine Forman Crane. 3 vols. Boston: Northeastern University Press, 1991.

Franklin, Benjamin. *Papers of Benjamin Franklin.* 42 vols. New Haven, CT: Yale University Press, 1959–2017.

Franks, Abigaill. *The Letters of Abigaill Levy Franks, 1733–1748.* Edited by Edith B. Gelles. New Haven, CT: Yale University Press, 2004.

Gambold, John, ed. *A Collection of Hymns of the Children of God in All Ages, from the Beginning till Now. In Two Parts. Designed Chiefly for the Use of the Congregation in Union with the Brethren's Church.* London, 1754.

Goldsmith, Oliver. *An History of the Earth and Animated Nature.* 8 vols. London, 1774.

Greene, Katherine. *The Journal of Mrs. John Amory (Katherine Greene), 1775–1777.* Edited by Martha C. Codman. Boston: privately printed, 1923.

Heaton, Hannah. *The World of Hannah Heaton: The Diary of an Eighteenth-Century New England Farm Woman.* Edited by Barbara E. Lacey. DeKalb: Northern Illinois University Press, 2003.

Hervey, John. *Meditations and Contemplations.* 2 vols. Bath, 1748.

Hills, George Morgan, ed. "A Summer Jaunt in 1773." *Pennsylvania Magazine of History and Biography* 10 (1886): 205–13.

Hiltzheimer, Jacob. *Extracts from the Diary of Jacob Hiltzheimer, of Philadelphia.* Edited by Jacob Cox Parsons. 3 vols. Philadelphia: William F. Fell & Co., 1893.

Hobart, John Henry. *The Correspondence of John Henry Hobart, 1757–1797.* Edited by Arthur Lowndes. New York: privately printed, 1911.

Hulton, Ann. *Letters of a Loyalist Lady: Being the Letters of Ann Hulton, Sister of Henry Hulton, Commissioner of Customs at Boston, 1767–1776.* Edited by E. Rhys Jones. Cambridge, MA: Harvard University Press, 1927.

Knight, Sarah Kemble. *The Journal of Madam Knight.* Edited by Perry Miller and Thomas H. Johnson. New York: American Book Company, 1938.

Letters of Abelard to Heloise. London, 1782.

The Litany-Book, According to the Manner of Singing at Present Mostly in Use Among the Brethren. London, 1759.

Morris, Margaret. *Margaret Morris, Her Journal.* Edited by John W. Jackson. Philadelphia: G. S. MacManus, 1949.

Morton, Robert. "Diary of Robert Morton, Kept in Philadelphia While That City Was Occupied by the British Army in 1777." *Pennsylvania Magazine of History and Biography* 1, no. 1 (1877): 1–39.

Murray, Judith Sargent. *From Gloucester to Philadelphia in 1790: Observations, Thoughts, and Anecdotes from the Letters of Judith Sargent Murray.* Edited by Bonnie Hurd Smith. Cambridge, MA: Judith Sargent Murray Society, 1998.

———. *The Letters I Left Behind: Judith Sargent Murray Papers, Letter Book 10.* Edited by Bonnie Hurd Smith. Cambridge, MA: Hurd Smith Communications, 2005.

———. *Letters of Loss and Love: Judith Sargent Murray Papers, Letter Book 3.* Edited by Bonnie Hurd Smith. Cambridge, MA: Hurd Smith Communications, 2009.

Norris, Deborah. "'A dear dear friend': Six Letters from Deborah Norris to Sarah Wister, 1778–1779." *Philadelphia Magazine of History and Biography* 108, no. 4 (1984): 487–516.

Osborne, Sarah. *Sarah Osborne's Collected Writings.* Edited by Catherine A. Brekus. New Haven, CT: Yale University Press, 2017.

Parnell, Thomas. *Collected Poems of Thomas Parnell.* Edited by Claude Rawson and F. P. Lock. Newark: University of Delaware Press, 1989.

Pinckney, Eliza Lucas. *Letterbook of Eliza Lucas Pinckney, 1739–1762.* Edited by Elise Pinckney. Chapel Hill: University of North Carolina Press, 1972.

Polwhele, Richard. *Discourses on Different Subjects.* 2 vols. London, 1791.

Pope, Alexander. *The Twickenham Edition of the Poems of Alexander Pope.* Edited John Butt. 11 vols. New Haven, CT: Yale University Press, 1939–67.

Radcliffe, Ann. *Romance of the Forest.* Edited by Chloe Chard. Oxford, UK: Oxford University Press, 2009.

Ramsay, Allan, ed. *The Tea-Table Miscellany; or, A Complete Collection of Scots Songs.* 4 vols. Dublin: E. Smith, 1729.

Ray, John. *A Compleat Collection of English Proverbs.* 3rd ed. London, 1737.

Rush, Benjamin. *The Letters of Benjamin Rush.* Edited by L. H. Butterfield. Princeton, NJ: American Philosophical Society, 1951.

Saltar, Frances. "Fanny Saltar's Reminiscences of Colonial Days in Philadelphia." Edited by Mrs. E. B. Hoskins. *Pennsylvania Magazine of History and Biography* 40, no. 2 (1916): 187–98.

Sansom, Hannah Callender. *The Diary of Hannah Callender Sansom: Sense and Sensibility in the Age of the American Revolution.* Edited by Susan E. Klepp and Karin Wulf. Ithaca, NY: Cornell University Press, 2010.

Sewel, William. *The History of the Rise, Increase, and Progress of the Christian People Called Quakers.* 1717. Burlington, NJ, 1774.

Shippen, Nancy. *Nancy Shippen, Her Journal Book: The International Romance of a Young Lady of Fashion of Colonial Philadelphia with Letters to Her and About Her.* Edited by Ethel Armes. Philadelphia: Lippincott, 1935.

Swift, Jonathan. *Gulliver's Travels.* Edited by Herbert Davis. Oxford, UK: Basil Blackwell, 1959.

Tapner, John. *The School-Master's Repository; or, Youth's Moral Preceptor.* London, 1762.

Warren, Mercy Otis. *Mercy Otis Warren: Selected Letters.* Edited by Jeffrey H. Richards and Sharon M. Harris. Athens: University of Georgia Press, 2009.

Watson, Thomas. *A Body of Practical Divinity: Consisting of Above One Hundred and Seventy Six Sermons on the Lesser Catechism.* London, 1692.

————. *Seven Sermons on Several Select Subjects Preached by Mr. Tho. Watson*. London, 1689.

Watts, Isaac. *Horæ Lyricæ: Poems Chiefly of the Lyric Kind*. London, 1727.

Windus, John. *A Journey to Mequinez, the Residence of the Present Emperor of Fez and Morocco: On the Occasion of Commodore Stewart's Embassy Thither for the Redemption of the British Captives in the Year 1721*. London, 1725.

Wister, Sarah. *The Journal and Occasional Writings of Sarah Wister*. Edited by Kathryn Zabelle Derounian. Rutherford, NJ: Fairleigh Dickinson University Press, 1987.

Zinzendorf, Nicholas Ludwig von. *Nine Public Lectures on Important Subjects of Religion, Preached in Fetter Lane Chapel in London in the Year 1746*, edited by George W. Forell. Iowa City: University of Iowa Press, 1973.

————. *Twenty-One Discourses or Dissertations upon the Augsburg Confession*. Translated by Francis Okely. London, 1753.

SECONDARY SOURCES

Albright, S. C. *The Story of the Moravian Congregation at York, Pennsylvania*. York, PA: Maple Press, 1927.

Alderfer, E. G. *The Ephrata Commune: An Early American Counterculture*. Pittsburgh: University of Pittsburgh Press, 1985.

Altman, Janet. *Epistolarity: Approaches to a Form*. Columbus: Ohio State University Press, 1982.

Andrews, Dee. *The Methodists and Revolutionary America, 1760–1800: The Shaping of an Evangelical Culture*. Princeton, NJ: Princeton University Press, 2002.

Arndt, Karl John Richard and Reimer C. Eck, eds. *The First Century of German Language Printing in the United State of America*. 2 vols. Göttingen: Pennsylvania German Society, 1989.

Atwood, Craig D. ed., *A Collection of Sermons from Zinzendorf's Pennsylvania Journey*. Bethlehem, PA: Moravian Church, 2001.

————. *Community of the Cross: Moravian Piety in Colonial Bethlehem*. University Park: Pennsylvania State University Press, 2004.

————. "Deep in the Side of Jesus: The Persistence of Zinzendorfian Piety in Colonial America." In *Pious Pursuits: German Moravians in the Atlantic World*, edited by Michele Gillespie and Robert Beachy, 50–64. New York: Berghahn Books, 2007.

————. *The Theology of the Czech Brethren from Hus to Comenius*. University Park: Pennsylvania State University Press, 2009.

————. "The Use of the 'Ancient Unity' in the Historiography of the Moravian Church." *Journal of Moravian History* 13, no. 2 (2013): 109–57.

————. "Zinzendorf's 1749 Reprimand to the Brüdergemeine." *Transactions of the Moravian Historical Society* 29 (1996): 59–84.

Bach, Jeff. *Voices of the Turtledoves: The Sacred World of Ephrata*. University Park: Pennsylvania State University Press, 2003.

Baker, William S. *Early Sketches of George Washington*. Philadelphia, 1894.

Balch, Thomas. *Letters and Papers Relating Chiefly to the Provincial History of Pennsylvania*. Philadelphia: privately printed, 1855.

Bancroft, Catherine. "Maria Beaumont: Race and Caribbean Wealth at the Early Nineteenth Century Moravian Boarding School for Girls in Bethlehem." *Journal of Moravian History* 13, no. 2 (2013): 158–96.

Beachy, Robert. "Manuscript Missions in an Age of Print: The Moravian 'Gemein Nachrichten' in the Atlantic World." In *Pious Pursuits: German Moravians in the Atlantic World*, edited by Michele Gillespie and Robert Beachy, 33–49. New York: Berghahn Books, 2007.

Beck, A. R. "Extracts from the Diaries of the Lititz Moravian Congregation Relating to the Occupancy of the Brethren's House as a U.S. Military Hospital." *The Moravian* 58, no. 44 (October 29, 1913): 701.

Beck, Herbert H. *A Century and Three-Quarters of Life and Service: Linden Hall Seminary, 1746–1921.* Lancaster, PA: Conestoga Publishing Co., 1921.

———. "The Military Hospital at Lititz, 1777–78." *Journal of the Lancaster County Historical Society* 23, no. 1 (1919): 4–14.

Beiler, Rosalind. *Immigrant Entrepreneur: The Atlantic World of Caspar Wistar, 1650–1750.* University Park: Pennsylvania State University Press, 2008.

Beneke, Chris. "'The Catholic Spirit Prevailing in Our Country': America's Moderate Religious Revolution." In *The First Prejudice: Religious Tolerance and Intolerance in Early America,* edited by Chris Beneke and Christopher S. Grenda, 265–85. Philadelphia: University of Pennsylvania Press, 2011.

Bloch, Ruth H. *Visionary Republic: Millennial Themes in American Thought, 1756–1800.* Cambridge, UK: Cambridge University Press, 1988.

Brickenstein, H. A. "Sketch of the Early History of Lititz, 1742–75." *Transactions of the Moravian Historical Society* 2, nos. 7–8 (1885): 343–74.

Brooks, Mary Uhl. *Threads of Useful Learning: Westtown School Samplers.* West Chester, PA: Westtown School, 2015.

Brückner, Martin. *The Geographic Revolution in Early America: Maps, Literacy, and National Identity.* Chapel Hill: University of North Carolina Press, 2006.

Brunsman, Denver. *The Evil Necessity: British Naval Impressment in the Eighteenth-Century Atlantic World.* Charlottesville: University of Virginia Press, 2013.

Chambers-Schiller, Lee Virginia. *Liberty, a Better Husband: Single Women in America: The Generations of 1780–1840.* New Haven, CT: Yale University Press, 1984.

Charnock, John. *Biographia Navalis, or Impartial Memoirs of the Lives and Characters of the Officers of the Navy of Great Britain.* 4 vols. London, 1795.

Clark, Edward L., ed. *A Record of the Inscriptions on the Tablets and Gravestones in the Burial-Grounds of Christ Church, Philadelphia.* Philadelphia: Collins, 1864.

Cooper, Wendy A., and Lisa Minardi. *Paint, Pattern, and People: Furniture of Southeastern Pennsylvania.* Philadelphia: University of Pennsylvania Press, 2011.

Crisp, Frederick Arthur. *Abstracts of Somersetshire Wills, etc., Copied from the Manuscript Collections of the Late Rev. Frederick Brown.* 4th ser. London: privately printed for F. A. Crisp, 1889.

Davies, Hywel M. *Transatlantic Brethren: Rev. Samuel Jones (1735–1814) and His Friends: Baptists in Wales, Pennsylvania, and Beyond.* Bethlehem, PA: Lehigh University Press, 1995.

———. "'Very Different Springs of Uneasiness': Emigration from Wales to the United States of America During the 1790s." *Welsh History Review* 15, no. 1 (1990): 368–98.

Dierks, Konstantin. *In My Power: Letter Writing and Communications in Early America.* Philadelphia: University of Pennsylvania Press, 2009.

Dine, Sarah Blank. "Diaries and Doctors: Elizabeth Drinker and Philadelphia Medical Practice, 1760–1810." *Pennsylvania History* 68, no. 4 (2001): 413–34.

Dresser, Madge. "Moravians in Bristol." In *Reformation and Revival in Eighteenth-Century Bristol,* edited by Jonathan Barry and Kenneth Morgan, 105–48. Bristol, UK: Bristol Record Society, 1994.

Dunn, Richard S. *A Tale of Two Plantations: Slave Life and Labor in Jamaica and Virginia.* Cambridge, MA: Harvard University Press, 2014.

Dupuy, Charles Meredith. "The Haskins Family." In *A Genealogical History of the Depuy Family,* 62–68. Philadelphia: Lippincott, 1910.

Durey, Michael. *Transatlantic Radicals and the Early American Republic.* Lawrence: University Press of Kansas, 1997.

Engel, Katherine Carté. *Religion and Profit: Moravians in Early America.* Philadelphia: University of Pennsylvania Press, 2009.

Erben, Patrick. *A Harmony of the Spirits: Translation and the Language of Community in Early Pennsylvania.* Chapel Hill: University of North Carolina Press, 2012.

Evans, Elizabeth, ed. *Weathering the Storm: Women of the American Revolution.* New York: Scribners, 1975.

Faber, Eli. *Jews, Slaves, and the Slave Trade: Setting the Record Straight.* New York: New York University Press, 1998.

Fatherly, Sarah. *Gentlewomen and Learned Ladies: Women and Elite Formation in Eighteenth-Century Philadelphia.* Bethlehem, PA: Lehigh University Press, 2008.

Faull, Katherine M., ed. and trans. *Moravian Women's Memoirs: Their Related Lives, 1750–1820.* Syracuse, NY: Syracuse University Press, 1997.

———, ed. and trans. *Speaking to Body and Soul: Instructions for Moravian Choir Helpers, 1785–1786.* University Park: Pennsylvania State University Press, 2017.

Ferguson, Leland. *God's Fields: Landscape, Religion, and Race in Moravian Wachovia.* Gainesville: University Press of Florida, 2011.

Fogleman, Aaron Spencer. *Two Troubled Souls: An Eighteenth-Century Couple's Spiritual Journey in the Atlantic World.* Chapel Hill: University of North Carolina Press, 2013.

Ford, Worthington Chauncey, ed. *British Officers Serving in the American Revolution, 1774–1783.* Brooklyn: Historical Printing Club, 1897.

Galson, David W. *White Servitude in Colonial America: An Economic Analysis.* Cambridge, UK: Cambridge University Press, 1981.

Garrett, Clarke. "Priestley's Religion." In *Joseph Priestley in America, 1794–1804,* edited by Peter M. Lukehart, 6–13. Carlisle, PA: Dickinson College, 1994.

Gaul, Theresa Strouth, and Sharon M. Harris, eds. *Letters and Cultural Transformations in the United States, 1760–1860.* Burlington, VT: Ashgate, 2009.

Gerber, David A. *Authors of Their Lives: The Personal Correspondence of British Immigrants to North America in the Nineteenth Century.* New York: New York University Press, 2006.

Gerstell, Vivian S. *Silversmiths of Lancaster, Pennsylvania, 1730–1850.* Lancaster, PA: Lancaster County Historical Society, 1972.

Gillespie, Michele, and Robert Beachy, eds. *Pious Pursuits: German Moravians in the Atlantic World.* New York: Berghahn Books, 2007.

Gipson, Lawrence Henry, ed. *The Moravian Mission on White River: Diaries and Letters, May 5, 1799, to November 12, 1806.* Indianapolis: Indiana Historical Bureau, 1938.

Gollin, Gilliam Lindt. *Moravians in Two Worlds: A Study of Changing Communities.* New York: Columbia University Press, 1967.

Gordon, Scott Paul. "Asylum: The Case of Mary Tippet." *Church Square Journal* 21 (Spring 2017): 4–5.

———. "Entangled by the World: William Henry of Lancaster and 'Mixed' Living in Moravian Town and Country Congregations." *Journal of Moravian History* 8 (2010): 7–52.

———. "Glad Passivity: Mary Penry of Lititz and the Making of Moravian Women." *Journal of Moravian History* 13, no. 1 (2013): 1–26.

———. "The Paxton Boys and the Moravians: Terror and Faith in the Pennsylvania Backcountry." *Journal of Moravian History* 14, no. 2 (2014): 119–52.

———. *The Power of the Passive Self in English Literature, 1640–1770.* Cambridge, UK: Cambridge University Press, 2001.

Graham, Jenny. "Joseph Priestley in America." In *Joseph Priestley, Scientist, Philosopher, and Theologian,* edited by Isabel Rivers and David L. Wykes, 203–30. Oxford, UK: Oxford University Press, 2008.

Gundersen, Joan R. *To Be Useful to the World: Women in Revolutionary America, 1740–1790.* Chapel Hill: University of North Carolina Press, 2006.

Haldeman, Eliza Jacobs. "Seventy-Seven Years Ago." *Linden Hall Echo* 2, no. 1 (September 1877): 1.

Haller, Mabel. *Early Moravian Education in Pennsylvania.* Nazareth, PA: Moravian Historical Society, 1953.

Handler, Bonnie S. *Linden Hall: Enduring Values, Changing Times.* Lititz, PA: Linden Hall, 1996.

Harvey, A. D. *Collision of Empires: Britain in Three World Wars, 1793–1945.* New York: Blooms-bury, 2003.

Hecht, Arthur. "Pennsylvania Postal History of the Eighteenth Century." *Pennsylvania History* 30, no. 4 (1963): 420–42.

Hocker, Edward W. *Genealogical Data Relating to the German Settlers of Pennsylvania and Adja-cent Territory: From Advertisements in German Newspapers Published in Philadelphia and Germantown, 1743–1800.* Baltimore: Genealogical Publishing, 1980.

Hogeland, William. *The Whiskey Rebellion: George Washington, Alexander Hamilton, and the Frontier Rebels Who Challenged America's Newfound Sovereignty.* New York: Scribners, 2006.

Hostetter, Albert K. "Newspapers as Historic Records." *Historical Papers and Addresses of the Lancaster County Historical Society* 26, no. 7 (1922): 155–63.

Jackson, Maurice. *Let This Voice Be Heard: Anthony Benezet, Father of Atlantic Abolitionism.* Philadelphia: University of Pennsylvania Press, 2010.

Jenkins, R. T., *The Moravian Brethren in North Wales: An Episode in the Religious History of Wales.* London: Honourable Society of Cymmrodorion, 1938.

Jennings, Francis. *Empire of Fortune: Crowns, Colonies, and Tribes in the Seven Years War in America.* New York: Norton, 1988.

Jones, Theophilus. *History of the County of Brecknock.* 2 vols. Brecknock, UK: George North, 1809.

Jordan, Helen. "Pennsylvania Marriage Licenses, Issued by Governor James Hamilton, 1748–1752." *Pennsylvania Magazine of History and Biography* 32, no. 1 (1908): 71–82.

Jordan, John Woolf. "Biographical Sketch of the Rev. John Meder." *The Moravian* 36, no. 4 (January 28, 1891): 51.

———. "John Okely." *The Moravian* 34, no. 7 (February 13, 1889): 100–101.

———. "Lewis Weiss, of Philadelphia, Conveyancer, Lawyer, Judge." *Pennsylvania Magazine of History and Biography* 15, no. 3 (1891): 361–65.

———. "The Military Hospitals at Bethlehem and Lititz During the Revolution." *Pennsylvania Magazine of History and Biography* 20, no. 2 (1896): 137–57.

Juster, Susan. *Doomsayers: Anglo-American Prophecy in the Age of Revolution.* Philadelphia: University of Pennsylvania Press, 2010.

Kahler, Gerald E. *The Long Farewell: Americans Mourn the Death of George Washington.* Char-lottesville: University of Virginia Press, 2008.

Kamensky, Jane. *The Colonial Mosaic: American Women, 1600–1760.* New York: Oxford Univer-sity Press, 1995.

Kerber, Linda K. *Women of the Republic: Intellect and Ideology in Revolutionary America.* Chapel Hill: University of North Carolina Press, 1980.

Klepp, Susan E. "Fragmented Knowledge: Questions in Regional Demographic History." *Pro-ceedings of the American Philosophical Society* 133, no. 2 (1989): 223–33.

Knouse, Nola Reed, ed. *The Music of the Moravian Church in America.* Rochester, NY: Univer-sity of Rochester Press, 2008.

Landis, Bertha Cochran. "Col. Timothy Matlack: A Revolutionary Patriot in Lancaster." *Papers of the Lancaster County Historical Society* 42, no. 6 (1938): 149–56.

Lerbscher, August, and Albert Calvin. "Items of Interest from the Neue Unpartheyische Lan-caster Zeitung, und Anzeigs-Nachrichten." *Papers Read Before the Lancaster County His-torical Society* 34, no. 5 (1930): 97–107.

Levering, Joseph Mortimer. *A History of Bethlehem, Pennsylvania, 1741–1892.* Bethlehem, PA: Times Publishing, 1903.

Lewis, Jan. "The Republican Wife: Virtue and Seduction in the Early Republic." *William and Mary Quarterly* 44, no. 4 (1987): 689–721.

Lloyd, John. *Historical Memoranda of Breconshire.* 2 vols. Brecon, UK: Ellis Owen, 1903.

Long, Dorothy. "Medical Care Among the North Carolina Moravians." *Bulletin of the Medical Library Association* 44, no. 3 (1956): 271–84.

Mason, J. C. S. *The Moravian Church and the Missionary Awakening in England, 1760–1800.* Suffolk, UK: Boydell, 2001.

Matar, Nabil. *British Captives from the Mediterranean to the Atlantic, 1563–1760.* Leiden: Brill, 2014.

McClinton, Rowena, ed. *The Moravian Springplace Mission to the Cherokees.* 2 vols. Lincoln: University of Nebraska Press, 2007.

McCullough, Thomas J. "'The Most Memorable Circumstances': Instructions for the Collection of Personal Data from Church Members, Circa 1752." *Journal of Moravian History* 15, no. 2 (2015): 159–76.

McKitrick, Eric, and Stanley Elkins. *The Age of Federalism: The Early American Republic, 1788–1800.* New York: Oxford University Press, 1993.

McMurran, Mary Helen. "Crèvecoeur's Transatlantic Bilingualism." *Early American Studies* 13, no. 1 (2015): 189–208.

———. *The Spread of Novels: Translation and Prose Fiction in the Eighteenth Century.* Princeton, NJ: Princeton University Press, 2010.

Miller, Kerby A., Arnold Schrier, Bruce D. Boling, and David N. Doyle, eds. *Irish Immigrants in the Land of Canaan: Letters and Memoirs from Colonial and Revolutionary America, 1675–1815.* New York: Oxford University Press, 2003.

Moglen, Seth. "Excess and Utopia: Meditations on Moravian Bethlehem." *History of the Present* 2, no. 2 (2012): 122–47.

Mullan, John. *Sentiment and Sociability: The Language of Feeling in the Eighteenth Century.* Oxford, UK: Oxford University Press, 1990.

Myers, Elizabeth Lehman. *A Century of Moravian Sisters: A Record of Christian Community Life.* New York: Fleming H. Revell Co., 1918.

Myrsiades, Linda. *Law and Medicine in Revolutionary America: Dissecting the Rush v. Cobbett Trial, 1799.* Bethlehem, PA: Lehigh University Press, 2012.

Nelson, Vernon H. *John Valentine Haidt: The Life of a Moravian Painter.* Edited by June Schlueter and Paul Peucker. Bethlehem, PA: Moravian Archives, 2012.

O'Connell, Sheila. *London 1753.* Boston: David R. Godine, 2003.

O'Neill, Lindsay. *The Opened Letter: Networking in the Early Modern British World.* Philadelphia: University of Pennsylvania Press, 2015.

Pasley, Jeffery L. *"The Tyranny of Printers": Newspaper Politics in the Early American Republic.* Charlottesville: University of Virginia Press, 2002.

Periodical Accounts Relating to the Missions of the Church of the United Brethren, Established Among the Heathen. London, 1846.

Petterson, Christina, and Katherine M. Faull, eds. "Speaking About Marriage: Notes from the 1744 Married Choir Conferences." *Journal of Moravian History* 17, no. 1 (2017): 58–103.

Peucker, Paul. "In the Blue Cabinet: Moravians, Marriage, and Sex." *Journal of Moravian History* 10 (2010): 10–38.

———. *A Time of Sifting: Mystical Marriage and the Crisis of Moravian Piety in the Eighteenth Century.* University Park: Pennsylvania State University Press, 2015.

Philp, Mark, ed. *Resisting Napoleon: The British Response to the Threat of Invasion, 1797–1815.* Aldershot, UK: Ashgate, 2006.

Podmore, Colin. *The Moravian Church in England, 1728–1760.* Oxford, UK: Clarendon Press, 1988.

Prince, Carl E. "The Passing of the Aristocracy: Jefferson's Removal of the Federalists, 1801–1805." *Journal of American History* 57, no. 3 (1970): 563–75.

Radbill, Samuel X. "Francis Alison, Jr: A Surgeon of the Revolution." *Bulletin of the History of Medicine* 9 (1941): 243–57.

Raley, Robert L. "John James Barralet in Dublin and Philadelphia." *Irish Arts Review* 2 (1985): 19–25.

Reichmann, Felix, and Eugene E. Doll, eds. *Ephrata as Seen by Contemporaries.* Vol. 17 of *The Pennsylvania German Folklore Society.* Allentown: Pennsylvania German Folklore Society, 1952.

Ritter, Abraham. *History of the Moravian Church in Philadelphia.* Philadelphia: Hayes and Zell, 1857.

Rosenberg, Nancy F. "The World Within, the World Without: Quaker Education in Philadelphia, 1682–1987." PhD diss., University of Michigan, 1991.

Roth, Anthony A. *Mayors of Philadelphia, 1691–1972: Some Genealogical Notes.* 8 vols. Philadelphia: Genealogical Society of Pennsylvania, n.d.

Rubicam, Milton. "The Wistar-Wister Family: A Pennsylvania Family's Contributions Toward American Cultural Development." *Pennsylvania History* 20, no. 2 (1952): 142–64.

Sachse, Julius F. *Wayside Inns on the Lancaster Roadside Between Philadelphia and Lancaster.* Lancaster: privately printed, 1912.

Salmon, Marylynn. *Women and the Law of Property in Early America.* Chapel Hill: University of North Carolina Press, 1986.

Schofield, Robert E. *The Enlightened Joseph Priestley: A Study of His Life and Work from 1773 to 1804.* University Park: Pennsylvania State University Press, 2004.

Schutt, Amy C. "Complex Connections: Communication, Mobility, and Relationships in Moravian Children's Lives." *Journal of Moravian History* 12, no. 1 (2012): 20–46.

Schwarz, Ralph Grayson. *Bethlehem on the Lehigh.* Bethlehem, PA: Bethlehem Area Foundation, 1991.

———. *Picturesque Sand Island.* Bethlehem, PA: Oaks Print Co., 1990.

Seeman, Erik R. "'It Is Better to Marry Than to Burn': Anglo-American Attitudes Toward Celibacy, 1600–1800." *Journal of Family History* 24, no. 4 (1999): 397–419.

Sensbach, Jon F. *Rebecca's Revival: Creating Black Christianity in the Atlantic World.* Cambridge, MA: Harvard University Press, 2005.

Sherlock, Peter, ed. *Monumental Inscriptions of Wiltshire.* Trowbridge, UK: Wiltshire Record Society, 2000.

Skidmore, Gil. *Strength in Weakness: Writings of Eighteenth-Century Quaker Women.* New Haven, CT: Yale University Press, 2010.

Smaby, Beverly Prior. "Forming the Single Sisters' Choir in Bethlehem." *Transactions of the Moravian Historical Society* 28 (1994): 1–14.

———. "Gender Prescriptions in Eighteenth-Century Bethlehem." In *Backcountry Crucibles: The Lehigh Valley from Settlement to Steel,* edited by Jean Soderlund and Catherine Parzynski, 74–103. Bethlehem, PA: Lehigh University Press, 2007.

———. "'Only Brothers should be accepted into this proposed council': Restricting Women's Leadership in Moravian Bethlehem." In *Pietism in Germany and North America, 1680–1820,* edited by Jonathan Strom, Hartmut Lehmann, and James Van Horn Melton, 133–62. Burlington, VT: Ashgate, 2009.

———. *The Transformation of Moravian Bethlehem: From Communal Mission to Family Economy.* Philadelphia: University of Pennsylvania Press, 1988.

Smith, Anna Maria Henry. "Communication from a Former Scholar of the Litiz Female Boarding School." *The Moravian* 1, no. 31 (August 1, 1856): 245.

Smith, Billy G. "Death and Life in a Colonial Immigrant City: A Demographic Analysis of Philadelphia." *Journal of Economic History* 37, no. 4 (1977): 863–89.

Sommer, Elisabeth. "Fashion Passion: The Rhetoric of Dress Within the Eighteenth-Century Moravian Brethren." In *Pious Pursuits: German Moravians in the Atlantic World,* edited by Michele Gillespie and Robert Beachy, 83–96. New York: Berghahn Books, 2007.

———. "Gambling with God: The Use of the Lot by the Moravian Brethren in the Eighteenth Century." *Journal of the History of Ideas* 59, no. 2 (1998): 267–86.

Southern, Ron. "Strangers Below: An Archaeology of Distinctions in an Eighteenth-Century Religious Community." In *Archaeologies of the British: Explorations of Identity in Great Britain and its Colonies, 1600–1945*, edited by Susan Lawrence, 87–101. London: Routledge, 2003.

Stanton, Domna. *The Female Autograph: Theory and Practice of Autobiography from the Tenth to the Twentieth Century*. Chicago: University of Chicago Press, 1984.

Stauffer, David McNeely, and Mantle Fielding. *American Engravers upon Copper and Steel, Part 2: Check-List of the Works of the Earlier Engravers*. 1907. New York: Burt Franklin, 1964.

Stead, Geoffrey, and Margaret Stead. *The Exotic Plant: A History of the Moravian Church in Great Britain, 1742–2000*. London: Epworth Press, 2003.

Stocker, Harry Emilius. *A History of the Moravian Church in New York City*. New York: n.p., 1922.

Tagg, James. *Benjamin Franklin Bache and the Philadelphia "Aurora."* Philadelphia: University of Pennsylvania Press, 1991.

Tolles, Frederick B. "Unofficial Ambassador: George Logan's Mission to France, 1798." *William and Mary Quarterly* 7, no. 1 (1950): 3–25.

Townsend, Mrs. Stockton. "Phillips Bible Record." *Publications of the Genealogical Society of Pennsylvania* 12, no. 2 (1934): 177–90.

Trimble, William F. *High Frontier: A History of Aeronautics in Pennsylvania*. Pittsburgh: University of Pittsburgh Press, 1982.

von Morzé, Leonard. "Cultural Transfer in the German Atlantic: Brown, Oertel, and the First Translation of a U.S. Novel." *Transatlantic Literature and Transitivity, 1780–1850: Subjects, Texts, and Print Culture*, edited by Annika Bautz and Kathryn Gray, 171–94. New York: Routledge, 2017.

Weber, Julie Tomberlin. "Translation as a Prism: Broadening the Spectrum of Eighteenth-Century Identity." In *Ethnographies and Exchanges: Native Americans, Moravians, and Catholics in Early North America*, edited by A. G. Roeber, 195–207. University Park: Pennsylvania State University Press, 2008.

Wellenreuther, Hermann. *Citizens in a Strange Land: A Study of German-American Broadsides and Their Meaning for Germans in North America, 1730–1830*. University Park: Pennsylvania State University Press, 2013.

Wells, Robert. "Quaker Marriage Patterns in a Colonial Perspective." *William and Mary Quarterly* 29, no. 3 (1972): 415–42.

Wessel, Carola. "Connecting Congregations: The Net of Communication Among the Moravians as Exemplified by the Interaction Between Pennsylvania, the Upper Ohio Valley, and Germany (1772–1774)." In *The Distinctiveness of Moravian Culture*, edited by Craig D. Atwood and Peter Vogt, 153–72. Nazareth, PA: Moravian Historical Society, 2003.

Williams, Greg H. *The French Assault on American Shipping, 1793–1813: A History and Comprehensive Record of Merchant Marine Losses*. Jefferson, NC: McFarland, 2009.

Williams, Gwyn A. *The Search for Beulah Land: The Welsh and the Atlantic Revolution*. New York: Holmes and Meier, 1980.

Wilson, Lisa. *Life After Death: Widows in Pennsylvania, 1750–1850*. Philadelphia: Temple University Press, 1992.

Winslow, Stephen N. "John Jordan." In *Biographies of Successful Philadelphia Merchants*, 24–29. Philadelphia: James K. Simon, 1864.

Withington, Lothrop. "Pennsylvania Gleanings in England." *Pennsylvania Magazine of History and Biography* 28, no. 4 (1904): 456–69.

Wokeck, Marianne S. *Trade in Strangers: The Beginnings of Mass Migration to North America*. University Park: Pennsylvania State University Press, 1999.

Wulf, Karin. *Not All Wives: Women of Colonial Pennsylvania*. Philadelphia: University of Pennsylvania Press, 2000.

Zacks, Richard. *The Pirate Hunter: The True Story of Captain Kidd*. New York: Hyperion, 2003.

INDEX